ORIGIN OF THE AMERICAN REVOLUTION: 1759–1766

ORIGIN OF THE AMERICAN REVOLUTION: 1759–1766

BERNHARD KNOLLENBERG

Edited and with a Foreword by
Bernard W. Sheehan

LIBERTY FUND

INDIANAPOLIS

This book is published by Liberty Fund, Inc., a foundation established to encourage study of the ideal of a society of free and responsible individuals.

The cuneiform inscription that serves as our logo and as the design motif for our end-papers is the earliest-known written appearance of the word "freedom" (*amagi*), or "liberty." It is taken from a clay document written about 2300 B.C. in the Sumerian city-state of Lagash.

Printed in the United States of America

06   05   04   03   02   C   5   4   3   2   1
06   05   04   03   02   P   5   4   3   2   1

Library of Congress Cataloging-in-Publication Data

Knollenberg, Bernhard, 1892–1973.
    Origin of the American Revolution, 1759–1766/Bernhard Knollenberg;
    edited and with a foreword by Bernard W. Sheehan.
       p.   cm.
    Originally published: New York: Free Press, 1960.
    Includes bibliographical references (p.   ) and index.
    ISBN 0-86597-382-2   IBSBN 0-86597-383-0 (pbk.)
     1. United States—History—Revolution, 1775–1783—Causes.
    I. Sheehan, Bernard W. II. Title.

E210.K65 2002
973.3′11—dc21   2002022817

Liberty Fund, Inc.
8335 Allison Pointe Trail, Suite 300
Indianapolis, Indiana 46250-1684

CONTENTS

CONTENTS

FOREWORD

Bernhard Knollenberg turned to scholarship only after a successful career in the law. But in many ways he remained a lawyer. Defense of a client's interest now became a relentless pursuit of historical truth. Some of his writings are directly works of advocacy, designed to make a historiographical point contrary to the conventional view. Even his narrative works offer a substantial component of argument, frequently in the text but also in the remarkably full note sections that he invariably attached to his works. And yet this penchant for advocacy and voluminous documentation never became either intrusive or pedantic. Knollenberg consistently crafted a good story with an interpretive thread, a tour of the pertinent literature, and an account of the author's adventures in the sources. Thus the discipline of the law has served both Knollenberg and his readers well.[1]

Born in Richmond, Indiana, in 1892 into the leading merchant family of the town, he attended Earlham, the local Quaker college, although he was not himself a Friend. After graduating he traveled east

---

1. For insight into the consequences of legal training for Knollenberg's historical writing see the exchange between him and Clifford K. Shipton in *William and Mary Quarterly*, 3rd ser., 10 (1953): 117–24; ibid., 10 (1953): 348–50; ibid., 10 (1953): 507.

to Harvard, where he took a master's degree in history. He soon found the financial rewards of academia unpromising and moved on to the law school, where he finished a degree in 1916. Through the two postwar decades Knollenberg forged a distinguished legal career, practicing in Hawaii, Indiana, Massachusetts, and New York and becoming a recognized authority on taxation. He had apparently never abandoned his early inclination toward scholarship, for in 1938 he became librarian at Yale. In both world wars he served his country in various bureaucratic posts, including a stint with the OSS. At the end of World War II he resigned from Yale and retired to Chester, Connecticut, where he devoted the rest of his life to the study of the founding years of the American republic.[2]

Knollenberg began his publishing career in 1940, while still at Yale, with the appearance of the first of his two volumes on George Washington.[3] They are both studies in interpretation, rather than biographical narratives, and reveal an important characteristic of Knollenberg's work. Even when he wrote narrative history, as he did in his two books on the coming of the Revolution, the problems presented by the past always engaged his mind more than the narrative itself. He took a cold-eyed view of the founding father, though his analysis fell considerably short of the kind of the debunking biographies that became popular in the 1920s and 1930s. Washington does emerge slightly bruised from Knollenberg's scrutiny, but his greatness remains intact.

By far the most significant and controversial aspect of these volumes is Knollenberg's discussion of the Conway Cabal. At the time that he wrote, most historians believed that in 1777–1778 a coterie of officers and congressmen led by Thomas Conway, a Franco-Irish general in the Continental army, conspired to replace Washington. After reviewing the sources, Knollenberg found the evidence thin and concluded that the plot was "probably a myth." The issue remains controversial, but

---

2. *The Palladium-Item*, Richmond, Indiana, July 8, 1973; Carl Bridenbaugh, "Bernhard Knollenberg," Massachusetts Historical Society, *Proceedings* 86 (Boston, 1974): 81–83.

3. Bernhard Knollenberg, *Washington and the Revolution: A Reappraisal. Gates, Conway, and the Continental Congress* (New York: Macmillan, 1940); Bernhard Knollenberg, *George Washington: The Virginia Period, 1732–1775* (Durham, N.C.: Duke University Press, 1964).

opinion has tended in Knollenberg's direction. There was no doubt that, after Washington's loss of Philadelphia, which compared unfavorably to Horatio Gates's victory at Saratoga, unhappiness spread concerning the commander's generalship, but an organized conspiracy existed more in the imagination of Washington and his staff than in reality. Knollenberg's interpretation has stood the test of time.[4]

Twenty years elapsed between the appearance of his first volume on Washington and the publication in 1960 of *Origin of the American Revolution*. It is a close study of the opening of the controversy leading to independence. Perhaps because Knollenberg remained outside of the formal ranks of academia, he writes an interpretively eclectic kind of history. Academic historians of early America tend to come in schools. In the immediate postwar period they were either imperial, neo-whig, or progressive. Knollenberg falls mainly into the neo-whig category. Although he never engages in anti-British polemics, there can be no question about where his sentiments lay. He believes that the American interpretation of the British constitution was correct, and that the colonists' actions in the 1760s served the cause of liberty. At the same time, he is conscious of the imperial context of the dispute between Britain and her overseas possessions, so the volume begins with an informative account of the English origins of the controversy. Although he plainly knows the intellectual background of the attack on British policy, his writing does not stress ideas.[5] And his work shows no interest in the progressive history that had been popular before World War II. In his version of the story, the Revolution hap-

4. Knollenberg, *Washington and the Revolution*, ch. 7 and *passim*. The fullest defense of Washington in the controversy can be found in Douglas Southall Freeman, *George Washington: A Biography*, vol. 4, *Leader of the Revolution* (New York: Charles Scribner's Sons, 1951), 586–611. Louis Gottschalk doubted Knollenberg's position in *Journal of Modern History*, 13 (March 1941), 97–98. But see also Don Higginbotham, *The American War of Independence: Military Attitudes, Policies, and Practice, 1763–1789* (New York: Macmillan Company, 1971), 116–22; Charles Royster, *A Revolutionary People at War: The Continental Army and the American Character, 1775–1783* (Chapel Hill: University of North Carolina Press, 1980), 178–89.

5. On the question of ideas and the coming of the Revolution, see Milton M. Klein's review of *Origin* (*William and Mary Quarterly*, 3rd ser., 18 [1961]: 278) in which he accuses Knollenberg of failing to credit the colonists with an attachment to principle and Knollenberg's response (*William and Mary Quarterly*, 3rd ser., 18 [1961]: 258).

pened in the political and constitutional realms, not in an internal social upheaval that by indirection spilled over into the empire.[6]

Most accounts of the beginnings of the revolutionary conflict center on the Stamp Act as the crucial event between the close of the Seven Years' War and the Declaration of Independence. Knollenberg recognizes the importance of the Stamp Act, but he thinks it the culmination of the first phase rather than the beginning of the controversy. He finds the origin of colonial discontent in 1759, in the midst of the Seven Years' War, when the British ministry made a number of critical decisions concerning imperial policy. In that year, according to Knollenberg, the British began the process of tightening the administration of their colonial possessions, in part as a war measure and in part as a more general effort to redefine the imperial bond. Thus Knollenberg conceives of the Anglo-American dispute as at base an argument over the nature of the empire, and he locates the source of the trouble in London. Throughout the 1760s and 1770s, the Americans responded to British initiatives; they did not start the argument.

Historians before and after Knollenberg have chosen different dates for beginning the march toward revolution. Recently, for much the same reason that led Knollenberg to fix on 1759, Jack P. Greene has stressed the importance of 1748.[7] Noting the significance of the French departure from North America at the close of the Seven Years' War, Lawrence Henry Gipson favored 1763, though in many ways his multivolume history of the entire British colonial experience is an account of the background of the Revolution.[8] Edmund S. Morgan, whose work did so much to elucidate the significance of the Stamp

6. Two brief accounts of the historiography of the Revolution are Edmund S. Morgan, "Revisions in Need of Revising," *William and Mary Quarterly,* 3rd ser., 14 (1957): 3–15, and Jack P. Greene, "The Reappraisal of the American Revolution in Recent Historical Literature" in *The Reinterpretation of the American Revolution,* ed. Greene (Westport, Conn.: Greenwood Press, 1968), 2–74.

7. Jack P. Greene, "The Origins of the New Colonial Policy" in *The Blackwell Encyclopedia of the American Revolution,* ed. Jack P. Greene and J. R. Pole (Oxford: Blackwell, 1991), 95–106. See further the bibliographical references on p. 106.

8. Lawrence Henry Gipson, "The American Revolution as an Aftermath of the Great War for Empire, 1754–1763," *Political Science Quarterly,* 65 (1950): 86–104, and John M. Murrin, "The French and Indian War, the American Revolution, and the Counterfactual Hypothesis: Reflections on Lawrence Henry Gipson and John Shy," *Reviews in American History,* 1 (1973): 307–18.

Act, knew that much had occurred during the war with France to dis-
rupt the contentment of the colonists.[9] So Knollenberg could find
little disagreement among historians over his contention that trouble
had been brewing for some time or even over the point at which the
historian should intrude into the flow of events. But the meaning of
the predating of the Revolution was another question.

By marking the change of policy that occurred beginning in 1759
as a decisive turn in imperial affairs, Knollenberg implies an earlier
age of harmony in Anglo-American relations. At least, he rejects the
kind of whiggish position made famous by George Bancroft in the
nineteenth century that detected the seeds of revolution in the very
establishment of colonies in the New World. Bancroft thought it inevitable, as did many Whigs, that American liberty should be realized
apart from Europe. Nor did Knollenberg credit the contention of
Charles M. Andrews that the story of Anglo-American relations was
fraught with difficulties that came to fruition in the 1760s and 1770s
but that plainly did not begin then.[10] For Knollenberg it is a matter of
emphasis. He knows that relations with the British had not always
been rosy, and he also sees that the navigation system extracted a cost
from colonial commerce. Certainly, with their trade confined by imperial regulations and their liberty circumscribed by a distant king
and bureaucracy, the colonists were not the free people they would be
after 1776. But the imperial system offered compensations. The colonies enjoyed the protection of Britain in a hostile world, especially
against the French. Colonial legislatures, whose power increased mea-
surably in the eighteenth century, exercised local autonomy. And even
the labyrinthine navigation system proved to be tolerable. Until the
1760s Britain enforced it loosely (described by Edmund Burke as
"salutary neglect"), and for the burdens it imposed on colonial commerce it offered numerous drawbacks and bounties. If the British government had not revised its colonial policy, Knollenberg sees no rea-

9. Edmund S. Morgan and Helen M. Morgan, *The Stamp Act Crisis: Prologue to Revolution,* 3rd ed.
(Chapel Hill: University of North Carolina Press, 1995), chs. 1 and 2.

10. Charles M. Andrews, *The Colonial Background of the American Revolution,* rev. ed. (New Haven,
Conn.: Yale University Press, 1931).

son why the colonists should not have lived into the future as reasonably contented subjects of the crown.

For good reason, then, Knollenberg seeks the origin of the Revolution mainly in Britain. In *Origin of the American Revolution,* he offers a
primer on the old colonial system and treats in detail the instability of
British politics in the sixties. By that decade the stable administration established by the Whigs after the Hanoverian succession had passed into
history. No longer could a politician of Sir Robert Walpole's stature
remain in power for twenty years as the king's first minister. Public men
of talent who understood the colonial situation and wished the Americans well still appeared on the scene, but they proved incapable of
holding power. The Duke of Newcastle was beyond his prime, William
Pitt suffered from physical and psychological infirmities, and the Marquis of Rockingham failed to maintain his office. Other figures, such
as the Earl of Bute, George Grenville, Charles Townshend, and the
Duke of Grafton, possessed only modest political capacities and were
unsympathetic to the colonies. Not until the crown maintained Lord
North in power in the 1770s did Britain once again have stable administration. Ironically, stability did nothing to save the empire. North
repeated the blunders of the sixties that had done so much to under-
mine the loyalties of the colonists.

By beginning his account in the late 1750s, before the Stamp
Act crisis, Knollenberg focuses on a long list of smaller issues, none
of which in itself would have induced the Americans to seek a
change in their relationship with Britain. It was the cumulative
effect of such minor grievances as the disallowance of colonial laws,
writs of assistance, the threat of an Anglican bishopric, enforcement of the White Pine Act, and appointment of colonial judges at
the pleasure of the king, together with the Sugar and Stamp acts,
that fueled the American conviction that the British government
had embarked on a long-term conspiracy to destroy American liberty. In these early stages, American responses were largely legal
and constitutional, but the groundwork had been laid for a shift in
American reactions that culminated in the language of conspiracy
adopted by Thomas Jefferson in the Declaration of Independence.
That founding document details the "Abuses and Usurpations,"

predating the Stamp Act, that supported the American case for a ministerial conspiracy.[11]

Of course the British intended no such conspiracy. The sources of their misguided policy could be found in ignorance, inattention, political instability, and a certain supercilious incapacity to take their colonial dependents seriously. Perhaps most important, many British politicians feared that, if the imperial bond were not clarified and tightened, the Americans would soon slip into independence.[12] But if the British ministries did not conspire to destroy American liberty, they did propose to initiate drastic changes in the long-established imperial connection that were unlikely to serve the interests of the colonies. The American reaction might occasionally have seemed overwrought, but in fact it arose from a reasonably clear-headed insight into the long-term significance of British policies.

Some of Knollenberg's most provocative writing concerns the movement of American settlers to the West. It was this development, according to the ministry, that justified the stationing of substantial forces in America and that required the raising of a revenue to pay for their support. Settlers on Indian lands brought trouble and expense. They stirred hostilities with the native warriors, and they disrupted trade. Garrisons in the backcountry would serve the dual purpose of protecting the border settlements and keeping the colonists from intruding farther into Indian territory. In addition to the retention of substantial forces in America and the building of frontier forts, the British government issued the Proclamation of 1763, which temporarily halted the movement of population beyond the Appalachians.[13]

11. Bernard Bailyn, *The Ideological Origins of the America Revolution* (Cambridge, Mass.: Harvard University Press, 1967), remains the basic work. But also see Forrest McDonald, *Novus Ordo Seclorum: Intellectual Origins of the Constitution* (Lawrence: University of Kansas Press, 1985). For a brief summary of the intellectual background of the Revolution, see Isaac Kramnick, "Ideological Background," in *Blackwell Encyclopedia*, 84–91.

12. Jack P. Greene, *Understanding the American Revolution: Issues and Actors* (Charlottesville: University Press of Virginia, 1995), 2–3.

13. On the proclamation, consult Jack M. Sosin, *Whitehall in the Wilderness: The Middle West in British Colonial Policy, 1760–1775* (Lincoln: University of Nebraska Press, 1961), 39–64. A discussion of Grenville's decision to station troops in America can be found in John L. Bullion, *A Great and Necessary Measure: George Grenville and the Genesis of the Stamp Act, 1763–1765* (Columbia: University of Missouri Press, 1982), 21–23.

Knollenberg finds the ministerial justification for its western policy unconvincing. He argues that long experience had demonstrated the ineptness of European troops against the wilderness warriors of North America. Such spectacular debacles as Braddock's defeat and later the failure of Sir Jeffrey Amherst to suppress Pontiac's Rebellion reinforced the case. Moreover, that backcountry fracas proved the futility of frontier garrisons. All of the smaller posts fell. Only Detroit and Fort Pitt held, and they became more prisons for their garrisons than bases from which troops could advance against the Indians. The warriors simply skirted the fortifications and with fire and pillage drove the settlers a hundred miles east.

Knollenberg contends that the garrisons served a purpose other than defense against marauding Indians. They preserved for the crown a source of patronage that otherwise would have been lost in time of peace. With what was in effect a standing army in America, the king had many more commissions to distribute. The Proclamation of 1763 derived more from a long-held eighteenth-century bias in favor of compact settlements more amenable to control and more likely to provide markets for British goods. Scattered primitive backcountry settlements tended to drift beyond imperial control and outside the orbit of mercantilist influence. As plausible as Knollenberg's contentions may be, they do not exclude the possibility that the ministers were simply misinformed about the best means of frontier protection and that they were eager to avoid the expense of war and to preserve the fur trade.

Knollenberg's interest in the West led him to the often-repeated accusation that the garrison at Pittsburgh had sent blankets infected with smallpox to the Indians besieging the fort during Pontiac's Rebellion. In his initial examination of the issue, Knollenberg concluded that, despite Amherst's suggestion (it was not really a command) in a letter to Simeon Ecuyer, fort commander, that blankets might be given to the Indians, blankets were not in fact sent out of the fort. Knollenberg added that it could not be established that smallpox could be spread in that manner and that in any case it was unclear that the British action was responsible, since the contagion was already rife in the neighborhood of the fort. No sooner had Knollenberg published his findings when Donald Kent of the Pennsylvania Historical and Museum Commission informed him that newly discovered evidence revealed that Ecuyer had anticipated Amherst and had distributed blankets from the smallpox hospital before the general's proposal arrived. Knollenberg immediately conceded the point publicly and corrected his original contention.[14] The episode confirmed two of Knollenberg's virtues as a historian: he possessed a sharp eye for original interpretation, and he was not unduly wedded to his own view when others knew better.

For all of his emphasis on the policy changes of the late 1750s and early 1760s, Knollenberg recognizes that those events were preliminary (albeit in many ways formative) to the dispute over taxation. Grenville opened the controversy with the Sugar Act[15] and the Stamp Act, both of which, contrary to precedent and constitutional principle, levied a tax in America. The colonists reacted slowly. They protested the economic burden imposed by the Sugar Act before making their constitutional objections clear. By the time news of the Stamp Act reached the New World, however, constitutional principle had become paramount. The resolves of the Stamp Act Congress claimed that the right to tax resided exclusively in the colonial legislatures.

Although historians have long agreed that at some point the colonists rejected all parliamentary taxation, the question of timing remains an issue. For many years imperial and progressive historians, for different reasons, doubted the early clarity of the American position. They contended that the colonists did not oppose all parliamentary taxation until the Townshend crisis. Initially, the argument goes, they distinguished external from internal taxation. Because external taxes (the Molasses and Sugar acts) could be seen as partly regulatory, they fell within the jurisdiction of Parliament. But authority over internal taxes (the Stamp Act) rested exclusively with the colonial legislatures.

14. Although Knollenberg does not treat the incident in the text, he cites his own work and Kent's letter in note 10 on p. 264. For a recent account of the subject, see Elizabeth O. Fenn, "Biological Warfare in Eighteenth-Century North America: Beyond Jeffrey Amherst," *Journal of American History* 86 (2000): 1552–80.

15. Knollenberg refers to the omnibus legislation of 1764 as the American Act. Most historians for convenience call it the Sugar Act because the tax on foreign molasses entering the North American colonies was its most significant component. The original legislation of 1733 governing the importation of molasses is probably best called the Molasses Act.

Beginning in the 1950s, Edmund S. Morgan tried to straighten out this tangle.[16] He contended that after some minor early hesitation the Americans rejected all parliamentary taxation, made no distinction between internal and external taxes, and maintained this position until 1773–1774, when they were well on the road to independence. The confusion arose because the colonists conceded Parliament's authority to pass general regulatory measures, which the British mistook for the right to levy external taxes. But in fact, according to Morgan, the colonies in their formal resolves and the pamphlet literature that grew up over the matter had been quite clear about parliamentary jurisdiction. They tied taxation to representation in a way that did not apply to imperial legislation. With only informal agents in London and no voting representation in Parliament, the Americans claimed exclusive authority to tax themselves.

The root of the problem lay deep in English history. Two constitutional principles had emerged from the Glorious Revolution of 1688 that concluded the century-long contest between crown and Parliament. Because it was the representative body, Parliament established its uncontested supremacy in the constitutional arrangement and assumed exclusive jurisdiction over taxation. Until the Sugar Act, it had exercised its taxing power only within Britain; the colonists had been taxed only by their legislatures. With the change in policy, parliamentary supremacy clashed with the identification of taxation with representation. British politicians opted almost entirely for supremacy. Only a minor faction of the Whigs joined the American side of the controversy. The colonists advanced no argument against parliamentary supremacy over the crown or even within the empire, but they insisted that supremacy could not trump the indispensable linkage between taxation and representation.

Although a little less certain than Morgan about the timing and clarity of the American position, Knollenberg is equally convinced

16. Morgan broached the issue first in "Colonial Ideas of Parliamentary Power 1764–1766," *William and Mary Quarterly*, 3rd ser., 5 (1948): 311–41. To support the case, he published the relevant documents in *Prologue to Revolution: Sources and Documents on the Stamp Act Crisis, 1764–1766* (Chapel Hill: University of North Carolina Press, 1959). For an alternative interpretation, see Bernard Bailyn, ed., *Pamphlets of the American Revolution 1750–1776* (Cambridge: Harvard University Press, 1965), 126, note 50.

that the colonists had the better of the constitutional dispute. Neither Morgan nor Knollenberg doubted the English roots of liberty. After all, they wrote a Whig version of history that saw the Anglo-American past as the saga of freedom.[17] But in one of those strange twists, in the 1760s and 1770s the agents of liberty resided now in the New World.

In understanding how the British stumbled into this debacle, much hinges on the personality and motives of George Grenville. He came to power convinced that the colonial regime required a major over-haul, which could not be accomplished without reining in the colonists and obtaining new sources of revenue. Although an unlikely candidate for the role, he saw himself as the preserver of the empire in its time of need. His connections (he was the younger brother of Earl Temple and Pitt's brother-in-law) might have made him a formidable political figure, but he lacked the personal qualities necessary to reach the first rank. Without the king's support he would never have gained the first office or held it even for the short tenure he was allowed. After the collapse of the Bute Ministry, George III wanted to keep the gov-ernment out of the hands of Pitt or the Whig magnates, and he chose Grenville because he knew that he would be dependent on the crown. But Grenville had other ideas. Driven by the fatal combination of am-bition and weakness, he mounted a scheme to save the empire and make his own career. He failed at both.[18]

Morgan stresses the shifty side of Grenville's character. Suspecting that the colonists would not react well to an effort to tax them, he met with the agents and with a show of sympathy hoped to maneuver them into accepting the new policy. His efforts came off as entirely too clever and succeeded only in alienating the agents and convincing Morgan that he played a deceptive game.[19] Knollenberg sees the Grenville charade as slightly more sinister. He argues that from the

17. The classic work remains Herbert Butterfield, *Whig Interpretation of History* (London: G. Bell, 1931).

18. Bullion, *A Great and Necessary Measure*, chs. 4 and 5, emphasizes the importance of contraband trade in Grenville's policy.

19. Morgan and Morgan, *Stamp Act Crisis*, ch. 5; Bullion, *A Great and Necessary Measure*, 125–32, 147; P. D. G. Thomas, *British Politics and the Stamp Act Crisis: The First Phase of the American Revolution 1763–1767* (Oxford: Clarendon Press, 1975), 78.

beginning he intended to "cram the tax down their throats" (p. 211). Grenville's thinly disguised sympathy was part of a broader design to revamp the colonial relationship without the colonists' consent and contrary to their interests. Knollenberg believes that through the navigation system the Americans already contributed more than their share to the upkeep of the empire and that they were on the right side of the constitutional question.

He remains a reliable chronicler of the past because he rooted his work in the sources and was never content to rely on others for his historical opinions. And in many ways it is his opinions that make his writings engrossing to peruse once again. In this first installment the reader will have the pleasure of following a well-told narrative of the early stages of the American Revolution and at the same time accompany a deeply informed scholar as he grapples with the perennial questions raised by the American founding.

AUTHOR'S NOTE

Those intending to use this volume as a text are referred to pages 253–58 of the Appendix in the original edition (1960) for explanations of footnotes, dating, quotations, sources, differences in meaning, and for other comments.

INTRODUCTION

THIS BOOK is the outgrowth of an effort to discover why the principal British colonies in North America were on the point of rebellion in 1765–1766, ten years before the outbreak of the American Revolution. My conclusion and thesis are that, while the British Stamp Act of 1765 greatly contributed to and touched off the colonial uprising of 1765–1766, the colonists had been brought to the brink of rebellion by a number of other provocative British measures from 1759 to 1764, most of which persisted after the Stamp Act was repealed in 1766 and contributed to the mounting colonial discontent culminating in the American Revolution of 1775–1783.

From 1759 to 1763 the chief causes of colonial discontent were:

The Privy Council's disallowance in 1759 of an important Virginia act accompanied by an order to the Governor of the colony forbidding him to sign any bill passed by the legislature of the colony repealing or amending an existing act, unless the bill contained a clause suspending its operation until approved by the Privy Council in England. Since many acts would be wholly or nearly useless if suspended until thus approved, this order struck at the very roots of self-government in Virginia. Soon afterward Massachusetts and South Carolina were likewise alarmed by steps taken to extend the order to these colonies;

Issuance in 1761 of general writs of assistance empowering officers of the English customs service in Massachusetts to break into and search homes and stores for supposed smuggled goods;

Issuance of an order by the Privy Council in 1761 forbidding governors of the royal colonies to issue judicial or other commissions not revocable at the pleasure of the King, an order particularly disturbing in New York and New Jersey because the judges of the Supreme Court in these colonies had heretofore been granted tenure during good behavior;

The activities from 1759 onward of Thomas Secker, Archbishop of Canterbury, assisted by the Society for the Propagation of the Gospel in Foreign Parts of which he was President, in planting a Church of England mission church in Cambridge near Harvard College, fountainhead of the Congregational clergy in eastern New England; in procuring the disallowance by the Privy Council of a Massachusetts act to establish a Congregational missionary society for work among the American Indians; and in attempting to secure the establishment of Church of England bishops in the colonies.

The Treaty of Paris between Great Britain and France and Spain, signed at Paris in February 1763, laid the basis for reestablishing cordial relations between Great Britain and the colonies. For the colonists were highly pleased and grateful to the British Government, as they had every reason to be, for the removal of the French threat to the security of the British colonies in North America by insisting on France's cession of the whole of Canada. But the favorable effect of the treaty on colonial opinion was almost immediately impaired by fresh and even more provocative British measures affecting the colonies.

The first was a movement in 1763 for rigid enforcement of the whole range of acts of Parliament restricting colonial trade, including the hitherto unenforced Sugar Act of 1733 imposing a prohibitive duty on imports of foreign colonial molasses. The enforcement of this would seriously cripple if not destroy the extremely important trade of the northern British colonies with the foreign colonial possessions in the West Indies and South America. This trade not only furnished the molasses which was the backbone of the flourishing northern colonial rum industry and was widely used for sweetening, but gave northern colonial farmers, fishermen, and lumbermen a favorable market for their surplus farm produce, fish, and lumber.

Irritating under any circumstances, the new measure was particularly so because it was implemented by sending a squadron of British warships to American waters as an arm of the English customs service. Even when British warships were in American waters to defend the colonies in time of war, impressment of colonial seamen to fill gaps in the crews from death and desertion had caused serious trouble. Now, with the ships in constant attendance on an obnoxious mission, impressment and other incidents connected with their presence were a source of acute friction.

Rigorous enforcement of the Sugar Act was accompanied by rigorous enforcement of long-unenforced acts of Parliament prohibiting (with certain exceptions) the cutting of white pine trees in the colonies.

Even more serious and far-reaching was the passage by Parliament, in April 1764, of an act, the American Act of 1764,* imposing new restrictions on colonial trade and levying taxes in the colonies to support an enlarged British standing army in America without consulting the colonial governments as to the number or composition and distribution of the troops and without offering commissions to any former colonial officers, many of whom had served creditably in the recent French and Indian War. So long as Great Britain paid the entire cost of the British forces stationed in America, the colonists had little cause for complaint if not consulted on these points; but when called upon to support or help support the British troops in America, it was unreasonable not to give them a share in determining the number, distribution, and kind of troops needed for their protection and in the apportionment of commissions.

The failure to consult the colonial governments was particularly galling because at the very time the new policy of taxing the colonists for the support of the British army in America was put into effect, the army was miserably failing to protect the colonial frontiers from the ravages of the western Indians in an uprising (Pontiac's Rebellion) attributable largely to blunders of the British Commander-in-Chief in North America, General Sir Jeffery Amherst.

*The American Act is usually referred to as the Sugar Act. [B. W. S.]

Furthermore, though in the Act of Union of England and Scotland, the Scots were protected not only by representation in Parliament but by a provision permanently limiting the proportion of the total land tax to be imposed on Scotland, neither the American Act itself nor any statement in Parliament concerning it offered assurance that, having established the precedent of taxing the colonies, Parliament would not shift an ever-increasing proportion of the imperial tax burden from British to colonial taxpayers. Moreover, since the colonists were now to be taxed for imperial purposes, they had reason to expect an offset by amelioration of the restrictions imposed by Parliament on colonial trade, whereas, far from easing existing restrictions, Parliament made them more onerous than ever.

In considering the alarming British measures before 1765, later discussed, it should be noted that, in at least two instances the alarm proved to be unfounded: The efforts of Archbishop Secker and others to secure the establishment of an Anglican bishopric in the colonies were frustrated by the refusal of the British government to approve a step so likely to provoke colonial antagonism; and colonial alarm over the establishment of a British admiralty court at Halifax having jurisdiction throughout the colonies proved to be unfounded because almost no suits in causes of action arising outside Nova Scotia were brought in that court. Nevertheless, fears which in the end prove to be unfounded may be as influential as those that are.

Had the alarming measures from 1759 to 1764 been distributed over a long period, the effect of each might have rippled away before the next was felt; but, concentrated in the span of a few years, all contributed to the colonial fear that the British Government would go further and further in depriving the colonists of the large measure of self-government in internal affairs they had so long enjoyed and justly valued.

This fear became conviction on Parliament's passing the colonial Stamp Act of 1765. Warned by a resolution of the House of Commons in 1764 and by their agents in London that a bill for such an act would probably be introduced in the next session of Parliament, the legislatures of the leading North American colonies petitioned against the proposed new act, only to have their petitions rejected and the act adopted by an overwhelming majority in both Houses. This was the last straw. There now seemed no other way to halt further British encroachment on colonial self-government than to resist the execution of this latest measure, even at the risk of war.

As indicated by the foregoing discussion, I differ from the view presented by Professor Charles Andrews in his well-known Presidential address to the American Historical Association in 1925, "The American Revolution: An Interpretation." The manifestations of colonial discontent in the half century preceding the Revolution were, said Andrews, "the outward and visible signs of an inward factual divergence. . . . On one side was the immutable stereotyped system of the mother country, based on precedent and tradition and designed to keep things comfortably as they were; on the other, a vital, dynamic organism, containing the seed of a great nation, its forces untried, still to be proved. It is inconceivable that a connection should have continued long between two such yoke-fellows, one static, the other dynamic, separated by an ocean and bound only by the ties of a legal relationship."[1]

To me, on the contrary, it seems reasonably clear that until the adoption of the provocative British measures from 1759 to 1765 described in this book, the stereotyped system of British Government, based on precedent and tradition and designed to keep things comfortably as they were, was, on the whole, satisfactory to the colonial "yoke-fellows." Far from being bound only by the ties of a legal relationship, they were, in most cases, bound also by a powerful bond of sentiment woven from many strands: a feeling for England as the ancestral homeland ("home" as many still called it); a strong sense of family kinship with its people; a common language, literature, and system of law; loyalty to a common sovereign. Had the relationship not been disturbed by the many new and vexing British measures introduced from 1759 to 1765 and afterward continued or renewed, it might, I think, have endured (subject to occasional political readjustments, notably such as were made a half century later in the British Empire and in Great Britain itself) for many generations, perhaps even to this day.

I regret that the letters on which I rely so largely for evidence of colonial discontent during the period under consideration are almost exclusively from writers who resided in the old settlements on or near the sea-cost or along the great navigable rivers. I have searched almost in vain for letters from frontier communities touching on the controversies with Great Britain. Probably few such were written. However, the legislative petitions and protests discussed in later chapters were supported by representatives from all sections of the several colonies—and when the call to arms came in 1775, the frontier communities in most of the colonies were among the readiest to respond.

In giving the names of members of the numerous colonial committees that opposed the disturbing British innovations of 1759 to 1765, I do so not from love for petty detail but to bring home the wide range of persons, especially among colonial merchants and legislators, who took part in this early opposition. In reading some accounts of the American Revolution, one gets the impression that, until the very eve of the outbreak of war, active colonial opposition was limited to a relatively few propagandists and hotheads, which is far from true.

Living as we do in a period when relatively few laymen sit as judges, readers not particularly familiar with our colonial period may think that colonial leaders other than lawyers must have had little participation or even interest in the controversies over fine points of law dealt with in this book, and that I have given undue space to them. But the colonial period was quite different in this respect from our own. In the colonies, as in eighteenth-century Britain, a man of position in the community was likely to serve during most of his adult life as a justice of the peace and, in some colonies, as a justice of a county court, so that knowledge of and interest in legal questions were more common among laymen in colonial days than now.

While most of this book deals with the causes and manifestation of discontent in the old British colonies in North America, three other related questions are considered: To what extent was the cession of Canada, freeing the old British colonies in North America from fear of French invasion and weakening their sense of dependence on Great Britain, responsible for the colonial uprising of 1765–1766? Why were the British island colonies and the new British colonies on the North American mainland so much less determined than the old mainland colonies in their resistance to the Stamp Act? Why were so many British measures obnoxious to the colonies adopted at this particular time?

Parkman and other distinguished historians have stated or implied that the British colonies in North America desired to shake off British rule long before 1765 and that the British conquest and retention of Canada, by relieving the residents of the old British colonies on the North American mainland of their need for British protection from French invasion, made rebellion practically inevitable.

Some of the colonists doubtless wished for independence; but I am convinced that Thomas Pownall, former royal Governor of Massachusetts, truly represented the feeling of the vast majority when he stated in 1764, "It has been often suggested that care should be taken in the administration of the plantations; lest, in some future time, these colonies should become independent of the mother country. But . . . if, by becoming independent is meant a revolt, nothing is further from their nature, their interest, their thoughts . . . nothing can eradicate from their hearts their natural, almost mechanical, affection to Great Britain, which they conceive under no other sense, nor call by any other name, than that of home," and that even after passage of the Stamp Act, all but a small minority were, as Jonathan Mayhew wrote in August 1765, "far, very far indeed, from desiring to be independent upon Great-Britain."[2]

In speaking of the small amount of colonial thought of or desire for independence at this period, I use, and believe Pownall and Mayhew used the term "independence" in the sense of complete freedom from British control. Even if, as later widely maintained in the colonies, Parliament had no right to legislate for them, there remained a wide range of unchallenged Crown jurisdiction, including control of the foreign relations of the colonies; settlement of colonial boundary disputes; appointment of the governor and members of the Council of most of the colonies; review by the Privy Council of legislation passed in most of the colonies, with power of disallowance; and the authority of the Privy Council to review and reverse the decisions of the highest courts of all the colonies.

The chief source for the view that a desire for, or at least the thought of complete independence was rather widespread in the colonies before 1765 seems to be a passage in *En Resa til Norra America* (1756) by a Finnish naturalist, Pehr Kalm, concerning a trip made by him through the middle and northern British North American colonies in 1748–1749, and a letter of John Adams in 1755 to Nathan Webb, recently a fellow student at Harvard.[3]

In the Resa, after describing the restrictions laid by Great Britain on colonial trade and industry, Kalm wrote, "These and some other restrictions occasion the inhabitants of the English colonies to grow less tender for their mother country. This coldness is kept up by the many foreigners such as Germans, Dutch and French, who live among the English and have no particular attachment to Old England. . . . ¶ I have been told by Englishmen, and not only by such as were born in America but also by those who came from Europe, that the English colonies in North America, in the space of thirty or fifty years, would be able to form a state by themselves entirely independent of Old England. But as the whole country which lies along the seashore is unguarded, and on the land side is harassed by the French, these dangerous neighbors in times of war are sufficient to prevent the connection of the colonies with their mother country from being quite broken off."

In his letter to Webb, Adams said, "Soon after the Reformation, a few people came over into this new world for conscience sake. Perhaps this apparently trivial incident may transfer the great seat of empire into America. It looks likely to me: for if we can remove the turbulent Gallicks, our people, according to the exactest computations, will in another century become more numerous than England itself. Should this be the case, since we have, I may say, all the naval stores of the nation in our hands, it will be easy to obtain the mastery of the seas; and then the united force of all Europe will not subdue us. The only way to keep us from setting up for ourselves is to disunite us. *Divide et impera.*"

My conviction that the statements of Kalm and Adams tend to give a misleading view of general colonial sentiment is based chiefly on the mass of colonial letters I read in preparing this volume. Among the many hundreds of these written from 1745 to 1763, I found only one besides Adams's that gives any intimation of a desire for independence,[4] and not a single one commented on, much less exulted over, the cession of Canada as probably paving the way for freedom from British rule.

This is not to say that the cession of Canada had no bearing on the American Revolution, for I think it did—not, however, by removing a barrier to the realization of a preexisting Colonial desire for independence but by making the colonists more self-reliant and thus giving them added boldness to resist the alarming British innovations brought out in this book.

The view that many of the colonists had long wished for independence stems, I think, partly from the evidence of British fear of this. As far back as 1721, Jeremiah Dummer in London wrote in his *A Defence of the New-England Charters*, "There is one Thing more I have heard often urg'd against the Charter Colonies, and indeed 'tis what one meets with from People of all Conditions and Qualities, tho' with due respect to their better Judgments, I can see neither Reason nor Colour for it. 'Tis said, *that their encreasing Numbers and Wealth join'd to their great Distance from Britain, will give them an Opportunity in the Course of some Years to throw off their Dependance on the Nation, and declare themselves a free state, if not curb'd in Time, by being made entirely subject to the Crown.*" Twenty years later, Acting Governor George Clarke of New York, urging the legislature to obey a Crown instruction to vote permanent salaries to certain officials in the colony, said, "only this will remove as to this province, a jealousy [suspicion] which for some years has obtained in England, that the plantations are not without thoughts of throwing off their Dependence on the Crown of England." And in 1746, the Duke of Bedford, Secretary of State for the Southern Department, wrote the Duke of Newcastle of the undesirability of colonial troops taking Canada without British aid because of "the independence it may create in those provinces towards their mother country, when they shall see within themselves so great an army possessed in their own right by conquest of so great an extent of country."[5]*

Expressions of this fear appear again and again during and immediately following the close of the French and Indian War of 1755–1760. In 1757 the anonymous author of *The Contest in America between Great Britain and France* (London, 1757) commented on "the false and groundless notion that seems to influence many people's opinions and conduct with regard to the colonies, . . . the fear of their rebelling, and

*John Bumstead, " 'Things in the Womb of Time,' Ideas of American Independence, 1633–1763," *William and Mary Quarterly*, 3rd ser., 31 (1974): 533–64. [B. W. S.]

throwing off their dependence on Britain. . . ." Soon after the capture of Quebec in 1759, Colonel James Murray, British military governor of the Quebec district, wrote Amherst, "Everybody will inform you how powerful and how flourishing this colony was, and how formidable it might be under any other government than that of Monsr. Vaudreuil: *En bonne politique* it should perhaps be destroyed, but there may be reasons why it should remain, as it is a guarantee for the good behaviour of its neighbouring colonies." And Bedford, questioning the advisability of Great Britain's retaining the whole of Canada, wrote Newcastle, "indeed my Lord, I don't know whether the neighbourhood of the French to our Northern American colonies, was not the greatest security of their dependence on their Mother Country, who I fear will be slighted by them when their apprehensions of the French are removed."[6]

Better known than Murray's and Bedford's letters is a pamphlet published anonymously by William Burke in 1760, *Remarks on the Letter Addres'd to Two Great Men*. In this tract, arguing in favor of British retention of Guadeloupe in preference to Canada, he said, "If, Sir, the People of our Colonies find no Check from Canada . . . What the Consequences will be . . . I leave to your own reflections. . . . This is indeed a Point that must be the constant Object of the Minister's Attention, but it is not a fit Subject for a Discussion. . . . The Possession of Canada, far from being necessary to our Safety, may in its Consequence be even dangerous. A Neighbour that keeps us in some Awe, is not always the worst of Neighbours."[7]

English suspicion of colonial desire for independence does not, however, prove that the suspicion was well grounded, and, for reasons previously stated, I am convinced it was not. Probably, when later antagonized by the British innovations discussed in this book, the colonists were less yielding than they might have been if still fearful of French invasion from Canada, but that does not signify that they previously wished for independence.

As to the failure of the island colonies and the newly acquired mainland colonies to resist the Stamp Act, the reasons for this are, I think, pretty clear. Enforcement of the prohibitive duty on foreign colonial molasses imposed by the Sugar Act of 1733 and perpetuated at a lower but still heavy rate by the American Act of 1764, far from injuring the West Indians as it did the mainland colonists, was for their benefit. Furthermore, Great Britain granted a large tariff preference in favor of British colonial over foreign sugar, and, since the British demand for sugar had long outstripped the British colonial sugar supply, the tariff differential in favor of British colonial sugar was effective in raising the price of sugar in the British market far above the world price. Because of its costliness to British consumers, the high protective tariff in favor of British colonial sugar had long been under fire, and, if Parliament was seriously antagonized, would almost certainly be reduced or repealed. Finally, apart from economic considerations there was a compelling reason for the British West Indian colonists to remain quiet, since, outnumbered seven to one by their slaves and in constant fear and danger of slave insurrection, they were utterly dependent on the continued protection of the British army and navy.[8]

Bermuda, the Bahamas, and Nova Scotia, though not benefited by the British tariff differential on sugar, were, like the West Indian colonies, exceptionally dependent on the British navy and army for protection. Moreover, they were politically and economically backward; Nova Scotia received direct financial aid from Parliament;[9] and Bermuda and the Bahamas were isolated from the currents of opinion and protest through which the leaders in the mainland colonies aroused and encouraged each other. Grenada, East Florida, and West Florida, formed out of the territory ceded by France and Spain in 1763, were too sparsely peopled and politically undeveloped (they did not even have representative assemblies yet) to resist. And Quebec, the colony formed from eastern Canada, though more populous than the other new colonies, was equally backward in political development.

As to the third question, the question why so many British measures obnoxious to the North American colonists were taken at this particular time, no summary answer is possible. As will be seen in the course of this book, many factors were involved. The most important, I believe, was the distracted state of British politics and government following the death in 1760 of George II, a state attributable chiefly to the shift in power from the experienced Duke of Newcastle and William Pitt to George III's inexperienced favorite, Lord Bute, and the audacity and art of the archdemagogue John Wilkes. Hence, in the opening chapter, I outline the developments in British politics and government during the early years of the reign of George III, believing that some knowledge of these is essential to an understanding of much that follows.

ORIGIN OF THE AMERICAN REVOLUTION: 1759–1766

CHAPTER I

BRITISH POLITICS
AND COLONIAL POLICY:
1759–1765

PART ONE

The Old Regime: August 1759–April 1762

WHEN OUR PERIOD opens in the summer of 1759 George II, aged seventy-six, was on the throne in the thirty-third year of his reign. The heir apparent was his twenty-one-year-old grandson, George, Prince of Wales (whose father Frederick had died in 1751), an unworldly young man deeply attached to and greatly under the influence of his Groom of the Stole, Lord Bute. The King's chief ministers were the Duke of Newcastle, in his sixty-seventh year, First Lord of the Treasury, and William Pitt, in his early fifties, Secretary of State for the Southern Department and Leader of the House of Commons. Their task in dealing with the crotchety old King was eased by the advice and influence of Lady Yarmouth, his devoted and sensible mistress.[1]

Newcastle had held high office almost continuously since 1717. Wellborn, rich, and married to a granddaughter of the great Marlborough, he became, in 1724, Secretary of State for the Southern Department, the Department dealing with the colonies, where he served for twenty-four years, gaining a knowledge of colonial affairs more extensive than that of any other leading minister. In 1748 he moved to the Northern Department, and, in 1754, on the death of his brother

1

Henry Pelham, to the headship of the Treasury Board, the most influential office in the Government, which he had since retained except for a few months in 1756–1757. Fussy, gushing, morbidly afraid of colds and of cabals to thrust him from office or weaken his influence, Newcastle has been the butt of much ridicule. But, as his tenure of high office, longer than that of any other British statesman of the period, and his undisputed leadership of the main body of the Whigs indicate, he had important elements of strength. Unstinting in the use of his wealth to establish and maintain his political influence, he was indefatigable as minister and politician at a time when many of his colleagues were devoted chiefly to sport, women, the bottle, and other private pursuits. Furthermore, he had the good sense to draw heavily on the wisdom of his close friend and advisor Philip Yorke, Earl of Hardwicke,[2] successively Attorney-General, Chief Justice of the King's Bench, and Lord Chancellor of England, one of the best heads in the nation.

"Newcastle," wrote the distinguished American scholar Theodore Calvin Pease, "was a typical politician and a good one—with an excessive geniality of manner the fruit of a kind heart and a real human interest. . . . He had fits of timorousness, suspicion, and procrastination; but they came and went; possibly sometimes they represented a pose. He was always in a hurry, but his voluminous correspondence with its multiplicity of interests explains why; explains why, also, with so many details constantly before him, he was sometimes careless about them. As a diplomat he had the experience of a quarter of a century and knew the personal foibles of most of the European statesmen of his generation."[3]

From the standpoint of the present book, the most significant fact about Newcastle that emerges from his massive correspondence was his interest in the defense of the colonies and his opposition to novel or harsh measures of colonial government likely to dampen or forfeit colonial good will and thus injure British trade with the colonies.

In 1750 he wrote his brother, "If you do not act with vigour, and support . . . our right to the extended boundaries of Nova Scotia you may not only lose that province but . . . all your northern colonies which are inestimable to us. If you do [act], you may run a risk of rup-

ture with France. But I think that is to be run." Later, in writing of the
Cabinet decision to send British troops to Virginia to resist French
penetration in the Ohio Valley, he said "I am very glad to be able to
tell you . . . the first point we have laid down is, That the Colonies
must not be abandon'd." And soon afterward he declared, "The Insults, and Encroachments of the French have alarm'd The Inhabitants
of Our Colonies to That Degree That Many of Them have left Their
Habitations, with Crops upon Their Lands. All North America will be
lost if these Practices are tolerated: and no War can be Worse to This
Country Than the Suffering such Insults." Furthermore, when the
question arose as to the disposition of Canada after its surrender by
the French in 1760, he was among those who favored demanding cession of the whole colony to Great Britain for the future security of the
British colonies in North America.[4]

In 1761, when thinking of resigning as First Lord of the Treasury,
one of the two measures Newcastle said he would consistently oppose,
whether in or out of office, was "any alteration, that may be proposed,
of the present Constitution, or receiv'd usage and practice, with regard either to *Scotland, Ireland, or our Settlements in America.*" In 1763, he
heartily endorsed Pitt's view that "Measures of Power and Force"
must be avoided in "the Settlement of our Colonies upon a proper
foot," and condemned the idea of giving the British governor of
Canada power to govern the colony without an elected provincial
Assembly. Such an innovation would, he thought, "shake the very
Foundation of our Colonies, who could, with entire Justice, expect
that that would be their fate very soon . . . [and] blow up all our Trade
& make such Confusion there, that neither our Old nor our new
Settlements would be of Use to this Country." Finally, not long before
his death, he wrote Lord Rockingham, "the measure of conquering
the colonies and obliging them to submit is become now more popular . . . [but] for my own part, whoever is for it, I must in conscience
enter my protest against it; and I hope our friends will well consider
before they give in to so destructive a measure."[5]

Moreover, of greater importance in Newcastle's relation to the
colonies than anything he said was the fact that, in spite of strong
pressure from British civil officials and military officers in America for

Parliamentary taxation of the colonies during the recent Seven Years' War, no bill for colonial taxes was introduced so long as he remained head of the British Treasury. Furthermore, though no evidence has been found of his opposing, while out of office, the American Act of 1764 or the colonial Stamp Act of 1765, after his return to office in July 1765, as Lord Privy Seal in the Rockingham Ministry, he was among the leading supporters of the repeal of the Stamp Act.

As indicated by his statement quoted above condemning the reported plan of governing Canada without any elected provincial Assembly, Newcastle's interest in the security and good will of the colonies probably stemmed chiefly from his conception of the value to Great Britain of her colonial trade and the importance of protecting the colonies and maintaining colonial good will as a means of preserving and enlarging this.[6] But even if dictated by a conception of British interest rather than a feeling of benevolence for the colonies, Newcastle's colonial policy was nonetheless wise and fruitful.

Pitt, a younger son in a family of less wealth and prestige than Newcastle's, did not attain an office of first rank until 1756, when, at the age of forty-eight, he became Secretary of State for the Southern Department, first briefly and, after June 1757, continuously until 1761.

Pitt had no such group of political followers—"friends" in British eighteenth-century parlance—as Newcastle, but he was generally supported in the House of Commons by the Tories or "country gentlemen," numbering something over a hundred members, and by William Beckford, an immensely wealthy merchant who was an outstanding member for London.[7] He also could count on the support of his wife's brothers, Lord Temple, an English peer holding the high office of Lord Privy Seal and a member of the inner Cabinet (hereinafter called simply the Cabinet),[8] and George Grenville, an important member of the House of Commons.

Until 1758 Pitt's reputation and influence were based chiefly on his effectiveness as a speaker in the House of Commons, of which we have an interesting description by Jared Ingersoll, a lawyer of New Haven, Connecticut, in a letter from London in December 1759 to a friend at home. "You seem desirous," wrote Ingersoll, "of some particular account of the characters of the more distinguished personages here, and of Mr. Pitt in particular. . . . As to his person, he is tall, rather slender than corpulent, not quite straight, but bending forward a little about the shoulders and head; a thin face somewhat pale; a Roman nose; his legs pretty small, and almost all the way of a bigness, — his angles being swelled with the gout, which makes him rather hobble than walk when he goes. His elocution is good, his voice clear, soft, and masculine. He delivers himself in the House, in public, in a manner distinct and forcible. If he has any fault I think it is in his language being a little too much swollen; seeming to border on bombast and fustian. . . . He makes use of a great many very brilliant and striking expressions, which, being attended with an air and manner sage and awful as a Cato, make a deep impression on the hearers; . . . [but] I believe he is a greater speaker than reasoner."[9]

Another source of Pitt's strength was his reputation for disinterestedness; many holders of public office were believed to be chiefly concerned with feathering their nests, but Pitt, who held the office of Paymaster-General of the army for over nine years (1746–1755), refrained from exploiting the office for his private profit. Finally, and of supreme importance as far as his popularity at this time was concerned, Pitt had proved to be a remarkably able and successful war minister, evidenced by a succession of British victories after he took over the direction of the British war against France, in brilliant contrast to humiliating defeats before.

Pitt seems to have fully shared Newcastle's interest in colonial security and good will. In 1754, he strongly recommended not only sending British troops to Virginia but raising and equipping, presumably at British expense, a large body of soldiers in America, and, in 1761 and 1762, advocated the retention of the whole of Canada even at the expense, if necessary, of giving up conquests in the West Indies. In 1763, he disapproved, as noted above, of using "Measures of Force . . . in the Settlement of our Colonies upon a proper Foot," and, though too ill to attend Parliament when taxation of the colonies for revenue was under consideration in 1764, made known his opposition. Again too ill to attend Parliament in 1765, he condemned the colonial stamp tax and, on returning to Parliament in 1766, came out strongly in favor of repeal.[10]

At the time our period opens in August 1759, on the continent of Europe neither side was winning; victory of the British and allied troops at Minden was offset by defeat of Great Britain's chief ally, Prussia, by the Russians and Austrians at Kunersdorf. But in North America the British capture of Fort Niagara, Amherst's occupation of the strongholds of Ticonderoga and Crown Point on Lake Champlain, abandoned by the French on his advance in great strength, and the taking of Quebec by a combined operation under General James Wolfe and Admiral Charles Saunders foreshadowed the collapse of French power in Canada. Furthermore, the threat of French invasion, which had long hung over Great Britain, was banished by a British naval victory over the French near Lagos, Portugal, in August, followed by the crushing defeat of the main French fleet at Quiberon Bay, north of the mouth of the Loire, on November 20, 1759.[11]

Fortified by British victory in North America and on the sea, the Ministry had practically no opposition in the 1759–1760 session of Parliament. On November 16, three days after the opening of Parliament, Horace Walpole wrote his friend Sir Horace Mann, "no battles are fought in Parliament now—the House of Commons is a mere war office, and only sits for the dispatch of military business," and, according to *Parliamentary History*, "there were no debates on any public measures in either House" during the long, quiet session which closed May 22, 1760.[12]

The war continued to go well for the British in 1760. In Germany victories and defeats again about offset each other, but a decisive British victory over the French at Wandewash in January practically assured the supremacy of the British East India Company in India, and the French capitulation to Amherst at Montreal on September 8, 1760, included the surrender of all of Canada not already in British hands.[13] Cheered and united by success, Newcastle and Pitt, though often at odds, managed, as Lord Chesterfield wrote his son, to "jog on like man and wife; that is, seldom agreeing, often quarreling; but, by mutual interest, upon the whole, not parting,"[14] and had George II remained on the throne, they probably would have continued to jog along together indefinitely. But on October 25, 1760, the King died suddenly of a heart attack, and the accession of George III introduced new and disturbing elements, which, even before the war was ended, led to the resignation of both of his grandfather's chief Ministers.

George III Becomes King: October 1760

Rarely has a reign opened under such fair auspices as George the Third's. The threat of Jacobite rebellion, long a menace, was gone; whatever loyalty to the Stuarts remained after the collapse of the Rebellion of 1745 had oozed away as the exiled old Pretender, James Stuart, sank into lethargy at Rome and his son, "Bonnie Prince Charlie," became a habitual drunkard.[15] Government bonds, which dropped a couple of points on news of the old King's death, quickly rallied, fully regaining their previous level by November first.[16]

The new King made an excellent impression. Lord Barrington, Secretary at War, whose office brought him into constant contact with the King, wrote of the pleasure of doing business with him, of his "most uncommon attention," his "quick and just conception, great mildness, great civility." Edmund Hooper of the Customs Board wrote how "wonderfully pleased" everyone was with him, and even Walpole, who was far more apt to disparage than to praise, reported to Mann, soon after the opening of the new reign, "The young King, you may trust me who am not apt to be enamoured with royalty, gives all the indication imaginable of being amiable. His person is tall and full of dignity; his countenance florid and good-natured; his manner is graceful and obliging."[17]

With winning thoughtfulness, George III dismissed the guards in attendance on himself to act as a guard of honor to the body of his grandfather; went out of his way to be kind to his uncle, the ailing Duke of Cumberland; and graciously granted the request of Lady Yarmouth for the appointment of a favorite of hers to office.[18] More importantly, he retained both of his grandfather's chief ministers in their posts, and, as we shall see, permitted Newcastle to proceed with the management of the election of a new House of Commons.[19]

The King made clear, however, that Pitt and Newcastle must share their power with Bute, whom he promptly appointed to the Privy Council and made Groom of the Stole to himself as King.[20]

Bute, whom the young King idolized, was almost twenty-five years older to the day than he. Both of Bute's parents were Scotch; his father, James Stuart, was a Scotch peer, his mother, Lady Anne Campbell, a daughter of the powerful Duke of Argyll. Bute succeeded to his father's peerage in 1723, and served as one of the representative Scotch peers in the British House of Lords from 1738 to 1741 when, failing reelection, he spent some years in retirement at his home on the island of Bute in the Clyde below Glasgow. But, though Scotch by blood, birth, and early residence, he had strong English ties. He went to Eton, had long (since 1736) been married to an Englishwoman, Mary Montagu, daughter of the famous Lady Mary Wortley Montagu, had been a resident of London or vicinity since around 1745, was a Lord of the Bedchamber to Frederick Prince of Wales at the time of his death in 1751, and had been Groom of the Stole and private counsellor to George since 1756.

As early as July 1756, George wrote to Bute, "I have had the pleasure of your friendship during the space of a year . . . [and hope] with the continuation of your advice, I may turn out as you wish. . . . ¶ I know few things I ought to be more thankfull for to the Great Power above, than for its having pleas'd Him to send you to help and advise me in these difficult times. ¶ I do hope you will from this instant banish all thoughts of leaving me, and will resolve, if not for my sake for the good of your country to remain with me." Friendship ripened, as the years passed, into ardent affection, and confidence into the most implicit trust, as we know from many surviving letters of the Prince to Bute from 1757 to 1760,[21] of which the following, in May 1760, is typical:

"My Dearest Friend,

"Your conversation last night makes me think it necessary to trouble you with this scrawl; undoubtedly nothing can be more friendly than your constant endeavours to point out those things in me that are likely to destroy any attempts of raising my character; but at the same time you have so gentle a manner of doing this painful though necessary office, that I can perceive it grieves you to be forced to mention them. . . . ¶ What I still flatter myself is, that some method may turn up of regulating affairs, which may still make the Treasury not unpalatable to you; if that should not happen, you will for all that be

Minister for all men will find the only method of succeeding in their desires, will be by first acquainting you with what they mean to request before they address themselves to me; in short all I interest myself in is your health, for whilst my Dearest is near me I care not who are the tools he may think necessary to be in Ministry provided the blackest of hearts [Pitt] is not one of them; for I look on the majority of politicians as intent on their own private interests instead of that of the public."[22]

The 1760–1761 session of Parliament (November 18, 1760, to March 19, 1761), like the preceding, was very quiet. An anonymous pamphlet, *Considerations on the Present German War,* published soon after the beginning of the new reign, advocating withdrawal of Great Britain from all participation in the war in Germany and concentration of British resources on the conquest of France's remaining possessions in the West Indies, quickly ran into six editions and was, wrote Walpole, "the only work I almost ever knew that changed the opinions of many."[23] But there was no movement in Parliament for a change of policy, and, when Pitt moved in the House of Commons to continue the military subsidy of £670,000 a year paid Frederick the Great of Prussia, only one member, Sir Francis Dashwood, demurred, and the subsidy was promptly voted without a division.[24]

While Parliament was running its quiet course, the King was absorbed in selecting a wife from the available Protestant princesses of Europe;[25] Pitt was deep in preparation for the proposed military campaigns of 1761, including attacks on Belle Isle at the mouth of the Loire and Martinique in the West Indies; and Newcastle was busy with plans for the election of a new House of Commons.[26] This went off smoothly for the Ministry—only 48 of the 315 constituencies[27] electing members to the House of Commons were contested and 410 of the 558 members of the old House were reelected.[28]

On March 25, 1761, immediately after the close of Parliament, the King, with Newcastle's approval, offered Bute the post of Secretary of State for the Northern Department,[29] which he accepted in a characteristically theatrical letter. "I have had the honor," he wrote, "of being nearest to your Person many years and to instill into your Royal mind, whatever virtue, honor or public spirit could suggest to me; ever looking up to your glory and happiness, my every thought has been pointed to that alone. . . . I may want talents for business, faction may overwhelm me, and Court intrigues destroy me; but all the power of man cannot take this heartfelt satisfaction; this comfortable retrospect from me; for I know and feel I have in serving you, done my duty to my God, my Country and my King; and that without permitting self or selfish considerations to mix an instant in the plan I followed. . . . The honorable station, which I have hitherto made subservient to your Royal interest, I now resign; to tread an unknown path I sacrifice peace, quiet, and all my little happiness to your commands, to your service; . . . but not without violent emotion and unpleasant forebodings . . . [and] desire in the most solemn manner that I may have your Royal promise to ensure me a safe retreat again near your person, in case I find myself unable to do what I wish."[30]

Several other changes were made in the Ministry, including the appointment of Lord Barrington as Chancellor of the Exchequer, replacing Henry Bilson Legge, and Lord Sandys as President of the Board of Trade in place of Lord Halifax who became Lord-Lieutenant (Viceroy) of Ireland. The change at the Board was accompanied by a royal order enlarging the power of Pitt as Secretary of State for the Southern Department by transferring the nomination of governors and other provincial officials appointed by the Crown from the Board to this office.[31]

Throughout the spring and summer of 1761, the reorganized Ministry was absorbed in negotiations for peace with France, conducted by Pitt for Great Britain and the Duc de Choiseul for France, in which it was agreed that Great Britain should have Canada.[32] The negotiation failed, chiefly because by the time Pitt had given way, under pressure from fellow Ministers and the King, to France's demand for an island or two near the Grand Banks as shelter for its Newfoundland fishing vessels,[33] France had made a secret treaty of military alliance with Spain which barred acceptance of the latest British terms.[34] In the negotiations Pitt and Temple were repeatedly at odds with various members of the Cabinet, and when, after several tempestuous Cabinet meetings from September 18 to October 2, they were outvoted on their proposal to attack Spain, as almost certainly the secret ally of France, they resigned.[35]

On resigning, Pitt accepted a pension from the King of £3,000 a year to continue for the lives of himself and any two persons named by him and a peerage for his wife descendable to their male issue.[36] "I think," wrote Hardwicke to his son Charles Yorke, "the peerage and pension . . . surely must produce some quiet, at least for this session," and, whether sharing Hardwicke's cynical view that Pitt had been bribed to keep quiet or merely disillusioned by the evidence that he, too, was not superior to the allurement of public money and family advancement, many of his former admirers turned against him.[37]

Pitt was succeeded as Secretary of State by Lord Egremont, who had previously not held Crown office except briefly as a Commissioner to the Congress of Augsburg which never met, and Temple as Lord Privy Seal by the Duke of Bedford, an influential politician momentarily out of office but at one time and another First Lord of the Admiralty, Secretary of State, and Lord-Lieutenant of Ireland. Pitt's Leadership of the House of Commons went to his brother-in-law, George Grenville,[38] Treasurer of the Navy and a brother-in-law of Egremont whose sister was Grenville's wife.

As Secretary in charge of Spanish relations, Egremont tried hard to avoid war; but the peace negotiations between France and Great Britain having failed, Spain was committed, under the secret treaty with France (August 15, 1761) mentioned above, to fight Great Britain, and by January the two nations were formally at war.[39]

The reorganized Cabinet agreed, January 6, 1762, on a massive expedition for the capture of Havana; but were sharply divided on the question of continued British participation in the war in Germany. The King, who had written Bute in 1759 condemning George II's partiality for "that horrid Electorate [Hanover] which has always liv'd upon the vitals of this poor Country," favored withdrawal[40] and was supported by Bedford and Grenville, while Newcastle was strongly opposed and Bute apparently fluctuated.[41]

The issue came to a head on April 30, when, at a meeting attended by nine members of the Cabinet, the majority, including Bute, Grenville, and Egremont, rejected the plea of Newcastle, Hardwicke, and the Duke of Devonshire to ask Parliament for an additional two million for the conduct of the war in 1762 and decided to ask for only one. This decision, which Newcastle believed was taken as a means of compelling withdrawal from the German war by denying the funds needed to continue it, was especially bitter to him because it was on a point relating particularly to his Department and because his opponents were supported by two of his associates on the Treasury Board and by a paper secretly prepared by Samuel Martin, joint Secretary to the Treasury.[42]

On May 3, the King upheld the majority of the Cabinet, telling Newcastle, "I can't bring myself to ask more than one million," whereupon Newcastle, though assuring Bute and the King that he would "avoid everything that could give any disturbance or raise any flame just at the end of the session," and would carry on until the arrangements could be made for his successor, tendered his resignation.[43] In the end, the British forces were continued in Germany for the 1762 campaign, and the one million, though by a narrow margin, proved sufficient to maintain them.[44]

Newcastle and the King thought Grenville was maneuvering for Newcastle's post, but George III, who had long wished Bute to be First Lord of the Treasury, insisted on his taking the place.[45] He was appointed May 29, 1762, with Grenville succeeding him as Secretary of State for the Northern Department and Sir Francis Dashwood replacing Barrington as Chancellor of the Exchequer. Lord Anson, First Lord of the Admiralty, dying soon afterward, was succeeded by Halifax.[46]

PART TWO

The Bute Ministry: May 1762–June 1765

From the standpoint of British relations with the colonies, the retirement of Newcastle was calamitous. Had he remained in office, the provocative colonial measures from 1763 to 1765 outlined in the Introduction, it is reasonable to believe, would not have been taken. There is no evidence that the new Ministers, some of whom later became hostile to the colonies, were so at this time; but ignorance and inexperience led them to adopt measures which Newcastle presumably would have avoided.*

The war continued to go well for Great Britain under the new Ministry. In Germany the balance at last tilted in favor of Great Britain and Prussia; the British defeated Spanish forces which had invaded Portugal; and in America, Havana fell in August 1762, and St. John's Newfoundland, seized by the French in a surprise attack in June, was recaptured by the British in September and the entire French force taken prisoners. Earlier in the year, Martinique, St. Lucia, and several other islands of less importance held by the French in the West Indies were taken by the British.[1]

The Ministry was engaged, both before and after Newcastle's retirement, in negotiations for peace, resumed in March 1762, through the good offices of the Sardinian ministers in Paris and London. The new negotiations began auspiciously with agreement that points conceded by France and Great Britain in the previous negotiations, including the understanding that Great Britain should have all of the Canadian mainland while France should have an island or two off the coast as a shelter for French fishermen, should stand. But in the ensuing negotiations other issues arose which were resolved only by the device of secret commitments. The first, by Bute alone, concerned the boundary line on the lower Mississippi between the part of Louisiana to be ceded to Great Britain and the part to be retained by France. The second, by Bute and Egremont jointly, was that the strategically important island of St. Lucia in the West Indies should go to France if agreement was reached on all other points.[2]

Furthermore, even after France and Great Britain were substantially in accord, there was a long impasse over what Spain should yield to Great Britain, an impasse finally broken, after Great Britain's con-

---

*A number of the changes in policy that Knollenberg cites in fact occurred under the administration of Pitt and Newcastle. See P. D. G. Thomas, *British Politics and the Stamp Act Crisis: The First Phase of the American Revolution* (Princeton, N.J.: Princeton University Press, 1975), 61–66; review of Knollenberg by Milton M. Klein in *William and Mary Quarterly*, 3rd ser., 18 (1961): 279–80; and the Klein-Knollenberg exchange, *William and Mary Quarterly*, 3rd ser., 18 (1961): 458–60. [B. W. S.]

quest of Havana, by Spain agreeing to cede Florida to Great Britain and Louis XV of France secretly engaging to cede western Louisiana to Charles III of Spain.[3]

In the protracted negotiations, Grenville contended for greater concessions than Bute and the King, eager for peace, were willing to settle for.[4] Vexed with Grenville's contentiousness in the Cabinet and fearing that, if he remained Secretary of State and Leader of the House of Commons, his known opposition to some of the terms of the treaty would prove embarrassing, Bute and the King required him, in October, to exchange Cabinet posts with Halifax and to surrender his leadership of the House of Commons to Henry Fox, Paymaster-General of the Army.[5] Hardwicke thought Fox would add no "real strength to the ministry"; but Newcastle disagreed. "My Lord Bute," he wrote, "has the sole power of this kingdom. . . . He does not know how to exert that power. He has therefore (wisely for his purpose) chose the man in the world who will stick at nothing . . . [and] no man knows better than he does, the weakness and wickedness of mankind, or to make the best use of it."[6]

The preliminary treaty of peace, the Treaty of Fontainebleau, signed November 3, 1762, though possibly not securing for the victorious British every possible concession to be wrung from France and Spain, was, as Charles Townshend said, a "damned good one," was indeed so favorable to Great Britain that Hardwicke thought "the generality of the Parliament and of the nation . . . would have been content with terms rather lower than all we have yet been told about these preliminaries."[7]

Spain agreed to relinquish all claim to share in the fishery in the vicinity of Newfoundland; accede to the British position concerning prizes and the cutting of logwood in Honduras; renew unconditionally all commercial treaties with Great Britain, which Spain had hoped to terminate; cede Florida; and evacuate all occupied Portuguese territory. France agreed to restore Minorca, taken by her in 1756; cede her stations on the coast of Senegal in West Africa; waive all claim to territory in India acquired since January 1749; evacuate all Prussian territory; and cede, or, as to previously disputed territory, waive all claim to Grenada, the Grenadines, St. Vincent, Dominica, and Tobago in the West Indies, and the islands of St. John's (present Prince Edward Island), Cape Breton, and Anticosti in North America. Most important of all, and of supreme importance from the standpoint of the British colonies in North America, France also agreed to waive any further claim to Nova Scotia, and to cede the immense St. Lawrence basin, including the Great Lakes, and the whole eastern watershed of the Mississippi except the town and island of New Orleans. Britain was to restore Belle Isle near the French coast and Martinique and Guadeloupe in the West Indies.[8]

Newcastle, who was uneasy in being out of power and office, tried to form an alliance with Pitt for opposition to the treaty and the overthrow of Bute. But Pitt, while disapproving the treaty and opposed to Bute's "transcendency of power," was not receptive to the proposed alliance, stating that "tho' it was necessary Lord Bute should be removed from the office he now held, he might not think it quite for his Majesty's service to have the Duke of Newcastle succeed there."[9] Consequently, in speaking against the treaty in Parliament, Pitt made clear that he was not doing so in alliance with Newcastle, and, on a motion in the House of Commons, December 9, to approve the treaty, the disunited opposition mustered only 65 votes to the Ministry's 319. In the House of Lords, where Newcastle and Hardwicke condemned the treaty and Bute (elected a representative Scotch peer in 1761) defended it with ability, it was approved without even a division, that is, count of votes.[10]

The most striking feature of the votes on the treaty in the House of Commons was the Tories' abandonment of Pitt. Soon after the 1762–1763 session of Parliament opened, Hardwicke wrote Newcastle that he believed most of the Tories would no longer support Pitt, who had "fed them with hopes of what he would do for them in a new reign . . . but all that was done was by my Lord Bute." Richard Rigby made a similar prediction, writing Bedford that the "Tories will certainly be with the Court; four or five at most will stick by Pitt," a forecast which proved to be accurate, for only five of them voted against the treaty.[11]

Following a preliminary test of strength in the House of Commons on December 1, which the Ministry won, 213 to 74, Bute's protégé Colonel Lord Shelburne, aide de camp to the King, wrote Bute,

"Before another question comes, let the 213 taste some of the plunder of the 74. Without you do somewhat of that kind, you'll find your cause want a necessary animation and your friends want encouragement," and, following the decisive vote on December 9, Fox wrote Bute in similar vein. "The impertinence," he said, "of our conquered enemies last night was great, but will not continue so if His Majesty shows no lenity. . . . Their connections spread very wide, and every one of them, their relations and friends, is in his heart your enemy. They all think themselves secure, and many talk with their own mouths, all by those of their relations and acquaintances, against your Lordship. Turn the tables, and you will immediately have thousands who will think the safety of themselves or their friends depends upon your Lordship, and will therefore be sincere and active friends."[12]

The King, too, urged Bute to dismiss from office some of the members of Parliament who had voted against the treaty, in order to "frighten others," and soon afterwards not only members of Parliament but many others who had been appointed to office on the recommendation of Newcastle and other leaders now in opposition were dismissed.[13] Thus holders of Crown office had sharp warning that in voting against ministerial measures approved by the King they did so at the peril of themselves and their friends.

Having secured Parliamentary approval of the treaty of peace, the final terms of which were signed at Paris, February 10, 1763, the King and Ministry turned to the reduction of the army and navy to a peacetime footing. The King, who had been considering the problem of the army for some time, by February 1, 1763, had tentatively agreed with the Commander-in-Chief, Lord Ligonier, as to what should be asked of Parliament. According to a memorandum of Newcastle of February 19 and a letter of Richard Rigby, a few days later, the King's plan called for eighty-five infantry regiments; but, at the last minute, ten regiments were lopped off in deference to Tory members of Parliament. This appears from a letter of Bute to Sir John Phillips, one of the leaders of the Tories (Country Gentlemen) in the House of Commons, on February 23, 1763, stating that, in view of the criticism of the plan by "many of the Country Gentlemen," the army "will be greatly reduced from the original Plan."[14]

The modified plan, approved at a meeting of leading supporters of the Ministry on February 24, called for approximately the same force as before the war in the British Isles but an increase from around 3,100 officers and men to around 7,500 in North America, and this plan was embodied in the army estimates for 1762 laid before the House of Commons on February 25 by Welbore Ellis, Secretary at War.[15]

Newcastle, who feared the proposed increase because of the addition it would make to the King's political power, intended at first to oppose; but, to avoid antagonizing Pitt, who favored a greatly enlarged postwar army and whom Newcastle and his allies were still wooing, they decided to remain silent. "Mr Pitt they say," wrote Newcastle to Hardwicke on March 3, "comes to town to support Every Part of the Court Plan of the Army, which is amazing. For such an Extensive Plan of Power, & Military Influence, was never thought of before in this Country. However, we have agreed . . . that, if Mr Pitt is there, Mr Legge [former Chancellor of the Exchequer] should just state His Own private Thoughts, but out of Deference to Mr Pitt, give them up to Him."[16] With Pitt approving and the rest of the opposition silent, the estimates were, of course, promptly voted,[17] and were embodied in the customary annual Mutiny Bill which rapidly passed both Houses.[18]

Newcastle and Rigby, Bedford's chief henchman in the House of Commons, heard that part of the Ministry's plan for the enlarged army was to require the colonies to pay the expense of the British forces stationed there, and this report was confirmed by Ellis, who, in laying the army estimates before the House on February 25, said the army in America was "to be supported the first year by England, afterwards by the Colonies."[19] This revolutionary plan to tax the colonies for the support of the British troops stationed in America had been under consideration for some months, as we know from a letter of the King to Bute in March 1763, condemning Charles Townshend, President of the Board of Trade, for speaking in the House of Commons in favor of an immediate tax for revenue on the colonies. "This subject," said the King, "was new to none, having been thought of this whole winter; all ought to have declar'd that next session some tax will be laid before the House but that it requires much information before a proper one can be stated."[20]

Governor Horatio Sharpe of Maryland heard that the colonists were to be compensated for being taxed by repeal of the British acts prohibiting colonial importation of all East Indian and most European products from any place except Great Britain;[21] but no evidence has been found of any such balanced plan, and the one later adopted gave the colonies no such compensation.

Newcastle's efforts to form a coalition with Pitt finally bore fruit when, after a felicitous political dinner at Devonshire House on March 7, Pitt and Temple joined forces with Newcastle and his followers to present a united front against a bill for an excise tax on domestic cider. But, though the vote was much closer than on the resolution for approval of the Treaty of Peace, the Ministry was again victorious.[22]

Ill, hounded by pamphleteers and cartoonists, attacked by rowdies on his way to Parliament,[23] and disgusted with the necessity or supposed necessity of governing by influencing members of Parliament through outright corruption or the distribution of government sinecures, pensions, and places,[24] Bute had long wished to retire, and now, having secured the adoption of his entire program for the session, obtained the King's consent to do so.[25]

Bute had suggested Fox as his successor; but the thought of Fox as chief Minister was extremely distasteful to the King, who wrote Bute, "I am ever hurt when my D. Friend and myself are in the least of different opinions . . . but in the case of Mr. Fox I fear we shall never think alike; I have one principle firmly rooted in my mind from the many seasonable lessons I have receiv'd from my D. Friend, never to trust a man void of principles; if any man ever deserved that character 'tis Mr. Fox; the seeing him at the head of the House of Commons was very unpleasant to me: but I consented to it, as that was the only means of getting my D. Friend to proceed this winter in the Treasury; . . . tis not prejudice but aversion to his whole mode of government that causes my writing so openly my thoughts to my only friend; has this whole winter been any thing else but a scene of corruption, and I am persuaded were he the acting Minister this would appear in more ways than he is now able to accomplish."[26]

Finally the King consented, but was spared the pain of having Fox as his chief Minister, when, heeding his wife's plea not to take a post which she said "would make him miserable and kill him," Fox declined the offer.[27]

With the King's approval, Bute turned next to Grenville, who was willing to accept but only on condition that Bute give up the idea of replacing Grenville's brother-in-law Egremont as Secretary of State for the Southern Department by Bute's young protégé, Shelburne. "As to Lord Egremont quitting the seals," wrote Grenville to Bute, "you will not wonder at my saying I can be no instrument in it." Besides, said Grenville, Shelbourne's appointment as Secretary of State would be extremely objectionable, particularly to the House of Lords, because of his "youth, his inexperience in business by having never held any civil office whatever, and from his situation and family, so lately raised to the [English] Peerage, however considerable both may be in Ireland." In the end, Shelburne was appointed President of the Board of Trade in place of Townshend and Egremont remained Secretary of State, while Grenville succeeded Bute as First Lord of the Treasury and replaced Dashwood as Chancellor of the Exchequer. (This office was commonly held by the First Lord of the Treasury unless, like Newcastle and Bute, he was a member of the House of Lords.) Grenville also resumed the Leadership of the House of Commons in place of Fox. Lord Sandwich succeeded to Grenville's place as First Lord of the Admiralty.[28]

The Grenville Ministry: April 1763–July 1765

Grenville was educated for the law, but had abandoned the profession in 1741, at the age of twenty-eight, on his election to the House of Commons. Three years later he was appointed to the Admiralty Board, and in 1747 was advanced to the Treasury Board, where he served until appointed Treasurer of the Navy seven years later. When his brother-in-law Pitt came to power in 1757, Grenville expected further advancement, but, though apparently industrious and an able speaker, he made no progress in ministerial rank, perhaps because of his boring prolixity, until after the accession of George III, and his rise then was under the auspices not of Pitt but of Bute.[29]

How intelligently Grenville would have dealt with colonial affairs, with which he had little prior experience, if he had been free to give them due attention and study is anybody's guess. But he was so beset with various distracting problems during the period when the decisions were made to enforce rigorously the whole range of British acts restricting colonial trade and to carry out the project of taxing the colonists that his apparent failure to foresee the disastrous effects on colonial opinion of these measures is not surprising.*

The chief of these distractions grew out of the activities of, and the Ministry's proceedings against John Wilkes, member of Parliament for Aylesbury, Colonel of the Buckingham County militia, and publisher of *The North Briton*.[30] This scurrilous weekly, begun in June 1762, had repeatedly attacked Bute with the utmost virulence.‡

One of Wilkes's chief weapons against Bute was exploitation of the anti-Scotism rampant in England during the eighteenth century. As Lord Holland said in the memorandum written shortly after *The North Briton*'s attack on Bute began, "The Press is, with more vehemence than I ever knew, set to work against Ld Bute. And it would be very surprizing to see how quick and fiercely the fire spreads, but for the consideration that it is fed with great industry and blown by a national prejudice which is inveterate and universal. Every man has at some time or other found a Scotchman in his way, and everybody has therefore damn'd the Scotch: and this hatred their excessive nationality has continually inflam'd."[31]

Though expressed more rudely among the so-called lower classes, the prevailing anti-Scotism was not confined to them, as we know from the writings of many in higher station, such as Dr. Johnson's remark (not in jest) in a letter to Boswell, "I am surprised that, knowing

---

* John L. Bullion, *A Great and Necessary Measure: George Grenville and the Genesis of the Stamp Act* (Columbia: University of Missouri Press, 1982); Philip Lawson, *George Grenville: A Political Life* (Oxford: Oxford University Press, 1989). [B. W. S.]

‡ Since Knollenberg wrote, a substantial body of work on Wilkes has appeared. See especially George F. E. Rudé, *Wilkes and Liberty: A Social Study of 1763–1774* (Oxford: Oxford University Press, 1962); P. D. G. Thomas, *John Wilkes: A Friend to Liberty* (Oxford: Oxford University Press, 1996); Pauline Maier, "John Wilkes and American Disillusionment with Britain," *William and Mary Quarterly*, 3rd ser., 20 (1963): 373–95; Jack P. Greene, "Bridge to Revolution: The Wilkes Fund Controversy in South Carolina, 1769–1775," *Journal of Southern History*, 29 (1963): 19–52. [B. W. S.]

as you do the disposition of your countrymen to tell lies in favour of each other, you can be at all affected by any reports [defending a Scot] that circulate among them" and Shelburne's statement in his autobiographical notes that, though Lord Mansfield had "contrived, like several of the Scotch, Lord Loughborough etc. to get rid of his brogue," he "always spoke in a feigned voice like Leoni the Jew singer" and "Like the generality of Scotch . . . had no regard to truth whatever."[32]

Another of Wilkes's methods of attack was to play up a foul rumor that Bute was the paramour of the King's mother, Princess Augusta. One whole issue of *The North Briton* was devoted to a résumé of the earlier years of the reign of Edward III, with the innuendo of similarity to the current reign, recounting the supposed adultery of Edward's mother with Roger Mortimer, Earl of March, and the evil influence of the adulterous pair on the young King.[33]

Finally, in issue No. 45, published April 23, 1763, Wilkes ventured to attack the King himself, asserting that the royal prerogative had been exercised with "blind favour and partiality" and the honor of the Crown "sunk even to prostitution"; denouncing, as a lie, a passage in the King's recent speech to Parliament mentioning the favorable terms of peace procured by Great Britain for her ally, Frederick the Great of Prussia; and declaring that "Every friend of his country must lament that a prince . . . can be brought to give the sanction of his sacred name to the most odious measures, and to the most unjustifiable, public declarations, from a throne ever renowned for truth, honour, and unsullied virtue."[34]

Three days later, Halifax issued a general warrant to several of the King's messengers (officers attached to the Secretaries of State's office) ordering the arrest of the authors, printers, and publishers of No. 45 of *The North Briton* and seizure of their papers. No particular persons or documents were specified in this sweeping order, under color of which Dryden Leach, printer of an early, innocuous issue of *The North Briton*, and at least fourteen of his workmen; George Kearsley the publisher and Richard Balfe the printer of No. 45; and Wilkes were arrested. Furthermore, Wilkes's home was ransacked and a mass of his papers carried away, and both Secretaries of State, Halifax and Egremont, jointly issued a warrant committing him to the Tower of

London as "author and publisher of a most infamous and seditious libel, intitled the North Briton, number 45" with orders to keep him "safe and close until he shall be delivered by due course of law. . . ."[35]

Wilkes applied to the Court of Common Pleas, presided over by Chief Justice Sir Charles Pratt, for a writ of habeas corpus, pleading the illegality of his confinement and petitioning for an order of release. This was promptly granted on the ground that, as a member of the House of Commons, Wilkes was entitled to privilege from arrest except for treason, felony, or breach of the peace, and that criminal libel (unless treasonable, which was not alleged in the warrant of commitment) was none of these.[36]

Soon afterward, Leach's workmen brought suits, also in the Court of Common Pleas, against the King's messengers for false arrest, and, on Pratt's instructing the jury that the arrests were illegal, were awarded extremely heavy damages—a further triumph for Wilkes, who was a conspicuous attendant at the trial and whose lawyers, headed by Sergeant John Glynn, represented the workmen. Swelling with self-esteem, Wilkes wrote Lord Temple, who was financing him, "The rod of oppression was lifted very high, but a few honest Englishmen have saved their country. . . . The joy of the people is almost universal," and later added, "I hear from all hands that the King is enraged at my insolence, as he terms it: I regard not his frowns nor his smiles. . . . Hypocrisy, meanness, ignorance, and insolence, characterize the King I obey. My independent spirit will never take a favour from such a man. ¶ . . . North Briton and Wilkes will be talked of together by posterity."[37]

During the summer of 1763, Pitt and Hardwicke were separately approached as to joining the Ministry, but the recent alliance between Pitt and the Newcastle group held firm; neither Pitt nor Hardwicke would consent to serve except in a Ministry which, it was intimated, must be formed largely from among the followers of Newcastle. The death of Egremont in August led to another attempt to strengthen the Ministry from the ranks of the opposition, and, after a preliminary talk between Bute and Pitt, the King himself conferred with the latter in two audiences, the details of which were reported in a long letter from Hardwicke to his son Lord Royston.[38]

"Mr Pitt," wrote Hardwicke, "received an open note unsealed, requiring him to attend His Majesty on Saturday noon, at the Queen's [now Buckingham] Palace, in the Park. In obedience hereto, Mr. Pitt went on Saturday [August 27] at noon-day, thro' the Mall in his gouty chair, the boot of which (as he said himself) makes it as much known as if his name was writ upon it. . . . His Majesty gave him a very gracious *accueil*, and heard with great patience and attention; and Mr. Pitt affirms that, in general, and upon the most material points, he appeared by his manner and many of his expressions to be convinced. . . .

"Mr Pitt went through the infirmities of the peace; the things necessary, and hitherto neglected, to improve and preserve it; the present state of the nation, both foreign and domestic; the great Whig families and persons which had been driven from His Majesty's Council and service, which it would be for his interest to restore. . . . The King . . . said now and then that his honour must be consulted; to which Mr. Pitt answered in a very courtly manner. His Majesty ordered him to come again on Monday, which he did, to the same place, in the same public manner."

On Monday, August 29, the King was again gracious; but, at the close, declined to accept Pitt's plan, saying "Well, Mr. Pitt, I see (or I fear) this won't do. My honour is concerned, and I must support it."

Hardwicke did not explain what the King meant by saying his honor was concerned, but the meaning clearly appears from a letter of Sandwich to Bedford saying Pitt had declared that Bedford and all others "who had been concerned in so disgraceful a measure as the peace" must be excluded from the new Ministry. Since the King had strongly encouraged the making of the very peace for which his ministers were to be proscribed, his honor was indeed "concerned," most deeply concerned, in not yielding to Pitt's demand, and a change of mind on Bedford's part made it unnecessary for the King to give in. Bedford had previously declined to enter public service again because, as he put it, of "the indolence of my disposition" and for other reasons explained to his friend Sandwich, but not now known. However, he was so incensed by Pitt's position that he now agreed to accept the Presidency of the Privy Council, thus enlisting the active support of one of the most wealthy, influential, and politically experienced of the great Whig Dukes.[39]

Shelburne, who had taken a leading part in initiating the negotiation with Pitt, resigned and was succeeded as President of the Board of Trade by Lord Hillsborough. Sandwich succeeded Egremont as a Secretary of State, with Lord Egmont taking Sandwich's place as First Lord of the Admiralty; and, of outstanding importance from the standpoint of colonial relations, Halifax now shifted from the Northern to the Southern Department of the Secretaryship of State.[40]

An inscription on the monument in Westminster Abbey to Halifax, who, as President of the Board of Trade from 1748 to 1761 had much to do with colonial affairs, says he was called "Father of the Colonies," but this does not seem to have been the general feeling while he was in office. Writing from London in 1759, Franklin said, "As to the Board of Trade, you know who presides and governs all there, and if his Sentiments were no otherways to be known, the fruitless Experiment he has try'd at the Nation's Cost, of a military Government for a Colony [Nova Scotia] sufficiently shows what he thinks would be best for us." Later, Franklin's son, William, wrote that Dean Tucker, "one of the bitterest Enemies N. America has in Britain," was "an Intimate of Lord Halifax's and patroniz'd by him." Joseph Trumbull of Connecticut charged Halifax with favoring the annulment of the remaining colonial charters, and Richard Jackson, Agent in London for Connecticut and Pennsylvania, deploring Halifax's transfer to the Southern Department, wrote that perhaps few were "so unfit for it."[41]

Various bits of evidence tend to show that colonial fear of Halifax was well-founded. He is known to have advocated Parliament's taxing the colonies in 1755–1756 and to have favored the establishment of English bishops in the colonies in spite of the strong objections to this project among colonial Dissenters; he told Barrington that a plan of Governor Francis Bernard of Massachusetts for the reorganization of the government of that colony, involving drastic revision of the colony's charter toward a less democratic form of government, was "the best thing of the kind by much that he ever read"; and he asked the Board of Trade in December 1763 to suggest means to restrain the colonists "from carrying on that very prejudicial Commerce with the French Islands," a commerce which, from the standpoint of the mainland colonies, was extremely beneficial. Furthermore, he favored a plan for the use of the funds to be raised by the proposed taxation of the colonies in a way that would be particularly obnoxious to the colonists, namely, for payment of the governors and other provincial officers out of the funds raised in the colonies by Parliamentary taxation, thus making them independent of the colonial legislatures and more dependent on the Crown.[42]

Shortly after its reorganization, the Ministry was again distracted by Wilkes. Following his arrest he discontinued publication of *The North Briton;* but, some months later, he practically challenged the Government to prosecute him by publishing a collected edition of those previously issued, including No. 45. He also put out an additional issue, No. 46, describing the chief Ministers as the "hackney'd tools" of Bute, "leagued together . . . for the plunder of the state," and denouncing the late Lord Egremont as having been as "universally odious in private, as he soon became in publick life," with "a savage disposition and brutal manners," "an ignorance scarcely to be credited and a mulishness which . . . rendered him the contempt of all who were so unhappy as to be under the necessity of attending him."[43]

Though, judging from his diary and correspondence, Grenville's thoughts were chiefly concerned, throughout the summer and fall of 1763, with keeping office and combatting Wilkes, he was taking steps, detailed in Chapters 7, 11, and 12, of the utmost importance to the colonies. A fleet of British warships was sent to colonial waters to secure rigid enforcement of hitherto laxly enforced British restrictions on colonial trade; a Proclamation was issued closing, for an indefinite period, the whole region west of the Alleghenies to white settlement; and plans were laid for bills in Parliament to impose further restrictions on colonial trade and to levy taxes for revenue on the colonies.

On the opening day of the 1763–1764 session of Parliament (November 15, 1763) Grenville informed the House of Commons that Wilkes, reputed author of No. 45 of *The North Briton,* had invoked his privilege as a member of the House to avoid arrest and prosecution for the publication of this libelous paper. The House promptly voted, 273 to 111, that the paper was in fact "a false, scandalous and seditious libel . . . most manifestly tending to alienate the affections of the people from his Majesty, to withdraw them from their obedience to the laws of the realm, and to excite them to traitorous insurrections against his Majesty's government," and agreed unanimously to consider the question of privilege raised by Grenville's statement.[44]

If the claim of privilege from arrest for alleged criminal libel had come before the House of Commons disassociated from Wilkes, the House, tenacious of its privileges, might well have supported the claim. But the plea of Pitt and others to consider the question apart from immediate circumstances was asking too much. Wilkes not only had aroused the burning enmity of the Scotch members by his virulent anti-Scotism but, before the question of privilege was brought to a vote, had been exposed as a man of the grossest impiety and obscenity. This was done by the Ministry's submission to the House of Lords of two pieces printed at a private press maintained by Wilkes, *An Essay on Woman by Pego Borewell Esq. With . . . A Commentary by the Rev. Dr. Warburton. Inscribed to Miss Fanny Murray* . . . (the Rev. Dr. Warburton was William Warburton, the distinguished Bishop of Gloucester, a member, ex officio, of the House of Lords; Fanny Murray had been a popular London courtesan) and *The Veni Creator paraphrased*.[45]

The *Essay* itself, a lewd parody of Pope's *Essay on Man*, is mildly amusing; but the commentaries, some of them attributed to Warburton, are of most disgusting obscenity and blasphemy; the Virgin Mary, for example, is compared to a woman of the town, and the ass described as a noble beast until made ridiculous by being chosen as "the vehicle of the Godhead into Jerusalem."[46] *The Veni Creator paraphrased* is a lubricious parody of the exceptionally beautiful and reverent hymn *Veni Creator Spiritus*.

Having listened to excerpts from these pieces, the Lords resolved that the *Essay*, "highly reflecting upon a member of this House, is a manifest breach of the privilege thereof" and that both pieces were "a most scandalous, obscene and impious libel; a gross profanation of many parts of the Holy Scriptures; and a most wicked and blasphemous attempt to ridicule and vilify the person of our blessed Saviour." Two days later, on evidence of Wilkes's having printed at least thirteen copies of the pieces, the House passed a resolution requesting the King to order "the immediate prosecution of the author, or authors of the said scandalous and impious Libel and for bringing them to condign punishment."[47]

Edward Gibbon, Captain in the Hampshire militia, later the great historian, had recently written, "Colonel Wilkes of the Buckingham Militia dined with us, and renewed the acquaintance Sir Thomas [Worsley] & myself had begun with him at Reading. I scarcely ever met with a better Companion . . . inexhaustible spirits, infinite wit, and humour, and a great deal of knowledge; but a thorough profligate in principle as in practice . . . his life stained with every vice and his conversation full of blasphemy and bawdy."[48] This was all very well among Wilkes's boon companions; but presumably many of a different cast, who had been attracted to Wilkes as the vigorous opponent of an unpopular Ministry, were repelled and alienated by the discovery that he was the author of the flagrantly obscene and blasphemous pieces laid before the House of Lords.

Having thus exposed Wilkes, the Ministry moved in the House of Commons "That Privilege of Parliament does not extend to the case of writing, and publishing, seditious Libels, nor ought to be allowed to obstruct the ordinary course of the laws, in the speedy and effectual prosecution of so heinous and dangerous an offence."[49]

Taking pains to disconnect himself from the "blasphemer of his God, and the libeller of the King" who did not "deserve to be ranked among the human species," Pitt led the opposition to the motion, arguing that its adoption was "neither consistent with the honour and safety of parliament, nor with the rights and interests of the people." But he had a hard case, not only because of the difficulty of disassociating the general principle from the person immediately involved but because, though much could be said in favor of granting immunity to members of Parliament for statements in debates in Parliament, there was little to justify their having special immunity for outside publications. (A better method, adopted in Fox's Libel Act of 1792, was to provide that in prosecutions for criminal libel the jury rather than the trial judge should decide whether or not the alleged libel was in fact libelous.) And the Ministry's motion, supported in a brilliant speech by Charles Yorke, was carried by a great majority—258 to 133.[50]

On December 1, the two Houses jointly resolved that No. 45 be burned by the common hangman, and, two days later, with the Sheriff of London and many constables, he appeared at the Royal Exchange,

London, to carry out this resolution. "On Saturday last," reported the *London Chronicle* of December 6, 1763, "there was the greatest mob assembled at the Royal Exchange that has been seen there for a long while, to see the *North Briton* burnt. About half after twelve a man appeared with a large bundle of billet [thick, firewood size] faggots, followed by Jack Ketch [the hangman] with a lighted link. . . . From this time to the coming up of the Sheriffs, there was one continued hustling of the Constables, accompanied with shoutings, hissings and pelting them with dirt. . . . Mr. Harley [Thomas Harley, the Sheriff of London] stept out of his chariot, and, attended by the City Marshall, Constables etc. came and read the order for burning the *North Briton* . . . the noises continued and some dirt fell on his head. When he had done reading, the *North Briton* was put on the link, and just as it began to blaze, great part of it was knocked off by the mob and fell on the ground . . . and the mob . . . seized the short billets and began to fall foul of the Constables, who were glad to retreat. Many persons were much hurt, and Mr. Sheriff Harley's front glass of his chariot was broke by a billet thrown at it." In the evening a large crowd again assembled, when "a large jack boot [a popular symbol of Bute] stuffed with straw was burnt in effigy amidst the acclamations of a large body of spectators."[51]

Three days later, Wilkes enjoyed an even more triumphant day, when a suit for damages for seizure of his papers in April brought in the Court of Common Pleas against Robert Wood, Under Secretary of State, who made or supervised the seizure, was heard before Chief Justice Pratt sitting in Westminster Hall. Pratt having declared his opinion that the general warrant under which the papers were seized was "unconstitutional, illegal and absolutely void," the jury gave Wilkes damages of a thousand pounds plus costs. Whereupon perhaps "the greatest concourse of people in Westminster-hall ever known," gave "the loudest acclamations that can possibly be imagined," and many trooped off to cheer Wilkes, housebound from a dueling wound, "with French horns, crying out Pratt, Wilkes, and Liberty For Ever."[52]

This, however, was the last of Wilkes's triumphs for many years. Bad days were just around the corner.

On January 19, 1764, the Commons found him guilty of having written and published No. 45, and passed a resolution expelling him.

A few days later, the House of Lords ordered that he be taken into custody for breach of privilege and contempt of that House. Furthermore, after the way had been cleared by the resolution of the House of Commons that the privilege of its members did not extend to criminal libel, Wilkes was prosecuted in the Court of King's Bench for republishing No. 45 of *The North Briton* and for publishing *An Essay on Woman,* and, on February 21, 1764, was found guilty in both cases. Failing to appear for sentence (Wilkes had slipped away to France on Christmas Day), he was declared an outlaw, and did not venture to set foot in England, except briefly, for over three years.[53]

Another important question arising out of Wilkes's case and one on which members of the opposition were united, was presented to the House of Commons by a motion of the opposition on February 14, 1764, "That a General Warrant for apprehending and seizing the authors, Printers and publishers of a seditious libel, together with their papers is not warranted by law." The debate, which continued until about seven o'clock the next morning, was postponed to the 17th when both sides assembled in full strength. "You would have almost laughed," wrote Walpole to his friend Lord Hertford, British Ambassador to France, "to see the spectres produced by both sides; one would have thought they had sent a search-warrant for Members of Parliament into every hospital. Votes were brought down in flannels and blankets till the floor of the House looked like the pool of Bethesda."[54]

The critical show of strength came on a motion to adjourn consideration of the resolution as to general warrants introduced by the Attorney-General, Sir Fletcher Norton, who argued that the question was one for the courts alone to pass on. "You are a peer," wrote Walpole to Hertford, "and therefore, perhaps will hear it with patience—but think how *our* ears must have tingled when he [Norton] told us, that should we pass the resolution, and he were a judge, he would mind it no more than the resolution of a drunken porter!" Norton was answered by his predecessor as Attorney-General, Hardwicke's son Charles Yorke, who had brilliantly supported the Ministry on the question of privilege, but now shone in the ranks of the opposition. "Joy, joy to *you* in particular," wrote George Onslow from the floor of the House to Newcastle; "I cannot a moment defer telling you that Mr Yorke has this moment closed the noblest performance that ever was heard. . . . We all think the thing is over. Nothing ever met with such applause as Charles Yorke. Pitt is in love with him, and so we are all. God be praised, I think now we shall, as Mr Pitt said, crush our domestic enemies as we have our foreign ones."[55]

Other speeches "we had without end," Walpole continued in his letter to Hertford, "one from Charles Townshend, so fine that *it amazed, even from him*. . . . At last, Pitt, who had three times in the debate retired with pain, rose about three in the morning, but so languid, so exhausted, that in his life, he never made less figure. Grenville answered him; and at five in the morning we divided. The Noes [against adjourning the debate] were so loud, as it admits a deeper sound than Ay, that the Speaker . . . gave it for us. They went forth; and when I heard our side was counted to the amount of 218, I did conclude we were victorious; but they returned 232."[56]*

The Ministry's victory was owing to members representing the Scotch constituencies, who voted to the tune of 31 to 5, in favor of Norton's motion. Eliminating these votes, the motion would have been defeated 213 to 201. Sir Lewis Namier attributes the heavy disproportion of Scotch votes for the Ministry "not so much to the 'unreformed' character of the Scottish constituencies as to their intense and very natural resentment of the unmeasured abuse which they were subjected to in England at this time from the Opposition, and most of all, from the writer in the *North Briton,* on whose case the vote was taken."[57] This interpretation of the Scotch votes seems eminently reasonable.

If Newcastle and Pitt had succeeded in overthrowing the Grenville Ministry on the issue of general warrants, it seems likely, judging from the record of their former Ministry, that they would have discarded the project of levying taxes for revenue on the colonies. But Grenville, having won, was now in a position to proceed with his colonial measures, and, on March 9, 1764, presented to the House of Commons resolutions for duties for revenue on a number of colonial imports and

*On Townshend, see Sir Lewis Namier and John Brooke, *Charles Townshend* (London: St. Martin's Press, 1964); Cornelius P. Foster, *The Uncontrolled Chancellor: Charles Townshend and His American Policy* (Providence, R.I.: Brown University Press, 1978). [B. W. S.]

exports. These resolutions, having been approved by the House, were embodied in a bill which also included provisions for additional restrictions on colonial trade, and, despite the novelty and questionable constitutionality of Parliament's taxing the colonies for revenue, the bill passed with little opposition of any kind and practically none based on constitutional grounds. Grenville also laid at this time the foundation for further taxation of the colonies by securing the adoption by the House of Commons of a resolution that, toward defraying the expenses of defending the British colonies in America, "it may be proper to charge certain Stamp Duties in the said Colonies."[58]

The curious lack of opposition in Parliament to the revolutionary proposal to tax the colonies was partly owing to concentration by the London agents of the northern colonies on securing reduction of the proposed high rate of duty on foreign molasses, which, if adopted, would be highly injurious to colonial commerce. Another important element was the decision of the opposition leaders to follow the policy outlined by Pitt, as reported in a letter from Newcastle to Charles Yorke stating, "Mr Pitt said very properly and very strongly, talking of the future proceedings, that nothing must be proposed, which could either renew former Points, in which we might have differ'd amongst ourselves; or bring on any Point, in which we could possibly differ now." And on the American Bill, the opposition would almost certainly be divided: Pitt was outspokenly "against all taxation" of the colonies, while Townshend, now an important member of the opposition, had favored a tax on the colonies during the recent war and spoken in favor of imposing a colonial tax for revenue on foreign molasses as recently as the preceding session of Parliament.[59]

Hopeful of overthrowing the Ministry at the next session of Parliament, Newcastle made every effort to cement the union with Pitt established in March 1763 and maintained during the attack on general warrants. But the latter, vexed by the failure of members of the opposition to defend him from criticism by Grenville in the House of Commons, blasted all hope of union at the next session of Parliament. Replying to a letter from Newcastle in October 1764, concerning a possible deal with members from the cider-producing counties for their support if the opposition would back the repeal of a recent excise tax on cider, Pitt wrote, "I could much have wished your Grace had not done me the great honour to ask my advice upon the matter proposed to your Grace; and I humbly and earnestly entreat, that, for the future, the consideration of me may not weigh at all, in any answer your Grace may have to make to propositions of a political nature. Having seen the close of last session, and the system of that great war, in which my share of the ministry was so largely arraigned, given up *by silence* in a full House . . . I have no disposition to quit the free condition of a man standing *single,* and daring to appeal to his country at large, upon the soundness of his principles and the rectitude of his conduct."[60]

The opposition also suffered a loss of strength by the death of the Duke of Devonshire, one of the most respected and influential members of the opposition, and by the defection of Charles Townshend and Charles Yorke, both of whom signified their intention of leaving the ranks of opposition. Moreover, even those remaining were divided in policy; Newcastle's old friend Sir William Baker and some of the younger members favored a consistent, aggressive attack on administration measures during the session of Parliament which opened January 10, 1765, while Newcastle and the King's uncle, the Duke of Cumberland, who was linked with the opposition, considered such a course undignified and improper.[61]

The hopelessness of Newcastle's plan to upset the Ministry was proved when, on January 29, the measure likely to muster the maximum number of opposition votes, renewal of the motion to declare general warrants illegal, was decisively defeated.[62] Eight days later, Grenville presented his budget for 1765, including a proposed colonial stamp tax, and, despite the strong protests from the colonies against such a tax, had little difficulty in pushing it through Parliament. A motion in the House of Commons to postpone consideration of the tax was defeated, 245 to 49, and a bill for the tax passed that House on February 27. In the House of Lords it passed without even a division (March 8), and in due course was assented to on behalf of the King.[63]

Four months later, the King, displeased with the Grenville Ministry on several counts, dismissed it.[64] But by that time Parliament was no longer in session and the mischief of the colonial stamp tax, effective

November 1, 1765, could not be undone without an extraordinarily early session of Parliament, which the new Ministry, though friendly to the colonies, apparently gave no thought to.

CHAPTER 2

ROYAL INSTRUCTIONS
AND THE THREAT TO HOME RULE
IN THE ROYAL COLONIES

IN 1759 THERE WERE twenty-two British colonies in America. The thirteen mainland colonies that later rebelled had at this time a population of somewhere around 1,250,000 whites and 340,000 Negroes,[1] mostly slaves. The other nine had a population of perhaps 55,000 whites and over 290,000 Negroes.[2] About two-thirds of the whites lived in the five most populous colonies, Virginia, Massachusetts (including present Maine), Pennsylvania, Connecticut, and Maryland. Practically all the colonists lived east of the Alleghenies, Indian raids during the French and Indian War having driven out the relatively few British settlers west of the mountains.[3] For purposes of comparison it may be noted that rough estimates of the population of the British Isles as of that time give around 6,700,000 in England and Wales, 1,275,000 in Scotland, and somewhat over 2,000,000 in Ireland.[4]

The colonies, governmentally speaking, were of three kinds: the corporate colonies of Connecticut and Rhode Island; the proprietary colonies of Maryland, Pennsylvania, and Delaware; and seventeen royal colonies embracing all the island colonies—Barbados, Jamaica, Bermuda, the Bahamas, and the four Leeward Island colonies of Antigua, St. Kitts, Nevis, and Montserrat—and the mainland colonies, Nova Scotia, Massachusetts, New Hampshire, New York, New

Jersey, Virginia, North Carolina, South Carolina, and Georgia.[5] The discussion in this chapter relates solely to the royal colonies.

The governors of all the royal colonies were appointed by and subject to dismissal at the pleasure of the King. In all except Massachusetts, which had a charter, the general form of government was established primarily by the Governor's commission, issued by the King under his Great Seal and made public on the Governor's taking office. "The King's commission," wrote Thomas Pownall, former royal Governor of Massachusetts, "becomes the known, established constitution of that province which hath been established on it, and whose laws, courts, and whole frame of legislature and judicature are founded on it: It is the charter of that province: . . . and cannot, in its essential parts, be altered or destroyed by any royal instructions or proclamation."[6] Pownall did not mention alteration by changes in the text of the commission itself; but, had any material change been made in the customary form (none was made in the period here considered), a colony adversely affected by the change would almost certainly have protested.

The outstanding feature of the commission was its provision for a Legislature composed of a Council appointed by the Crown and a House or Assembly more or less popularly elected, which, in conjunction with the Governor, was given "full Power and Authority to make constitute and ordain Laws, Statutes and Ordinances for the publick Peace, Welfare and good Government of our said Province," provided, however, they were not "repugnant but as near as may be agreable to the Laws and Statutes of this Our Kingdom of Great Britain." This proviso in the commission was fortified by an act of Parliament, passed in 1696, providing that any colonial laws "repugnant to this present act, or to any other law hereafter to be made in this kingdom, so far as such law shall relate to and mention the said plantations ["plantations" was another name for colonies], are illegal, null and void."[7]

The Governor's assent was essential for a bill to become law (an "act," as commonly called), and even then the act was subject to review and possible disallowance by the Privy Council in England, where it might not be passed upon for years, either from inattention or to give the act a fair trial before passing judgment on it.[8] However, unless otherwise provided in the bill, it became operative when approved by the Governor; subsequent disallowance took effect only from the date official notice reached him.[9] Disallowance, in short, ordinarily operated as a repeal from the date notice reached the Governor, not as making the act void from its inception.[10]

Massachusetts, though a royal colony in the sense of having its Governor appointed by the Crown, differed from the other royal colonies in the enjoyment of a charter, which provided, among other things, for a provincial Council elected by the Legislature, and for limiting the period of disallowance to three years after acts of the colony were received by the Privy Council. (The charter of the proprietary colony of Pennsylvania likewise provided for transmission of the acts of the colony to England for review and possible disallowance by the Privy Council, with a limitation on the period for rejection of six months after receipt of the acts.)[11]

Once an act was allowed, it could thereafter be repealed only by the provincial Legislature or by Parliament; it could not be repealed by the King.[12] This principle was of great importance to the colonists because, as a colony accumulated a body of allowed acts dealing with such matters as the mode of election to the provincial Assembly, the establishment of courts, and the formation of town, parish, and county governments, this body of law protected the people of the colony against arbitrary or otherwise undesirable action by the Crown in matters of basic importance to them.

As indicated in the opening paragraphs of the Introduction, the provocative measures of tightening the restrictions on colonial trade and taxing the colonies for revenue, introduced by the harassed Bute and Grenville Ministries, were not the sole cause of the rising tide of colonial discontent. Even while Newcastle and Pitt were still in power and office, Lord Granville, President of the Council, and the Board of Trade took action, which, as we shall see, struck at the amplitude of legislative power long enjoyed in the colonies.

The Privy Council had another highly important part in the government of the colonies, in that, through its Committee for Hearing Appeals from the Plantations, it was the final court of judicial appeal in cases arising in all the colonies, royal, proprietary, and corporate.[13]

Supervision of the details of colonial affairs, including preliminary review of acts of the royal colonies and Pennsylvania, was in The Lords Commissioners for Trade and Plantations. This body, commonly known as the Board of Trade, established by William III in 1696, had eight more or less active members. It also had a number of members ex officio, but in our period (1759–1766) none of these attended the meetings of the Board. Among its officers, John Pownall, Secretary to the Board from 1753 to 1768, and Sir Matthew Lamb, its legal advisor from 1746 to 1768, were particularly important.[14] The President of the Board from 1748 to March 1761 was Lord Halifax, who was very regular in attendance at meetings of the Board, and, according to Franklin, writing in 1759, "governs all there."[15]

The ex officio members of the Board included the Bishop of London, who was consulted by the Board in matters affecting the Anglican church or clergy in the colonies.[16] The instructions to the royal Governors, except the Governor of Massachusetts, directed them to "give all countenance and encouragement" to the exercise of the Bishop's "ecclesiastical jurisdiction" in the colonies, but the nature and extent of this jurisdiction were not defined.[17]

The Secretary of State for the Southern Department also had, among other responsibilities, general supervision of colonial affairs. But the colonial correspondence of the Secretaries dealt chiefly with military affairs;[18] civil affairs were left largely in the hands of the Board of Trade and a committee of the Privy Council, the Committee on Plantation Affairs.

Action in England at this period on a colonial act involved four steps: the legal advisor to the Board of Trade examined the act to see if it was objectionable from any legal standpoint, such as ambiguity or exceeding the power of the legislature; the Board then made a recommendation concerning the act to the Committee on Plantation Affairs; the Committee in turn made a recommendation, usually, but not always, in agreement with the Board's to the Privy Council; and the Council then issued an order promulgating the Committee's recommendation. Approval by the Committee was the decisive action in the review; the Council invariably followed the Committee's recommendation.[19]

Most of the colonies had an agent in London to follow developments affecting the colony, one of whose most important duties was to keep in touch with proceedings in the Board of Trade and the Committee on Plantation Affairs with respect to acts of the colony which he represented.[20]*

The meetings of the Committee from 1759 to 1762 were regularly attended by the President of the Council, Lord Granville, better known in history as Lord Carteret, his title during the period (1730–1744) when he was the leading opponent of Sir Robert Walpole and for a time Secretary of State. Granville was concerned with colonial affairs not only by reason of his office but as one of the greatest owners of colonial land. A colonial claim inherited by him from his father had been settled in 1744 by the Crown's granting Carteret its entire property interest in the northern half of North Carolina, later known as the Granville District, extending from 35° 34′ north latitude to the southern boundary of Virginia.[21]

Three other members regularly attended the meetings of the Committee: Lords Cholmondeley, Falmouth, and Berkeley of Stratton. Cholmondeley (son-in-law of Sir Robert Walpole), who had earlier held high office, including Master of the Robes and Lord Privy Seal, was the father of the Reverend Robert Cholmondeley, Surveyor and Auditor General of the King's Revenues arising in America, and may have been regularly present as a substitute for his son, who was not a member of the Privy Council. Why, among the scores of members of the Privy Council, the relatively obscure Lords Falmouth and Berkeley of Stratton should have been the ones, along with the President and Cholmondeley, to attend the Committee meetings regularly, and what special qualifications, if any, they had for dealing with colonial affairs, is not known. These same members were also regular attendants at the meetings of the Committee for Hearing Appeals from the Plantations but with the important addition of some mem-

*Jack M. Sosin, *Agents and Merchants: British Colonial Policy and the Origins of the Revolution, 1763–1775* (Lincoln: University of Nebraska Press, 1965); Michael G. Kammen, *A Rope of Sand: The Colonial Agents, British Politics, and the American Revolution* (Ithaca, N.Y.: Cornell University Press, 1968); Michael G. Kammen, "The Colonial Agents, English Politics and the American Revolution," *William and Mary Quarterly,* 22 (1965): 244–63. [B. W. S.]

ber of the Council who held or had held high judicial office[22] and whose opinion was presumably given great if not decisive weight.

Besides his Commission, the Governor of a royal colony brought with him two sets of instructions from the Crown, general and trade, issued under the King's signature but not under the Great Seal, relating to his various responsibilities, executive, legislative, and judicial. The instructions, numbering over a hundred in 1759, were added to or revised from time to time and varied somewhat from colony to colony. They were not made public; the Governor was required to show some of them to the members of his Council, but in general they were for the Governor's eye only.[23]

From 1734 to 1749, there were proceedings in Parliament relating to colonial legislation and instructions which, if carried through, would have drastically curtailed the large measure of self-government enjoyed in the colonies. In 1734, the House of Lords passed a resolution for the preparation of a bill to be introduced at the next session of Parliament to provide that no future law passed in any of the colonies shall "have any effect, until the same shall have received his Majesty's approbation in Council . . . excepting such laws only as, through any emergency, may become necessary in the respective colonies for the immediate defence of the kingdom." But the proposed bill was not introduced, perhaps because of the protests on behalf of some of the colonies,[24] and nothing further was heard of the matter until 1744 when, during the brief ascendancy of Granville (then Lord Carteret), a bill was introduced in the House of Commons declaring that colonial acts not conforming to royal orders or instructions were invalid. Parliament was prorogued before the bill passed beyond the first reading. A similar bill introduced in 1749 met the same fate.[25]

One of the instructions to the royal Governors to be given the force of law if a bill such as Carteret favored had been passed, directed the Governor not to approve any bill to repeal or amend an existing act of the colony unless the bill contained a clause suspending operation of the new act until it was approved by the Privy Council.[26] Since most new acts of a public nature would amend to a greater or less degree some existing act, giving the force of law to this suspending clause instruction would have struck at the very roots of self-government in the royal colonies.

Despite an early legal opinion to the contrary, action by a royal governor was not treated as invalid because deviating from his instructions,[27] as was recognized in the following circular letter of June 3, 1752, from the Board of Trade to the Governors of all the royal colonies:

"Having taken into our consideration the General Instructions given by His Majesty to his Governors of the several Colonies and Plantations in America, we observed with concern that the experience of late years furnishes too frequent instances in which many of those Instructions have been dispensed with and neglected, upon slight & unwarrantable pretences. . . . We therefore think it our duty to recommend it to you and to all the Governors of His Majestys Colonies and Plantations strictly to adhere to your instructions and not to deviate from them in any point, but upon evident necessity, justified by the particular circumstances of the case; and whenever that happens you are forthwith to transmit to us, in the fullest and most explicit manner, your reasons for such deviation. But at the same time we must acquaint you, it is expected that you do apply for previous directions from hence in all cases where the occasion will admit of such a delay.

"The passing of laws in a method inconsistent with His Majesty's Instructions (which has been too often practised) is manifestly of great detriment to the publick service and the occasion of many difficulties; in as much as those laws, though they contain the most salutary provisions, cannot receive the Royall approbation, but by His Majesty's dispensing with his Instructions. We must therefore in a particular manner insist, that in the passing of all laws, you have a proper regard to the regulations contained in your Instructions."[28]

The rule thus stated was just and practical, recognizing on the one hand that satisfactory local self-government was possible in colonies remote from England, only if the Governors were given some discretion, and on the other that the Crown should have protection against careless or corrupt disregard of instructions by requiring a full explanation of any deviation. If the deviation was not approved, the Governor would be subject to censure, and if so grave or oft repeated as to warrant dismissal, he could be immediately dismissed since all the royal Governors held office merely at the pleasure of the King.

However, shortly before this circular letter was issued, the Board had recommended that no deviation from the suspending clause instruction be permitted in the case of bills to amend acts already allowed by the Privy Council, and this recommendation was followed in 1753 and 1754 with respect to acts of Virginia[29] and Jamaica.[30] The rule was not rigidly enforced after outbreak of the war with France in America,[31] but a letter in March 1759, from Benjamin Franklin in London as Agent for the Pennsylvania Assembly, concerning a recent interview with Granville, indicated that rigid enforcement of all the instructions, including the suspending clause instruction described above, was about to begin.

"An absolute Subjection to Orders sent from hence in the Shape of Instructions," wrote Franklin, "is the Point to be carried if possible. L_____d G_____, . . . told me frankly . . . 'Your People in the Colonies refuse obedience to the King's Instructions, and treat them with great Slight, as *not binding*, and *no Law*, in the Colonies; where as, says his L_____p, those Instructions are not like little Pocket Instructions given to an Ambassador or Envoy, in which much may be left to Discretion; . . . The King in Council is *the Legislator* of the Colonies; and when his Majesty's Instructions come there they are the *Law of the Land; they are*, said his L_____p, repeating it, THE LAW OF THE LAND, and as such *ought to be* OBEYED.' The whole of this Conversation was curious, of which, if I live to have the Pleasure of seeing you again, I shall show you the Minutes; they are too long for a letter."[32]

Granville would probably not have made so frank and alarming a statement to a colonial Agent six months earlier. After Braddock's defeat revealed that the struggle between Great Britain and France for hegemony in North America was likely to be close, the British Government had taken pains to conciliate the British colonial legislatures by avoiding disputes over matters of colonial government. Thus, when Governor Sir Charles Hardy of New York notified the Board of Trade that the New York Assembly refused to comply with a Crown instruction to secure an act providing a permanent revenue for payment of the Governor's salary and other governmental expenses in New York, the Privy Council Committee approved a letter from the Board to the King in February 1756, stating, "we should humbly submit, whether it may not be advisable, in the present situation of affairs, when peace, unanimity and a good understanding between Your Majesty's Governor and the People are so absolutely necessary for the good of the province, that the Governor should be directed, not to press this establishment of a perpetual Revenue for the present." And, two years later, the Board wrote Governor Pownall that while, "at a proper time," the Massachusetts Assembly should be required to abandon the practice of exercising various executive functions, it would not be advisable "in the present situation of things" to raise an issue over this point.[33]

By March 1759, the situation in America had radically changed. With Fort Duquesne and Louisbourg in British hands and British troops preparing to strike in overwhelming force at Niagara, Ticonderoga, and Quebec, the fate of France in North America was apparently sealed. Wholehearted cooperation by the British colonies in America was, of course, still desirable but was no longer vital to British success. Granville's desire for rigid enforcement of instructions to the royal governors need no longer be deferred.

CHAPTER 3

THE TWOPENNY ACT DISPUTE
IN VIRGINIA

IN 1758 VIRGINIA SUFFERED a severe drought, foreshadowing a very short crop of tobacco. The overseer of one of Colonel George Washington's plantations wrote him in July, "This Serves to inform you that all's Well Since you left this or my seeing you last. Likewise Serves to inform you of the great Drought Since then, that I have not had a Season to Plant one Single Plant. Every thing fit to Burn up with heat; . . . if there's no Tobacco Made Should be glad of Advice . . . as I am very Willing to do the best I can." Throughout the summer, similar letters complaining of one of the worst droughts in the history of Virginia continued to pour in on Washington, advancing with his Virginia regiment on Fort Duquesne. By the end of the growing season, William Allason, a Scotch storekeeper on the Rappahannock, wrote his brother in Scotland, "There never was so poor times in Virginia as is at present; there wonnt be above 5000 hhds. Tobacco made this present Crop; in a tolerable good Crop they have ten times that quantity."[1]

In Virginia, many private contracts and public acts stipulated for payment in pounds of tobacco rather than money, a practice facilitated by the widespread use as money of tobacco notes issued to cover deposits of tobacco in public warehouses under the colony's tobacco inspection system.[2] Among the public acts for payment in tobacco was an act of 1748 providing that members of the established, tax-supported Church of England clergy in Virginia should be paid 17,280 pounds of tobacco a year.[3]

By the time the Virginia Legislature met in September 1758, the great drought and consequent tobacco shortage had shot the price of tobacco up to four and a half pence a pound Virginia currency,[4] which was about triple the normal price.[5] To alleviate threatened hardship, the Virginia Legislature passed a bill authorizing the liquidation of tobacco obligations during the next year at sixteen shillings eightpence per hundred pounds,[6] the equivalent of twopence a pound.

Governor Francis Fauquier deviated from his instructions by approving the bill, which would temporarily amend acts providing for payment in tobacco, without requiring a suspending clause, but observed the Board of Trade's circular letter of June 1752, quoted in Chapter 2, by explaining to the Board the reasons for the deviation. "As the Bill," he wrote, "was a temporary Law to ease the people from a Burthen which the Country thought too great for them to bear, for one year only, a Suspending Clause would have been to all Intents and purposes the same as rejecting it. A Bill of the same Nature in a like Time of Scarcity of Tobacco had been passed [in 1755] without such a Clause, in the late Governor's Time and he incurred no Censure for having pass'd it. The Country were intent upon it, and both the Council and the House of Burgesses were almost unanimous in their pressing it. And I conceived it would be a very wrong Step for me to take who was an entire Stranger to the Distresses of the Country, to set my Face against the whole colony by refusing a Bill which I had a Precedent for Passing. Whatever may be the Case now, I am persuaded that if I had refused it, I must have despaired of ever gaining any Influence either in the Council or House of Burgesses."[7]

Most Virginians adversely affected by the act made no protest, but a number of the Anglican clergy in Virginia sought to have the act disallowed and sent one of their members, the Reverend John Camm, to England for this purpose. Camm, whom Fauquier described as one "whose Delight . . . is to raise a flame and to live in it," was Professor of Divinity (later President) of William and Mary College and rector of York-Hampton Parish. A Yorkshire man and graduate of Cambridge, he had been in Virginia for some fifteen years.[8]

In May 1759, the act was considered by the Board of Trade, together with petitions to the Board and the King signed by Camm on behalf of the protesting clergy of Virginia, asking that the act be declared void from its inception and that the King issue a command prohibiting the passage of any future act altering the act of 1748 in so far as it affected the established clergy of Virginia.[9] The Board sent a copy of the current act to its counsel, who apparently found no objection to it, and also sent copies of the act and of the petitions to Thomas Sherlock, Bishop of London, who replied in a long, bitter letter.

"I have," wrote Sherlock, "considered the act from Virginia referred to me. It seems to me to be the work of Men conscious to themselves that they were doing wrong, for tho' it is very well known, that the intention of the act is to abridge the maintenance of the Clergy, yet the Framers of the act have studiously avoided naming them, or properly describing them throughout the act; so that it may be doubted whether in a legal construction they are included or no.

"But to take the act as they meant it, and as everybody understands it, we must consider first by what authority the assembly acted in passing such a Law, and in the next place, how consistent the provisions of the said act are with Justice and Equity.

"The subject matter of this act, as far as the Clergy are concerned was settled before by act of Assembly [of 1748] which had the Royal assent and confirmation, and could not be repealed by a less power than made it, and to make an act to suspend the operations of the Royal Act, is an attempt which in some times would have been called Treason, and I do not know any other name for it in our Law. . . . Surely it is time to look about us, and to consider the several steps lately taken to the diminution of the prerogative and influence of the Crown.

"Lately taken, I say, because within a few years past, Virginia was a very orderly and well regulated colony, and lived in submission to the power set over them. They were all members of the Church of England and no Dissenters among them,[10] the Clergy were respected and well used by the people, but these days are over, and they seem to have nothing more at Heart than to lessen the influence of the Crown and the maintenance of the Clergy both which ends will be effectually served by the act now under consideration.

"It was not till the year 1748 that this spirit began to shew itself; at which time, an act of assembly passed by which the patronage of all the livings in the Colony were taken from the Crown and given to the Vestry in the several parishes, . . . [but] in the same act of 1748 there is the strongest confirmation of the Clergy's right to their full proportion of Tobacco, without any diminution whatsoever, which provision was meant to silence the complaints of the Clergy against the other part of the act. . . .

"As to the want of Justice and Equity shewed in this Bill, to the Clergy, the case is too plain to admit of any reflections upon it; and if the Crown does not, or cannot support itself in so plain a case as is before us, it would be in vain for the Clergy to plead the act confirmed by the King, for their right must stand or fall with the authority of the Crown."[11]

This letter was not only intemperate in making the reckless assertion that the Virginia Legislature was virtually guilty of treason, but contained gross misstatements of fact.

As indicated earlier in this chapter, the Twopenny Act was not leveled particularly at the established clergy. It was a general provision containing only a single, honorable exception—if a person under contract to deliver tobacco had received payment in money or goods on the basis of valuing tobacco at more than twopence a pound, he must fulfill the contract either by delivering the tobacco contracted for or by paying an amount equal to the value of what he had received. The charge that clerical patronage had been "taken from the Crown and given to the Vestry in the several parishes" by the act of 1748 was equally untrue. The vestries had had this patronage since 1643; the act of 1748 merely cleared up a doubt as to the time within which the vestry must make its decision.[12]

Furthermore, the Bishop's statement concerning the obvious unfairness of the act, echoed by Professor Tyler in his well known life of Patrick Henry (pp. 42–43): "Such, then, in all its fresh and unadorned rascality, was the 'two-penny act' . . . having there the sort of frantic popularity that all laws are likely to have which give a dishonest advantage to the debtor class," was open to question. There was a good deal to be said for affording protection of some kind to tobacco debtors against the sudden, severe inflation in the price of tobacco, and the price of twopence a pound at which tobacco debts might be temporarily liquidated, was, as previously noted, well above the usual price of tobacco.

Having considered the Bishop's letter and granted a hearing on the act to lawyers for Virginia and the protesting Virginia clergy, the Board of Trade, headed by Lord Halifax, submitted a report in July 1759, recommending disallowance of the act because of its supposed injustice and lack of a suspending clause and issuance by the King of an order to Fauquier commanding him "for the future strictly to observe and obey" the sixteenth article of his Instructions which included the suspending clause instruction.[13]

The Board's report, together with a protest against the Twopenny Act from British merchants engaged in trade with Virginia, was considered by the Committee on Plantation Affairs of the Privy Council, which, after hearing arguments of counsel, on August 3, 1759, likewise recommended disallowance of the act and the issuance of a peremptory instruction to Fauquier along the lines recommended by the Board.[14]

The members present at this important meeting of the Committee[15] were the four regulars mentioned in the preceding chapter (Lord Granville, President of the Council, and Lords Cholmondeley, Falmouth, and Berkeley of Stratton), Halifax, Thomas Secker, Archbishop of Canterbury, and former Lord Chancellor Hardwicke, whose presence was presumably desired because of the legal question raised by the Bishop of London's argument that the Virginia Legislature had no power to repeal or amend a Virginia act which had been assented to by the Crown.

In line with the procedure described in the preceding chapter, the Privy Council formally adopted the recommendations of the Committee on Plantation Affairs by orders of August 10 and 29, disallowing the act of 1758 and adopting a peremptory instruction to Fauquier, stating, in the King's name, "We do therefore strictly command and require you, for the future, upon pain of our highest displeasure and of being recalled from the government of our said colony, punctually to observe and obey the several directions contained in the 16th article of our said instructions."[16]

If Pitt and Newcastle, neither of whom attended meetings of the Committee on Plantation Affairs, had been aware of the significance of this order, which was bound to arouse colonial antagonism, they presumably would have insisted on its withdrawal.[17] But, so far as is known, they had no conception that Granville was laying the foundation for obtaining in the royal colonies much the same control as the bill of 1744, introduced during his brief ascendancy as chief Minister, was designed to obtain with respect to the colonies as a whole—that is, to make colonial acts not strictly conforming to instructions or other orders issued by the Crown void from their inception.

On learning of the sweeping order of August 29, 1759, official notice of which was delivered by Camm to Fauquier in June 1760, the Virginia Legislature petitioned the King for relief, pointing out that, if not modified, the order would "necessarily involve the Colony in the most insuperable Difficulties since many unavoidable Changes in our Circumstances do frequently happen which require the immediate Assistance of the Legislature before it is possible for us at so great a distance to make any Application to your Majesty." But, so far as is known, the Legislature received no reply, nor was the peremptory order of August 1759, modified or withdrawn.[18]

Exasperation was added to alarm over the order of August 1759, when Virginians learned the contents of the Bishop of London's letter, a copy of which, exultingly circulated among the clergy in Virginia, was obtained by Richard Bland and Landon Carter, prominent members of the Virginia House of Burgesses and of the established church.[19]

Bland, a planter and lawyer, just turned fifty, was the son of Richard Bland, Sr., and Elizabeth Randolph Bland. He had many influential family connections, including his first cousins Peter Randolph, a member of the Council, and Peyton Randolph, King's Attorney (Attorney-General) for the colony and member for Williamsburg in the House of Burgesses. Bland had served in the House with distinction since 1742 as a member for his home county, Prince George, and opposed Governor Robert Dinwiddie in the so-called pistole fee controversy of 1753–1755. No description of Bland at this time has been found, but at sixty-four, he was said to be "staunch and tough as white-leather [leather pounded and treated with alum and salt] —has something of the look of the musty old Parchments which he handleth and studieth much."[20]*

Carter, son of Robert ("King") Carter and Elizabeth Landon Carter, a little older than Bland, was also a member of the House (from Richmond County) and of one of the most influential families in Virginia. Peyton Randolph and William Byrd III, a member of the Council, were married to his nieces; Mann Page and Benjamin Harrison, important members of the House, were married to his sisters; and his brother Charles, representative for King George County, was likewise a leading member of the House. Carter, described by the rector of his parish as a "wealthy, Great, powerful Colonel . . . very proud, haughty, imperious and fickle," had previously crossed swords with the clergy in a dispute as to the right of a majority of the members of the vestry to dismiss the rector of their parish at pleasure, and had also actively opposed Dinwiddie in the pistole fee controversy.[21]

Carter and Bland published the Bishop's letter in pamphlets entitled respectively *A Letter to the Right Reverend Father in God, the Lord B_____p of L_____n;* and *A Letter to the Clergy of Virginia in which the Conduct of the General Assembly is vindicated Against the Reflections contained in a letter . . . from the Lord-Bishop of London.* They pointed out the lapses from truth and fairness in the Bishop's letter and denounced those in Virginia who had presumably misled him. Nor was the Crown wholly spared. "The Royal Prerogative," wrote Bland, "is without Doubt, of great Weight and Power in a dependent and subordinate Government: like the King of Babylon's Decree, it may, for aught I know, almost force the People of the Plantations to fall down and worship any Image it shall please to set up; but . . . it can only be exerted, while in the Hands of the best and most benign Sovereign, for the Good of his People, and not for their Destruction."[22]

*Jack P. Greene, ed., *The Diary of Colonel London Carter of Sabine Hall, 1752–1778,* 2 vols. (Charlottesville: University Press of Virginia, 1965); the introduction has been published separately as Jack P. Greene, *Landon Carter: An Inquiry into the Personal Values and Social Imperatives of the Eighteenth-Century Virginia Gentry* (Charlottesville: University Press of Virginia, 1967). [B. W. S.]

Another exasperating development was the institution of suit by Camm and at least three other members of the Virginia clergy against the officers of their several parishes to recover the full value of the tobacco payable to members of the established clergy under the act of 1748, on the ground that the Twopenny Act of 1758 was void from its inception and the act of 1748 remained in full force. Various grounds were alleged in support of this contention, the most sweeping and alarming of which was along the following lines: The Governor's commission is the organic law of the colony, and any act of the colony in conflict with it is void. The Governor's instructions are incorporated in the Commission by reference to them there. The Twopenny Act is clearly in conflict with the instructions. Therefore the act is void.[23]

This argument was virtually the same as that advanced by Granville in his conversation with Franklin, quoted in Chapter 2, which, as there pointed out, if sustained and enforced, would strike a crushing blow at self-government in internal affairs long enjoyed in the royal colonies. For the instructions, covering as they did so many details of governmental activity, were consistent with self-government only if construed as flexible guides, not, like the Governor's commission, as having the force of superior law.

The first two suits went against the clergy. In the case of the Reverend Alexander White, rector of St. David's parish, the King William County Court left the questions both of law and of fact to the jury, which brought in a general verdict for the defendant. In the case of the Reverend Thomas Warrington, rector of Charles City parish, the judges of the Elizabeth City County Court, George Wythe presiding, sustained the validity of the act of 1758 and held in favor of the defendant.[24] In the third, the case of the Reverend James Maury, rector of Fredericksville parish, the Hanover County Court on grounds unknown (the record of the trial was destroyed in the great Richmond fire of 1865) held the act of 1758 void from its inception, and set the case down for trial by jury on the question of the amount of damages.[25]

At the jury trial in December 1763, Maury's lawyer introduced evidence, which was not rebutted, that, when Maury's salary for 1758 became payable in May 1759, the market value of tobacco was sixpence a pound,[26] indicating damages of fourpence (six less the twopence paid under the act of 1758) a pound on 17,280 pounds of tobacco amounting to 69,120 pence or £288. But Patrick Henry, counsel for the defense, undertook to persuade the jury to ignore the evidence.

Henry, son of a leading Hanover county planter and nephew of a local rector, had unsuccessfully tried his hand at farming and storekeeping when, at the age of twenty-three, he found his calling. Securing admission to the bar in April 1760, he set up an office in his father-in-law's tavern at Hanover Court House, and had already built a large practice by the time he was retained as counsel in the Maury case.[27]

According to a letter from Maury to Camm, written shortly after the trial, the sheriff, after a feeble, unsuccessful effort to muster some "gentlemen" to serve on the jury, had resorted to "the vulgar herd," and, to Maury's disgust, selected jurors who, with one exception, he had never even heard of. Worse still, two or three of them were "Dissenters of that denomination called New Lights." Under the laws of Virginia, Dissenters, though supporting ministers of their own, had to pay taxes on the same basis as others for the support of the established clergy, and would presumably resent with special bitterness the clergy's attempt to increase taxes for clerical salaries by upsetting the Twopenny Act.[28] Maury's lawyer protested against the sheriff's selection; but Henry "insisted they were honest men, and, therefore unexceptionable," whereupon, they "were immediately called to the book and sworn."

"Mr. Henry," Maury continued, "harangued the jury for near an hour . . . to prove that the act of 1758 . . . was a law of general utility and could not consistently with what he called the original compact between King and people, stipulating protection on the one hand and obedience on the other, be annulled. Hence, he inferred, 'that a King, by disallowing Acts of this salutary nature, from being the father of his people degenerated into a Tyrant, and forfeits all right to his subjects' obedience.'" Whereupon "Mr. Lyons," Maury's lawyer, "called out aloud and with an honest warmth to the Bench 'that the gentleman had spoken treason,' and expressed his astonishment 'that their worships could hear it without emotion, or any mark of dissatisfaction.'" But the court did not even admonish Henry, and one of the jury, said Maury indignantly, "was so highly pleased with these doctrines . . . he every now and then gave the traitorous declaimer a nod of approbation."

Having paid his compliments to the Crown, Henry turned to the Church. "The Clergy of Virginia," he declared, in "refusing to acquiesce in the law in question . . . ought to be considered as enemies of the community," and "Mr. Maury instead of [obtaining] damages, very justly deserved to be punished with signal severity." Unless, he continued, the members of the jury "were disposed to rivet the chains of bondage on their own necks, he hoped they would not let slip the opportunity which now offered, of making such an example of him [Maury] as might, hereafter, be a warning to himself and his brethren, not to have the temerity, for the future to dispute the validity of such laws." The jury was evidently in sympathy with Henry's views, for, despite the evidence of damages amounting to £288, it brought in a verdict for one penny — and the Court denied the plaintiff's motion for a new trial.[29]

In Massachusetts, as we shall see in Chapter 5, controversies arose in 1760 to 1763 that revived old antagonisms between Anglicans and Congregationalists and tended to divide the members, both lay and clerical, of the two creeds into hostile camps. But in Virginia, as strikingly illustrated by the action of the jury in the Maury case, the controversy between part of the local Anglican clergy, the Bishop of London, and the Crown, on the one hand, and the Anglican and dissenting laity, on the other, tended to draw the latter together in common defense. The Maury case also plainly brought out that, so long as trial by jury prevailed, British laws or decrees could not be enforced in the colonies by ordinary civil process unless supported by local public opinion. Probably this practical consideration, even more than traditional, sentimental attachment to the principle of trial by jury, accounted for colonial opposition to the wide jurisdiction conferred by acts of Parliament on the colonial admiralty courts, in which, as a rule, questions of fact as well as of law were decided by the admiralty judge without a jury.

The fourth and last of the clergy's suits to come to trial was Camm's own, which was decided in favor of the validity of the act by the Council of Virginia sitting in its judicial capacity, in April 1764. Camm thereupon appealed to the Privy Council (which, as brought out in the preceding chapter, not only functioned as a kind of supergovernor in reviewing the acts of the royal colonies and Pennsylvania, but also sat as a final court of judicial appeal in cases arising in all the colonies) where the case hung fire until dismissed on a technicality in 1766.[30]

Removal of Camm's suit to England did not, however, quiet the controversy in Virginia, where it was kept alive by a fresh crop of angry pamphlets. In the latter part of 1763, Camm published *A Single and Distinct View of the Act, Vulgarly Entitled, The Two-Penny Act* maintaining that, while Carter and Bland professed to be much concerned over the hardship on the poor if the act was held void, they and other rich planters were the chief beneficiaries of the act. In February 1764, Carter replied in *The Rector Detected: Being a Just Defence of the Two-Penny Act* to which Camm, anonymously, soon afterward made a bitter rejoinder in *A Review of the Rector Detected: or the Colonel Reconnoitered.*[31]

No reply to Camm's second pamphlet appeared until August when, using the signature "Common Sense," Bland published his well-known *The Colonel Dismounted . . . Containing a Dissertation upon the Constitution of the Colony*, dealing with the recent new issue of Parliament's right to tax the colonies for revenue and also with the fundamental issue in the Twopenny Act controversy, the right of the Crown to straitjacket local self-government in the royal colonies by rigid enforcement of the suspending clause instruction. As to this latter point, Bland declared, "I have . . . a high reverence for the Majesty of the King's Authority, and shall upon every occasion yield a due Obedience to all its just Powers and Prerogatives; but Submission, even to the supreme Magistrate, is not the whole Duty of a Citizen . . . : Something is likewise due to the Rights of our Country and to the Liberties of Mankind. To say that a royal Instruction to a Governour, for his own particular Conduct, is to have the force and Validity of a Law, and must be obeyed without Reserve, is, at once, to strip us of all the Rights and Privileges of British Subjects, and to put us under the despotic Power of a French or Turkish Government; for what is the real Difference between a French Edict and an English Instruction if they are both equally absolute?"[32]

Coming from one of the leading men in Virginia, colonel of the militia of his county and its senior representative in the House of Burgesses, these words, if they reached officials in England, should have given warning that the people of Virginia would not lightly yield what they believed to be their rights.

CHAPTER 4

IRRITANTS IN OTHER
ROYAL COLONIES

In MAY 1761, William Bollan, London Agent for Massachusetts, reported a recent conference in the Board of Trade at which the Board
objected to a Massachusetts act of 1760 regulating official fees. The
Board, said Bollan, did not object to the amount of the fees specified
in the new act; its objections were to the temporary nature of the act
and to its amending an act which had been allowed by the Privy
Council, without including a clause suspending operation of the new
act until approved by the Council. The latter point, said Bollan, was
the one chiefly dwelt on.[1]

As pointed out in Chapter 2, Massachusetts differed from Virginia
and the other royal colonies in having its form of government established by charter, and the charter grant of legislative power to the
colony contained no provision stating or implying a reservation by the
King of authority to require a suspending clause in acts of the colony.[2]
Charter rights could not be revoked or modified at the pleasure of the
King,[3] and opposition to an attack on such rights was likely to secure
strong support in England because powerful vested interests there
were based on the security of royal charters.[4]

The Massachusetts House and Council promptly instructed Bollan to "defend to the utmost the General Court's power of legislation in its full extent according to the aforesaid charter." And in June 1762, a joint committee of the Legislature, including Thomas Hutchinson, Chief Justice of the Superior Court (the highest court) of Massachusetts and a member of the provincial Council, wrote a strong additional instruction to Bollan's successor, Jasper Mauduit.[5]

Declaring, "Our political or Civil Rights will be best understood by beginning at the Foundation," the Committee quoted the well-known passage in John Locke's *Two Treatises of Government,* "The Liberty of all Men in society is to be under no other legislative power but that established by Consent in the Commonwealth, nor under the Dominion of any Will or Restraint of any Law, but what such legislative shall enact, according to the trust put in it." The successful struggle against arbitrary rule in England, "from the Grant of *Magna Charta* to the Revolution [of 1688]," the Committee continued, had established the liberty of British subjects not merely in England but throughout the empire as a whole, since no reason "can be given why a man should be abridg'd in his Liberty, by removing from Europe to America, any more than by his removing from London to Dover, or from one side of a street to the other. So long as he remains a British Subject, so long must he be intitled to all the privileges of such an one: . . . Frenchmen, Portugals, and Spaniards are no greater Slaves abroad than at home, and by Analogy Britains should be as free on one side of the Atlantic as on the other."

From these generalizations, the Committee turned to the provisions of the Massachusetts charter relating to the legislative authority of the colony, and, after pointing out the absence of anything in the charter justifying the suspending clause instruction, declared that rigid enforcement of it would not only overthrow the constant usage of over half a century, but "in Effect . . . take away our Charter without act of Parliament, or the Ordinary process at Common law." "Surely," the Committee concluded, "the laws of England will never make such Construction of the King's Charter, as to put it in the power of the donor or his Successors to take it away when he pleases." The protest was apparently effective, for there is no evidence that the act was disallowed.[6]

Meanwhile, however, a serious controversy had arisen in Massachusetts over a petition by English customs officers, following the death of George II in October 1760, for the renewal of general writs of assistance issued to them by the Massachusetts Superior Court during the war. These writs, designed to help combat a pernicious, wartime trade with the French and other foreign West Indies by some northern colonial merchants and shipowners, would expire, under British law, six months after the death of the sovereign during whose reign they were issued.[7]

General writs of assistance authorized customs officers during daylight hours and accompanied by a local constable to enter and, if necessary, break into warehouses, stores, or homes to search for smuggled goods, without presenting any grounds for suspecting the presence of any such goods there. The merchants of the colony, the class most immediately affected, apparently did not oppose the original issuance of the writs, perhaps because of public opinion in favor of stamping out all commerce with France and its colonies during the war. But the new writs would probably continue to run long after the war, since the new King, George III, was only twenty-two and likely to live a long time. (He lived in fact until 1820.) Sixty-three Boston merchants united to oppose the petition for renewal, retaining James Otis, Jr., and Oxenbridge Thacher, well-known Boston lawyers, to represent them. The opposition was solely to the renewal of general writs; special writs for particular searches based on specific evidence presented under oath to the judge issuing the writ were not opposed.[8]

At the first hearing during the February 1761 term of the Superior Court, Jeremy Gridley, counsel for the customs officers, argued in favor of renewal on the grounds that, by act of the Massachusetts Legislature, the Massachusetts Superior Court was created a court of exchequer, and that by an act of Parliament of 1662, extended to the colonies in 1696, courts of exchequer were empowered to issue general writs of assistance.[9]

Thacher based the opening argument against renewal of the writs on several grounds. He asserted but offered no substantial proof that the Massachusetts court had renounced its statutory power to act as a court of exchequer. He maintained that if the court had exchequer powers it ought not to issue general writs because the English Court of Exchequer did not. He also argued that even if the English court issued general writs and the Massachusetts court was a court of exchequer it ought not to issue general writs because it did not have the supervisory authority over customs officials exercised by the Court of Exchequer in England and hence, unlike the English court, could not prevent abuse of the writs. (In 1776 Sir William De Grey, Attorney-General of England, gave an opinion that the act of 1662 authorized general writs of assistance by only one particular court, the English Court of Exchequer, and that the extension of this act to the colonies did not authorize colonial courts to issue such writs because no appropriate form of process for such writs was in force there.)[10]

Then came the turn of Otis, "a plump, round-faced, smooth skin, short-necked, eagle-eyed politician," a lawyer "of good reputation" but "of great Warmth . . . and much Indiscretion."[11] Basing his arguments on constitutional grounds, he contended that if the acts must be construed to authorize the writs, the acts were void as contrary to basic principles of the British constitution and must therefore be disregarded by the court. "An Act against the Constitution," Otis asserted, "is void: an Act against natural Equity is void; and if an Act of Parliament should be made, in the very words of this Petition, it would be void. The Executive Courts must pass such Acts into disuse."[12]

The court, Chief Justice Thomas Hutchinson presiding, reserved judgment until fall, when having received information from England that the Court of Exchequer there issued general writs, the Court held in favor of renewing the writs, and a number of general writs were issued in Massachusetts during the next few months.[13] The Massachusetts Legislature tried to annul the effect of the decision by passing a bill forbidding courts in the colony to issue general writs but Governor Bernard declined to approve the bill.[14]

Over fifty years later, John Adams wrote, "Otis was a flame of fire!—with a . . . profusion of legal authorities, a prophetic glance of his eye into futurity, and a torrent of impetuous eloquence, he hurried away everything before him. . . . Every man of a crowded audience appeared to me to go away, as I did, ready to take arms against writs of assistance. . . . Then and there the child Independence was born."

This is almost certainly a gross exaggeration; contemporary accounts, including Adams' own report of Otis' argument, give no indication of any such immediately electrifying effect as later described.[15] But the argument doubtless gave added currency to the colonial view, of major importance in strengthening colonial opposition to British taxation of the colonies, that Parliament's right to legislate was subject to constitutional limitations and that an act transgressing these limitations was void.

South Carolina was the next scene of disturbance—a disturbance arising out of a step toward rigid enforcement there of the instruction for a suspending clause in acts of amendment but embittered by other factors.

In May 1761, the Board of Trade recommended disallowance of a South Carolina act of 1759 amending an election act of 1721 on the ground among others of its lack of "the Clause of Suspension required in all such Cases by Your Majesty's Instructions," and the recommendation was adopted by the Privy Council which issued a formal order of disallowance in June 1761. Notice of this disallowance was proclaimed in December 1761, by Thomas Boone, newly arrived Governor of the colony, who announced at the same time that the House, elected the preceding winter for a term of three years, was dissolved because the election had been held under the disallowed act.[16]

When the new House met in March 1762, Boone sent a message, "Having had occasion lately to consider the Election Act passed in 1721, I have found it so loose and General, so little Obligatory on the Church Wardens, and so difficult in prescribing the forms to be observed . . . that I think a new Law absolutely necessary," adding that, to be approved, the bill must include a suspending clause. The House declined to pass the suggested bill, stating "they do not know or have ever heard of any . . . Objection to the Method . . . for issuing and Executing Writts of Election."[17] The reason for the House's nonaction is not known. Perhaps it was unwilling to accede to the demand for a suspending clause; perhaps it wished to show its disapproval of the recent dissolution. But in any event the Governor seems to have thought it appropriate to prove his power to retaliate.

At a special election, held some months later to fill a vacancy in the House for St. Paul's parish, Christopher Gadsden was elected by a large majority. Though there was a possible technical flaw in his election because the controlling election act of 1721 could be construed to require the parish churchwardens, whose duties included the conduct of elections to the House, to be specially sworn for this particular duty, whereas the wardens who conducted the recent election in St. Paul's had taken only the general oath required at the time they assumed office, he was seated without complaint or contest when the House convened in September 1762. However, upon his appearance before Boone to take the qualifying oaths the Governor not only refused to administer them, but, as he said, "to manifest in as public a manner as I can my disavowal of so undeniable an infraction of the election-act," again dissolved the House,[18] thereby putting the members and their constituents to the trouble and expense of still another election.

The members of the House, nearly all of whom, including Gadsden, were reelected, soon after assembling in November adopted a resolution denouncing Boone for his "precipitate, unadvised and prejudiced procedure" to which he retorted that, though he had no doubt as to his rightness on the point at issue, this was immaterial. For, whether right or wrong, he had absolute power "of adjourning, proroguing or dissolving an assembly, abruptly, precipitately, unadvisedly, for a good, insufficient or no reason at all." This led to an exchange of sharp messages between the House and Boone, ending in a vote by the House in December 1762 that, until the Governor "shall have done justice to this house in this important point," it would have no further dealings with him. On orders of the House, the proceedings were published in the local newspapers for the information of the people of the colony, and a copy was sent to the colony's Agent in London with instructions to have it printed and distributed among the other colonial Agents and to vindicate the Assembly's conduct in all quarters.[19]

The feud between the House and Boone continued until May 1764, when he left for England on leave of absence, never, as it proved, to return.[20] Even so, there was a brief aftermath when the Crown-appointed Council refused to concur in an appropriations bill passed by the House unless a salary for Boone was included; but the Council soon gave way on this point.[21]

The Crown also took steps at this time to tighten its control in New York and New Jersey, not, however, as in Virginia, Massachusetts, and South Carolina, by rigid enforcement of the instruction for a suspending clause in acts of amendment but by securing greater influence over the judges of the Supreme Courts through reducing their existing "during good behavior" tenure merely at the pleasure of the Crown.

For many years the instructions to the Governors of the royal colonies provided that "You shall not displace any of the judges . . . without good and sufficient cause to be signified unto us . . . , and to prevent arbitrary removals . . . you shall not express any limitation of time in the commissions." As apparently authorized by this instruction, Governors of New Jersey beginning in 1739 and of New York beginning in 1744 issued commissions to judges of the provincial Supreme Court granting tenure during good behavior. These commissions were in harmony with a provision in the Act of Settlement of 1701, effective on the death of Queen Anne, requiring that commissions of judges in England be granted to run during good behavior (*"quamdiu se bene gesserint"*), subject to removal upon the address of both houses of Parliament.[22] But the English Act provided that salaries of the judges in England "Shall be ascertained and established," whereas in New York and New Jersey the salaries were subject to reduction or nonrenewal at the pleasure of the Legislature,[23] thus giving the latter power to influence the judges.

If the Crown had taken steps to bring the colonial system into line by authorizing the grant of judicial commissions during good behavior, only if provision was made by the colonial legislature for permanence of the salary paid at the time the judge took office, there would have been no reasonable ground for colonial objection. But this was not what the Board of Trade had in mind. Beginning in 1754, instructions issued from time to time under its auspices to newly appointed Governors of the royal colonies ordered, without qualification, that judicial commissions "be granted during pleasure only,"[24] and acts of Jamaica and Pennsylvania providing for judicial tenure during good behavior, coupled with permanent salaries, were disallowed by the Privy Council pursuant to the Board's recommendation.[25]

Chief Justice James De Lancey, while acting Governor of New York in 1758, ignored the new instruction and appointed David Jones to the Supreme Court on the same tenure as the other judges, that is, tenure during good behavior. But when De Lancey died, his successor as acting Governor, Cadwallader Colden, played safe by consulting Halifax, President of the Board of Trade, whether to follow New York practice or the new instruction in filling De Lancey's place on the bench. And soon afterward the question was raised on a broader scale by the death of George II, requiring renewal, within six months of his death, of royal commissions generally, including those of the judges in New York and New Jersey.[26]

In a letter to the Board of Trade, Colden suggested the possibility of granting good behavior tenure provided the New York Legislature would grant permanent salaries. But in reporting to the Privy Council concerning the questions raised by Colden's letters the Board made no mention of this possible solution. Pointing out that New York failed to grant permanent salaries and asserting without proof that the salaries of colonial judges were inadequate and the caliber of the colonial judges was low, the Board recommended rigid enforcement of the instruction as to judicial tenure, declaring that to permit the granting of good behavior tenure to colonial judges would be "Subversive of all true Policy, destructive to the Interests of Your Majesty's Subjects and tending to Lessen that just dependance which the Colonies ought to have upon the Government of the Mother Country."[27] The Board's recommendation was adopted in November 1761 by the Privy Council, whose order, in the form of a circular instruction to Governors of the royal colonies to grant judicial commissions "during pleasure only," included a threat of dismissal for disobedience of the order.[28]

Meanwhile, the King had issued an order (mandamus) to Colden to appoint as Chief Justice of the New York Supreme Court, under a commission revocable at the pleasure of the Crown, Benjamin Prat,[29] Advocate-General for the Crown in Massachusetts. Some months earlier John Adams had jotted down a statement of Prat that "The people ought to be ignorant; and our free schools are the very bane of society; they make the lowest of the people infinitely conceited." "These words," Adams remarked, "would come naturally enough from the mouth of a tyrant, or of a king or ministry about introducing an arbitrary power, or from the mouth of an ambitious ecclesiastic; but they are base, detestable principles of slavery. He [Prat] would have ninety-nine hundredths of the world as ignorant as the wild beasts of the forest, and as servile as the slaves in a galley, or as oxen yoked in a team." Further light on Prat is furnished by a letter of his to the Board of Trade suggesting the advisability of the Crown's paying him a salary as New York's Chief Justice of £400 or £500 a year sterling, since "Such a salary independent of the People . . . could not fail to render the Office of great service to his Majesty, in securing the Dependence of the Colony on the Crown and its commerce to Great Britain."[30]

While Colden was waiting for a reply to his request to the Board for specific instructions as to tenure, the New York House passed bills providing that judges of the provincial Supreme Court should hold office during good behavior, and both the House and Council passed bills making the judges' salaries conditional on their being granted such tenure.[31]

After the arrival of the Privy Council's order of November 1761, forbidding the granting of good behavior tenure, Prat appealed (March 1762) to the House through its Speaker, William Nicoll, to vote salaries for the judges without any proviso as to tenure, pointing out that the judges could not be expected to serve without salary and that the existing act therefore threatened a failure of justice in New York. Nicoll replied that members of the House were well aware of this danger, but were also "sensible of the value of the essential Rights and security of the People, the concern for which has occasioned their granting the Judges Sallaries in the manner they have."[32] This was probably only a gesture of protest, since it was obviously impracticable for the colony to get along indefinitely without judges of the Supreme Court. In any event, two of the associate judges, soon afterwards, accepted "at pleasure" commissions, and, at its fall session, the Legislature voted the judges' salaries without imposing any condition as to tenure. The House accompanied its vote by a petition to the King requesting his approval of good behavior tenure provided it was accompanied by permanent judicial salaries.[33] But the petition was not granted; the circular instruction of 1761 as to tenure of judges remained in force, without change, until the Revolution.[34]

In New Jersey, Governor Josiah Hardy, less cautious than Colden, followed local practice rather than his instructions, and, in December 1761, renewed the Supreme Court judges' commissions on good behavior tenure, explaining his reasons for this in a letter to the Board of Trade. But though this deviation from instructions was warranted by the circular letter of 1752 quoted and discussed in Chapter 2, the Board recommended Hardy's dismissal "as a necessary example to deter others in the same situation from like Acts of Disobedience." In August 1762, he was dismissed and William Franklin, Benjamin Franklin's natural son, was appointed in his place.[35]

In response to a question of the Board of Trade as to the validity of Hardy's appointments in deviation from instructions, the Attorney-General, Charles Yorke, advised in January 1763 that the "appointment of Judges of the Supreme Court, during *good behaviour*, instead of during *pleasure*, contrary to the King's instructions, in Governments subsisting solely by his Majesty's authority, is illegal and invalid." The instructions, he declared, being referred to in the Commissions of the royal Governors, were incorporated into them and "regulate the mode of their [the royal colonies'] Constitution,[36] thereby in effect confirming Lord Granville's novel view, discussed in Chapter 2, that the royal instructions were on a parity with the Governor's Commission and had the force of superior law.

CHAPTER 5

THE DISTURBING ACTIVITIES OF ARCHBISHOP SECKER

FOR MANY YEARS after the founding of the Anglican church in Massachusetts there was much antagonism between the Congregational majority and the Anglican minority in the colony. Anglicans were aggrieved because, except in the town of Boston, where the ministers and churches were supported by voluntary contribution, members of the Church of England were compelled by law to contribute to the maintenance of the ministers selected by the Congregational majorities.[1] The Congregationalists, in turn, had been vexed by the action of the Society for the Propagation of the Gospel in Foreign Parts (hereafter called "the Society") in establishing nine missions in old, settled communities in Massachusetts supplied with Congregational churches,[2] apparently more to proselyte than to propagate the Gospel among those unfamiliar with its message.[3]

However, after 1742, relations improved. In that year the Massachusetts Legislature passed an act permanently providing that taxes for church purposes collected from any member of the Church of England be turned over to the minister of the Anglican church which he "usually and frequently attends," and from 1742 to 1759 the Society authorized only one more mission in the old, settled towns of the colony.[4] The change for the better was illustrated in 1745 when Andrew Oliver, Thomas Hancock, and other well-to-do Congregationalists were among the subscribers to the set of bells for Christ Church, one of Boston's three Anglican churches, and again in 1753 when, during the rebuilding of Anglican King's Chapel, Boston, the churchwardens of the Chapel requested two nearby Congregational churches to permit members of the Chapel to hold services in their churches and the requests were granted. Friendly relations were further strengthened by the French and Indian War, which drew together colonial members of all Protestant denominations, exhorted by their ministers to stand together to avert the common danger from Catholic France.[5]

The moderation of the Church of England on the one hand and the greater tolerance toward Anglicans among New England Congregationalists on the other, had, wrote Franklin in 1759, largely effaced the old bitterness in New England between Churchmen and Congregationalists, and this statement was borne out, as far as it concerned Massachusetts, by reports from the Society's missionaries there concerning the harmony between the members of their communion and the Congregationalists.[6]

This reciprocal tolerance was, however, not relished by some of the more militant Anglican ministers in the northern colonies. The Reverend Charles Brockwell, associate minister of King's Chapel, for example, protested against the use of a non-Anglican church when King's Chapel was under repair in 1753, declaring, "My conscience tells me that to perform any part of Divine Service there when here are two Episcopal Churches in the Town (to which we are welcomed) is sin." And, in 1761, the Reverend Thomas Bradbury Chandler, rector of St. John's Church, Elizabeth, New Jersey, wrote, "The Church seems to be in a state neither of encreasing nor of losing ground in regard to its numbers. This appears to me to be in some measure owing to that general harmony and good understanding which subsists between the Church and the Dissenters. The points in controversy between us, some years ago were disputed with warmth and some degree of animosity. Then the Church visibly gained ground. But . . . Dissenters have become so charitable as to think there is no material difference between the Church and themselves . . . [and] I fear that such is the moderation of the Church, as to return the compliment in their opinion of the Dissenters and possibly in time we may come to think the unity of Christ's body is a chimerical doctrine — that Schism is an Ecclesiastical Scarecrow — and that Episcopal is no better than the leathern mitten ordination; or in other words that the authority derived from Christ, is no better than that which is given by the mob. I hope the Clergy do not countenance these notions; but if they are suffered to prevail amongst our own people, the Clergy must in some measure be accountable for it."[7]

In the militant spirit desired by Chandler, the Reverend Henry Caner, rector of King's Chapel, addressed himself in 1759 to Thomas Secker, Archbishop of Canterbury and President of the Society. Born in 1693, the son of a Dissenter and educated in Dissenting academies, Secker did not join the Church of England until about 1720 and was not ordained priest until he was around thirty. Through ability, the influence of William Talbot, Bishop of Durham, whose acquaintance he had made some years earlier, and the favor of Queen Caroline, he rose rapidly in the Church and was consecrated Bishop of Bristol in 1735. Two years later he became Bishop of Oxford, "the jesuitical Bishop of Oxford," as Horace Walpole called him, and while holding his See, preached a sermon, in 1741, deploring the shocking state of irreligion among the colonists, many if not most of whom he described as "wicked, and dissolute, and brutal in every Respect." In 1758 he was made Archbishop of Canterbury.[8]

"May It Please Your Grace," wrote Caner to the Archbishop, "Nothing less than the Interest of Religion and the advancement of the Church over which you worthily preside could have given me the confidence of this Address. With a view only at promoting these good ends, I have presumed to mention to your Grace a Petition now to be laid before the Society for the Propagation of the Gospel, requesting their settling a Mission at Cambridge, in New England. . . . The College, my Lord, is placed in that Town. It is the only Seminary of Learning for this Province. Socinianism, Deism and other bad principles find too much countenance among us. To prevent these and the like errors from poysoning the Fountain of Education, it will undoubtedly be of great service to erect a Church there, agreeable to the desire of many of the Inhabitants. . . . Mr. Apthorp, a gentleman now in orders, and who had his Education at the University of Cambridge in England . . . offers himself to this service."[9]

The opening of a new mission church by the Society in Cambridge, fountainhead of the Congregational ministry of eastern New England, would obviously be particularly alarming and obnoxious to New England Congregationalists, and particularly ungracious, too, because while Oxford barred conscientious Dissenters even from matriculating and Cambridge from receiving degrees, Harvard laid no restrictions on Anglicans.[10] Nevertheless, Caner's suggestion was warmly seconded by the Reverend Samuel Johnson,[11] former missionary of the Society at Stratford, Connecticut, and, since 1754, President of King's College (now Columbia University), New York City.

The Archbishop's reply was favorable. "Good Mr. Caner," he wrote, "The Society have unanimously agreed to do what Dr Johnson and you recommend in relation to Mr Apthorp; for although they are apprehensive that settling a Mission at Cambridge will raise a great clamour, yet they hope for much greater good from his Abilities, Temper and Discretion," and to Johnson he gave the additional interesting information that "On a Consultation amongst the Bishops it was agreed . . . it would be best to propose the matter in the Society, without taking notice of its being liable to any peculiar objections; which was done accordingly, and the resolution taken unanimously."[12]

Construction of the new mission church, present Christ Church, Cambridge, within a stone's throw of the Harvard Yard, was begun in 1760, and the church opened for services in October 1761.[13]

In 1762 Caner had occasion to write Secker again, this time concerning a Massachusetts act incorporating a new missionary society for work among the North American Indians, organized by a group of influential Congregationalists of Boston and vicinity, including the Secretary of the province, Andrew Oliver; its Treasurer, Harrison Gray; outstanding merchants such as John Erving, James Bowdoin, and Thomas Hancock; and Edward Holyoke, President of Harvard, Joseph Sewall, Charles Chauncy, Jonathan Mayhew, Andrew Eliot, Thomas Foxcroft, and other leading members of the Congregational ministry.[14]

"Had any one here," wrote Caner, "Authority to convene the rest of his brethren, I presume this would not have been a single, but a joint address from all the clergy in these parts, who cannot look on with Indifference while the Dissenters are using every possible method of Giving a check to the Progress of the Church of England. Of this nature I esteem an Act of this province, past at the Sessions of the General Assembly in May last, of which I have enclosed a copy for your Grace's perusal; for notwithstanding the Specious Preamble it contains, I am well assured that the real design of it is to frustrate the pious designs of the Society for the Propagation of the Gospel in Foreign Parts."[15]

The Archbishop replied, "I have now the remains of Gout in both my hands, and a fresh attack upon one foot and knee, not without some threatening Symptoms in the other . . . but I see the necessity of taking immediate notice of your last Favor . . . I see the matter just in the same light that you do, and think your observations very just and material. . . . I am of opinion that our Society must not appear against it—the answer would be that they have done little in this way themselves, and ought not to hinder others. . . . But I conceive it may be shewn that several improprieties and Defects in the Present Frame of it, make it unfit for the Royal Assent. Possibly, also, one may venture to suggest with due caution to some persons, that no Act for this purpose will come from Boston, which is not so framed as to add more influence to the Dissenters than will be expedient."[16]

The first step was to have the Board of Trade recommend disallowance of the act. To this end, Secker collaborated with the Reverend William Smith (former missionary of the Society in Pennsylvania, in England on a fund-raising tour for the College and Academy of Philadelphia of which he was Provost) in preparing and submitting to the Board a memorandum of reasons why the Massachusetts Indian missions act should be disallowed. This memorandum was eminently successful. The Board recommended disallowance in a report to the King that was practically a paraphrase of the memorandum, and in May 1763, the Privy Council disallowed the act. The Board's report, of course, said nothing of the part played by the Archbishop and the Society, but Jasper Mauduit, London Agent for Massachusetts, got wind of this, and passed on the information to a correspondent in Boston.[17]

Mauduit's report naturally confirmed Congregationalists' fears of the Church of England as a menace to their ecclesiastical independence and leadership. The Reverend Andrew Eliot, minister of the New North Congregational Church, Boston, wrote Mauduit, "We find by your Letter to Mr Bowdoin that the Act . . . is not like to have the Royal Approbation. . . . It is strange that Gentlemen who profess Christianity will not send the Gospel to the Heathen themselves nor permit it to be sent by others. . . . ¶ [We] find by the Fate of our Charter, that our Enemies are more and greater than we were aware of." Others wrote in similar vein, including a committee of Boston Congregational ministers, who begged the London Committee representing the so-called Dissenting Deputies, an influential body consisting of two members from each Presbyterian, Congregational (Independent), and Baptist congregation in and within a ten-mile radius of London, for their assistance in counteracting the influence of Secker and the Society.[18]

Early in January 1763, Caner complained of the "bitterness of spirit which seems thus of a sudden" to break out among Dissenters, but an open clash did not occur until after the publication of a letter by an unknown writer in the *Boston Gazette* of February 18, 1763, commenting on the death of the Society's missionary in Braintree and ridiculing the Society's establishment of missions in old, established Congregational communities like Braintree and Cambridge. Galled by this letter, the Reverend East Apthorp, minister of the new Cambridge mission, published a pamphlet *Considerations on the Institution and Conduct of the Society for the Propagation of the Gospel in Foreign Parts,* defending the Society's activities and lauding its work in the colonies.[19]

This drew a reply, *Observations on the Charter and Conduct of the Society,* by the Reverend Jonathan Mayhew, pastor of the West Church (Congregational) of Boston,[20] "a man . . . of good abilities, but of a turbulent and contentious disposition," who had demonstrated his polemical talent, some years before, in a powerful sermon denouncing the Church of England for annually memorializing the beheading of Charles I as if he were among the Christian martyrs.[21]

Mayhew took Apthorp to task on some indiscreet statements he had made, such as that services in a Congregational church were no satisfaction "to him whose conscience cannot use or does not approve them, no more than Popery or Mahometonism affords the means of Religion to a good Protestant who happens to be in Popish or Mahometan countries," and that the Anglican churches in the colonies had freed religious doctrines there from the "senseless horrors with which Fanaticism had perverted them." The latter charge must have been particularly provoking to Mayhew. All ministers of the Church of England, including, of course, Apthorp himself, were compelled to subscribe, as a condition to ordination, the Thirty-Nine Articles of Religion, including the horrible Calvinist Article 9 "Of Original or Birth-Sin" and Article 17 "Of Predestination and Election," while ordination could be had by Congregational ministers without subscription to Calvinist doctrine, as strikingly exemplified by Mayhew, who, before as well as after ordination, was an outspoken anti-Calvinist (Arminian).[22]

Mayhew's chief object of attack, however, was the Society itself for establishing the new church at Cambridge; for frequently applying its funds to establish churches and ministers in communities already well supplied with Protestant churches instead of among the heathen and in frontier communities where the settlers were too poor to maintain a minister without external help; and for trying to secure the establishment of Church of England bishops in the colonies.[23]

In 1751–1752, Secker, then Bishop of Oxford, had been a leading supporter of the revival of a movement for colonial bishops recently launched by Thomas Sherlock, Bishop of London,[24] whom we met in Chapter 3. This movement had been defeated, chiefly, it seems, through the influence of the Duke of Newcastle, the Archbishop of Canterbury (Thomas Herring), Lord Hardwicke, and Horatio Walpole, member of Parliament for Norwich, a stronghold of English dissent,[25] who stated his grounds for opposition in an interesting letter to Sherlock.*

*Carl Bridenbaugh, *Mitre and Septre: Transatlantic Faiths, Ideas, Personalities, and Politics, 1689–1775* (New York: Oxford University Press, 1962); Paul K. Longmore, " 'All Matters and Things Relating to Religion and Morality': The Virginia Burgesses' Committee for Religion, 1769–1775," *Journal of Church and State*, 38 (1996): 775–97; Frederich V. Mills, Sr., "The Internal Anglican Controversy over an American Episcopate," *Historical Magazine of the Protestant Episcopal Church*, 44 (1975): 257–76. [B. W. S.]

"Your Lordship," wrote Walpole, "having been pleased to communicate to me . . . a paper containing a State of the Church of England in his Majesty's Dominions in America . . . , I carefully perused and considered [it] . . . as became a Member of the Church of England whose Education and profession have always been agreeable to her form and Doctrine.

"But your Lordship may remember that . . . I took the liberty to tell you that however desirable and reasonable a Scheme for settling Bishops for some purposes in the American Colonys might be, abstractly considered, yet having weighed this measure, with a due regard at the same time to what appears to be the inclination of those colonies, and what might be the consequences of it as a matter of State to our present happy Establishment, I was apprehensive [it] . . . might be attended with very Mischievous effects to the Government. . . . The [English] dissenters of all Sorts . . . will by the instigation and complaints of their brethren in the Colonys, altho' with no solid reasons, be loud in their discourses and writings upon this intended innovation in America, and those in the Colonys will be exasperated and animated to make warm representation against it. . . . And your Lordship will pardon my friendly freedom for adding that many persons of Consideration who have a true Value for your Lordship's great Learning and Understanding, are not without jealousy [suspicion] of your extraordinary Zeal and desire to increase Ecclesiastical Power in this Country, and that jealousy my Lord will carry with it an apprehension that this first motion for settling Bishops in America to perform certain functions only as Ordination and Confirmation is laying a foundation for giving them gradually the same Authority and power as the Bishops here enjoy and exercise . . . [and] will in a great degree have the effect and be attended with the same consequences of ill humor and discontent as if Ecclesiastical Government was now to be settled there in its full extent."[26]

The same practical objection was urged against the project by Josiah Willard, Secretary of Massachusetts, who wrote acting Governor Spencer Phips, "I need say but little in that Matter considering how fully and freely I expressed myself in a letter I wrote to your Excellency in June last. . . . I can only add that the universal dissatisfaction to that

Scheme among Persons of our Communion is . . . [from] expecting that if once Bishops should be settled in America, it would be judged for some Reason or other necessary to extend their Jurisdiction equally to what that Order of Men are possessed of in Great Britain."[27]

The extension in full of English ecclesiastical government to the colonies would include the establishment of separate ecclesiastical courts, having jurisdiction over testamentary and matrimonial causes and a variety of offenses such as adultery, fornication, and various kinds of defamation, and the expense of maintaining bishops appointed for the colonies who, in the course of time, would presumably press for incomes comparable to those of English bishops, some of whom had princely revenues. (From a statement prepared for George III in 1762 it appears that "the reputed Yearly Value" of the office of the Archbishop of Canterbury was approximately £7,000, Archbishop of York, £4,500, Bishops of Durham, Winchester, and London, £6,000, £5,000, and £4,000 respectively, and most of the other bishops from £1,400 to £3,400 a year—compared with £20 to £50 a year for thousands of English curates.)[28] And how was the revenue to support colonial bishops to be raised except, largely at least, from colonial taxation?[29]

Judging from the tolerance of Episcopal bishops in the states after the American Revolution, when fear of their temporal power had passed, most Dissenters would not have objected to visits from a bishop of the established church of England, Ireland, or the Isle of Man to alleviate the hardship of colonial Anglicans having to go abroad for confirmation or ordination according to Anglican rites, which only an Anglican bishop had authority to perform. But though such visits were repeatedly asked for by colonial Anglicans and there were forty-three Anglican bishops to draw on,[30] none ever came.

When Secker became Archbishop of Canterbury and President of the Society in 1758, it naturally seemed a propitious time for reviving the project for colonial bishops which he had warmly supported, and, in writing the new Archbishop of their pleasure at his elevation, a group of Anglican clergymen of New York and New Jersey, headed by President Samuel Johnson, took occasion to express the hope that "the immediate Inspection of a Bishop . . . may be one of the Blessings of your Grace's Archiepiscopate."[31]

Despite the known objections of the Dissenters, English and colonial, to the project, Secker replied in September 1758, assuring Johnson that the matter of colonial bishops was one he had "long had at heart," and would be brought before the King's advisors as soon as practicable, though "pushing it openly" would be unwise. In 1760 he again warned Johnson that it was best to lie low until the time came to apply "privately to the persons, whose advice the King will take," but gave the encouraging word that Lord Halifax, President of the Board of Trade, was "very earnest for Bishops in America."[32]

In March 1763, soon after the end of the Seven Years' War, Secker advised Johnson that the time was at last almost ripe for pushing the project. "Probably," said he, "our ministry will be concerting schemes this Summer against the next Session of Parliament for the settlement of His Majesty's American Dominions. And then we must try our utmost for Bishops." Apparently launched soon afterward, the plan was still in the balance a year later, as appears from the following letter from Secker to Johnson in May 1764. "The affair of American Bishops," wrote Secker, "continues in suspense. Lord Willoughby of Parham, the only English Dissenting Peer, and Dr. Chandler have declared, after our scheme was fully laid before them, that they saw no objection against it. The Duke of Bedford [Granville's successor as President of the Privy Council] . . . hath given a calm and favorable hearing to it . . . and promised to consult about it with the other ministers at his first leisure. Indeed, I see not how Protestant Bishops can decently be refused us, as in all probability a Popish one will be allowed, by connivance at least, in Canada. . . . ¶ But . . . what relates to Bishops, must be managed in a quiet, private manner. Were solicitors to be sent over prematurely from America for Bishops, there would come also solicitors against them; a flame would be raised, and we should never carry our point."[33]

Colonial dissenters, of course, had no such direct and detailed evidence of what was going on as we have today; but rumor of the project was alarming Congregationalists in Boston as early as April 1762, and by October 1763, the alarm had spread southward. According to the Reverend Richard Peters, rector of Christ and St. Peter's Churches, Philadelphia, writing in that month, "The manner in which this affair has been mentioned in the newspapers, both of England & of these Colonies, has raised much jealousy [anxiety] among the Dissenters, and many of them have come open-mouthed to me to know what is going on of this sort."[34]

To this project Mayhew, as previously stated, now addressed himself in his *Observations*.

"When we consider," he wrote, "the real constitution of the church of England; and how aliene her mode of worship is from the simplicity of the gospel, and the apostolic times: When we consider her enormous hierarchy ascending by various gradations from the dirt to the skies" and that "all of us be taxed for the support of *bishops* and their *underlings*," can we help crying out "Will they never let us rest in peace, except *where all the weary are at rest?* Is it not enough, that they persecuted us out of the old world? Will they pursue us into the new to convert us here? — *compassing sea and land to make* US *proselytes*, while they neglect the heathen and heathenish plantations! What other new world remains as a sanctuary for us from their oppressions, in case of need? Where is the COLUMBUS to explore one for, and pilot us to it, before we are . . . deluged in a flood of episcopacy?"[35]

So far as is known, Apthorp did not reply to the *Observations*, but some other New England Anglicans attacked Mayhew with intense bitterness. In a pamphlet attributed to the Reverend Arthur Browne, rector of Queen's Chapel, Portsmouth, New Hampshire, some of Mayhew's remarks were compared to "the fanatic ravings of his predecessors the Oliverian holders-forth, whose spittle he hath licked up, and coughed it out again, with some additions of his own filth and phlegm"; and an anonymous broadside, defending Apthorp, declared he was unhurt by "the Blast of a foul Mouth" and had received no more damage from Mayhew's reply "than if a Dog had belched in his Face after feeding upon Carrion." Caner, too, attacked Mayhew in a bitter pamphlet, pointing out the errors or weakness of several of Mayhew's statements, to which Mayhew replied with similar asperity.[36]

A far abler and more conciliatory reply to Mayhew, *An Answer to Dr. Mayhew's Observations* (1764), appeared in London, which Thomas Hollis, ardent English admirer of Mayhew, was convinced came from Secker's own pen. To this Mayhew responded in *Remarks on an Anon-*

ymous Tract (1764), repeating with less asperity and some modifications what he had said before. The battle of tracts did not end until 1765 when Apthorp reentered the lists with a reply to Mayhew's *Remarks*, which Mayhew, tired of strife and on the advice of friends, ignored.[37]

Harrison Gray, Treasurer of Massachusetts, said of Mayhew's *Observations*, "I think I never knew any performance of a Controversial nature meet with so general approbation and applause, excepting among some bigoted high Churchmen." The Reverend Solomon Palmer, an Anglican minister of Connecticut, wrote of its influence there, and Secker informed the Reverend Jacob Duché of Philadelphia that, although Lord Halifax favored the plan for colonial bishops, it was doubtful if "he hath zeal enough to undertake what will certainly meet with opposition, and the more for Dr. Mayhew's late Pamphlet which I presume you have seen."[38]

Mayhew had been in the bad graces of some of his Congregational brethren for his liberal doctrinal views, and, as recently as 1762, Harvard's disregard of strict orthodoxy was under fire by Congregationalists in western Massachusetts. But there now seems to have been a drawing together of the New England Congregationalists similar to the development at Boston in 1682 described by Edward Randolph in a letter to the Bishop of London. "There was a great difference," wrote Randolph, "betwixt the old church and the members of the new church about baptisme . . . ; but now, heereing of my proposals for [Anglican] ministers to be sent over . . . they are now joyned together, . . . and pray to God to confound the devices of all who disturbed their peace and liberties."[39]

In considering the antagonism aroused by Archbishop Secker's activities, it must be borne in mind that the Congregationalists greatly outnumbered (probably by at least thirty to one)[40] the Anglicans in New England. Consequently, though the revival of bitterness between these denominations would tend to draw New England Anglicans closer to England for protection and support, the net effect was to weaken the ties between New England and Old.

CHAPTER 6

THE BRITISH ARMY IN AMERICA
AND THE DECISION TO
TAX THE COLONIES

ONE OF the chief reasons for the British conquest and retention of Canada was to free the British colonies from danger of French invasion. In announcing the allotment of twelve thousand men to capture Quebec, the heart of French power in Canada, Pitt wrote General Amherst in December 1758, that the object was to establish the King's just claims and "to avert all future Dangers to His Majesty's Subjects in No. America." After Quebec had fallen, Franklin wrote from London that the argument for conquering the rest of Canada having the most weight in England was that "in Case of another War, if we keep Possession of Canada, the Nation will save two or three Millions a Year, now spent in defending the American Colonies, and be so much the stronger in Europe, by the Addition of the Troops now employ'd on that Side of the Water." And, when the conquest of Canada was completed, the King gave thanks for this as of the utmost importance to the "security of our colonies in North America," an advantage likewise stressed in pamphlets and newspapers of the day.[1]

Yet, when the war was ended and the whole of Canada ceded to Great Britain, the British forces stationed in North America, instead of being reduced, as might be expected, were greatly increased over prewar strength.

In 1754, before the war, the British infantry stationed in North America, including two companies detached to Bermuda and the Bahamas, consisted of two British regiments numbering 1,630 officers and men, nine British independent companies (companies not included in any regimental unit) numbering 998, a company of 117 rangers, a regiment from Ireland numbering 404, giving a total of 3,149 officers and men.[2] To these must be added two companies of British artillery, including a few engineers, totaling around two hundred men.[3]

After the war, the independent companies in North America were not revived or continued but the aggregate of British infantry stationed there was raised to 7,501 officers and men embodied in fourteen regiments and the artillery to ten companies totalling 550 officers and men. One regiment on the Irish establishment, the fifty-fifth, was also temporarily retained in North America, sailing for Ireland early in 1765.[4] The rangers, the distinctively North American corps, were discontinued.[5] The infantry for the British West Indies were increased; those for the British Isles, Minorca, and Gibraltar, slightly reduced.[6]

The lack of opposition in Parliament to the proposal for an increase of the British standing army in America, brought out in Chapter 1, made it unnecessary for the Ministry to explain the proposal to Parliament, and no explanation has been found in the correspondence of the period. (The letters of Lord Bute to the King during the winter of 1762–1763, which might well throw light on the question, are missing.)[7] Consequently the reason or reasons for the measure can only be surmised.

In 1907, the distinguished American historian George Louis Beer, in his *British Colonial Policy 1754–1765*, gave what may perhaps be termed the classic explanation of the increase.

"The experiences during the war," wrote Beer, "convinced the government that, on account of their particularism, the colonies could not be trusted to provide adequately for their own defence, and that the safety of the Empire demanded the permanent establishment of a relatively strong force in the colonies. Besides, as a result of the conquest of Canada, the Indian question had, from the military standpoint, assumed large proportions. Formerly almost all the land indisputably British had been settled, and the question of defence against the Indians had been a comparatively simple one. Now, the numerous forts in the interior had to be garrisoned, and this necessitated a large increase in the number of troops permanently stationed on the continent. Owing to their lack of union, the colonies did not desire, nor were they able, to undertake this clearly indispensable work. Besides, they had a tendency to underrate the military power of the Indians. Consequently, the British government could not do otherwise than establish a permanent standing army in America. There was no alternative course. Furthermore, apart from the facts that brought about this decision, the return of peace with France would not of itself have allowed the withdrawal of the British troops, as they were absolutely essential in suppressing the formidable Indian rebellion that Pontiac had organized."[8]

So far as this explanation is based on "the formidable Indian rebellion that Pontiac had organized," it is clearly fallacious. The rebellion did not begin until after the addition to the British standing army in America had been voted, and there is no evidence of the rebellion having been foreseen in England.[9]

Beer's general thesis is vulnerable, too, because if the increase had been designed for defense against the Indians, the British units — the Eightieth regiment, Goreham's corps and Hopkins' company of unmounted rangers and two companies of mounted rangers in Georgia — established during the war particularly for scouting and fighting under conditions peculiar to America, would almost surely have been retained, whereas no provision was made for retaining a single one of them. (Through a misunderstanding, the mounted rangers in Georgia were not immediately disbanded; but as soon as this was made known to the home government, they, too, were discharged.)[10]

The inability of forts and ordinary British troops, unaided by units specially equipped and trained for Indian warfare, to protect the colonial frontiers from Indian attack, proved by experience in the late war, was known in England as well as in the colonies. In *An Historical Review*, published in London in 1759, Richard Jackson pointed out that forts in the interior, garrisoned solely by British regulars, though valuable in opposing the advance of regular French troops, afforded no protection against Indian raids on the colonial frontiers. The way to protect the frontier settlements was to have "parties of rangers" fight the Indians "in their own way," that is, "to send parties frequently into the Indian country to surprise them in their hunting and fishing, destroy their cornfields, burn their habitations, and by thus continually harassing them, oblige them either to sue for peace, or retire further into the country"; except as bases for such roving troops, forts were worthless against the Indians since they could slip "between the forts, murder and scalp the inhabitants, and burn and destroy their settlements with impunity."[11]

The point was further developed by Franklin in his famous pamphlet *The Interest of Great Britain Considered*, published both in the colonies and in London in 1760. Dismissing the ordinary regular soldiers huddling in their forts in the Indian country as almost valueless, Franklin pointed out that "If the Indians when at war, march'd like the Europeans, with great armies, heavy cannon, baggage and carriages, the passes thro' which alone such armies could penetrate our country or receive their supplies, being secur'd, all might be sufficiently secure; but the case is widely different. . . . They pass easily between your forts undiscovered; and . . . When they have surpriz'd separately, and murder'd and scalp'd a dozen families they are gone. . . . The inhabitants of Hackney might as well rely upon the tower of London to secure them against highwaymen and housebreakers." And Colonel Sir William Johnson, Superintendent of the Northern Indians, informed the Board of Trade in 1762 that "altho' our frontier Forts . . . may prove a means of retarding the progress of an Army, or oppose an European force, they can in no wise prevent the Incursions of the Indians, who need not approach them in any of their inroads, and can destroy the inhabitants and their Dwellings with very little risque."[12]

The truth of these statements was again tragically demonstrated during the great Indian rebellion of 1763–1764 discussed in Chapters 8 and 9, yet no change in the kind of troops stationed in America was made during or after this rebellion. Some of the regiments initially stationed in North America after the war were replaced by others but the new regiments were of the same type as the old, and the same was true of the additional regiment—the Fourteenth—sent to North America in 1766.[13]

Another point militating against Beer's theory is the omission of the British Government to consult General Sir Jeffery Amherst, Commander-in-Chief of the British forces in North America, as to the number and kind of troops needed for defense of the colonial frontier from Indian attack. As we shall see in Chapter 8, Amherst was later discredited by the disastrous failure of his Indian policy, but this was not until months after the decision to enlarge the British peacetime army in America was made. Until then he was evidently highly regarded by Egremont and the King, and presumably would, as a matter of course, have been consulted concerning the number and kind of troops needed to control the Indians if protection of the colonial frontiers had been the chief reason for enlarging the British army stationed in North America.[14]

Some of the colonists had a far different explanation than Beer's for the increase. In their view, the large peacetime army now stationed in America was designed chiefly not to protect but to coerce the British colonists in America. Eliphalet Dyer of Connecticut, for example, wrote from London to a friend at home in April 1764, "it seems determined to fix upon us a large Number of regular Troops under pretence for our Defence; but rather designed as a rod and Check over us," while John Dickinson of Pennsylvania denounced the "formidable force established in the midst of peace, to bleed her [America] into obedience."[15] And such suspicion was not farfetched in view of the frequent references which had been made in recent years to the value of a large British army in North America to prevent or suppress rebellion in the old British colonies in North America, if Canada was conquered and retained by Great Britain.*

At the beginning of the French and Indian War, Governor William Shirley of Massachusetts, who favored the British conquest and retention of Canada even at the supposed risk of encouraging rebellion in

---

*John J. Shy, *Toward Lexington: The Role of the British Army in the Coming of the American Revolution* (Princeton, N.J.: Princeton University Press, 1965). [B. W. S.]

the old British colonies, wrote Secretary of State Sir Thomas Robinson, "Apprehensions have been entertained, that they will in time unite to throw off their dependency upon their mother country, and set up one general government among themselves. But if it is considered how different the present constitutions of their respective governments are from each other, how much the interests of some of them clash, and how opposed their tempers are, such a coalition among them will seem highly improbable. At all events, they could not maintain such an independency without a strong naval force, which it must for ever be in the power of Great Britain to hinder them from having. And whilst his majesty hath seven thousand troops kept up within them, and on the Great Lakes upon the back of six of them, with the Indians at command, it seems easy, provided his Governors and principal civil officers are independent of the Assemblies for their subsistence, and commonly vigilant, to prevent any step of that kind from being taken."[16]

Later, after the fall of Quebec, various suggestions were made as to the necessity of having a strong British army in North America to keep the colonists from throwing off British rule when freed from the menace of the French in Canada. Robert R. Livingston, Jr., of New York wrote his father of a British officer, a guest at their home, who asserted that if Canada was not restored to France, it would be "necessary to have garrisons to check us," and the anonymous author of *Reasons for Keeping Guadaloupe* declared that if the British colonists in North America were no longer held in check by the French in Canada, Great Britain "must keep a numerous standing army to over-awe them."[17] Another British officer, Captain Walter Rutherfurd, made the ingenious proposal to divide Canada, Great Britain keeping part for the protection of the old British colonies but leaving enough to the French to give "a good pretext to oblige each Colony to support a certain quota of [British] troops, apparently for their defence, but also to keep them in proper subjection to the Mother country" — a suggestion of particular interest because addressed to Gilbert Elliot, member of Parliament and of the Treasury Board and a confidant of Lord Bute.[18] Furthermore, papers in the files of Lord Shelburne, President of the Board of Trade in 1763, disclose that similar suggestions were made in official circles after the cession of Canada.

One of these papers, partly in the hand of Shelburne's secretary, Maurice Morgann, dealt with a number of questions concerning North America raised in an important letter of May 5, 1763, from Lord Egremont to the Board of Trade during Shelburne's Presidency of the Board. The questions included, "What Military Establishment will be sufficient? What new Forts should be erected? and which, if any, may it be expedient to demolish?"[19]

As to these, the writer stated, "I have no idea that we want Military Establishments against the Indians, and as We have now no Enemy to the Northward, I do not know that any Forts or Soldiers will be wanted there. I think no Danger is to be apprehended from the Canadians. . . .[20] Yet if Canada is to be made a Military Government and a Place of Arms, I suppose it will be proper to imitate the Policy of the French; They have already marked the proper Places for the stationing of Troops in order to awe the British Colonies. The Lines of Forts so much talked of before the war will restrain the colonies at present as well as formerly. The Pretences for this regulation, must be, the keeping of the Indians in subjection, and making of Roads, in which last Work the Troops ought actually to be employed, that they may be kept disciplined, and Hardy."[21]

Another, entitled "Plan for securing the future Dependance of the Provinces on the Continent of America," undated and unsigned but wholly in Morgann's hand, recommends: "That the Military Force on that Continent be increased and stationed in East Florida, Nova Scotia, Canada and in Posts the whole Length of the Navigation between Montreal and the Mouths of the Mississippi, so that with the aid of a Naval Force, the whole of the Provinces shall be surrounded.

"That, in the next Place, under Pretence of regulating the Indian Trade, a very straight line be suddenly drawn on the Back of the Provinces and the Country beyond that Line thrown, for the present, under the Dominion of the Indians, and the Indians be everywhere encouraged to support their own Sovereignty. . . .

"The Provinces being now surrounded by an Army, a Navy and by hostile Tribes of Indians . . . It may be time (not to oppress or injure them in any Shape but) to exact a due obedience to the just and equitable Regulations of a British Parliament."[22]

However, though keeping the colonists, old as well as new, under control was evidently considered in connection with the decision to enlarge the British standing army in North America, this probably was not the chief reason for the proposed increase. If it had been, Amherst would presumably have been consulted as to the number and kind of troops needed for this service, and he was not. Moreover, stationing most of the additional troops in Canada, Nova Scotia, and the Floridas indicates that prevention or suppression of rebellion in the old British colonies in North America was not the chief object of the increase, since the coercive effect of the troops in the old colonies would presumably be greater if stationed there.

Another possible explanation of the increase was the intention of the King to augment his political influence by increasing the number of army officers subject to his power of promotion and dismissal. This explanation was suggested at the time by Newcastle in a letter of March 1763, quoted in Chapter 1, and by the anonymous author of *Serious Considerations on the Measures of the Present Administration* (1763) who wrote, "Why should there be an increase in the army except that by the increase of Colonels, Lieutenant-Colonels . . . with all the other terms of command, the m_____ [Ministry] may create . . . an additional dependency on the Crown in the members of the two Houses of Parliament." It was again advanced long afterward (1774), by Edmund Burke in his famous speech on American Taxation. "At that period [1763]," said Burke, "the necessity was established of keeping up no less than twenty new regiments, with twenty colonels capable of seats in this House . . . at the very time that, by your conquests in America, your danger from foreign attempts in that part of the world was much lessened or indeed rather quite over."[23]

One of the outstanding sources of the King's dominant influence in Parliament unquestionably was his power to appoint, dismiss, replace, and transfer officers in the armed services at pleasure,[24] and colonelcies of regiments were particularly useful political pawns because, though honorable and very lucrative, they required little service. When, for example, the French suddenly attacked Minorca in 1756, not one colonel of the four British regiments stationed there was with his regiment,[25] and at the time of the great American Indian rebellion of 1763–1764, discussed in later chapters, only two of the colonels in command of the seventeen battalions in North America were present,[26] both of whom held other offices requiring their presence—Gage as Commander-in-Chief of the British army in North America and James Murray as Governor of Quebec. Nor can George III's readiness to make political capital out of his power to dismiss or transfer officers at pleasure be doubted. In November 1762, when Parliament's approval of the preliminary treaty of peace was at issue, he wrote Bute, "I cant help hinting again what I did last night that every officer that votes against government at a time like this ought to be made an example of"; he told Fox, a few months later, that he might promise the Duke of Richmond transfer to the colonelcy of the regiment of the Blues, a crack cavalry regiment, if his Parliamentary conduct was as the King desired; and, in November 1763, when the question of Parliamentary privilege in cases of criminal libel was at issue, he favored "dismissing General Conway from both his civil and military commissions; also Mr. Fitzherbert and any others who have equally with these gone steadily against us, and giving it out that the rest would have the same fate if they do not amend their conduct."[27]

Nevertheless, it would be rash, in the absence of clear-cut evidence, and none has been found, to suppose that the King would employ so extravagant a method to enhance his political power as the establishment of superfluous new regiments.

All things considered, it seems probable that the thoughts of the King and Ministers ran along somewhat the following lines. The army ought to be increased as a matter of general defense. Because of the traditional British prejudice[28] (weakening perhaps, but still apparently strong)[29] against a large standing army, it would presumably be easier to secure Parliament's approval of the desired increase by proposing to station the additional troops in America rather than in the British Isles. This proposal would have the further advantage of fitting in nicely with the Ministry's assurance to Parliament that, after the first year, the increase would no longer be burdensome to British taxpayers because the colonies would be required to maintain the troops stationed there.

Troops for general defense could be stationed as advantageously in North America as any place in the empire. They would be at hand in case of renewed war with France and Spain, to attack the French and Spanish West Indies, which the late war had demonstrated were particularly vulnerable to British attack,[30] and, in time of peace, could be usefully employed in various ways: helping to enforce the British acts of trade; guarding against surprise attack by France or Spain on British North American ports; garrisoning forts in the Indian country; keeping the inhabitants of the territory recently ceded by France and Spain under control; and, if required, nipping in the bud any movement toward rebellion that might appear in the old British colonies.[31]

Turning to the Ministry's related proposal, the proposal for Parliamentary taxation of the colonies for revenue, we again encounter a perplexing question, not as to the reason for the decision, which obviously was to shift part of the burden of taxation from British to colonial taxpayers, but as to the minister or ministers chiefly responsible for the decision to introduce this revolutionary proposal,[32] a proposal urged in vain upon Ministry after Ministry for over half a century.

In 1703 Colonel Robert Quary, Surveyor-General of Customs for North America, proposed such a measure, and in 1710 Governor Hunter of New York, following the refusal of the New York Assembly to pass a provincial revenue bill along the lines desired by the Crown, recommended a tax on all the northern colonies. Suggestions for taxing the colonies as a whole were made during the next thirty years by various British officials or former officials, including Colonel David Dunbar, Surveyor-General of the King's Woods in North America, who proposed a tax to maintain two or three regiments in Massachusetts to make the people there "sensible of their duty" and Sir William Keith, former Governor of Pennsylvania, who submitted a number of proposals for colonial taxation by Parliament.[33]

The War of the Austrian Succession ("King George's War" in America) brought a large crop of suggestions from British officials in America for Parliamentary taxation of the colonies for revenue, and, following the outbreak of the French and Indian War in 1754, officials in England were again bombarded with letters from colonial governors suggesting such taxation. The most persistent, Robert Dinwiddie of Virginia, repeated the suggestion at least a dozen times.[34] Similar recommendations were made by British officers serving in America, including General Lord Loudoun, Commander-in-Chief of the British army in North America, who wrote the Duke of Cumberland urging an act of Parliament to raise a revenue in the colonies independent of the colonial legislatures "to pay the governors, and new model the governments." Loudoun urged immediate action because "if you delay until a peace, you will not have force to exert any British Act of Parliament here."[35]

Even before this bombardment, the Board of Trade, in April 1754, had written Robinson proposing the building and garrisoning of a line of forts along the colonial frontier in North America, the expense, along with "the other stated & certain Expences of Government in the Colonies," to be met by an act of Parliament consolidating the revenue heretofore raised by the several provincial legislatures "into one permanent and fixed Fund, and applied by Directions from home to the Services for which it is appropriated in Such manner as His Majesty shall think best." And in response to a request from the Cabinet for a plan for the suggested "mutual and common Defence" of the colonies, the Board proposed a common defense fund, the quota of each colony in North America to be determined at a meeting of commissioners from every colony, with the proviso that, if the colonies failed to cooperate, the Ministry should apply "for an interposition of the Authority of Parliament."[36]

Newcastle sent copies of the Board's plan to members of the Ministry, at least two of whom, Charles Townshend of the Admiralty Board and William Murray, the Attorney-General, favored immediate taxation of the colonies by Parliament. A year later, Lord Halifax, President of the Board of Trade, likewise suggested immediate Parliamentary taxation of the colonies, preferably by a stamp tax.[37] But as long as Newcastle remained head of the Treasury no action was taken either on the Board's plan or on the proposals of Townshend, Murray, and Halifax.

As brought out in Chapter 1, Lord Bute succeeded Newcastle as First Lord of the Treasury in 1762. The year before, Henry McCulloh, former Commissioner for Crown lands and quit rents in the Carolinas,[38] had submitted a memorandum to Bute recommending an act of Parliament along the lines later adopted, namely a lower colonial import duty, designed for revenue, on foreign molasses and a colonial stamp tax.[39] Bute was evidently favorably impressed by the proposal for colonial taxation, and, presumably supported by Halifax and Murray (now Lord Mansfield), members of the Cabinet during the winter of 1762–1763, and Townshend, Secretary at War until the middle of December 1762, decided to adopt it.

THE PROCLAMATION OF 1763 AND LIMITATION OF WESTWARD EXPANSION

ONE OF the most important responsibilities facing the new Grenville Ministry in April 1763 was to establish civil government and make plans for dealing with the Indians in the territory in America ceded or confirmed to Great Britain by France and Spain in the Treaty of Paris. Some of the new territory lay in the West Indies but much the greater part was in North America, stretching southward from the Hudson's Bay Company's domain in the far north to the Gulf of Mexico and westward from the Alleghenies to the Mississippi.

Except for a relatively small section along the banks of the St. Lawrence, the whole of this great, fertile land mass was very thinly peopled. There were probably less than 90,000 whites in the whole of Canada and under 10,000 in Louisiana, while the white population of Florida was almost negligible. The Indian population was almost equally sparse; Sir William Johnson and John Stuart, Superintendents of the Northern and Southern Indians, estimated the fighting men in their departments at only around 25,000 and 14,000 respectively, which, adopting Johnson's ratio of five persons to each fighting man, gives a total of less than 200,000 Indians in both departments.[1]

For many years this vast region had been a place of menace to the British colonists—the menace of invasion, devastation, and death from the French and their Indian allies. But the British capture of Quebec, foreshadowing the conquest of the whole of Canada, threw a new light on this once forbidding land. The Reverend Samuel Cooper of Boston doubtless spoke the sentiment of thousands of his fellow countrymen when he exclaimed in his sermon of thanksgiving for Wolfe's far-reaching victory, "What fair Hopes have we of being compleatly delivered from that Enemy, that has so often interrupted our Tranquility and checked our Growth! What Scenes of Happiness are we ready to figure to ourselves, from the Hope of enjoying, in this good Land, all the Blessings of an undisturbed and lasting Peace; . . . our Settlements extending themselves with Security on Every Side, and changing a Wilderness into a fruitful Field!"[2]

The laboring oar in making plans for governing this domain was given to the Board of Trade, headed by Lord Shelburne. On May 5, 1763, Secretary of State Lord Egremont wrote the Board enclosing many papers bearing on the new possessions and asked its views on a wide range of questions respecting them. The Board replied on June 8, recommending among other things the establishment of a single new colony in the West Indies and three new colonies in North America: East Florida and West Florida, carved out of former Spanish Florida and French Louisiana, and Canada. The latter was to be confined to only the most easterly part of the old French province—the rest together with most of British Louisiana should, the Board proposed, "be left . . . to the Indian Tribes for their hunting Grounds; where no Settlement by planting is intended, immediately at least, to be attempted; and consequently where no particular form of Civil Government can be established." The form of government proposed for each of the new colonies was a Governor and Council appointed by the King but not an elected Assembly. A "considerable military Force must be likewise kept up in these Governments, as well in respect to the neighbourhood of the French and Indians, as to the security of the Settlers, till their numbers enable them to have Security by their own internal Force."[3]

The only practicable form of government for the territory reserved for the Indians was, the Board suggested, a military one. Free trade with the Indians should be open to all British subjects on equal terms under the protection of British troops, who would also be useful to secure "the good Treatment of the Indians" and "the maintenance of Your Majesty's Sovereignty and the general defence of North America." Recommendation as to the number of troops and the particular posts and forts to be maintained for these purposes was deferred by the Board until it received further information from the Commander-in-Chief and Indian Superintendents in North America. As to Egremont's question "In what Mode least Burthensome and most palatable to the Colonies can they contribute towards the Support" of whatever arrangements were proposed, the Board replied that it was unable to answer this. Only July 14, Egremont informed the Board of the King's general approval of its recommendations and instructed it to prepare commissions and instructions for the governors of the proposed new colonies and to consider and report the best method of settling the new colonies "with useful and industrious Inhabitants."[4]

The Board replied on August 5 recommending that inhabitants of the old colonies and all foreign Protestants be encouraged to settle East and West Florida and Nova Scotia and that particular encouragement to settle in those places be given to officers and soldiers in the late war by offering every field officer five thousand acres, captains three, subalterns twenty-five hundred, noncommissioned officers a hundred, and privates fifty, provided they should personally apply for and live on the land and abide by such terms as to cultivation as the King might impose. The Board's letter, it will be seen, implied that no encouragement should be given to settlement in Canada or to emigrants from Great Britain and Ireland. In view of the Indian uprising in North America, discussed in the next two chapters, the Board proposed that, to help quiet the Indians, the King immediately issue a proclamation defining the boundaries of the territory reserved to the Indians and announcing that no white settlement would be permitted under any pretext in the territory thus reserved.[5]

No reply was made for several weeks. During the interval, as brought out in Chapter 1, the King had been negotiating unsuccessfully with Pitt for a change in the Ministry; Egremont had died and been succeeded by Lord Halifax as Secretary of State for the Southern Department; and Lord Hillsborough had succeeded Shelburne as President of the Board of Trade, the rest of the Board remaining unchanged. In answering the Board, Halifax directed it to draft a Proclamation with a few suggested changes, including limitation of the proposed offer of land to such retired officers as had served in America during the late war and to privates who were disbanded there; and to change the name of the proposed new northern colony from Canada to Quebec. Halifax also sent the Board for consideration a statement from Colonel James Grant, Governor-to-be of East Florida, suggesting a northward extension of the boundaries of this colony.[6]

The Board, now headed by Hillsborough, replied on October 4, enclosing a draft of the proposed Proclamation, prepared along the lines projected in the correspondence, with one important change, namely the insertion of an announcement that the Governors of the new colonies were authorized and directed to convene an elected Assembly in each, similar to those in the existing royal governments, "so soon as the state and circumstances of the said Colonies will admit thereof." This, the Board thought, would help to "give Confidence and Encouragement to such Persons as are inclined to become Settlers in the new Colonies."[7]

The Proclamation, including this change, issued by the King on October 7, 1763, provided for a new colony, Grenada, in the West Indies and three new North American colonies, named and bounded as follows:[8]

East Florida: The present state of Florida as far west as the Apalachicola River;

West Florida: The region between the Apalachicola and Mississippi rivers, extending north from the Gulf of Mexico to the 31° or north latitude, about twenty-five miles north of Mobile in present Alabama;

Quebec: A strip along the south bank of the St. Lawrence River from its mouth to where it meets the 45° of north latitude, (across from the present town of Cornwall, Ontario) and a vast area north of the river extending northwestward to Lake Nipissing and from there northeastward to the St. John River, now called Rivière St. Jean.

Additions of territory to several old British colonies or possessions were also included in the Proclamation. The area north of the

St. Lawrence and east of the St. John River together with the island of Anticosti and the Magdalen Islands in the Gulf of St. Lawrence were added to Newfoundland. Cape Breton Island and St. John's (present Prince Edward) Island were added to Nova Scotia, and the region between the northern boundary of East Florida and the Altamaha River was added to Georgia.[9]

The rest of the vast territory westward of "the Heads or Sources of any of the Rivers which fall into the Atlantic Ocean from the West and North West" (roughly the line of the Appalachian Mountains from Georgia to Quebec) including the whole of the present states of Ohio, Indiana, Illinois, Michigan, Wisconsin, Kentucky, and Tennessee and parts of present Minnesota, New York, Pennsylvania, Maryland, West Virginia, Virginia, North Carolina, South Carolina, Georgia, Alabama, Mississippi, Ontario, and Quebec, was reserved by the King, "for the present, and until our further Pleasure be known," for the Indians. In addition, any tracts east of the mountains to which Indian title had not been relinquished were reserved to the Indians.[10] Nothing was said as to the government of the Indian territory, which, as a practical matter, was taken over by the Commander-in-Chief of the British army, assisted by the Indian Superintendents.[11]

Four years after the Proclamation was issued, the Board of Trade made a statement tending to imply that the sole reason for having reserved the region west of the Alleghenies as an Indian reservation was to protect and pacify the Indians, and, citing this statement, Farrand, in his "The Indian Boundary Line" maintained that the protection of the Indians from encroachments upon their lands is "a sufficient explanation of the adoption of this feature of policy."[12] But, though protection and pacification of the Indians was unquestionably an important motive for the reservation, there is abundant evidence of another.

Writing the Privy Council Committee on Plantation Affairs in 1772, the Board of Trade said, "We take leave to remind your Lordships of that principle, which was adopted by this Board, and approved and confirmed by his Majesty, immediately after the treaty of Paris, viz. the confining the western extent of settlement to such a distance from the seacoast, as that those settlements should lie within the reach of the trade and commerce of this kingdom, upon which the strength and riches of it depend, and also of the exercise of that authority and jurisdiction which was conceived to be necessary for the preservation of the colonies in due subordination to, and dependence upon, the mother country."[13]

This statement, in so far as it relates to British trade and commerce, is sustained by a passage in the Board's report of June 8, 1763, referred to above. In explaining the reasons for restricting the boundaries of the proposed British colony of Canada to much narrower limits than those of the former French province and reserving the rest for the Indians, the Board pointed out, as one of the advantages, the "preventing by proper and natural Boundaries, as well the Ancient French Inhabitants as others from removing and settling in remote Places, where they neither could be so conveniently made ameanable to the Jurisdiction of any Colony nor made subservient to the Interest of the Trade and Commerce of this Kingdom by an easy Communication with and Vicinity to the great River St. Lawrence."[14]

The Board's proposal to discourage settlement in the West as a means of conserving the colonial market for British exports was not novel. Captain Walter Rutherfurd, in the letter quoted in Chapter 6 suggesting the advantage of letting France retain western Canada, pointed out that if the British got the whole of Canada, the "poorer sort" of colonists, freed from fear of the French, "would retire far into the woods . . . where they would raise and manufacture every thing for their own use, without consuming any thing from Britain, or being the least benefit to that country."[15] And there are several interesting papers along this same line in Shelburne's files.

One of these, by an unidentified writer, entitled "Hints relative to the Division and Government of the conquered and newly acquired countries in America," recommended establishment of a western boundary beyond which the colonists, for the present, should not be permitted to settle. Thus those seeking new homes would be compelled "to emigrate to Nova Scotia or to the provinces on the Southern Frontier, where they would be usefull to their Mother Country, instead of planting themselves in the Heart of America, out of the reach of Government, and where from the great Difficulty of procuring

European Commodities, they would be compelled to commence Manufacturs to the infinite prejudice of Britain."[16]

A second, entitled "Mr Pownall's Sketch of a Report concerning the Cessions in Africa and America," recommended prohibition of all settlement beyond the Alleghenies, at least for the present, both as sound Indian policy and because the colonists, if permitted to settle away from the seaboard, might "ingage in the production and manufacture of those articles of necessary consumption which they ought, upon every principle of true policy, to take from the mother country."[17]

A third, partly in the hand of Shelburne's secretary, Maurice Morgann, is the most explicit of the three. It declares that colonies are "to be regarded in no other Light, but as subservient to the Commerce of their Mother Country," that colonists are "merely Factors for the Purposes of Trade," and that "in all Considerations concerning the Colonies, *this* must be always the leading idea." From which it followed that the colonists "must be kept as near as possible to the Ocean," and, since furs were the article the back settlers could best exchange for British commodities, the interior should be kept "as open and Wild as possible for the Purposes of Hunting."[18]

The Proclamation, designed for the public eye, of course said nothing about restricting colonial settlements to regions where the colonist could be "made subservient to" British commercial interests and apparently created little or no immediate concern in the colonies. But when the Crown deferred opening the West to settlement and used British troops to keep white settlers out of the western territory, the Proclamation's restriction of settlement became a source of acute discontent in several of the North American colonies.[19]*

---

*Woody Holton, "The Ohio Indians and the Coming of the American Revolution in Virginia," *Journal of Southern History*, 60 (1994): 453–78; Jack M. Sosin, *Whitehall and the Wilderness: The Middle West in British Colonial Policy* (Lincoln: University of Nebraska Press, 1961). [B. W. S.]

CHAPTER 8

AMHERST AND THE INDIAN
UPRISING OF 1763

IN WRITING Secretary of State Egremont concerning the frightful Indian uprising of 1763–1764, sometimes called Pontiac's Rebellion, General Amherst said, "It is difficult my Lord, to account any Causes, that can have induced these Barbarians to this perfidious attempt: they have pretended to be very dissatisfyed at not getting of Rum, When in every formal meeting that has been held it has generally been a request of their Chiefs not to permit any: from a declaration of one of their Prisoners it appears they strike the blow, to revenge the death of two of their Chiefs, that were killed in the Action at Niagara [in 1759]: I think it most likely to have derived from the belt that was sent to the Miamis; which Sir William Johnson supposed to have come from the French some time ago, and has lain by, and I believe the Savages have really long meditated this mischief, and have been waiting an opportunity."[1]

As brought out in Peckham's recent admirable study of Pontiac's Rebellion, many factors besides those mentioned by Amherst contributed to the uprising, chief among which, as will be seen from this chapter, were Amherst's own blunders in arousing the Indians' fear of white encroachments on their lands, which the British Government and the Penns had in recent years taken steps to allay, and suddenly stopping gifts of ammunition to the Indians.[2]*

During the war the British Government had sought to cultivate the good will of the western Indians within reach of British influence by assuring them of the future protection of their land from white aggression and fraud. In 1755 and 1756 the King prohibited the governors of New York and Virginia from making further grants of Crown land until the prospective grantee had received a license from the governor to purchase the Indian title, the license to be issued only on the filing of a sworn survey showing the exact bounds of the land to be purchased attested by the reputed Indian owners in the presence of an official interpreter. No grants whatever were to be made in a tract extending sixty miles southward from lakes Erie and Ontario and running westward from the Salmon River in present Oswego County, New York, to the Cuyahoga River in present central Ohio, which the Iroquois had deeded in 1726 to the British Crown to be held in trust for them. And in 1760 the governor of Virginia was forbidden to make any further grants on the Ohio River or its tributaries.[3]

Furthermore, Thomas and Richard Penn, Proprietaries of Pennsylvania, in the important Indian Treaty of Easton of 1758, released all claim to the soil of Pennsylvania west of the Alleghenies and of a large section east of the Alleghenies and north of present Sunbury, on agreement by the Indians not to sell the land to anyone else.[4]

In presenting the Penns' release to a gathering of Indian chiefs in April 1759, Colonel Sir William Johnson,[†] the Crown's Superintendent of Indians north of the Ohio, said, "I hope this Surrender will convince you and all other Indians how ready Your Brethren the English are to remove from Your hearts all jealousies [suspicions] and uneasiness of their Desiring to Encroach upon Your Hunting Lands, and be a con-

---

*On Indian unrest after the Seven Years' War, see Richard White, *The Middle Ground: Indians, Empires, and Republics in the Great Lakes Region, 1650–1815* (Cambridge: Cambridge University Press, 1991), ch. 7; Gregory Evans Dowd, *A Spirited Resistance: The North American Indian Struggle for Unity, 1745–1815* (Baltimore: Johns Hopkins University Press, 1992), ch. 2; Michael M. McConnell, *A Country Between: The Upper Ohio Valley and Its Peoples* (Lincoln: University of Nebraska Press, 1992), ch. 8. [B. W. S.]

[†]James Thomas Flexner, *Mohawk Baronet: Sir William Johnson of New York* (New York: Harper, 1959). [B. W. S.]

vincing proof to You how false the accusations of the French are that we are at war with them, in order to get Your Country from you; for you see, while the French keep their forts in the midst of Your Country and fight with us in order to secure the possession of them, we give up those lands which you had sold us." And when General John Stanwix was sent to strengthen Fort Pitt on the Ohio after its capture from the French, Johnson's deputy, George Croghan, explained to a large number of deputies from the Six Nations (Iroquois), Delawares, Shawnees, Wyandots, and eight other western nations assembled at the Fort that Stanwix was coming merely to "build a Trading House, to secure the Goods brought by the English Traders." "I assure you," he continued, "as soon as the Enemy are drove out of your Country, which I expect you will be assisting in, the General will depart your Country after securing our Trade with you and our Brethren to the Westward."[5]

However, as soon as Canada was conquered, Amherst disregarded the wise land policy adopted during the war. In April 1761, he issued a permit to Captain Walter Rutherfurd and others to establish a settlement at the carrying-place or portage around Niagara Falls, deep in the country of the Senecas and within the very region where the governors were ordered to make no grants whatever. Amherst wrote Johnson that the officers were told they must "Buy the Soil of the Indians if necessary";[6] but the permit contained no such condition, and there is not the slightest evidence of arrangements for any such purchase.

From the standpoint of convenience there was reason to authorize and encourage the settlement; it would provide food for the garrison at Fort Niagara and furnish horses, oxen, and a source of dependable manpower for transporting supplies around Niagara Falls from Lake Ontario to Lake Erie and the upper Great Lakes, Huron, Michigan, and Superior. But from the standpoint of Indian relations, the permit was most pernicious, since the establishment and maintenance of the settlement under Amherst's protection would inevitably alarm the Indians as to the security of their land. After strong protest by a group of Albany merchants engaged in the Indian trade, the Privy Council ordered Amherst to disperse the Niagara settlement; but this order was not carried out until October 1762,[7] by which time the Senecas and the western Indians were well on the way to rebellion.

Soon after the settlement was begun, two Seneca chiefs appeared among the Indians in the neighborhood of Detroit inviting them to join a projected uprising against the British. "The English," they were reported as saying, "treat us with much disrespect, and we have the greatest reason to believe by their behavior they intend to cut us off entirely; they have possessed themselves of our Country; . . . there is no time to be lost; let us Strike imediately." A report of the complaint among the Senecas that "the General is giving away their Country to be Settled, which the King of England long ago Promised to secure for their use," also reached Fort Pitt, the British outpost on the Ohio.[8]

Johnson heard complaints of the new settlement when he reached Fort Niagara, late in July 1761, en route to a great Indian conference in Detroit. He immediately wrote Amherst, "I plainly discover an universal Jealousy and uneasiness appear amongst those of every Nation, on account of the hasty Steps they look upon it we are taking towards getting possession of their severall Countrys, which uneasiness I am certain, will never subside whilst we encroach within the Limits, which Your Excellency may recollect have been actually put under the Kings protection in the year 1726, and . . . Which Your Excellency in your speech of the 22d April 1760 (delivered to them by Brigadier General Monkton) was pleased to promise to secure to them. . . . I should be glad to know whether I can acquaint the Indians that those People [at the Niagara settlement] will be ordered to remove, or not, and hope by your Excellencys answer to be able to Satisfie them on that Head." Amherst, however, refused to give way. The settlers were there only upon sufferance until the King's pleasure was known, "and untill that is known," he wrote Johnson, "they must not be removed."[9]

Amherst's next move, again apparently without any arrangement with the neighboring Indians, was to order the establishment of a blockhouse and garrison at Sandusky Bay on the southwest shore of Lake Erie. The building of this new fort was all the more menacing and provocative because of the recent rebuilding of forts at Presque Isle, Le Boeuf, and Venango,[10] which, now that the French power in Canada had been broken, naturally seemed to the Indians to be a concerted movement directed against them.[11] Johnson warned Amherst that erecting the blockhouse at Sandusky would, he feared, greatly alarm the Indians; but Amherst was adamant. "With regard to their objection against our Erecting a Blockhouse at Sandusky," he replied, "that has no manner of weight with me; a post at that place is absolutely necessary, not only for the above purposes of keeping up the Communication, but also to keep the Canadians in proper Subjection; I must and will therefore, say what they will, have one at that place."[12]

Amherst's indifference to the Indians' good will, particularly evident from this time on, was perhaps attributable in large measure to the success of a punitive expedition of British and South Carolinian provincial troops under a British Officer, Colonel James Grant, in severely punishing the Cherokees who had risen against the British. According to Amherst's triumphant report to Johnson in August 1761, Grant had "not only destroyed Fifteen of their Towns . . . but also 1400 Acres of Corn, pease and Beans, and has driven near 5000 Men, Women, and Children, into the Woods, where, if they do not make a proper Submission, they cannot fail of starving in the Winter."[13]

Another British measure for cultivating Indian good will during the war had been to shower the Indians in the British interest with gifts of ammunition, clothing, and other articles, which were regarded by the Indians not as charity but as compensation for their acquiescence in the British occupation and retention of posts at Niagara, Detroit, Pittsburgh, and elsewhere in the Indian country. This giving of presents was expensive; but, at least so long as the French retained possession of eastern Louisiana, including the Illinois country, a change in policy would be extremely dangerous.[14] Their post at Fort Chartres in present Illinois gave the French easy access to various Indian nations under British jurisdiction, among which they could and unquestionably would exploit any adverse change in British policy as confirming their warnings of what the Indians must expect if the French were no longer at hand to befriend them.

However, some months after the conquest of Canada, Amherst decided it was no longer necessary to cultivate the Indians' friendship by further bounty, being obsessed with the belief that they must be too greatly impressed by British military power to dare rebel, or, if they did rebel, that they could be immediately subdued and punished. He would deal with them justly according to his lights; if they did not like what he did, so much the worse for them.

In February 1761, he announced the change of policy to Johnson, who, by the terms of his commission, was subject to Amherst's commands. The Indians, wrote Amherst, were to be properly rewarded for particular services rendered, but "as to purchasing the good behavior either of Indians, or any Others, is what I do not understand; when men of what race soever behave ill, they must be punished but not bribed."[15]

In June 1761, Johnson, who had had much more experience with the Indians than his commanding officer, warned Amherst that the Indians allied with them were "uneasy at the coolness and indifference which they think is shewed towards them," and that he feared "something not right is abrewing." Amherst replied, "I am sorry to find that you are Apprehensive, that the Indians are Brewing something privately amongst them; if it is Mischief, it will fall on their own Heads, with a Powerfull and Heavy Hand." To similar letters from Johnson later in the summer, he gave similar replies. He declared that a reported Indian plot "never gave me a moment's Concern, as I know their Incapacity of attempting anything Serious, and that if they were rash enough to venture upon any ill Designs, I had it in my power not only to frustrate them, but to punish the delinquents with Entire Destruction"; that "upon the first Hostilities they [the western Indians] May be Guilty of, they must not only Expect the Severest Retaliation but an Entire Destruction of all their Nations, for I am firmly Resolved Whenever they give me an Occasion, to Extirpate them Root and branch, but I am hopefull they will not force me to that cruel Necessity."[16]

The most important of the British gifts to the Indians was ammunition, of which they were in dire need after the close of the French and Indian War.[17] But, far from regarding their predicament as a reason for excepting powder and lead from the general policy of drastically cutting down gifts to the Indians, Amherst, desiring, as he said, to keep them short of ammunition, ordered the commanding officers at the western posts to deal it out to them "very Sparingly." Captain Donald Campbell, in command at Detroit in 1761–1762, wrote in

October 1761 to his commanding officer, Colonel Henry Bouquet at Fort Pitt, "I am certain if the Indians knew General Amherst Sentiments about keeping them Short of Powder it would be impossible to keep them in temper," and, nine months later, he again warned Bouquet that "if the Indians in this Country had the least hint that we intended to prevent them from the use of Ammunition it would be impossible to keep them Quiet; I dare not trust even the Interpreters with the Secret." But Bouquet could do nothing, having had similar orders himself from Amherst.[18]

Johnson, who had evidently heard of Amherst's instruction as to ammunition before leaving for the Indian conference at Detroit, warned him that "Unless all our Old, as well as New Indian Allies are allowed Ammunition for their Livelyhood, or hunting, all Treaties held with, or Presents made to them will never secure their friendship, for they will in such case ever be Jealous [suspicious] of Us, as I find they are a good deal so already, by reason of their not being able to get, or purchase any from us." On receipt of this letter, Amherst promised to include three hundred pounds of powder among the presents to be distributed at the Detroit conference; but this took care of only a single situation, and, as Johnson pointed out, left unremedied the general complaint among the Indians as to the shortage of powder.[19]

The only important exceptions were the substantial gifts of powder and lead at Fort Pitt, during and shortly after the British-Cherokee War of 1760–1761, to parties of Senecas and other Six Nations Indians on their way south to attack the Cherokees, and, after Spain entered the Seven Years' War as the ally of France, to parties of various northern Indians on their way to attack southern Indians reportedly in the Spanish interest.[20]

To Johnson's warnings that the Indians, angered by the denial of ammunition, might rebel, Amherst replied that "nothing can be so impolitick as to furnish them with the means of accomplishing the Evil which is so much Dreaded," and that keeping the Indians "scarce of Ammunition," was the way "to abolish entirely every kind of apprehension on that account."[21]

This, of course, was true of the strong forts at Detroit, Pittsburgh, and Niagara, since a siege of these would have little or no chance of success so long as the Indians were low in ammunition. But what of the smaller forts, and, above all, what of the frontier settlements? If the Indians should rebel, were they likely to leave these settlements in peace? And equipped with tomahawk and firebrand, how much powder would they need to destroy them?

Amherst's failure to give weight to this danger was evidently of long standing, as appears from a letter of General John Forbes, who wrote him in 1759, "I Delayed hearing what those Indians had to say who came lately down, still flattering myself I might have the pleasure of seeing you soon, and imagining that the consideration of Indian affairs and the fixing and settling those Scoundrals to be of more consequence to those Colonys in the neighborhood than you seem at present to be aware of; — I agree with you that they always will incline to the Strongest. . . . But this requires a long and serious Confab to discuss; only I beg in the mean time that you will not think trifflingly of the Indians or their friendship; when I venture to assure you that twenty Indians are capable of laying half this province [Pennsylvania] waste, of which I have been an eye witness."[22]

After a visit to Amherst's headquarters at New York City in the summer of 1763, Croghan wrote Johnson that "the people who frequent there, as well as Sir J. [Amherst] himself, Seem Nott to feel for the Distress of thire felow Creturs [on the frontier] and Talk of Nothing Butt the Country of the Indians being Now Conquered and every B_____t of p_____e haveing a grant for a Large Tract of Land."[23] But Amherst's besetting weakness was apparently not so much indifference to the fate of the frontier settlers as his overconfidence that, no matter how much the Indians might be angered, they would not dare rebel.

Ominous reports of widespread discontent and suspicion, chiefly because of the small amount of ammunition allowed the Indians, flowed in from the Indian country during the fall of 1762 and winter of 1762–1763, and were known to Amherst.[24] But the warnings apparently made no impression. His reply, in April 1763, to one of the last of them was typical. The reported Indian plots were, he said, "Meer *Bugbears,* and can never have any other Effect than that of hurting themselves by makeing Us Treat them as Enemies and Withdraw Our Friendship from them."[25] The final straw was the Indians' learning of the preliminary treaty of peace ceding the whole of Canada and most of eastern Louisiana to Great Britain. It was "like a thunderclap to them," declared Captain Simeon Ecuyer, commanding at Fort Pitt, and Croghan wrote Amherst that "this last Account . . . has allmost drove them to despair. . . . they say . . . the French had no right to give away their country"[26] — to which Amherst replied characteristically "whatever idle notions they may entertain in regard to the cessions made by the French Crown can be of very little consequence, as it is their interest to behave peaceably."[27]

The gathering storm broke on May 7, 1763, when a detachment of soldiers and sailors taking soundings on Lake St. Clair near Detroit was attacked by a band of Chippewas, and all the whites were killed or captured. Two days afterward, having tried unsuccessfully to take the fort at Detroit by stratagem, parties of Ottawas, under the leadership of their chief, Pontiac, killed several British civilians in the immediate neighborhood of the fort, and began firing on the fort itself, which by May 14 was besieged by six hundred or more warriors. Smaller bands captured Fort Sandusky on May 16, Fort St. Joseph (Niles, Michigan) May 25, and Fort Miamis (Fort Wayne, Indiana) May 27. On June 1 and 2 Fort Ouiatanon (below Lafayette, Indiana) and Fort Michilimackinac (Mackinaw City, Michigan) were taken, and about the same time a detachment of nearly a hundred troops en route from Niagara to Detroit was attacked as it neared Detroit and over half of the men were killed or captured.[28]

The uprising quickly spread eastward. On May 28, a party of Delawares and Mingoes killed several whites in the neighborhood of Fort Pitt, and, a few days later, Fort Ligonier, forty-odd miles southeast of Pittsburgh, was fired upon.[29] On June 18, Fort Le Boeuf (Waterford, Pennsylvania) was taken, and some time before June 20 a band of Chenussios of the Seneca nation burned Fort Venango at present Franklin, Pennsylvania, and killed all of its small garrison. On June 22 there was a sharp attack by Delawares and Shawnees on Fort Pitt, and, on the same day the fort at Presque Isle (Erie, Pennsylvania) surrendered to a force of about two hundred Huron and other Indians.[30]

Amherst's heavy share of responsibility for the Indian uprising was widely recognized. In December 1763, Thomas Penn, in England, wrote Governor James Hamilton of Pennsylvania, "Sr. Jeffery Amherst's conduct is extremely injurious to the Colonys, and his Schemes not approved of here, so that I suppose he will speedily come home and leave his plan to one who will judge better what is fit to be done"; George Washington's friend Captain Robert Stewart wrote him from London a few weeks later, "the Conduct of the late Commander in Chief in that Country . . . his Errors, contempt of Indians, ill tim'd parsimony . . . is expos'd to the publick by some very keene and able Pens"; a letter in the *London Chronicle* of January 14, 1764, named Amherst as "the sole cause of the cruel war, which inflicts horror and desolation on our suffering colonies";[31] and, in March 1764, William Livingston of New York attributed the uprising to Amherst's "blundering and disdainful Conduct towards the distant Tribes."[32]

Amherst's contribution to provoking the uprising is, however, only part of the story. The other is the failure of the British army, when the long-threatened rebellion at last broke out, to protect the Pennsylvania and Virginia frontiers from the horrors of Indian raids or to carry out Amherst's confident threats of prompt and crushing punishment of any Indians who might dare rebel.

CHAPTER 9

FAILURE OF THE BRITISH ARMY

THANKS TO the quiescence of the Six Nations, apart from some of the Senecas, and to the protection furnished by the militia of New York and New Jersey, the frontier settlements in New York seem to have suffered relatively little damage and those in New Jersey none whatever.[1] But, despite the calling into service of a thousand militia in Virginia and over seven hundred recruits in Pennsylvania, the frontiers of these colonies, and to a less extent of Maryland, were terribly stricken.[2] A brief respite was afforded while the Indians were gathering to attack the convoy for the relief of Fort Pitt, described later in the chapter, but after the convoy reached its destination the raids in Pennsylvania and Virginia began again.[3] Writing from the Pennsylvania frontier in September 1763, Colonel Henry Bouquet said there were "upwards of 600 Persons already lost," and George Croghan, Deputy Indian Agent, later estimated that the Indians had killed or captured at least two thousand whites, besides driving several thousands more "to Beggary and the greatest distress."[4] Even if these estimates were too high, the torture, the loss of life and property, and the suffering of those driven in terror from their homes on the Pennsylvania and Virginia frontiers were dreadful enough.

As foreshadowed by his threats quoted in the preceding chapter, Amherst prepared for immediate and drastic punishment of the Indians implicated in the uprising. There must be, he wrote Secretary of State Egremont, "a severe Chastisement now, to keep them hereafter within bounds"—a view generally shared by colonists concerned in Indian affairs.[5]

As to his ability promptly to inflict this punishment, Amherst was supremely confident. On first hearing of the outbreak around Fort Pitt, he wrote Bouquet at Philadelphia that the three companies he was placing at his disposal would, he presumed, not only be "more than Sufficient to Quell any Disturbances the Whole Indian Strength could raise," but would fully enable Bouquet "to Chastize any nation, or Tribe of Indians that Dare to Commit Hostilities on His Majesty's Subjects." Even after he was aware of the magnitude of the uprising, Amherst continued to write in similarly confident vein,[6] though the bad news pouring in from the Indian country induced him to send substantial reinforcements to Detroit, held by about a hundred and twenty men, including traders, under the command of Major Henry Gladwin, and to Fort Pitt, held by about three hundred and forty British regulars, Indian traders, and backwoodsmen commanded by a junior officer, Captain Simeon Ecuyer.[7] The object in each case was not only to strengthen the posts but to punish the rebellious tribes as a deterrent to future attack.[8]

On June 10, 1763, Amherst dispatched one of his aides, Captain James Dalyell, to gather some troops for Detroit at various points in New York, and, on July 29, with about two hundred and sixty men, Dalyell reached Detroit by water, slipping past the besieging Indians under cover of night. A month earlier an armed schooner had arrived with an officer and fifty men from Niagara, who, with the addition of Dalyell's force, brought the force at Detroit to well over four hundred.[9] Dalyell's orders, which have not been found, were probably similar to those of Captain Valentine Gardiner, in command of a detachment sent out later, to whom Amherst wrote, "It is my intention that you should act with the Corps under your Command offensively against the Indians; and, that No opportunity may be lost of Punishing them in the most effectual manner for the Enormous Cruelties committed by them, You have, by these Instructions, a Latitude . . . in Attacking the Savages and Destroying their Hutts and Plantations" and dealing with them "Not as a Generous Enemy but as the Vilest Race of Beings that Ever Infested the Earth and whose Riddance from it, must be Esteemed a Meritorious Act, for the good of Mankind."[10]

Two days after Dalyell's arrival at Detroit, Gladwin authorized him to lead a surprise attack on an Indian camp about four and a half miles from the fort. The expedition consisting of about two hundred and fifty officers and men set out before daylight and was well on its way when, as the advanced party was approaching a stream later known as Bloody Run, heavy firing began on the front and left from well-covered parties of Indians who evidently had been forewarned. Dalyell himself was killed, about sixty of his party were killed or wounded, and the survivors were driven back into the fort. On learning of Dalyell's defeat and death, Amherst (September 3, 1763) ordered Major John Wilkins, commanding at Niagara, to proceed immediately with all the men who could be spared from Niagara to Presque Isle, advise Gladwin of his movements, and be prepared to join him or take such other action as he might direct.[11]

The critical point in the movement of troops and supplies from Fort Niagara to Presque Isle and Detroit was at the so-called Carrying Place, the road around Niagara Falls over which supplies were hauled in wagons drawn by horses and oxen from Lake Ontario below the Falls to Lake Erie above. The rest of the journey, by water, was relatively safe. Since the wagon train was vital to the movement of supplies, and could not easily be replaced, prudence dictated a powerful, alert escort at the Carrying Place to prevent surprise; but a large wagon train hauling supplies over the Carrying Place had an escort of only a sergeant and at most twenty-eight men when it was surprised and nearly wiped out by a party of several hundred Indians lurking in ambush. A small body of troops, hearing the firing, rushed to rescue the stricken train, only to be ambushed, too, with a total British loss of about eighty officers and men killed and about twenty wounded. Even more disrupting, from the standpoint of Wilkins's detachment reaching Detroit in good season, was the loss of horses, oxen, and wagons in the train, all of which were destroyed or carried away by the Indians.[12]

This disaster and the wreck of one of the British armed vessels on Lake Erie, prevented Wilkins's detachment from setting out for Detroit until October 19,[13] by which time frequent high winds and seas made navigation of Lake Erie by small boats very hazardous. On the night of November 7, when the expedition, consisting of around six hundred officers and men in forty-six bateaux, was still about a hundred miles from Detroit, a storm wrecked sixteen of the bateaux, with the loss of seventy officers and men and almost all the ammunition, whereupon the whole expedition returned to Niagara.[14]

As it turned out, the shipwreck made little or no difference in the project of punishing the Indian nations in the region of Detroit, because Gladwin had already entered into a truce with them, described in a letter from him to Amherst. "On the 12th October," wrote Gladwin, "the enemy sued for peace in a very submissive manner. At that time I was so circumstanced for want of flour that I must either pass [flee?] or hear them. Of the two I chose the latter, thinking it of the utmost consequence to keep possession of the country. Nevertheless I made them no promises. I told them the affair of peace lay wholly in your breast, but I did not doubt when you was thoroughly convinced of their sincerity everything would be well again, upon which hostility ceased and they disbursed to their hunting grounds. This gave me an opportunity of getting flour from the country to serve from hand to mouth."[15]

Pontiac, leader of the band of Ottawas participating in the siege, held aloof from the truce until he received a letter from Neyon de Villiers, French commandant at Fort Chartres in the Illinois country, confirming the treaty of peace between Great Britain and France, advising the Indians they were not to expect further military supplies from the French and urging them to make friends with the British. Pontiac sent Gladwin a copy of this, declaring that all his warriors had now buried their tomahawks ("enterré leurs Casse-têtes") and proposed that bygones be bygones. Gladwin replied that Amherst must have the final word, but "if you conduct yourself well in the future, as soon as the General is convinced of this, I have no doubt that everything will be well."[16]

The expedition for the relief of Fort Pitt and punishment of the hostile Indians on the upper Ohio, consisting of about five hundred rank and file of the Forty-second and Seventy-seventh (Scotch High-lander) regiments under the command of Colonel Henry Bouquet, a Swiss who had served with distinction in the British army in North America since 1756, set out on July 18 from Carlisle, Pennsylvania. Though this expedition was to march overland to Fort Pitt and was en-cumbered by a large wagon train of flour for the garrison there, Am-herst, who had a "very poor Opinion" of colonial rangers or "woods-men," scouts as they were later called, had provided none.[17] Apologizing to Amherst for incurring the extra expense, Bouquet explained that he had been compelled to recruit about thirty of these woodsmen be-cause "the Highlanders loose themselves in the woods as soon as they go out of the road . . . and cannot . . . be employed as Flankers,"[18] es-sential to avoid ambush.

At Fort Ligonier, fifty-six miles from Fort Pitt by road, Bouquet transferred the flour from wagons to pack horses, and, on August 4, began the final and most dangerous leg of his march with about four hundred men (some of the troops had been left behind to strengthen Fort Ligonier and another fort en route) and a pack train of four hun-dred horses. The next day, an hour after noon, as the convoy ap-proached a stream called Bushy Run, the enemy struck, and in the course of the attack, which lasted until nightfall and was resumed early the next morning, Bouquet lost forty-nine killed and sixty wounded.[19] Thanks to the coolness of his officers and men and to a successful stratagem by which the Indians were lured into the open, they were finally driven off, and, after destroying part of the flour to keep it out of the Indians' hands, Bouquet and his surviving men pro-ceeded to Fort Pitt.[20]*

Bouquet's detachment was expected to advance from Fort Pitt to Presque Isle on Lake Erie, punishing the Ohio Indians by destroying their settlements within striking distance of the line of march. But so many of his men were killed, wounded, or ill by the time the expedi-tion reached Fort Pitt that he was compelled to give up the projected

---

*Most accounts of Bushy Run note the narrowness of Bouquet's victory. See Howard Peckham, *Pontiac and the Indian Uprising* (Princeton, N.J.: Princeton University Press, 1947), ch. 14; White, *The Middle Ground*, 288–89; McConnell, *A Country Between*, 191–94; Don Daudelin, "Numbers and Tactics at Bushy Run," *Western Pennsylvania Historical Magazine*, 68 (1985): 153–79. [B. W. S.]

advance. On learning of this, Amherst hoped Bouquet would use the force at Fort Pitt to act "offensively against the Indians . . . in such Operations as can most distress the Savages who have committed the Depredations." But even sorties against the nearest Delaware towns were impracticable, since the survivors of the colonial rangers recruited at Bedford had been dismissed, and, as Bouquet wrote Amherst, "Without a certain number of woodsmen I cannot think it advisable to employ regulars in the woods against Savages, as they cannot procure any intelligence and are open to continual surprise, nor can they pursue to any distance the enemy when they have routed them, and should they have the Misfortune to be Defeated, the whole would be Destroyed if above one Days March from a Fort."[21]

Thus, while the Detroit and Fort Pitt expeditions succeeded in strengthening the British garrisons at these posts, neither was able to give more than brief relief to the frontier settlements or to achieve the important long-range object of punishing the Indians as a deterrent to future outbreaks.

Fortunately, though the Cherokees and Creeks were restless, neither they nor any other of the southern Indian nations joined the uprising. For one thing, Lord Egremont had prudently arranged for a great congress of southern Indians to be held at Augusta, Georgia, to explain that France's transfer of Canada and eastern Louisiana to Great Britain was not a threat to them and to reconcile them to the change by a lavish distribution of presents.[22] For another, the recent terrible punishment of the semicivilized Cherokees, whose settlement in agricultural villages within relatively easy striking distance from the seacoast made them much more vulnerable to British attack than the western Indians, had been an object lesson not only to them but to their neighbors the Creeks, whose settlements were nearly if not quite as vulnerable as those of the Cherokees.[23]

In October 1763, Amherst received permission he had long sought to return to England on leave of absence,[24] and turned over to his second in command, Major-General Thomas Gage, the task of "Crushing the Indian Insurrection, and Punishing those Tribes who have so ungratefully Attacked their Benefactors."[25] Before leaving, Amherst called on the Governors of New York, New Jersey, Pennsylvania, and

Virginia for 3,500 men, to be armed and fed by the British but re-cruited, clothed, and paid by the colonial governments, "to proceed early in the Spring in Conjunction with such regular Troops as can be collected . . . for reducing the Savages, and securing Peace and Quiet to the Settlements hereafter,"[26] thus, in effect, as William Smith, Jr., of New York remarked, giving "the despised Indians so great a mark of his [Amherst's] Consideration, as to confess he could not defend us."[27]

The two outstanding problems facing Gage were whether or not to ratify the truce between Gladwin and the nations of the Detroit re-gion; and how best to punish the nations and bands with whom no truce had been made — the Shawnees, Delawares, Mingoes (an Ohio Valley band chiefly of Six Nation Indians), and the Wyandots (Hurons) of Sandusky.

As to the first, Gage decided in favor of ratification. He wrote Gladwin on December 22, 1763, "Lieut. Montresor arrived here on the 16th Inst. with your dispatches. . . . ¶ Considering the circum-stances of your Affairs, the Overtures made you by the Savages was a lucky incident. . . . ¶ I would have you inform them, that we accept of the proposals they have made Us, of concluding a peace, provided they will convince us of the Sincerity of their Overtures. . . . ¶ You will by Spring, be able to discover whether their dispositions are really pacifick or not, and if you shall be satisfied they are sincere, I autho-rise you, to close with them till affairs can be finally concluded in a more formal manner."[28]

As to the second, punishment of the rest of the rebel Indians, Gage planned a sort of pincer movement to be executed by two detach-ments, one under Colonel John Bradstreet, based on Fort Niagara, the other, under Bouquet, based on Fort Pitt.

The first to get under way was Bradstreet's, consisting of about twelve hundred British regulars, three hundred Six Nations and other friendly Indians, two hundred Canadians, and six hundred officers and men from New York, New Jersey, and Connecticut, which left Niagara on August 9, 1764. As will be seen later, Gage intended Brad-street not to make peace with the Shawnees, Delawares, and Sandusky Wyandots until they were severely punished, but a statement in his instructions to Bradstreet, "You will give the Savages in general to un-

derstand ... you go with a Body of Troops, to chastise such nations
who shall continue in Arms against us, to offer peace, and his Majesty's protection to those who shall chuse to conclude a lasting Peace
and live in Amity and Friendship with us," seemed to imply that any
of the Indian nations offering to make peace and be future friends
should be granted peace without punishment.[29]

A few days after he set out, Bradstreet was approached on the
south shore of Lake Erie at L'Ance aux Feuilles near present Dunkirk,
New York, by a peace delegation of Indians, representing themselves
as deputies of the Delawares, Shawnees, and Wyandots of Sandusky,
to whom, on August 12, 1764, he granted extremely easy terms of
peace. The most important articles were that the Indians' captives,
white or black, were to be delivered to him at Sandusky, in present
northwestern Ohio, within twenty-five days; that a number of
specified chiefs were to come there to ratify the peace; and that the
British, Bouquet's detachment as well as his own, would not attack the
Indians provided their engagements were fulfilled.[30]

Bradstreet then proceeded to Detroit, where he ratified with the
Ottawas, Ojibways, and other Indian nations the truce made by Gladwin the preceding fall. Finding that he could not reach Sandusky by
the appointed date, Bradstreet dispatched an advance party with provisions, and soon afterward set out with the rest of his detachment, arriving at Sandusky on September 18, only to find that the Indian chiefs
and the captives to be restored had not yet come. He sent word to the
Delawares and Shawnees that he would give them another week in
which to keep their engagements; but neither the chiefs nor captives
appeared.[31]

On the day the extension expired, Bradstreet received a blistering
letter dated September 2 from Gage. "I have this Day," wrote Gage,
"received your letter of the 14th of August, inclosing to my great astonishment, Articles of Peace which you have taken upon you to conclude with the Shawnese and Delawares; which do not contain the
smallest satisfaction to the Nation for the Traitorous Proceedings or
the horrid and cruel Massacres those Indians have been Guilty of from
their first Insurrection to within these few Weeks; or any one Article
that might serve to deterr them from recommencing their Butcheries

the next year and cutting our Throats the first Opportunity. . . . ¶ The Peace you have thought proper to conclude with the Shawnese and Delawares, you had no Powers to Conclude nor do I approve or will I ratify or confirm any Peace so derogatory to the Honor and Credit of His Majesty's Arms amongst the Indian Nations, so unsafe to the future Peace and Tranquility of His Majesty's Subjects, and so apparently productive of future Wars. . . . ¶ You will attack as Ordered, unless you get the Promoters of the War into your Hands, to be put to Death."[32]

Bouquet wrote in similar vein to Gage. "The terms," he said, "fill me with Astonishment. After the massacre of our officers and Garrisons and of our Traders and Inhabitants, in time of a profound Peace, after the Immense Expence of the Crown and some of the Provinces to punish these infamous murders not the least satisfaction is obtained."[33]

The colonists, too, were, of course, indignant over Bradstreet's conduct. *The New-York Mercury* of September 10, for example, denounced the treaty as tending to encourage future outbreaks "on every little occasion" and growled further over the affair in its issues of September 17 and October 1, while Governor Sharpe of Maryland wrote of the general dissatisfaction over giving the Indians peace before they had been punished.[34]

Pursuant to Gage's letter of September 2, Bradstreet made plans to march part of his force against the Delawares and Shawnees; but inadequate food supplies and refusal of the Six Nations Indians to cooperate in the proposed attack led him to defer action. And in the end he left with his entire detachment for Niagara (October 18) without having struck a single blow.[35]

This left the task of punishing the Delawares, Shawnees, and others exclusively to Bouquet, whose force consisted of about four hundred British regulars, twenty Indians, and seven hundred provincial troops recruited in Pennsylvania and Virginia and paid by Pennsylvania.[36] His plan, approved by Gage, was to clear the whole country from Fort Pitt westward to the Scioto river in the central part of the present state of Ohio by attacking and killing the Shawnees and Delawares found in this region and sending out parties of soldiers and Indian auxiliaries "to burn all the small towns, left behind us." Having beaten the Indians to their knees, peace would be made on condition that "they deliver up the murderers of the Indian traders and the first settler killed; pay indemnity over seven years to the traders for their losses; surrender all captives; and renounce their claim to all land east of the Ohio river."[37]

On October 2, when Bouquet was just about to set out from Fort Pitt for the Scioto, two Iroquois who had been sent by Bradstreet to help round up the chiefs and prisoners due to assemble at Sandusky, appeared. They declared that the Indians with whom Bradstreet had made peace were collecting their prisoners to be handed over at Sandusky in five days and begged Bouquet to wait to see if this was done or, if he insisted on proceeding, "to take the road leading to Sandusky where you will meet with Col. Bradstreet, and there settle everything with him."[38]

Pursuant to an order from Gage to proceed without regard to Bradstreet's treaty, Bouquet refused to defer his march, and crossed the Ohio on his way to the Indian country the next day. However, he authorized the Iroquois messengers to tell the Delawares and others that he would not attack them on his march if they remained quiet. He would talk peace with their chiefs if they would meet him at Tuscarawas, a Delaware Indian settlement on the Tuscarawas river in present east central Ohio, and there surrender their captives.[39] Though constantly spied on, the expedition reached Tuscarawas on October 13, without molestation, and on the following day Bouquet received word that representatives of the Indians were on their way there for the suggested peace talk with him. At ensuing conferences on October 17 and 20 the Indians surrendered eighteen white captives and promised to deliver all the others, while Bouquet, on his part, promised lenity if the Indians surrendered these (including Negro slaves and the children of white captives by Indian fathers) by November first at a place appointed near the confluence of the Tuscarawas and the Muskingum in the heart of the Delaware Indian settlements.[40]

By the specified date, only forty-three more captives, far less than the number held, had been handed over to Bouquet; but many more were said to be on the way, and by November 9 all the captives held by the Delawares and Mingoes were delivered. Whereupon, having recently received a letter from Gage giving him carte blanche as to terms if the Indians seemed genuinely desirous of peace, Bouquet concluded a tentative agreement of peace with these two nations, who promised to send representatives to Johnson's headquarters on the Mohawk in New York to conclude a formal treaty of peace with him and gave hostages for the fulfillment of this promise.

Though the Shawnees still had not delivered all their captives, Bouquet was apparently satisfied that they had brought all those near at hand (many of them had been taken to Shawnee settlements far beyond the Muskingum) and, some days later, on their promise to surrender the rest as soon as possible, he granted similar terms to them, adding the stipulation that, to ensure delivery of the remaining captives, the hostages given by the Shawnees were to be held until the promise had been fulfilled.[41]

Soon afterward, Bouquet and his men, together with the liberated captives numbering over two hundred, set out for Fort Pitt, where they arrived without incident on November 28.[42] The Shawnee hostages soon decamped, but chiefs of the three nations assembled, as promised, at Johnson's headquarters in the spring of 1765, when more prisoners were delivered and a final peace was concluded. Here again, however, no punishment (other than the required surrender of their captives) was imposed on the Indians except the exaction of a promise that they would grant whatever land should be agreed upon by the King and the Six Nations to indemnify British and colonial Indian traders for losses suffered by them during the uprising.[43] For the ravaged frontier settlers, no indemnity whatever was demanded or received.

The value of Bouquet's services in securing the release of the Indians' captives and demonstrating that the Indian settlements were vulnerable to British attack was recognized and highly appreciated by the colonies chiefly affected.[44] Nevertheless, it was perfectly clear that the British army had dismally failed not only to protect the colonial frontiers but even to punish the Indians promptly, and that when at last the Indians had yielded, the invading force had consisted chiefly of colonial troops recruited and paid by the colonists themselves.

CHAPTER 10

ENFORCEMENT OF THE
WHITE PINE ACTS

THE NEW ENGLAND frontiers, though spared the horror of Indian warfare in 1763, were not undisturbed. For in the spring of 1763, after an interval of many years, vigorous efforts to enforce British acts for the conservation of colonial white pine for masting the royal navy were resumed.*

The value of the so-called mast trees of New England for naval purposes was recognized by officials in England at least as early as 1654, and, in 1666, the arrival of naval masts from New England played a critical part in the second Anglo-Dutch War, as we know from the diary of Samuel Pepys, Secretary to the Admiralty, who jotted down on December 3 of that year, "There is also the very good news come of four New-England ships come home safe to Falmouth with masts for the King; . . . without which, if for nothing else, we must have failed the next year. But God be praised for thus much good fortune, and send us the continuance of his favour in other things."[1]

In granting the Massachusetts charter of 1691, William and Mary, "for the better provideng and furnishing of Masts for Our Royall

---

*See Joseph J. Malone, *Pine Trees and Politics: Naval Stores and Forest Policy in Colonial New England, 1691–1775* (Seattle: University of Washington Press, 1964). [B. W. S.]

Navy," reserved certain trees in the province to the Crown,[2] and in 1711, 1722, and 1729 Parliament passed acts for the conservation of colonial white pine. The two later acts and a relatively unimportant section of the first were still on the statute books when our period begins. The act of 1722 prohibited the felling, without license from the Crown, of "any white pine-trees, not growing within any township" in New England, Nova Scotia, New York, and New Jersey. (In New England, the words "town" and "township" were used interchangeably.) The act of 1729 prohibited the felling, without license from the Crown, of "any white pine trees, except only such as are the property of private persons, notwithstanding the said trees do grow within the limits of any township," in any "province or country in America, that now belongs or hereafter shall belong to the crown of Great Britain." The act further prohibited the unlicensed cutting in Massachusetts of white pine trees of twenty-four inches or more in diameter measured a foot from the ground, even on privately owned land within township bounds, unless the land had been "granted to some private person or persons" before October 7, 1690.[3]

Enforcement of the acts was in the hands of the Surveyor-General of the King's Woods in America, hereafter called the Surveyor, an officer appointed by the Treasury Board but whose reports commonly were sent to the Board of Trade.[4]

The penal provisions introduced in the act of 1722 and not repealed by the act of 1729 were very severe. The penalties for illegal felling of white pines ranged from five pounds per tree if twelve inches in diameter or under, to fifty pounds per tree if twenty-four inches or more, with imprisonment for three months to a year, at the judge's discretion, if the penalty adjudged was not paid. Of greater practical importance, the Surveyor was empowered to seize any illegally felled white pine trees, or masts or logs cut from them, and sue for their forfeiture in the admiralty court of the colony in which the trees were felled. Such courts were presided over by a judge appointed by and dismissible at the pleasure of the Crown, sitting without a jury[5] and usually in a town remote from the region where the loggers lived and worked.

Moreover, the act of 1722 put the burden on the claimant of the seized trees, masts, or logs to prove that they had not been cut outside township bounds. Thus, since the unlicensed felling of any white pines outside township bounds was illegal under the act, the Surveyor, by alleging that the trees in question were felled outside township bounds, could secure the forfeiture of any white pine trees, masts, or logs he saw fit to seize unless the owner appeared and was able to prove to the satisfaction of the court that the trees had been felled within township bounds.

Efforts to enforce these acts in Massachusetts (which from 1691 to 1820 included most of the present state of Maine) and New Hampshire aroused intense hostility, especially in Massachusetts, where the acts plainly violated the colony's royal charter.[6]

The decision of the English Government to conserve this important colonial resource is quite understandable, and, if carried out wisely, with due regard for colonial needs and without infringement of colonial charters or property rights, might well have had general colonial support. For most of the colonists, living on or near the seacoast, were largely dependent for protection against foreign attack on the strength of the British navy and this in turn was dependent on an assured, ample supply of the great trees needed for naval masts, yards (spars), and bowsprits. Furthermore, since the trees suitable for naval masts brought a higher price as masts than if cut into lumber,[7] the colonists would have found it profitable to conserve the mast trees on privately owned land or even on public land owned by the colonial governments if the British Government had been willing to pay a fair price for them.

The British measures were, however, far from wise.

A basic defect was the failure to reserve only such trees as were or might become fit for naval masts, yards, or bowsprits and permit the cutting into lumber or shingles of those forking near the ground or otherwise obviously not fit for naval use. This was early called to the attention of the English Government by Governor Joseph Dudley of Massachusetts, and later by Governor William Burnet of New York; and the instructions to the Governors of Nova Scotia, New York, and New Hampshire, requiring a reservation of white pine in grants of Crown land, properly limited the required reservation to trees "fit for masts." But the White Pine Acts of 1722 and 1729 contained no such limitation; they reserved all white pine irrespective of size or quality on all land not privately owned and even on privately owned lands outside township bounds.[8]

David Dunbar, Surveyor from 1725 to 1743, ventured to temper the acts by issuing a proclamation permitting the cutting of white pine trees that forked within fifty-four feet of the ground, which took reasonable account of colonial needs without, it seems, unduly sacrificing those of the navy. But when he sent a copy of the proclamation to the Board of Trade with a request for sanction to continue it from year to year, the Board sharply reprimanded him and ordered him to revoke it. He promptly did so, and apparently no similar proclamation was ever again issued, nor were the acts amended.[9]

The unfortunate effect of the failure of Parliament to draw a line similar to Dunbar's was well described by John Wentworth, Surveyor from 1766 to long after the American Revolution, who wrote in 1778, "The Acts of Parliament relative to the preservation of pine timber in America, being merely penal, and too general, operated so much against the convenience and even necessities of the inhabitants, that . . . it became almost a general interest of the country to frustrate laws, which comprehend nearly an unlimited reservation. This will appear more evident, when we consider that the country from Skuylkill in Pennsylvania to the river St. Lawrence, was, with little exception, generally interspersed with white pine trees; in many places it was the principal growth, [and] the greater part of these were utterly unfit for masts, yards, or bowsprits, and would remain so till they perished . . . [yet] were useful to cut into the different species of lumber requisite for their [the colonists'] own buildings, or profitable at market for exportation, the proceeds supplying the poor settlers with provisions, West India produce, and British manufactures:—but the whole being equally reserved, it naturally rendered the real object disagreeable to the people."[10]

Similar comments on the unwisdom of the acts as they stood were made by Thomas Pownall, former Governor of Massachusetts, in his *Administration of the Colonies* published in 1764 and by Chief-Justice Thomas Hutchinson of Massachusetts in his *History of the Province of Massachusetts Bay* published in 1767.[11]

However, though the failure to discriminate between trees that were or might some day be valued for naval use and those that would evidently never have any value except as lumber was doubtless largely responsible for the frequent clashes between the Surveyors and the people of New England, disagreement over the interpretation of the acts and of the provision in the Massachusetts charter reserving certain trees in the province to the Crown, was another important factor. Read out of context, the Surveyors' complaining letters give the impression that the New Englanders were an utterly lawless lot, whereas in many if not most cases they were standing for what they believed, with reason, were their legal and equitable rights in trees growing on their own lands.

An early difference of opinion arose over the meaning of the words "private person" in the White Pine Act of 1711 exempting trees which were "the property of any private person." Surveyor Bridger maintained that until land held in common by town (township) proprietors was divided, the trees on it were not the property of any "private person" within the meaning of the act,[12] while the colonists maintained the contrary. The act of 1722 eliminated dispute on this point by exempting all trees "growing within any township"; but the act of 1729 revived the issue by exempting only those trees within township bounds that were "the property of private persons."

Pownall pointed out in 1764 that the act of 1729 ought to be changed because based on "a mistaken apprehension of a township, there being no lands within such but what are private property,"[13] but the act stood without amendment and without a final judicial decision as to whether trees on town land held in common were the "property of private persons," until the Revolution.

Another serious issue arose out of a ruling by the Surveyor that the word "logs," as used in the act of 1722 authorizing the Surveyor or his deputies to seize white pine logs from trees alleged to have been illegally felled, included lumber.[14] The colonists' refusal to accept this farfetched construction of the word "logs" naturally led not only to litigation but to clashes with the Surveyor or his deputies, notably the Exeter, New Hampshire, riot of 1734. In this a band of about thirty colonists attacked and drove away ten deputies of Surveyor Dunbar who were attempting to put the Crown mark—a broad arrow—on some lumber (boards) that the Surveyor claimed had come from white pine trees illegally felled.[15]

Another bitter controversy arose over the ruling by the Surveyors that the great white pines in the Gorges tract, now part of Maine but then part of Massachusetts, had been reserved to the Crown in the Massachusetts charter of 1691. This tract, extending eastward from the eastern boundary of New Hampshire to the Sagadahoc (Kennebec) river and inland one hundred and twenty miles from the sea, granted by Charles I to Sir Ferdinando Gorges in 1639, had been sold by his grandson and sole heir in 1678 for £1,250 to John Usher, acting as agent for Massachusetts.[16]

The controversy was particularly bitter and hard fought not only because this region, according to Surveyor Bridger, was "better furnished with Mast Trees both for Number and Large Sizes more than all besides" but because the claim on behalf of the Crown involved violation of the cherished Massachusetts charter, the "Magogg or Idoll of these people," as Bridger angrily called it.[17]

The Massachusetts charter granted by William and Mary on October 7, 1691, gave to "Our good Subjects the Inhabitants of Our said Province or Territory of the Massachusetts Bay and their Successors" all property rights of the Crown in the province with the following reservations: joint control over the disposal of land in the undeveloped region extending eastward from the Sagadahoc river in the present state of Maine to the Nova Scotia boundary; one-fifth of the gold, silver, and precious stones in the province; and "all Trees of the Diameter of Twenty Four Inches and upwards . . . Twelve Inches from the ground growing upon any soyle or Tract of Land within Our said Province or Territory not heretofore granted to any private persons. . . ." These reserved trees could not be felled "without the Royall Lycence of Us, Our Heires and Successors first had and obteyned."[18]

The charter seemed clearly to reserve to the Crown none of the trees in the Gorges tract, inasmuch as all the land in that tract admittedly had "heretofore," i.e., before the date of the charter, been granted to a private person, namely, Gorges. What later disposition was made of the land was irrelevant under the terms of the charter.

Nevertheless, successive Surveyors, supported after 1718 by a flimsy opinion of Richard West, Counsel to the Board of Trade,[19] maintained that the trees in this tract, twenty-four inches or more in diameter a foot from the ground, were reserved by the charter to the Crown.[20]

The Surveyors' leading opponent was Dr. Elisha Cooke, a prominent politician and capitalist of Boston, who had large holdings of land in the district.[21] Under his leadership a joint committee of the Massachusetts Legislature in 1718 condemned Bridger for having "obstructed the Inhabitants of this Province in their just Rights and Privileges of Logging" in the towns of Kittery and Berwick in the Gorges tract and recommended that "some effectual Care be taken by this Government to Secure . . . the aforesaid Privileges and just Properties . . . from further Invasions." Cooke long continued to oppose the Surveyors on the point, and the issue finally came to a head in 1734 in *Frost* v. *Leighton,* one of the most famous law suits in our colonial history.[22]

In 1709 and 1710, four hundred and twenty acres of land were conveyed by the proprietors of Kittery, one of the towns in the Gorges tract, to Charles Frost, whose son John Frost inherited the land in 1724 and still owned it in 1733. In 1730, the Crown issued a license to Ralph Gulston, a mast contractor of London, to cut a stated number of the Crown's white pine trees in the colonies of the dimensions mentioned in a contract between Gulston and the British Navy Board, provided the trees were first viewed and approved by the Surveyor. Gulston sent his license to a subcontractor, Samuel Waldo of Boston, who hired William Leighton to cut the masts and bring them to the waterside. Among the trees viewed and approved by Surveyor Dunbar to be felled for the contract were six great white pine trees on Frost's land. These, Leighton cut and hauled away in the winter of 1733–1734 without Frost's consent and apparently without offer of payment either for these or for ninety-one other trees cut down in getting out the white pines.[23]

In March 1734, Frost brought suit against Leighton in the County Court of York County, Massachusetts, alleging the facts as to the felling of trees stated above and asking £200 damages under a recent Massachusetts statute. Leighton pleaded in defense that the white pines felled by him belonged to the Crown under the Massachusetts charter; that he had a license from the Crown to cut them; and that the Crown's ownership of the trees included the right to cut adjacent trees so far as necessary to utilize the white pines and that he had not cut more than was necessary for this purpose. The Court gave judgment for damages of £121 and costs, and this judgment was sustained on appeal to the highest Court of Massachusetts, which added more costs.[24] Neither Court stated the basis for its judgment, nor does the amount of the judgment indicate the Courts' view on the chief question at issue—whether or not the Crown had reserved ownership of the great white pines in the Gorges tract.

On appeal by Leighton to the Privy Council in England, Frost's counsel consented to an order to the Massachusetts Superior Court for repayment of the damages and costs collected by Frost and for a new trial along lines laid down in the order, which was designed to secure a record of the pertinent facts for consideration by the Privy Council if the case was again appealed. But Frost failed to repay Leighton, and the Superior Court declined, even after a second order from the Privy Council in 1739, to issue process to compel Frost to do so.[25]

Finally, in October 1743, after a third order from the Privy Council, the Superior Court directed the Clerk of the Court to prepare and lay before it the draft of a summons to Frost to show cause why the Privy Council's order, so far as it concerned him, had not been complied with. No evidence has been found that the contemplated summons was drafted, much less served on Frost; but shortly afterward Governor William Shirley of Massachusetts, at one time Leighton's counsel, reported to officials in England that Frost had repaid Leighton.[26] Frost, discouraged perhaps by the prospective cost of another appeal to England,[27] apparently did not ask for a new trial, and the case thus ended after nine years without a decision of the crucial question whether or not the trees in the Gorges tract belonged to the Crown. (This question seems never to have been finally determined.)*

Soon after the Frost case was ended by Frost's repaying Leighton, Governor Benning Wentworth of New Hampshire, a native of the colony, was appointed Surveyor, and for the next twenty years there seem to have been only two serious efforts to enforce the White Pine Acts.[28]

*Richard B. Morris (*Journal of Modern History*, 33 [1961]: 321–22) disputes Knollenberg's interpretation of the Gorges controversy. [B. W. S.]

The first was in Connecticut, whose charter, granted by Charles II in 1662, reserved no timber rights whatever to the Crown. (The only reservation was a fifth of the gold and silver ore extracted in the colony.) However, the acts of 1722 and 1729 included Connecticut, and, in January 1753, Wentworth gave Daniel Blake of Middletown, Connecticut, a commission authorizing him to "seize all White pine trees that you may find Cutt within the said Colony [Connecticut] also all Logs or other timber into which the said trees or Masts may be Cut."[29]

This commission, it will be observed, plainly went beyond the wording of the acts in that it made no exception in favor of trees which were in townships and "the property of private persons." Yet, when Governor Roger Wolcott of Connecticut pointed out to Wentworth that all land in Connecticut was within township bounds and privately owned, Wentworth replied that this was immaterial because trees were not considered private property within the meaning of the act of 1729 unless growing on "Lands under Actual improvement and Inclosures . . ." — an utterly untenable position.[30]

However, Wentworth's illegal effort to conserve the white pine trees of Connecticut was short-lived. In June 1753, Wentworth complained that Blake, while in the execution of his office, was thrown into a mill-pond by Daniel Whitmore of Middletown and nearly drowned, and, though Blake was reported in May 1754 to be about to have Whitmore prosecuted,[31] nothing further has been found as to any prosecution by Blake or further effort by the Crown to apply the White Pine Acts to Connecticut.

Wentworth's other effort at enforcement before 1763 was the seizure in 1758 of over fifteen hundred white pine logs in New Hampshire and nearly two thousand near the mouth of the Merrimac River in Massachusetts, the results of which may well have disheartened him. Some of the logs seized in Massachusetts were retaken by persons unknown and the rest "turned into the river on the Ebb-tide, which soon carried them to sea." In New Hampshire, where Wentworth was having the seized logs sawed into boards and planks, the sawmill was burned down by unidentified incendiaries and all the logs, boards, and planks were destroyed.[32]

A new chapter opened in 1763 when Wentworth seized over two thousand white pine logs along the Connecticut River Valley, chiefly in Massachusetts, and brought suits for their forfeiture in the admiralty court at Boston, alleging that the trees from which the logs were cut grew in New Hampshire outside township bounds.[33]

This allegation would require forfeiture under the act of 1722 unless the respective owners appeared and were able to prove that the particular logs claimed had come from trees growing within township bounds. Where the trees were actually felled or whether any owners appeared is unknown, but the cost of a trip to Boston with witnesses to prove the source of a given log or parcel of logs was probably prohibitive. Some of the logs were under twenty-four inches in diameter, some over, but how large a proportion were from trees fit, immediately or potentially, for naval use is unknown. Judging from the statement of John Wentworth, quoted earlier in this chapter, the great majority were probably of no possible use for the navy and would have rotted away, without value to anyone, if not cut for lumber.

Hundreds of white pine logs were also seized in Connecticut, as appears from letters to Jared Ingersoll of New Haven, Connecticut, who had recently begun operations along the Connecticut River as a mast contractor for the British navy.[34]

Why Wentworth suddenly made these sweeping seizures is unknown. Perhaps he was influenced by the new program of strict enforcement discussed in the next chapter. Possibly he had heard of complaints in England concerning his laxity and wished to make an impressive display of enforcement to forestall censure or dismissal.[35] Possibly, as suggested by Ingersoll's biographer, Wentworth's sudden activity was caused by commercial rivalry between his family, which had long had important masting interests in Maine and southern New Hampshire, and Ingersoll.[36] Be that as it may, hostility to the White Pine Acts immediately broke into flame again.

Governor Bernard of Massachusetts issued a proclamation ordering provincial officials to assist the Surveyor and his deputies, but justices of the peace to whom Wentworth's deputies, threatened with beating and death, applied for assistance in their work, gave them no help. One justice at first refused even to read the proclamation, and, when persuaded to do so, said, "the Governor did not understand the affair for, if he had, he would never have put out such a proclamation." The other, though less openly hostile, rejected the request for an order requiring the inhabitants to assist the deputies, stating that if the latter were "abused and beaten and applied to him as a Justice he was ready to take cognizance of the Same but nothing more."[37] A letter from two of Ingersoll's assistants in April 1764 gives a similar picture of rearoused colonial hostility.[38]

At the very time renewed enforcement of the obnoxious White Pine Acts of 1722 and 1729 was arousing violent antagonism in the upper Connecticut Valley, rigorous enforcement of another hitherto laxly enforced British act, the so-called Sugar Act of 1733, was causing widespread discontent along the seaboard from Massachusetts to Pennsylvania.

CHAPTER 11

ENFORCEMENT OF THE
SUGAR ACT OF 1733

By various acts from 1660 to 1732, fully described in Chapter 14, Parliament imposed a wide range of restrictions on colonial trade. After a long struggle between West Indian sugar interests and London Agents for the British mainland colonies, Parliament added a further restriction by passing the Sugar Act of 1733, which imposed heavy duties on colonial imports of foreign colonial molasses, sugar, and rum, primarily not for revenue but to give British West Indian sugar interests a monopoly of the market for these products in the British mainland colonies.[1] The duty of sixpence a gallon on foreign molasses was particularly heavy, amounting to about 100 per cent ad valorem. Though initially enacted to run for only five years, the act was repeatedly extended, the last extension carrying it forward into 1764.[2]*

The acts restricting colonial trade were ameliorated by a practice of British customs officers in the colonies to "indulge," as it was called, cer-

*On economics, sugar, and rum, see Thomas Barrow, *Trade and Empire: British Customs Service in Colonial North America, 1660–1775* (Cambridge, Mass.: Harvard University Press, 1967); John W. Tyler, *Smugglers and Patriots: Boston Merchants and the American Revolution* (Boston: Northeastern University Press, 1986); John J. McCusker, *Rum and the American Revolution: The Rum Trade and the Balance of Payments of the Thirteen Continental Colonies*, 2 vols. (New York: Garland, 1989). [B. W. S.]

tain open violations of the acts. Spanish vessels were permitted to enter Jamaican ports to bring in Spanish colonial products and carry away slaves and goods of various kinds in violation of acts of 1660 and 1696,[3] while, on the mainland, domestic (British colonial, British, or Irish) vessels were permitted to import fresh fruit and wine direct from southern Europe in violation of an act of 1663 prohibiting colonial importation of most European products from any place but Great Britain,[4] and to import foreign colonial molasses on payment of only a small fraction of the prohibitive duty imposed by the Sugar Act of 1733.[5] An effort was made at Boston in the early forties to enforce the full duty on foreign colonial molasses; but this was apparently short-lived.[6]

James Otis of Boston said the custom there was for the officers to settle for "about one tenth" of the statutory duty on foreign molasses, and at New York the customary rate was said to be a fourth to a half-penny a gallon.[7] At Salem, Massachusetts, a leading port of entry for foreign molasses, the rate before 1758 was less than a halfpenny a gallon, as disclosed in a letter of 1758 from Timothy Orne, prominent merchant and shipowner of the town, to the master of one of his ships. "Since you Sailed from here," Orne wrote, "our Officers have received Orders not to Enter foreign Melasses as heretofore. The Vessells that have arrived since those Orders have been admitted to Enter about One Eight or Tenth part of their Cargo paying 6 d sterling per gallon Duty for what is Entered—which is more than twice as much as was given before. How it will be settled hereafter I know not but it is generally thought that the Vessels that Saile from here before the Officers Received those Orders will be admitted to Enter a Small part of their Cargo paying the 6 d Sterling per gallon for what they Enter."[8]

The customs officers apparently treated the molasses duty collected by them prior to 1760 as a perquisite of office, since, except for one year, the total amount reported in the mainland colonies from this source never amounted, before 1760, to as much as £1,000 a year and was often less than £100.[9]

The foreign colonial molasses trade was extremely valuable to the northern British colonies, since it gave them a favorable outlet for their surplus lumber, fish, and farm products not absorbed by other markets. (Beef, pork, and bacon, colonial as well as foreign, could not legally be imported into Great Britain at all, wheat and other grains were subject to heavy British import duties, and the importation of salt fish was severely restricted.) Furthermore, the molasses received in exchange was not only a favorable form of sweetening in the colonies but was the source of the cheap rum distilled in the northern colonies widely used for home consumption and in the fisheries, the African slave trade, and the Indian trade.[10]

The bulk of the molasses trade was with the French West Indian colonies of Guadeloupe (then spelled Guadaloupe), Martinique, and St. Domingo (now Haiti), where, presumably because of the French policy of protecting the market for French brandy by discouraging the distillation of molasses into rum, molasses was much cheaper than in the British West Indies.[11] The trade with the French West Indies was threatened by the English Navigation Act of 1660 forbidding foreign vessels to enter English colonial ports for trade, coupled with a French ordinance of 1670 forbidding foreign vessels to enter French colonial ports for trade;[12] but the threat did not materialize because French governors ignored the ordinance to the extent of permitting British colonial vessels to bring in lumber, horses, fish, and other food in exchange for molasses.

In 1726 this practice was legalized to some extent by the French Minister of Marine, in charge of colonial affairs, authorizing the Governors to issue permits to foreign vessels to import horses, mules, lumber, shingles, staves, and firewood.[13] And in April 1763, this permission was widened by a general order from France authorizing the governors of all French colonies in America to permit foreign vessels to import horses, mules, lumber of all kinds, bricks, furniture, and a wide variety of foodstuffs in exchange for molasses—permission which the governors promptly acted on.[14]

The British colonial merchants would have liked to secure foreign sugar as well as molasses, but got relatively little sugar because officials in the French and other foreign colonies would not permit its export in foreign vessels. There was likewise apparently little foreign colonial rum imported. It seems that in earlier days but little rum was distilled in the foreign colonies,[15] while, in the later period, after the French began to distill more, northern colonial distillers probably saw to it that the ninepence a gallon import duty levied by the Sugar Act of 1733 was rigidly enforced for their protection against French competition.

Another foreign colony with which the northern British colonies carried on an extensive molasses trade was the Dutch settlement at Surinam (Dutch Guiana) on the northeast coast of South America. Rhode Island in particular carried on a flourishing trade with Surinam, taking molasses in exchange for horses, foodstuffs, and Rhode Island tobacco. The evidence is conflicting as to whether or not this trade was in violation of Dutch law; but, whether legal or not, the northern colonial vessels seem to have brought in their produce and carried away the molasses received in exchange openly and without molestation. The British colonies in general also carried on an extensive trade with the tiny Dutch island of St. Eustatius ("Statia") which, though producing little itself, was an important entrepot in the West Indies.[16]

Three other nations had sugar-producing colonies in the West Indies or on the mainland of South America: Denmark held St. Thomas and St. Croix, the more important of the Virgin Islands, Portugal held Brazil, and Spain, Hispaniola (now the Dominican Republic), Cuba, and Porto Rico. There was some trade in sugar and molasses between the northern British colonies and the Danish islands but it was apparently small compared to that with the French and Dutch Colonies. Though Brazil was an important sugar-producing colony, no evidence has been found of any sugar or molasses trade between it and the British colonies. In 1764 Nicholas Brown & Company of Providence, Rhode Island, extensively engaged in the molasses trade with Surinam, wrote the captain of one of its ships to inquire closely into "trade of the Brazil for hope Something may be done there to advantage from this part of the world";[17] but apparently nothing came of the suggestion.

Sugar cane was successfully introduced into the Spanish West Indies as early as 1520, and, considering the immense sugar and molasses exports from Cuba and Puerto Rico to the United States today, one might expect to find a large, clandestine sugar and molasses trade between the Spanish West Indian colonies and the northern British colonies; but there is little evidence of such trade, except in time of war between France and Great Britain when great quantities of sugar of

French colonial origin were shipped from Monte Cristi in Hispaniola to the British colonies.[18]

Though conducted in plain violation of the Sugar Act of 1733, the indulged foreign molasses trade was on a very different footing from clandestine smuggling of European or East Indian goods. The latter was frowned on by the so-called fair traders among the colonial merchant-importers,[19] while the indulged foreign molasses trade was apparently locally regarded by all as perfectly respectable. The magnitude of the indulged trade in foreign molasses is indicated by the amount entered for duty from 1767 to 1771, after the rate of duty had been reduced to a penny a gallon, totaling over three million gallons a year.[20] Efforts were made by British West India sugar interests to secure British legislation to put a stop to the colonial importation of foreign molasses, in the course of which the nonenforcement of the act of 1733 was brought out. But no change was made in existing legislation or in enforcement measures until the latter part of the Seven Years' War, when the Sugar Act was rigorously enforced as a means of stopping the pernicious colonial trade with the enemy referred to in Chapter 4.[21]

When peace came, Charles Townshend, President of the Board of Trade, proposed in Parliament (March 1763) that the foreign molasses duty be reduced to twopence a gallon and its enforcement continued as a means of raising a revenue in the colonies. But his proposal was not then adopted and the old prewar indulgence was evidently soon restored. Chief Justice Hutchinson of Massachusetts wrote in September 1763 that vessels there engaged in the foreign West Indies trade had lately been "arriving and making their entries for some small acknowledgments as openly as from our own Islands without paying the duties,"[22] and evidence brought out later in the chapter indicates that the restoration was general.

The restoration was, however, short-lived. In April 1763, Parliament passed an act laying the basis for use of the British navy in time of peace as an arm of the British customs service to enforce the British acts of trade and customs throughout the empire. Eight warships and twelve armed sloops were assigned to service in North American waters, whose commanders were deputed by the Commissioners of Customs, hereafter referred to as the Customs Board, "to seize and proceed to condemnation of all such Ships and Vessels as you shall find offending against the said Laws [of trade]" and "to seize any Goods, wares and Merchandize prohibited to be exported out of, or imported into any of his Majesty's Dominions."[23] Supplementing this measure, customs officers holding posts in the colonies but farming them out and living in Great Britain were summoned to take their stations, and orders were issued to colonial governors to render them all possible assistance. General Amherst, too, as Commander-in-Chief in North America was ordered to require the officers under his command to assist in preventing illicit trade.[24]

At first it appeared that the new measures were to be directed solely to better enforcement of acts which the customs officers had habitually tried to enforce and that the usual indulgence to the foreign molasses trade was not to be disturbed. John Temple, Surveyor-General for the Northern Customs District, was said to have assured merchants of his district that "they might expect the same Indulgence, with regard to the Sugar Act, as had been heretofore usual," and on November 15, Tench Francis, a merchant of Philadelphia in the Southern Customs District, wrote Nicholas Brown & Company of Providence, "I find the consequences on Account of the Men of War station'd on our Coast are not so bad as I at first thought I had reason to fear. . . . They have no intention to meddle . . . with any Molasses or Sugar Ships . . . but will leave them to the several Collectors to settle with them as usual."[25]

However, in November 1763, the Customs Board sent a circular letter to all customs officers in America threatening them with instant dismissal for failure to do their full duty. Presumably alarmed by this warning, Temple, in January 1764, published notice to the masters of all vessels engaged in the West Indian trade that customs officers would board their vessels to see that the act of 1733 was "fully carried into execution"—a notice which, according to an oft-quoted statement of Governor Francis Bernard of Massachusetts, "caused a greater alarm in this country than the taking [by the French] of Fort William Henry did in 1757."[26]

Here again the reason for the British decision is obscure; but it may well have been a bid by the Ministry for the political support of British

West India sugar interests. Israel Mauduit, brother of the London Agent for Massachusetts and active in politics, wrote in March 1764 that it was a very bad time for the northern colonies to try to secure abolition of the duty on foreign molasses since "the state of parties is such that 50 or 60 West India voters [in Parliament] can turn the balance on which side they please,"[27] and George Grenville's action when West India merchants called his attention to the adverse effect of the new enforcement measures on the indulged Spanish trade at Jamaica, indicates his eagerness to appease them.

In April 1764, Charles Jenkinson, joint Secretary to the Treasury, wrote Grenville, "Mr. Long and Mr. Payne, West India merchants, yesterday came to me to complain that our men of war, under the orders they had received from hence to prevent contraband trade, had interrupted our commerce with the Spanish Main; they said that fresh instructions were going from the Admiralty, and they wished that great care was taken in the manner of wording them, so as not to include the commerce to the Spanish Main. I told them that I was convinced it was not within your intention to include that." Grenville replied, "I entirely approve of your doing all you can to prevent any inconvenience, from what Mr. Long mentioned, to our trade with the Spaniards, in America; . . . I will talk to you upon that subject as soon as we meet"—a talk which evidently was favorable to the West Indians, for, shortly afterward, orders were given that the indulged Spanish trade at Jamaica be winked at.[28]

While still uncertain whether or not the Sugar Act would be enforced, Thomas Cushing, a Boston merchant and one of the town's representatives in the Massachusetts House, wrote privately to Jasper Mauduit, the colony's London Agent, describing the importance of the foreign molasses trade to Massachusetts, particularly to its fishing industry, and urging him to cooperate with Agents of the other northern colonies to secure a reduction of the foreign molasses duty to a halfpenny or, at most, a penny a gallon. This, said Cushing, was "the utmost the trade wou'd bare." He wrote Mauduit again, a few weeks later, reemphasizing the importance of having the duty reduced to a halfpenny or penny a gallon, which, he thought, would be cheerfully and universally paid and would thus yield a considerable revenue to the Crown. Cushing added, however, "It's a difficult affair for you to conduct at present, as the Generall Court [Massachusetts Legislature] have heretofore instructed Mr. Bollan [former London Agent of the colony] to oppose any duty at all, as of Dangerous precedent. What their mind will be now I can't say, but . . . I'm inclined to think they would be willing the affair should take this Turn, provided it's done without their explicit Agreement."[29]

Cushing's view as to the general acceptability of a low rate of duty on foreign molasses was shared by Hutchinson, who wrote an English correspondent in August 1763, "To reduce the duty to a penny per gallon I find would be generally agreeable to the people here, and the merchants would readily pay it." But, he added, "do they see the consequence? Will not they be introductory to taxes, duties and excises upon other articles, and would this consist with the so much esteemed privilege of English subjects—the being taxed by their own representatives?"[30]

The "merchants and traders" of Boston, Salem, Marblehead, and Plymouth, Massachusetts, were also active, and, shortly after the Massachusetts Legislature met in December 1763, presented petitions asking for appropriate action against renewal of the Sugar Act.[31] These petitions were supplemented by a detailed statement, a State of the Trade, prepared by a committee of Boston merchants, bringing out the importance to Massachusetts of the foreign molasses trade, asserting that the margin of profit was too narrow for the trade to bear any duty and urging nonrenewal of the Sugar Act on its expiration in 1764. According to this statement, 15,000 hogsheads or 1,500,000 gallons of molasses and rum a year were imported into the colony, part of the molasses for direct consumption, part to be made into rum and beer, of which only a small part came from the British West Indies, where the price was much higher than in the foreign islands. About three-fifths of the molasses was consumed locally; the rest was exported, much of it as rum, to the southern colonies, Nova Scotia, Newfoundland, and Africa. As in Cushing's letter to Mauduit, particular stress was laid on the importance of the foreign molasses trade to Massachusetts fishermen, whose prosperity, it was said, depended on the exchange of their otherwise almost worthless low-grade fish for foreign molasses.[32]

In response to the merchants' petitions, the legislature appointed a joint committee, including Cushing and Otis, to prepare instructions for Mauduit, which, together with a copy of the merchants' statement, was sent to him. The instructions are missing, but their tenor is indicated by a letter of Cushing to Mauduit stating, "I find the Committee in general are of oppinion that this Act is at this time of dangerous consequence as it will be conceding to the Parliaments having a Right to Tax our trade which we can't by any means think of admitting, as it wou'd be contrary to a fundamentall Principall of our Constitution vizt. That all Taxes ought to originate with the people."[33]

A committee of Boston merchants also took steps to enlist the co-operation of merchants in Rhode Island and Connecticut by writing correspondents in these colonies. "The Act commonly known as the Sugar Act," they wrote, early in January 1764, "has long & justly been complain'd of by the Northern Colonies as a great Grievance; and should it be continued and put in Execution with any Degree of Rigour (as is like to be the Case hereafter) it will give a Mortal Wound to the Peace of these Colonies. ¶ As this Act is now about to expire, it behoves us all to unite our endeavours to prevent, if possible, the revival of it . . . [and] defeat the iniquitous Schemes of these overgrown West Indians."[34]

In October 1763, Elisha Brown of Providence had suggested a "Meaten . . . So as wee may Stand by Each other," and merchants and traders of Newport and Providence now applied to Governor Stephen Hopkins of Rhode Island for a special session of the Legislature, which was summoned to consider not only the threat to the colony's trade but also a call from General Gage for troops to help punish and thus secure a "lasting and durable" peace with the western Indians. At this special session, which opened on January 24, no recorded action was taken on the call for troops; but the threat to the colony's trade called forth a strong remonstrance to the Board of Trade to be presented by Joseph Sherwood, the colony's London Agent, if the Agents of at least three other northern colonies would join.[35]

According to this interesting document, Rhode Island, though having an estimated population of only about 48,000, annually imported 14,000 hogsheads of molasses, all but 2,500 of which came from foreign colonies. This molasses, distilled by the colony's thirty or more distilleries into rum, was "the main hinge upon which the trade of the colony turns." The rum was particularly important in the colony's trade with the west coast of Africa, to which eighteen Rhode Island vessels, carrying 1,800 hogsheads of rum, resorted annually to barter "for slaves, gold dust, elephants' teeth, camwood etc." The slaves were sold in the British West Indies, North and South Carolina, and Virginia; the other items in Europe.[36]

Nicholas Brown of Providence wrote his firm's New York correspondent, David Van Horne, telling of developments in Rhode Island and expressing the hope that New York was taking similar action. A few days later the New York merchants met and chose a committee which prepared a statement, approved by the New York Council and later by the House, for submission by the colony's London Agent to the House of Commons. The statement pointed out that the colony shipped flour, beef, pork, lumber, and horses to the foreign West Indies in exchange for sugar and for molasses "consumed amongst us in the brewing of Beer, and by the poor sort of People in great Quantities in the Room of Sugar" or distilled into rum, a staple in the trade with the Indians, who "will deal with no Traders destitute of this Spirit, and resent the Thoughts of being stinted in their favourite Liquor, with the highest Indignation."[37]

Merchants in Connecticut and Pennsylvania were active, too. At a special session of the Connecticut Legislature in January 1764, Jared Ingersoll of New Haven filed a petition "in behalf of Gurdon Saltonstall Esq. and others Merchants & Traders of this Colony," reciting that "his Majesty has been pleased of late to Inforce the Execution of the Sugar Act," to the distress of the northern colonies, and requesting that a committee be appointed to collect pertinent information and assist the colony's London Agent, Richard Jackson, in opposing renewal of the act. But there is no record of any action by the Legislature on this petition until the next (March 1764) session, when a committee consisting of Saltonstall, Nathaniel Shaw, and Thomas Mumford, Jr., all of New London, was appointed to collect reasons against renewal of the act to be sent to Jackson.[38]

In Philadelphia some merchants met and appointed a committee to draw a petition to the Pennsylvania Assembly requesting that its

London Agent be ordered to cooperate with those of other colonies in opposing renewal of the Sugar Act;[39] but, so far as is known, the petition was not presented or even prepared, perhaps because of word from England indicating it was too late for a petition to have effect.

These activities and statements of the northern colonial merchants are interesting and important for the light they shed on the nature of the economy of the northern colonies and as the first intercolonial movement of the pre-Revolutionary period designed to exert political pressure in England. But the petitions probably had little or no influence since even the one from Massachusetts, apparently the first to arrive, did not reach London until March 17, 1764, by which time a bill for taxing the colonies for revenue, including a tax of threepence a gallon on foreign colonial molasses, had been laid before Parliament.[40]

In December 1763, Mauduit believed the Ministry would be satisfied with a duty of twopence a gallon on foreign molasses; but, by February 1764, he was afraid that, under pressure from West Indian interest, the rate would be fixed at threepence. Apparently hoping to prevent this by winning the good will of the Treasury Board, Mauduit filed a statement with the Treasury dilating on the importance of the foreign molasses trade to Massachusetts, in which, after stating that the principal merchants of Massachusetts were unanimous in declaring the trade would not bear a duty of more than a penny a gallon, he nevertheless added that his "Deference to your Lordships" would make him "silently acquiesce in a Duty of Two Pence." Jackson, London Agent for Connecticut and for the Pennsylvania Assembly, proposed a rate of a penny and a half a gallon; but, in the end, he and also John Huske, a former New Englander, now an English resident and member of Parliament to whom the committee of Boston merchants had appealed, likewise acquiesced in a rate of twopence.[41] (Huske justified his readiness to go as high as twopence by referring to the French proclamation of 1763 which, by permitting foreign vessels "to carry off Molasses without the expence of passports or the risque of seizure," would, he thought, now enable the northern colonial merchants to afford twopence a gallon as easily as the penny they were previously willing to pay.)[42]

Their strategy was, however, unsuccessful. The bill as introduced and passed April 5, 1764, levied a duty of threepence a gallon on foreign colonial molasses, to take effect September 29, 1764, and to run for an unlimited time. The duty on foreign colonial refined sugar was sharply increased and the importation of foreign colonial rum into the British colonies prohibited. To bridge the gap between the ending of the old act, which by its terms was to expire at the close of the current session of Parliament, and the beginning of the new, the old act was temporarily extended.[43]

The Ministry's decision to lay a permanent duty of threepence a gallon on foreign colonial molasses, coupled with its stoppage of the previous indulgence to the foreign molasses trade, though understandable in the light of the West Indians' political power, was a serious error.

Colonial merchants had influence within their several communities far greater, proportionately, than the merchants of our time. They were not only wholesale and in many cases retail dealers, but the principal importers, exporters, shipowners, bankers, insurers, wharfingers, and warehousemen in the chief port cities, with influence comparable to that of the combined mercantile, banking, shipping, import and export, and marine insurance interests in these cities today. Furthermore, the merchants and their lawyers were constantly in touch with each other across colonial lines. By fixing the duty on foreign molasses at a rate higher than the merchants believed the traffic would bear, the Ministry particularly exasperated members of this especially influential group at a time when, along with the colonists generally, they were antagonized and alarmed by other British measures discussed in this volume.

CHAPTER 12

PARLIAMENT TAXES THE COLONIES
FOR REVENUE

"In what Mode," wrote Secretary of State Lord Egremont to the Board of Trade in May 1763, "least Burthensome and most palatable to the Colonies can they contribute toward the Support of the Additional Expence, which must attend their Civil and Military Establishment upon the Arrangement [for governing the territory acquired from France and Spain] which your Lordships shall propose?" The Board, as observed in Chapter 7, failed to answer this perplexing question, leaving the Treasury to its own devices in carrying out the decision of the Bute Ministry in the winter of 1762–1763 to levy taxes for revenue on the colonies.[1]

In September 1763, the Treasury Board directed the Commissioners of the British Stamp Duties to draft a bill for extending stamp duties to the colonies, and in March 1764, the House of Commons laid the basis for a future colonial stamp tax by adopting the resolution declaring, "it may be proper to charge certain Stamp Duties in the said Colonies and Plantations."[2] But, as brought out in Chapter 1, the budget for 1764 presented by Grenville on March 9, 1764, included a proposal for colonial customs duties only.[3]

139

Duties were to be paid in the colonies on colonial imports of foreign sugar, molasses, wine, silk, lawn, cambric, and printed calico and
on colonial exports of native coffee and pimento to any place but
Great Britain; and in Great Britain on a wide range of foreign and
Irish products reexported from Great Britain to the colonies. These
latter duties could not be legally avoided by direct colonial importation of the dutied products from the country of origin, because, as we
shall see in Chapter 14, the colonists were forbidden to import European, East Indian, or Irish products, with few exceptions, from any
place but Great Britain. Most of the duties payable in Great Britain
were to take effect May first, those payable in the colonies, September
29, 1764.[4] The act levying these duties will hereafter be referred to as
the American Act of 1764 or simply as the Act of 1764.

Unlike the duties previously levied by Parliament in the colonies,
some at least of those imposed by the Act of 1764 were clearly for the
purpose of raising a colonial revenue; and the act explicitly recited
that "whereas it is just and necessary, that a revenue be raised, in your
Majesty's said dominions in America . . . we, your Majesty's most dutiful and loyal subjects, the commons of Great Britain, in parliament
assembled, . . . have resolved to give and grant unto your Majesty the
several rates and duties herein after-mentioned." The duties thus
raised were to be disposed of by Parliament "towards defraying the
necessary Expences of defending, protecting and securing the British
Colonies and Plantations in America,"[5] meaning, Grenville indicated,
the cost of maintaining the British army stationed in America, toward
which the colonists were to contribute £225,000 to £400,000 a year.[6]

The constitutional and other grounds for challenging Parliamentary taxation of the colonies for revenue are discussed at length in the
next chapter. Suffice to point out here that, in proposing this revolutionary measure, the Ministry made no effort to render it as acceptable as possible to the colonists. No assurance whatever was given as
to either the amount or the proportion of future taxes that Parliament
might levy on the colonists without their consent; for all they knew or
were given to understand, there was no limit to the burden of taxation
that Parliament might later lay on them if they acquiesced in the present innovation. And, far from offering to relieve them from the many

burdensome restrictions on their trade, described in Chapter 14, which were regarded in the colonies as already imposing a kind of indirect tax on them, the restrictions were made more severe than ever. Though Burke's famous words, "Whether you were right or wrong in establishing the colonies on the principles of commercial monopoly rather than on that of revenue, is at this day a problem of mere speculation. You cannot have both by the same authority. To join together the restraints of an universal internal and external monopoly with an universal and external taxation is an unnatural union—perfect, uncompensated slavery," were not spoken until later, they were as valid in 1764 as when thundered to the House of Commons in 1774.[7]

Moreover, linking colonial taxation with maintenance of the British army in America was particularly galling to the colonists, because, as brought out in earlier chapters, none of the commissions in the army had been offered to colonial officers and the troops, consisting almost exclusively of regiments inexperienced in the woods and untrained for Indian fighting, were ill fitted to protect the colonies from the only serious danger, Indian attack, to which they were now exposed—as had just been tragically demonstrated in the great Indian uprising of 1763–1764.

Considering the importance and revolutionary nature of the bill for the American Act of 1764, the small amount of opposition to it in Parliament is remarkable. Introduced in the House of Commons on March 14, 1764, it passed that House on March 30 and the House of Lords on April 4 and was formally assented to next day by the King. Agents of several of the northern colonies were to have talked with Grenville on March 27 concerning the bill, but he left before they arrived.[8]

At one stage of the proceedings on the bill, Sir William Baker, a London merchant having extensive interests in the northern colonies and Member for Plympton, proposed a reduction in the rate of duty on molasses,[9] and John Huske, Member for Maldon, and Richard Jackson, London Agent for Connecticut and Pennsylvania and Member for Weymouth and Melcombe Regis, spoke in favor of this.[10] But apparently the only opposition in Parliament to the bill as a whole was by Huske, who maintained that "as the Bill was [a] peculiar step on the Colonies, the colonies ought to have first notice thereof, giving them opportunity to lay . . . any objections they might have to such a Bill to the House, by their Agents."[11]

Jackson, who plays an important part in our colonial history, was an English lawyer of a rich, Dissenting, Norfolk family and was not only a member of Parliament but Grenville's private Secretary.[12] His connections with Connecticut extended, we know, as far back as 1753, when he wrote the Reverend Jared Eliot of Killingworth, Connecticut, whose *An Essay upon Field-Husbandry in New-England* had attracted his favorable attention, concerning the proposed purchase of some land in Connecticut. Later he was kind to visitors from Connecticut, including the Reverend William Johnson, in England for ordination, and Jared Ingersoll, the New Haven lawyer we have met before. Upon the death of Agent Richard Partridge, he was appointed the colony's London Agent. His connection with Franklin and through him with Pennsylvania went back even farther than with Eliot, as appears from a letter from Peter Collinson to Franklin in 1752 saying he had "delivered a pacquet" from Franklin to Jackson.[13]

John Huske, elected for Maldon in April 1763, was the son of Ellis Huske, a distinguished New Englander. The date and place of John's birth are elusive, but we know he lived in America for twenty-four years and was in London by January 1761, where, young John Hancock wrote, he was "very intimate with him."[14] Huske's defeated rival at Maldon, Bamber Gascoyne, alleged that Huske was supported by "Wilkes and his crew"; that his campaign was conducted with "great violence and open bribery"; and that "Guineas and scraps of North Britons" were "scattered all over the town"; but the election seemingly was not contested, perhaps because Gascoyne's own campaigning methods did not bear close scrutiny.[15]

As brought out in Chapter 1, the easy progress of the American Act bill through Parliament was owing in large measure to the determination of Pitt, Newcastle, and other opposition leaders to avoid issues on which they might disagree among themselves. But the failure to put up a fight against the bill was also attributable to the inexperience of the colonial Agents in London (Partridge, the highly experienced and resourceful Agent for Rhode Island, New Jersey, Pennsylvania, and Connecticut, had died in 1759, and William Bollan, long the Agent for Massachusetts, had recently been dismissed)[16] and to the lack of proper instructions from America.

If the legislative committees of correspondence or others charged with the duty of corresponding with London Agents had instructed them vigorously to oppose any kind of colonial duties or other taxes for revenue, the Agents, however inexperienced, would presumably have obeyed instructions. But, though warnings were sent to America when the matter was mentioned in Parliament in February 1763,[17] apparently no instructions were given any of the Agents to oppose the tax on principle; and, as brought out in Chapter 11, Mauduit, Agent for Massachusetts, and Jackson, Agent for the Pennsylvania Assembly and Connecticut, expressly approved a duty for revenue on foreign colonial molasses if it was at a low rate. The failure of Agent Jackson to protest against the proposed taxes for revenue was particularly unfortunate because, as a member of Parliament and one of Grenville's secretaries, he was in a position to make himself heard on behalf of the colonies.

Jackson's failure seems to have been largely the responsibility of Benjamin Franklin, who, having been chosen a member of the Pennsylvania Assembly's Committee of Correspondence in April 1763, wrote Jackson of this, adding, "I shall shortly send you the Minutes of the late Session, and from time to time whatever may be necessary to inform you of our Affairs. And I hope to receive from you early Notice of such Proceedings at home, as it may be useful for our Assembly to be acquainted with."[18] Jackson was thus given to understand that Franklin was the mouthpiece for the Committee. Yet Franklin, though he had warned Governor Shirley of Massachusetts in 1754 that taxing the colonists "by Act of Parliament where they have no Representative" would probably give them "extreme Dissatisfaction,"[19] and was now advised by Jackson of the Ministry's proposal to bring in a bill taxing the colonies for revenue, gave no warning that the colonies would object.

On March 10, 1763, Jackson wrote Franklin of the Ministry's proposal to station fourteen battalions of troops in North America to be paid for by the colonies. Franklin replied with seeming indifference, "You mention a Proposal to charge us here with the Maintenance of

10,000 Men. I shall only say, it is not worth your while. All we can spare from mere Living, goes to you for Superfluities. The more you oblige us to pay here, the less you can receive there." Later in the year, Franklin was informed by Jackson that Parliament would raise £200,000 a year on the colonies, and that, while he planned to oppose any "Inland Duties," he did not intend to oppose a duty for revenue on colonial imports of foreign molasses. To this Franklin replied, "I am not much alarm'd about your Schemes of raising Money on us. You will take care for your own sakes not to lay greater Burthens on us than we can bear; for you cannot hurt us without hurting your selves. All our Profits center with you, and the more you take from us, the less we can lay out with you"[20]—as if it made no difference to the colonists whether their money was exacted in taxes or was voluntarily paid for goods purchased by them!

Why Franklin took a course so inconsistent with his earlier stand is unknown. Presumably he was influenced by the movement for a change of government in Pennsylvania, discussed in Chapter 18, which he strongly supported and which could not be hoped for without the favor and support of the British Ministry. But he also had strong personal reasons for desiring to stand well with the Ministry since his office of joint Deputy Postmaster-General in North America, carrying a salary of £300 sterling a year, was held at the pleasure of the Crown.[21]

Weighing on the same side was the recent appointment of Franklin's son, William Franklin, to the governorship of New Jersey in place of Governor Josiah Hardy, referred to in Chapter 4. This was likewise terminable at the pleasure of the Crown. The probable influence of this appointment on the elder Franklin was noted in a letter from Thomas Penn to Governor James Hamilton of Pennsylvania, saying, "I am told you will find Mr. Franklin more tractable, and I believe we shall in matters of prerogative; as his son must obey instructions, and what he is ordered to do, the father cannot well oppose in Pennsylvania." Franklin's friend, Joseph Chew, wrote in similar vein, prophesying that Franklin would not support the land claim of the Susquehanna Company, since the claim was frowned upon by the British

Ministry, and Franklin would "on no Terms interfer in any matter disagreeable to the Ministry—this it is Reasonable to immagine."[22]*

At a conference with several of the colonial agents in May 1764, Grenville expressed the belief that the colonial assemblies would instruct their agents to assent to the proposed stamp tax;[23] but, if this was anything but idle talk, he was sadly deceived, for, though there was division of colonial opinion concerning the duties levied in the colonies by the Act of 1764, the Assembly of every important mainland colony that met in 1764 protested, as we shall see, against the proposed stamp tax. But before turning to the colonial protests, three important factors bearing on them will be examined: the British constitution in relation to British taxation of the colonies; the British acts restricting colonial trade and manufacturing before 1764; and the additional restrictions on colonial trade and currency imposed by Parliament in 1764.

---

* On Franklin, see Robert Middlekauff, *Benjamin Franklin and His Enemies* (Berkeley: University of California Press, 1996); Sheila L. Skemp, *Benjamin and William Franklin* (Boston: St. Martin's Press, 1994); Cecil B. Currey, *Road to Revolution: Benjamin Franklin in England, 1765–1775* (Garden City: Anchor Books, 1968). For Knollenberg's view of Franklin, see his letter to the editor: *William and Mary Quarterly,* 3rd ser., 4 (1947): 549. [B. W. S.]

CHAPTER 13

THE ENGLISH CONSTITUTION AND COLONIAL TAXATION

In the reigns of James I and Charles I, during which Virginia and Massachusetts were founded, the King claimed and exercised sole jurisdiction over the colonies. When, in 1621, a bill was introduced in the House of Commons relating to fishing in English colonial waters, one of James's ministers opposed it on the ground that in the "new Plantations, the King is to govern . . . only by his Prerogative, as his Majesty shall think fit," and three years later, on learning of a petition to the House of Commons concerning affairs of the Virginia Company, James himself wrote that it was "very unfitt for the Parliament to trouble themselves with these matters," whereupon the petition was dropped.[1]

During Charles's reign, two acts were passed applying in general terms to England and any of its "Dominions," but no evidence has been found that they were published or enforced in the colonies.[2] The absence of any known protest in Parliament against the broad powers granted by Charles to Lord Baltimore in the charter of Maryland of 1632, including a clause that neither the King nor his successors would cause any custom duties or other taxes to be imposed in the colony and commanding his ministers never "to attempt any Thing to the contrary,"[3] also indicates that the King's power to deal with the colonies, exclusive of Parliament, was claimed and recognized at that time.

However, during the Commonwealth period, following the execution of Charles I, the Rump Parliament passed an act in 1649 declaring that "the People of England, and of all the Dominions and Territories thereunto belonging . . . shall from henceforth be Governed . . . by the Supreme Authority of this Nation, The Representatives of the People in Parliament." This was followed in 1650 by an act forbidding any foreign vessel to trade with the colonies without special license from Parliament or the Council of State; and in 1651 by an act forbidding the importation of any products of Asia, Africa, or America into the colonies except in ships owned exclusively and manned chiefly by Englishmen. These ordinances might later have been explained away as a mere usurpation of royal power by the Rump Parliament if, on the restoration of the monarchy, Parliament had ceased to deal with colonial affairs. But one of the first acts passed by Parliament after the Restoration was the famous Navigation Act of 1660, restricting colonial navigation and trade, and, by 1764, Parliament had passed scores of acts dealing with or bearing on colonial trade, navigation, and manufacturing. (A typical set of trade instructions issued to the Governor of New Hampshire in 1761 listed nearly a hundred such acts.)[4]

Yet, while firmly establishing its authority over colonial trade and related matters despite initial colonial opposition,[5] Parliament had consistently abstained from taxing the colonies for revenue, disregarding repeated suggestions from royal Governors and other British officials in the colonies that such taxes be laid. Thus usage, a powerful force in establishing legal rights and constitutional principles under English law, had drawn a line between Parliament's legislating for the colonies as to trade and related matters and Parliament's levying taxes for revenue on the colonies.

Various acts of Parliament pertaining to the colonies and having revenue aspects had, indeed, been passed; but they were either designed primarily for the regulation of trade or had other features distinguishing them from ordinary revenue acts. Even though it might be difficult in some cases to determine whether an act was designed primarily for revenue or for regulation of trade, there was an obvious difference in principle between the two classes, as was recognized in the Declaratory Act of 1778 stating that Parliament would thereafter impose no duties whatever in the colonies "except only such duties as it may be expedient to impose for the Regulation of Commerce."[6]

The duties laid by the Act of 1733, as noted in Chapter 11, were imposed primarily for the protection of British West Indian sugar, molasses, and rum, not primarily for revenue. The duties under the act of 1673 on intercolonial shipments of products enumerated in the Navigation Act of 1660 were chiefly to discourage shipment of these products to any place but England rather than to raise a revenue.[7] The postage chargeable under the Post Office Act of 1711 was for particular services rendered, and the Greenwich Hospital Acts, requiring seamen throughout the empire to contribute to the maintenance of a hospital for themselves and their families, were of a similar character. The Prize Goods Act of 1708, levying duties in the colonies on prize goods condemned and sold in the colonies at the same rates as on similar goods brought into Great Britain and reexported, merely ensured that captors should not obtain undue advantage by bringing their prizes into colonial rather than British ports for condemnation.[8]

Nor were the acts in fact revenue producing. On the contrary, according to Grenville, writing in 1764, the gross revenue amounted to less than two thousand pounds a year, at a cost of collection amounting to between seven and eight thousand pounds.[9] The net loss thus indicated was exaggerated because the expenses included the cost of enforcing acts wholly prohibiting certain branches of colonial trade, which, of course, produced no revenue at all. But the essence of the statement—that the duties did not produce enough revenue to pay the cost of collection—was doubtless true.

Moreover, even compulsory charges for services rendered and the Sugar Act duties were protested against by or on behalf of the colonists because of the dangerous precedent they might tend to establish. Virginians sought to nullify the British Post Office Act; the Massachusetts Legislature objected to the Greenwich Hospital Acts; and Richard Partridge, London Agent for Rhode Island, protested that the prohibitive duties proposed in the Sugar Act bill of 1733 were more ob-noxious than outright prohibition, as previously proposed, because of the danger of setting a precedent for duties for revenue.[10]

A similar distinction between acts for revenue and acts for the reg-ulation of trade and manufacturing was observed in dealing with Ire-land. the British Parliament declared in 1719 that it had "full power and authority to make laws to bind the kingdom and people of Ire-land," and widely exercised this power in regulating Irish trade and manufacturing;[11] but it never levied taxes for revenue on Ireland until a legislative union was established by the Act of Union of 1800 which gave Ireland a hundred seats in the united House of Commons and thirty-two in the united House of Lords.[12]

Parliament's abstinence from levying taxes for revenue on Ireland or on the colonies before 1764 was in harmony with principles of the English constitution recognizing the existence of certain basic, unal-terable rights of Englishmen, one of which was no taxation without representation.

The concept of basic principles constituting permanent limita-tions, reaching back at least as far as Magna Carta, had been affirmed in one of the great documents of English political and constitutional history. The Bill of Rights, enacted by Parliament in 1689, declared that a number of fundamental rights and privileges "shall stand, re-main and be the law of this realm forever."[13] Furthermore, in the Act of Union with Scotland (1707) certain of the articles were declared to be binding "for ever."[14]

England's great and influential philosopher, John Locke, asserted in his *Two Treatises of Government* (1690), that the law of Nature com-prising certain principles of government "stands as an eternal rule to all men, legislators as well as others,"[15] a view reflected again and again in Trenchard's and Gordon's *Cato's Letters* published in 1720–1723 and often republished during the succeeding half century.[16] Sim-ilar views were expressed by statesmen of the period. Lord Boling-broke, for example, gloried in the English constitution, that "Assem-blage of Laws, Institutions and Customs, derived from certain fixed Principles of Reason . . . according to which the Community hath agreed to be governed," and Chesterfield, writing to his son in 1750, spoke of England's "fixed laws and constitutional barriers for the security of our liberties and properties."[17]

Furthermore, the English Courts had indicated in several early opinions that Englishmen had certain basic rights which could not be infringed by Parliament, and leading textbooks and encyclopedias of English law current in England around 1760, Coke's *Institutes,* Wood's *Institutes,* Bacon's *Abridgment,* and Viner's *Abridgment,* recognized limitations on the legislative power of Parliament.[18]

Blackstone, it is true, in his popular *An Analysis of the Laws of England,* first published in 1756, stated that "In all States there is an absolute Supreme Power, to which the Right of Legislation belongs; and which, by the singular Constitution of these Kingdoms, is vested in the King, Lords, and Commons." He slightly qualified this in his *Commentaries* (1765), where, though repeating that "the power of Parliament is absolute and without control," he states that the "law of nature . . . is of course superior in obligation to any other."[19]

But assuming that Blackstone held to the doctrine of unlimited legislative power in Parliament, some Englishmen disagreed, as shown, for example, by Furneaux's masterly *Letters to Blackstone,* published in 1770, stating "the learned author observes that 'the bare idea of a state without a power somewhere vested to alter every part of its laws is the height of political absurdity.' . . . I say, in every free state there are some liberties and privileges, which the society have not given out of their own hands to the governors, not even to the legislature; and to suppose the contrary (if I may be allowed the expression) would be the height of political absurdity; for it is saying a state is free and not free at the same time; or, which is the same thing, that its members are possessed of liberties, of all which they may be divested at the will of the legislature. . . . In our own government . . . the whole legislature is so far from having an *absolute power,* that . . . they cannot dispense with any of those essential rights of the people, respecting their liberties, properties, or lives, the preservation of which ought to be the great object of government in general, as it is of our constitution in particular."[20]

If there were any principles which Parliament was obliged, morally at least, to observe, "no taxation without representation" was surely one of them. Article 12 of Magna Carta declared, "No scutage nor aid shall be imposed in our kingdom, unless by the common council of our kingdom, excepting to redeem our person, to make our eldest son a knight, and once to marry our eldest daughter, and not for these, unless a reasonable aid shall be demanded." Among the principles which the Bill of Rights declared to be "the law of the realm forever" was "levying money for or to the use of the crown, by pretence of prerogative, without grant of parliament, for longer time, or in other manner than the same is or shall be granted, is illegal." And one of the three fundamental rights specifically mentioned by Locke was that no taxes shall be raised "on the property of the people without the consent of the people given by themselves or their deputies."[21]

These statements dealt primarily or exclusively with the relationship between the King and parliament and with the rights of Englishmen in England; but the principle of no taxation without representation logically and equitably applied with equal force whether the King or Parliament sought to impose the tax, and colonial Englishmen were entitled, by repeated declarations, to the same basic rights as those at home.

Colonial charters, beginning with the first charter of Virginia (1606), stated that all the King's subjects dwelling in the colony "shall have and enjoy all Liberties, Franchises and Immunities . . . as if they had been abiding and born within this our Realm of England" and the principle had recently been reaffirmed in the British colonial Naturalization Act of 1740 declaring that, "Whereas the increase of people is a means of advancing the wealth and strength of any nation or country; and whereas many foreigners . . . might be induced to come and settle in some of his Majesty's colonies in America, if they were made partakers of the advantages and privileges which the natural born subjects of this realm enjoy," persons naturalized in the colonies under the act "shall be deemed, adjudged, and taken to be his Majesty's natural born subjects . . . as if they, and every of them, had been or were born within this kingdom."[22] If naturalized subjects in the colonies were made "partakers of the privileges of natural born subjects" of Great Britain, surely native colonists were entitled to these privileges.

The right of English subjects, whether at home or in the colonies, not to be taxed without representation was supported by Chief Justice Lord Camden in the House of Lords in 1766. Denouncing a bill to accompany the repeal of the Stamp Act, which asserted the authority of Parliament to legislate for the colonies "in all cases whatsoever," he declared the bill to be "illegal, absolutely illegal, contrary to the fundamental laws of nature, contrary to the fundamental laws of this constitution." The "British parliament," he maintained, "have no right to tax the Americans," for "taxation and representation are coeval with and essential to this constitution."[23] Even the British advocates of colonial taxation paid implied tribute to the principle of no taxation without representation by advancing the far-fetched argument that the colonies were "virtually" represented in Parliament.[24]

In one important respect, however, many colonists at this time held a view of the British constitution which most Englishmen probably did not share. For, in England, the doctrine of Chief Justice Coke and other English judges that they had the power and duty to hold void and refuse to execute an act of Parliament which, in their opinion, was in conflict with fundamental rights (a doctrine now definitely repudiated in Great Britain) was becoming obsolete,[25] while in the colonies it still was vigorously upheld. "Our friends to liberty," wrote Chief Justice Hutchinson of Massachusetts to an English correspondent in 1765, "take advantage of a maxim they find in Lord Coke that an act of Parliament against Magna Charta or the peculiar rights of Englishmen is *ipso facto* void. This, taken in the latitude the people are often enough disposed to take it . . . seems to have determined great part of the colonies to oppose the execution of the act [Stamp Act of 1765] with force and to show their resentment to all in authority who will not join with them."[26]

The best known exponent of this thesis was the Boston lawyer, James Otis, whose argument based on Chief Justice Coke's famous dictum in *Dr. Bonham's Case*, "when an act of parliament is against common right and reason . . . the common law [i.e., judges applying common law] will controul it and adjudge such act to be void," was referred to in the discussion of the writs of assistance controversy in Chapter 4. Otis reenunciated this thesis in his popular pamphlet *The*

Rights of the British Colonies Asserted and proved, published at Boston in 1764, maintaining, "If the reasons that can be given against an act, are such as plainly demonstrate that it is against *natural* equity, the executive courts will adjudge such acts void. It may be questioned by some, tho' I have no doubt of it, whether they [the judges] are not obliged by their oaths [of office] to adjudge such acts void."[27] But, as Hutchinson indicated, this view was not peculiar to Otis or to Massachusetts.

In 1762 the Superior (Supreme) Court of Rhode Island, presided over by Chief Justice Samuel Ward, in effect held an act of Parliament, providing for naturalization of members of the Jewish faith in the colonies, void in so far as it concerned Rhode Island since such naturalization would be "absolutely inconsistent with the first Principle," namely, "quiet enjoyment of the Christian Religion and a Desire of propagating the same" upon which the colony was chartered and founded.[28]

In 1764 Governor Sharpe of Maryland wrote that people there were saying, "surely the Judges will never in case of a Dispute with the Collectors of such Taxes [levied by act of Parliament] give Judgment against the express words of the Charter in which the King has declared that neither he nor his Successors would ever lay any Impositions or Taxes on the Inhabitants of the province."[29]

And in February 1766, the County Court of Northampton county, Virginia, Justice Littleton Eyre presiding, unanimously advised the officers of the court to proceed without regard to the Stamp Act "in as much as they conceive the said Act to be unconstitutional." At almost the same time, Edmund Pendleton, one of the leading lawyers of Virginia, was expressing a similar opinion to his fellow justices of the County Court of Caroline county, Virginia.[30]

The continued vitality in the colonies of the concept of the courts having the power and duty to declare acts of Parliament void is not surprising, since the commissions of the royal Governors, colonial charters, and an act of Parliament provided that acts of the colonial legislatures "are not to be repugnant, but as near as may be agreeable unto the Laws and Statutes of this Our Kingdom of Great Britain," or words to similar effect;[31] and, pursuant to these limitations, the Privy Council and colonial courts had repeatedly held colonial acts void.[32]

But probably an even more important factor was the deeply felt need in the colonies for some legal protection from arbitrary legislation by a body, the British Parliament, in which they were not represented.

So long as the King or Queen exercised the royal prerogative to disallow bills passed by both Houses of Parliament, this, theoretically at least, afforded the colonists some protection, since the sovereign would presumably be more inclined than Parliament to think and act in terms of the empire as a whole rather than of particular British interests. But the prerogative of disallowance had long been abandoned; no bill had been rejected since Queen Anne refused assent to a bill for a Scotch militia in 1711.[33] Consequently the recognition that legislative power was limited by fundamental law binding on the courts of law was the colonists' only legal protection against Parliament's legislating for them as arbitrarily as it pleased.

The colonists also had a strong equitable claim related to but in addition to the claim on constitutional grounds of freedom from taxation by Parliament. This additional clam was based on the particular object for which the colonists were to be taxed, namely the support of the army stationed in America. As brought out in Chapter 6, there was ground for doubt that the British Ministry's chief object in stationing so large a body of British troops in North America after the war was, as stated by Grenville, the defense of the colonies. But even if Grenville was truthful, taxation of the colonists for protection infringed a basic principle of the relationship between the colonies and the Mother Country, repeatedly expressed, that the latter should and would protect the colonies as the *quid pro quo* for the restrictions on colonial trade and manufacturing, described in the next chapter, imposed on the colonies.

In 1763, Richard Jackson, the member of Parliament and colonial Agent previously mentioned, wrote Franklin, "it is not disputed that the Mr [mother] Country is Mistress of the Trade of its Colonies; this Right has always been challenged [claimed] & exercised by England & all other Countries . . . And the Colonys have a Compensation in Protection." Some months later Chief Justice Hutchinson wrote, "it is highly reasonable that by the Laws of the mother Country a restraint should be laid . . . in any branch of Trade or in any other matter or thing which shall cause advantage to a foreign State and prejudice the mother Country . . . ; it is no more than is reasonable to part with in return for the Protection received against foreign Enemies." And in *Late Occurrences in North America* (1766), the anonymous author wrote, "The duties of a mother country and its colonies are reciprocal; the one expects encouragement and protection; and the other clams and secures to itself every advantage that an extensive commerce can produce."[34]

Similar statements were made by the Board of Trade and by Crown officials in the colonies. Thus, the Board, in reporting to Governor Shirley of Massachusetts the disallowance by the Privy Council of a recent act of Massachusetts to promote the manufacture of linen in the colony, pointed out that "The passing of Laws in the Plantations for encouraging manufactures, which anyways interfere with the Manufactures of this Kingdom, has always been thought improper and has ever been discouraged. The great expence which this Country has been and still is at for the defence and protection of the Colonies, while they on the other hand contribute little or nothing to the taxes with which it is burthen'd, gives it a just claim to restrain them in such attempts." In 1752, Archibald Kennedy, Collector of the Port of New York, quoting "A Late Elaborate Author" (Montesquieu), wrote, "The Disadvantage of a Colony that loses the Liberty of Commerce, is visibly compensated by the protection of the Mother-Country, who defends it by her Arms or supports it by her Laws." And in 1764, Governor Dobbs of North Carolina defended British restrictions on colonial trade for the benefit of Great Britain as a "tribute we ought to pay to our Protectors."[35]

The desire of the British Ministry to have the colonies, some of which had very light public debts and taxes compared with the British,[36] contribute to the cost of imperial defense was reasonable. And if, following the lines adopted in 1705–1707 when the abolition of the Scotch Parliament and the consolidation of Scotland with England was desired,[37] the Ministry had taken steps to secure the appointment of commissioners to negotiate with the colonial governments and to offer the colonies compensation, the proposal to change the prevailing relationship between Great Britain and the colonies would have been a statesmanlike move. But to act unilaterally, to change a constitutional relationship established for over a century without prior effort to negotiate a settlement and without any offer of compensation or assurance against future exploitation, was high-handed, reckless, and unjust.

BRITISH RESTRICTIONS ON COLONIAL TRADE AND MANUFACTURING

IN 1660 AND 1663, Parliament passed acts laying extensive restrictions on colonial trade.

The first, the famous Navigation Act of 1660, prohibited vessels owned by or manned to the extent of more than one-fourth by foreigners to import or export any "goods or commodities" into or out of colonial ports. (An act of 1696 extended the prohibition to foreign-built vessels even though owned and chiefly manned by English, Irish, or colonials.)[1] Furthermore, vessels permitted to trade in the colonies were forbidden to export colonial sugar, tobacco, cotton, indigo, and dye wood, known as "enumerated commodities," to any place except England, Ireland, or an English colony. Scotland was classified, for purposes of the Act, as a foreign nation until its union with England in 1707[2] when it was placed on the same footing as England with respect to this and other acts relating to colonial trade.

The second, the act of 1663, prohibited the direct importation of most European products into the colonies even in domestic vessels.

These products could henceforth be legally imported only by way of England. The only exceptions were wine of Madeira and the Azores and Irish and Scotch horses and servants, which might be imported directly into any of the colonies, and European salt, which might be imported directly into the New England colonies and Newfoundland and (by later amendments) into New York, Pennsylvania, Nova Scotia, and Quebec.[3]

From 1670 to 1750 many additional British restrictions were laid on colonial trade, and restrictions were also laid on colonial manufacturing.

In 1671 the act of 1660 was amended to prohibit shipment of colonial enumerated commodities directly to Ireland and to prohibit colonial-owned ships from carrying enumerated commodities, even if produced outside the English colonies, to any place in Europe except England.[4]

In 1673 Parliament levied duties on shipments of enumerated commodities from one English colony to another,[5] primarily, as brought out in Chapter 13, to discourage intercolonial trade in these commodities rather than for revenue.

In 1696 Parliament passed an important act dealing chiefly with clarifying and providing for better enforcement of prior acts relating to colonial trade, but also forbidding the direct export of any colonial products to Ireland. (In 1731 this was amended to forbid direct export to Ireland of enumerated commodities only.)[6]

In this same year Parliament included the colonies, along with foreign countries, in an act designed to protect the English knitted wear industry by forbidding any export from England of knitting frames.[7] (The colonists were forbidden to obtain European-built frames by the act of 1663 prohibiting colonial importation of European products from any place but Great Britain.)

In 1698 Parliament passed an act forbidding all English subjects, except members of the English East India Company, to carry on any trade whatever, import or export, with the "East Indies," which was defined to include not only India but the whole continent of Asia and adjacent islands, the east coast of Africa, and the west coasts of North and South America. Later extended, the act was still in force until after 1775.[8]

Complaints by English woolen manufacturers that Irish competitors were capturing the colonial and foreign markets led to consideration by the Board of Trade of ways to stop this competition. In suggesting measures with respect to Ireland, the Board added, "We do also observe that . . . New-England and other northern colonies, have applied themselves . . . to the improvement of woolen manufacturers amongst themselves; which in its proportion, is as prejudicial to this kingdom, as the working of those manufacturers in Ireland; wherefore it is submitted, that, upon occasion, the like prohibitions be made with relation to those northern colonies as to Ireland."[9] Pursuant to this recommendation, Parliament passed an act, in 1699, prohibiting the export from Ireland of Irish woolen goods to any place but England and any export of wool or wool products from the colonies, even from one colony to another.[10]

In 1704 rice, molasses, tar, turpentine, hemp, masts, and other naval stores were added to the list of enumerated commodities. Though the restriction on the export of rice was later eased to permit shipment direct from Carolina and Georgia to Europe south of Cape Finisterre (in northwestern Spain), vessels built and owned in the colonies were excluded from this trade, which was reserved exclusively for vessels "built in Great Britain or belonging to any of his Majesty's subjects residing in Great Britain"[11]—a deviation from the spirit of the act of 1660, which had put colonial ships on nearly the same favored footing in the colonial trade as English ships.

In 1721 Parliament prohibited the importation into the colonies of any East India products, including tea, pepper, spices, drugs, and silk and cotton fabrics, from any place except Great Britain.[12]

A year later, fur and copper were added to the list of enumerated commodities.[13]

In 1732 the export of colonial-made felt or hats was prohibited even from one colony to another. The act also forbade anyone in the colonies to make felt or hats who had not served an apprenticeship for at least seven years and any master to employ more than two apprentices other than his own sons. (Martin Bladen, a member of Parliament and of the Board of Trade, complaining that the colonies were "running into all sorts of manufactures, which must be stopped," even went so far as to propose that persons acquitted in colonial courts of having violated the act be retried in England,[14] but this extreme proposal was not adopted.)

In this same year on complaint by a member of Parliament that colonial hops were successfully competing with English in the Irish market, direct export of hops from the colonies to Ireland was prohibited.[15]

In 1733 came the Sugar Act discussed in Chapter 11.

In 1736 Parliament struck at the manufacture of colonial canvas (sailcloth) by enacting that the initial set of sails of all vessels thereafter built in the colonies must be of British-made cloth.[16]

In 1750 Parliament prohibited the erection of any new mill in the colonies for slitting, rolling, or plating iron or of any new furnace for making steel.[17]

In 1732 the Privy Council supplemented the acts of Parliament restricting colonial trade and manufacturing by an order peremptorily forbidding colonial governors to assent to any act of levying import duties on any British products, thus preventing the colonies from encouraging domestic industries by protective tariffs against British competition.[18]

The penalties for violation varied somewhat from act to act; but in general they involved forfeiture of the vessel and either the part of the cargo illegally imported or exported or the entire cargo. In some cases there was provision for a fine in addition to forfeiture, but imprisonment was provided for only in cases of violence or intimidation of customs officers.[19]

At first the colonial Governors, assisted by civilian deputies, known as "naval officers," and commanders of English naval vessels when at hand, were responsible for enforcement of the acts,[20] but, long before 1764, officers of the English customs service stationed in the colonies had become the most important enforcement agency.[21]

In 1763 there were three colonial customs districts, each having several ports of entry and supervised by a Surveyor-General. The Northern District comprised Nova Scotia, the New England colonies, New York, New Jersey, Newfoundland, and Bermuda; the Southern District, Pennsylvania, Maryland, Virginia, the Carolinas, the Bahamas, and Jamaica; and the Barbados District, Barbados, Antigua, St. Kitts, Nevis, and Montserrat.[22] According to a list prepared in 1765 or 1766, there were about two hundred officers of the colonial branch of the English customs service at that time.[23]

To assist enforcement of the restrictions on colonial navigation and trade, vessels entering or leaving colonial ports were required by acts of Parliament to give bonds and inventories for each trip and to obtain clearance papers from designated officers. Furthermore, vessels (with some specified exceptions) engaged in colonial trade must be registered in England, Ireland, or one of the colonies. In 1696, Parliament gave colonial admiralty courts, in which the judge decided questions of fact as well as of law without trial by jury, jurisdiction over certain suits for alleged violations of the English acts restricting colonial trade, and the next year several admiralty courts with judges appointed by and subject to dismissal at the pleasure of the Crown were established in the colonies.[24]

At first glance it is puzzling that, until 1764, the mainland colonists should have submitted, apparently without much protest, to this extensive British network of restrictions on their trade and manufacturing. But extensive smuggling eased the severity of some of the acts restricting colonial trade, and, as we saw in Chapter 11, important indulgences were allowed with respect to the importation of molasses from the foreign West Indies and of fresh fruit and wine from southern Europe. As to the acts restricting colonial manufacturing, these seem to have been almost dead letters before 1764.[25] Probably British manufacturers found their interest in colonial trade adequately protected by the well-enforced royal instruction forbidding governors to assent to legislation favoring local industry over British.

Furthermore, British tariff preferences and import bounties were granted to a number of products of the mainland colonies imported into Great Britain—tariff preferences on tobacco, pot and pearl ashes, hemp, pig and bar iron, raw silk, whale oil ("train oil"), pitch, tar, whalebone ("whale-fins"), and various timber products;[26] import bounties on naval stores (tar, pitch, turpentine, masts, yards, and bowsprits) and indigo. The colonists, of course, did not benefit to the full amount of the bounties. If, for example, a colonial rice planter who could sell his rice crop for £1,000 switched to indigo, for which he got, say, £900 plus a bounty of £150, his net benefit from growing indigo rather than rice would obviously be not £150, the full amount of the bounty, but only the excess of £1,050 over £1,000, or £50. But even so, the bounties, totaling £1,028,584 on naval stores for the years 1729 to 1774 and £145,022 on indigo from 1749 to 1773,[27] doubtless were of much value to the colonies where the bountied products were produced.*

Other economic benefits enjoyed by the colonists were access of colonial-built vessels to the carrying trade in Great Britain on nearly the same favorable footing as British-built vessels, thus providing a favorable market for colonial-built vessels in Great Britain; participation in the monopoly of the colonial carrying trade under the Act of 1660; liberty of colonial fishermen to cure fish on the shores of Newfoundland, Labrador, and Nova Scotia;[28] the issuance of Mediterranean passes to colonial as well as British-owned vessels as a security against capture and confiscation by North African (Barbary) corsairs;[29] and, of course, general protection by the British navy.

Also of great importance to the mainland colonies was the unrestricted freedom of exporting their products in their own ships to the British West Indies — a trade perhaps of even more value to them than the trade with the foreign West Indies and Dutch Guiana (Surinam) discussed in Chapter 11. The volume of exports from the British mainland colonies to the British West Indies in the later colonial period has been estimated at around £725,000 sterling a year, of which £500,000 represented the value of the products before shipment and £225,000 freight to the West Indies, with corresponding returns in sugar and rum, cash, and bills of exchange, all of great value to the economy of the northern colonies.[30]

It seems a fair guess that prior to 1764, except for Virginia and Maryland, the two great tobacco exporting colonies, the cost to the mainland colonies of the laxly enforced restrictions on colonial trade and manufacturing was very largely offset by the commercial advantages outlined above.

At first glance, it would seem that the British tariff preference in favor of British colonial tobacco[31] would have more than compensated

---

*Charles Ritcheson (*Mississippi Valley Historical Review*, 47 [1961]: 682–83) disputes Knollenberg's reasoning. [B. W. S.]

Virginia and Maryland for the cost to these colonies of British restrictions on colonial trade. But, unlike colonial sugar, colonial tobacco received little benefit from the British tariff preference. The British demand for British colonial tobacco was only a small fraction of the
British colonial supply available for export, over nine-tenths of the tobacco shipped to Great Britain being reexported.[32] When supply of a
commodity regularly far exceeds demand, a tariff preference is inoper-
ative unless supplemented by other protective legislation, which British
colonial tobacco did not enjoy.[33] Hence, the price of even the relatively
small part of the colonial tobacco consumed in Great Britain must
have been determined by the world price, and the price of the tobacco
reexported for sale abroad would, of course, necessarily be determined by the price in the unprotected world market. Consequently,
colonial tobacco had little if any price benefit from the British protective tariff, and the extra cost imposed by the act of 1660 of shipping the tobacco for foreign markets to Great Britain, and unloading,
reloading, and reshipping it there, was almost if not wholly a net loss.

Daniel Dulany, distinguished Maryland lawyer and pamphleteer,
calculated in 1765 that the extra freight and other expenses, incident to
the British restrictions on the export of British colonial tobacco, cost
Virginia and Maryland tobacco planters about £270,000 a year. And
Professor Lawrence A. Harper in his impressive pioneer study, "The
Effect of the Navigation Acts on the Thirteen Colonies," calculates, on
the basis of 1773, a seemingly typical year of the period involved, that
this restriction cost colonial tobacco planters at least $2,000,000 a year,
most of which fell on Virginia and Maryland. These colonies were, of
course, also burdened with a share of the extra cost incident to the
provisions of the Acts of 1663 and 1721 forbidding colonial importation of most European and all East Indian products except by way of
Great Britain, which, Harper estimates, cost the thirteen colonies at
least $500,000 a year.[34]

Another distinguished historian of our colonial period, Professor
Oliver M. Dickerson, has argued, chiefly on the basis of the falling off
in tobacco exports from the former British North American colonies
after the Revolutionary War, that the restriction on the export of colonial tobacco was not disadvantageous to the colonies. But his argu-

ment is not convincing. According to his figures, the average exports for 1790–1794, the earliest period after the Revolution tabulated by him, actually exceeded the average exports for 1767–1775, and the sharp falling off in 1805–1809[35] was during the general disruption of overseas trade incident to the Napoleonic Wars.

It seems reasonably clear that even before the more severe restrictions on colonial trade imposed by Grenville's new enforcement policy and by the American Act of 1764 discussed in the next chapter, Virginia and Maryland were, on balance, heavy losers by the British regulation of colonial trade.

CHAPTER 15

NEW RESTRICTIONS ON COLONIAL
TRADE AND CURRENCY

THE AMERICAN ACT of 1764 not only laid taxes for revenue on the colonies but imposed the following new restrictions on colonial overseas trade. Hides, skins, potash, and several other colonial products were added to the list of enumerated commodities which, under the Act of 1660, could legally be exported from the colonies only to Great Britain or another British colony; direct export of colonial lumber and iron to continental Europe or Ireland was prohibited; and vessels were now prohibited from going from Great Britain to the colonies unless, with a few exceptions, their entire cargo had been loaded in Great Britain.[1] Heretofore, a vessel qualified to engage in the colonial trade could carry a cargo of, say, fish from Boston to Jamaica, pick up some sugar there, proceed to London for further cargo and return with a full cargo to a colonial port. Henceforth, if the vessel on its return voyage took cargo in Great Britain it must first unload its other cargo there, pay the British customs duties, if any, and reload before it could legally proceed to the colonies. The act also discouraged the flourishing direct wine trade between the colonies and Madeira, the Azores, and the Canary Islands, not by outright prohibition but by levying an extremely heavy duty payable in the colonies on wine of these islands directly imported.[2]

Far more serious, however, than the additional restrictions on over-seas trade was the burden on intercolonial trade imposed by Sections 29 and 23 of the Act. Section 29 provided that "no Goods, Wares or Merchandizes, of any Kind whatsoever, shall be shipped or laden on board any Ship or Vessel in any of the British Colonies or Plantations in America, to be carried from thence to any other British Colony or Plantation, without a Sufferance or Warrant first had and obtained from the Collector or other proper Officer of the Customs . . . : and the Master . . . shall . . . take out a Cocket or Cockets expressing the Quantity and Quality of the Goods, and Marks of the Package, so laden." And Section 23 specified that every vessel carrying any non-enumerated colonial product, such as corn, wheat, lumber, meat, dairy products, etc., must give bond to pay duty on any foreign colonial mo-lasses taken aboard during the course of the voyage. A new bond (£1,000 if the vessel was under a hundred tons, £2,000 if a hundred tons or over) must be given each trip and failure to give the bond or to observe its terms subjected the vessel and its entire cargo to forfeiture.[3]

Under these provisions, a farmer or merchant shipping local farm produce on a small sloop from one colony to another was now re-quired to go to the nearest customs office, no matter how far from his home or place of business, file a detailed invoice of what he planned to ship, give bond, and obtain a customs cocket, or run the risk of hav-ing his vessel and cargo seized and forfeited. As William Allen of Pennsylvania wrote to an English correspondent in November 1764, the owner of a boat on the Delaware river carrying merely a load of staves, pig iron, or tar from New Jersey to Philadelphia must now "go thirty or forty miles or more to the nearest customs house to give Bond, the charge of which and his travelling, makes this Burthen In-tollerable," and similar complaints were made by others.[4]

Heretofore customs officials in the colonies had not required clear-ances from small vessels carrying nonenumerated products in coast-wise and river trade. In 1733, Governor Jonathan Belcher of Massa-chusetts at Boston, asking for the appointment of a Collector of Customs at Plymouth, wrote, "the inhabitants along that shore have thought it a great fatigue and inconvenience to come hither to enter and clear every vessel . . . that goes upon a foreign voyage," thus implying that shippers were not required to enter and clear vessels engaged in coastwise trade. In 1753, Governor James Glen of South Carolina, writing from Charleston, center of the trade of South Carolina and large parts of North Carolina and Georgia, said, "as our Produce is bulky, most Planters keep large decked boats to bring it to market from the distant Rivers and Plantations . . . ; these Boats are kept as Coasters, but they are capable of performing foreign Voyages, and [yet] are under no regulation of entering, or Clearing at any Office." And in 1761, Allen, reporting a shipment of wine from Philadelphia to Virginia, said, "I have shipped them in a Shallop . . . ; she has not cleared out from our Custom-House, it not being usual for these small Coasters."[5]

Furthermore, the act of 1757, a British war measure limiting the export of grain, pork, and several other nonenumerated colonial products during the war and requiring a cocket and bond to control the shipments of these products, exempted shipments "across rivers by common ferries, or up or down the said rivers, or across harbours where clearances have not usually been taken" thus showing that the practice of not requiring customs clearances for shipments of this kind was known and sanctioned by the British Government.[6]

To appreciate the immense value to the colonies of the previous freedom of coastwise traffic from customs regulations, it must be recalled that in colonial days when roads were few and extremely bad, bridges at or near the mouths of the larger rivers not yet built, and railroads, of course, nonexistent, carriage by water was of much greater relative importance than it is in this same region today. Among the most animated sights in colonial America, frequently commented on by visitors from abroad, was the throng of small sailing vessels, the trucks and freight cars of the period, carrying cargo along the Atlantic coast and in the bays and tidal reaches of the rivers.[7]

The new regulation of coastwise traffic would unquestionably assist the enforcement of the export duties levied by the act of 1673 on intercolonial shipments of enumerated commodities and of the ban on intercolonial shipments of wool, woolen goods, felt, and hats imposed by the acts of 1699 and 1732. But a British Minister who had any serious concern for colonial well-being and the retention of colonial good will would nevertheless have refrained from enforcement measures so disruptive of the free flow of intercolonial commerce.[8]

Several other enforcement provisions of the new act, though less serious, were extremely galling.

The first was designed to make colonial customs officers, including naval commanders stationed in colonial waters, less cautious than before in seizing and bringing suit for condemnation of suspected vessels and cargo. Heretofore, though tempted to seize and sue for condemnation by a reward of a third or half of the net proceeds of sale if the seized property was condemned,[9] officers were deterred from proceeding without strong evidence, because of the common law rule holding them personally liable for damages to the owner if the suit was dismissed. The new act encouraged less caution by providing that, no matter what the owner's actual damages might be, he should recover only twopence damages from the officer making the seizure if the trial judge certified probable cause for the seizure. Moreover, if such certification was refused by the trial judge, any four members of the English Customs Board could authorize reimbursement of the officer for any damages collected from him.[10]

Another provision authorized the establishment of a new admiralty court for the trial and condemnation of vessels and cargo for alleged violations of the acts of trade anywhere in colonial waters. Previously such suits could be brought only in a court within the colony where the alleged violation occurred. Now the seizing officer could bring suit for condemnation no matter where in America the alleged offense took place.[11] This provision would have been harsh enough even if the new court had been established at an important, centrally located port, such as New York or Philadelphia, but it was in fact established at the raw, struggling village of Halifax, Nova Scotia, remote from all the more important British settlements in America.[12]

This choice was apparently made at the suggestion of Admiral Lord Colville, in command of the British fleet in North American waters, who wrote from Halifax to the Secretary to the Admiralty suggesting that judges of admiralty courts elsewhere than at Halifax might be unduly influenced by mobs or "interest in the Welfare of their Neighbours"; and that this would be "avoided by sending the

Prizes to be tried at this Place, which would besides give great Encouragement to this young Colony, and the Produce turn to very good account, as Commissions for purchasing [ships and cargo condemned by the new court] would be sent from several of the other provinces."[13]

Establishment of the new court at remote Halifax was the more embittering because of a collateral section, Section 45, of the Act of 1764 providing that "if any ship or goods shall be seized for any cause of forfeiture, and any dispute shall arise whether the customs and duties for such goods have been paid, or the same have been lawfully imported or exported, or concerning the growth, product or manufacture of such goods, or the place from whence such goods were brought . . . the proof thereof shall lie upon the owner or claimer of such ship or goods, and not upon the officer who shall seize or stop the same; any law, custom, or usage, to the contrary notwithstanding."[14] So, under the new act, the commander of one of the British naval vessels now stationed in colonial waters could seize a ship or goods or both at New York, Philadelphia, Norfolk, Virginia, or Charleston, South Carolina, for an alleged violation of one of the acts of trade, hire a lawyer to bring suit against the seized property in the distant admiralty court at Halifax, and, without offering any evidence in support of the allegation, have the property condemned and sold (pocketing half the net proceeds) unless the owner appeared and proved there had been no violation.

The Act of 1764 also made clear for the first time that all suits for penalties imposed by any of the acts of trade or customs applying to the colonies could, at the election of the person bringing suit, be brought in admiralty, thus enabling the plaintiff to deprive the defendant of trial by jury in any suit brought under these acts.[15]

Most of the enforcement provisions in the Act of 1764 were proposed by the Commissioners of Customs who, at the order of the Treasury, submitted a long, detailed report in September 1763 recommending many changes in the acts of trade and customs pertaining to the colonies, almost all of which the Treasury ordered the Commissioners to embody in the draft of a bill for submission to Parliament.[16]

The only known official opposition to the proposed bill came from William Wood, venerable Secretary to the Commissioners, a holdover from the Newcastle regime, who wrote Charles Jenkinson, joint Secretary to the Treasury, "I wish that everything which may have been thought of respecting the Plantations may be defered another year, except continuing the Act of the 6th of George 2nd [the Sugar Act] for a year, or longer. For if what I have occasionally heard mentioned be true, I conceive you want [lack] information of several things from the Plantations . . . I was once young but am now old; yet as they are of such advantage to their Mother Country, their welfare is still uppermost in my thoughts."[17]

Besides laying new restrictions on colonial trade, Parliament also greatly restricted the issue of colonial currency.* In response to the complaints of merchants trading to Virginia and North Carolina of their losses from colonial currency inflation, the Board of Trade and Privy Council recommended passage of an act of Parliament applying to the colonies outside New England, similar to an act already applying to those in New England.[18] The recommendation was adopted, and a bill forbidding the issue of paper currency having the quality of legal tender by the colonies previously not restricted, was passed by Parliament in 1764.[19]

The new British restrictions on colonial trade and currency were accompanied by a business depression of exceptional severity in most of the mainland colonies.[20]

In May 1764, Nicholas Brown and Company of Providence, Rhode Island, wrote their New York correspondent, David Van Horne, that "all business seems to wear a gloom not before seen in America." Van Horne was equally unhappy. He had never, he wrote, known a time "when money was so scarce and difficult to get" nor trade "so dull and extremely declined." This was confirmed by Jonathan Trumbull, Jr., of Connecticut who wrote from New York City in June 1764, "Business in this town is very much stagnated, Cash excessive scarce. . . . The Prospect is really discouraging, the Sound of Terror every Day encreasing."[21]

Connecticut was no less hard hit. In July 1764, Jared Ingersoll of New Haven wrote, "I have lately travailed through the interior parts

---

* See Joseph Albert Ernst, *Money and Politics in America, 1755–1775: A Study in the Currency Act of 1764 and the Political Economy of Revolution* (Chapel Hill: University of North Carolina Press, 1973). [B. W. S.]

of this and New York Province, and every where found the farmer complaining that he could not Sell his wheat etc. The English West-Indians by monopolising (their great object) the above trade have so lowered the prices of the Several articles abovementioned that the Merchant here cannot buy them without loss, nor can they be raised by the farmer so as to answer; indeed the English West-Indians cannot take off the half of what we raise and have to spare." Likewise, John Ledyard of Hartford bemoaned "the Strange Scene of Bankruptcy and ruins" in the colony, and Joseph Trumbull of Connecticut, on returning from England in January 1765, wrote that business was "embarrassed and Clog'd . . . even beyond what I had imagined."[22]

Business was bad in Boston, too. Trade was reported very dull there as early as June 1764, and the failure of a number of well-known Boston merchants in the latter half of the year culminated in the bankruptcy of Nathaniel Wheelwright, one of the leading merchants of New England, whose failure, in January 1765, according to a letter from James Otis to English clients, "has given as great a shock to credit here as your South Sea Bubble did in England some years ago." The genial Boston merchant John Rowe, as we know from his familiar diary, was so "much out of order today, occasion'd by the distress this town is in" over Wheelwright's failure, as to keep him home from church. The picture was apparently much the same in New Hampshire, where, it was said, "Merchants and Farmers are breaking and all things going into confusion."[23]

Conditions at Philadelphia were little better. In May 1764, Samuel Rhoads, Jr., wrote his London correspondents, "scarcity of Money added to the Probability of having no more Paper Currency made here, Renders Trade very dull as well as very precarious. Have therefore contracted my Fall order, which I have enclos'd," and in October reported "the late Acts of Parliament for restraining our Trade and the medium of it, our Paper Currency, and the Prospect of further Impositions [so] damps the Spirits of our Customers that they now handle English Goods with fearful apprehensions, least the Means of making Payment shou'd be utterly out of their Power." The letterbooks of Benjamin Marshall, Daniel Roberdeau, and William Allen, merchants of Philadelphia, tell much the same story, epitomized in the words of a contributor to the *Pennsylvania Journal*, "Trade is become dull, Money very scarce, Contracts decrease, Law Suits increase."[24]

Virginia was apparently hardest hit of all. In June 1764, William Allason, a Scotch merchant on the Rappahannock river, wrote a British correspondent, "Goods in the retail way sells at a very great profit; very few articles sold for less than 200 pcent advance and often higher, but the misfortune is the Planters are so much in Debt, they are not able to pay their former Ballances . . . I believe there never was so many suits depending in this Country as is at this time; . . . in some Countys the People have agreed to defend one another against the officers — money . . . so scarce that there is exceeding few purchasers for any thing that is sold by virtue of Execution etc.; negroes that was purchased 2 years ago are now to be sold at not much more than half of what was given for them."[25]

A month later, Allason wrote another of his correspondents for "a pair of Pistols . . . small, for the conveniency of carrying in a side Pockett," because, "as it is sometimes Dangerous in Travelling through our wooden Country, Particularly at this time when the Planters are pressed for old Ballances, we find it necessary to carry with us some defensive Weapons." "Poor Virginia," exclaimed John Baylor of Caroline County, "what art thou reduced to, held in scorn and derision by the merchants of great Brittain and torn to pieces by theirs and our [own] country law suits." And Arthur Lee of Virginia denounced "the British merchants, who fix, like cankers, on their [the colonial planters'] estates, and utterly consume them."[26]

Some compensating benefits or seeming benefits to colonial trade were, to be sure, granted by Parliament in 1764. Acts were passed permitting salt to be imported directly from any part of Europe to Quebec and rice to be exported from South Carolina and Georgia to any part of America south of these colonies;[27] granting a bounty on British imports of colonial hemp and flax[28] (to discourage the manufacture of cordage and linen in the colonies by drawing off the colonial supply of raw material);[29] permitting the importation into Great Britain, nearly duty free, of whalebone ("whale-fins") from whales caught by colonial as well as by British vessels in the river or Gulf of St. Lawrence or along the colonial coasts; and extending for some years several existing acts favorable to colonial trade.[30] But these benefits were far more than offset by the new restrictions on colonial trade and the much more rigorous enforcement of those already on the statute books.

Hard times; British warships patrolling the American coast to break up the once flourishing trade with the foreign West Indies; British officials in the interior enforcing uneconomic and confiscatory laws against the cutting of white pine; the highest prelate of the Church of England encouraging measures alarming and offensive to colonial Dissenters; drastic steps by the Board of Trade and Privy Council to curtail home rule in the royal colonies; a British Commander-in-Chief embroiling a number of colonies in one of the most costly Indian wars in their history and then failing to protect the frontier settlers or even to punish the rebel Indians; and, above all, the recent acts of Parliament levying taxes towards the upkeep of a large, unrequested, and ineffective force of British troops stationed in North America and imposing new and severe restrictions on colonial trade and currency— this was the accumulation of grievances giving rise to the surge of protest by British colonists of North America, individually and through their legislatures, to which we now turn.

CHAPTER 16

INDIVIDUAL PROTESTS

THE COLONIAL reaction to the American Act of 1764 was foreshadowed, before the bill for the act had come before Parliament, in a letter of about March 1, 1764, from Colonel Eliphalet Dyer of Windham, Connecticut, in London, to an unidentified correspondent in America. Dyer, forty-two years old, a graduate of Yale and the leading lawyer of northeastern Connecticut, had served for fifteen years in the Connecticut Assembly, headed a Connecticut regiment during the French and Indian War, and, in 1762, was elected to the Governor's Council, of which he was still a member.[1]

"About a Fortnight since," wrote Dyer, "Mr. G_____lle moved the House of Commons for Liberty to bring in a Bill in order to provide a Fund for Defraying the Expences of protecting, securing and defending America, which contains the several Articles of Duties mentioned in the enclosed Resolves. . . . But may it not be concluded that those Regiments destined for America, for the support of which those Methods are taking, are not primarily for our Defence (as they are undesired by us) but rather as a standing Army, to be as a Rod and Check over the Colonies, to enforce those Injunctions which are to be laid upon us, and at the same Time to oblige us to be at the Expence of their Support."

"If the Colonies," he continued, "do not now unite, and use their most vigorous Endeavours in all proper Ways, to avert this impending

Blow, they may for the future, bid Farewell to Freedom and Liberty, burn their Charters, and make the best of Thraldom and Slavery. For if we can have our Interests and Estates taken away, and disposed of without our Consent, or having any Voice therein, and by those whose Interest as well as Inclination it may be to shift the Burden off from themselves under Pretence of protecting and defending America, why may they not as well endeavour to raise Millions upon us to defray the Expences of the last, or any future War?"

Another early protest came from thirty-two-year-old Richard Henry Lee of Chantilly, Westmoreland County, Virginia, third of the six well-known sons of Thomas Lee and Hannah Ludwell Lee. (Philip Ludwell and Thomas Ludwell were older brothers, Francis Lightfoot, William, and Arthur, younger.) Four of the six brothers were at this time members of the Virginia Legislature; Philip had succeeded his father as a member of the Council, while Thomas, Richard, and Francis were members of the House of Burgesses for Stafford, Westmoreland, and Loudoun counties respectively.[2]

"Many late determinations of the great, on your side of the water," wrote Lee to a British correspondent, "seem to prove a resolution, to oppress North America with the iron hand of power, unrestrained by any sentiment, drawn from reason, the liberty of mankind, or the genius of their own government. 'Tis said the House of Commons readily resolved, that it had 'a right to tax the subject here, without the consent of his representative'; and that, in consequence of this, they had proceeded to levy on us a considerable annual sum, for the support of a body of troops to be kept up in this quarter. Can it be supposed that those brave adventurous Britons, who originally conquered and settled these countries, through great dangers to themselves and benefit to the mother country, meant thereby to deprive themselves of the blessings of that free government of which they were members, and to which they had an unquestionable right? . . . And as certain it is, that 'the free possession of property, the right to be governed by laws made by our representatives, and the illegality of taxation without consent,' are such essential principles of the British constitution, that it is a matter of wonder how men, who have almost imbibed them in their mother's milk, whose very atmosphere is charged with them, should be of opinion that the people of America were to be taxed without consulting their representatives!"

"It will not avail," Lee continued, "to say that these restrictions on the right of taxation, are meant to restrain only the sovereign, and not Parliament. The intention of the constitution is apparent, to prevent unreasonable impositions on the people; and no method is so likely to do that, as making their own consent necessary, for the establishment of such impositions. . . . Possibly this step of the mother country, though intended to oppress and keep us low, in order to secure our dependence, may be subversive of this end. Poverty and oppression, among those whose minds are filled with ideas of British liberty, may introduce a virtuous industry, with a train of generous and manly sentiments, which, when in future they become supported by numbers, may produce a fatal resentment of parental care being converted into tyrannical usurpation. I hope you will pardon so much on this subject. My mind has been warmed, and I hardly know where to stop."[3]

Even John Watts, the New York merchant whose letters are usually models of geniality, was somewhat soured by the new act. "The Colonys," he wrote, "are extremely incensed at the Treatment they have received from the Mother Country. . . . They seem to wish Canada again French; it made them of some Consequence, which Consequence they lost when it was conquered, if their reasoning be just. They certainly would not grant a Man for that or any other use was it to be done over again. I hear so much of it in Conversation, I have no Stomach left to write upon the Subject."[4]

An exceptionally able statement of the colonial position was made by Chief Justice Hutchinson of Massachusetts in a memorandum enclosed in a letter of July 23, 1764, to Richard Jackson, replying to a letter from Jackson of April 16, now missing but evidently written in defense of the recent revenue act. The memorandum was important not only in content but because of the person who wrote it, for Hutchinson, "tall, slender, fair complexioned, fair spoken," a "gentleman of capacity and erudition,"[5] was easily one of the most distinguished New Englanders of his day.*

---

*For Hutchinson's ideas on the empire, see Bernard Bailyn, *The Ordeal of Thomas Hutchinson* (Cambridge, Mass.: Harvard University Press, 1974), especially ch. 3. [B. W. S.]

Graduated from Harvard in 1727, Hutchinson entered business with his father, a Boston merchant who was long a member of the provincial Council. A member himself of the New Brick Church of Boston, the younger Hutchinson had highly influential connections in the dominant Congregational fold in Boston. His sister Sarah was the wife (by 1764, the widow) of the Reverend William Welsteed, pastor of the New Brick Church, and his sister Hannah was the wife of the Reverend Samuel Mather, son of the famous Cotton Mather and pastor of the Bennet Street Church. Hutchinson was also closely connected by marriage and friendship with Andrew Oliver, a pillar of Old South Church as well as Secretary of Massachusetts. In 1737, Hutchinson was elected one of Boston's four representatives in the Massachusetts Assembly, and from then until 1765 was almost continuously a member of the Assembly or of the provincial Council. In 1758 he was appointed Lieutenant-Governor of Massachusetts by the Crown and two years later, though not a lawyer by training, was appointed Chief Justice of the Superior Court by Governor Francis Bernard—to the chagrin of James Otis who had expected his father, James Otis, Sr., to get the next vacant seat on the Court.[6]

Hutchinson's part in the Court's decision to issue general writs of assistance was discussed in Chapter 4. A few months later, he joined with the other judges in deciding against the province in a suit by Massachusetts against Charles Paxton, Surveyor of Customs and Register of the Vice-Admiralty Court in Boston. Writing in March 1762 to a correspondent in England concerning the latter case, Hutchinson said, "This trial, the writs of Assistance and my pernicious principles about the currency, have taken away a great number of friends." But he evidently still had more friends than opponents in the Legislature, for he was reelected to the Council soon afterward and again in 1763, 1764, and 1765.[7]

In his memorandum to Jackson, Hutchinson conceded the right of Parliament to levy taxes for revenue on the colonies in an emergency; but he strongly argued against the propriety of doing so under existing circumstances. Pointing to the compact between England and Scotland in the Act of Union of 1707, guaranteeing that Parliament would not tax the Scotch except in the manner and proportion specified in the act, and maintaining that Parliament could not disregard this compact except "for the sake of the publick safety," Hutchinson argued that the provisions in the colonial charters and commissions to the royal Governors granting the colonists the privileges and immunities of English subjects, having been acted on by the colonists in settling the colonies, were likewise compacts. Hence, these too could not honorably be disregarded except for the sake of the public safety, which was not then in danger.[8]

Another important point made by Hutchinson was in reply to a distinction drawn by Jackson between so-called "external" taxes, import and export duties, on the one hand, and "internal" taxes, including stamp taxes, on the other. Jackson thought the first acceptable in principle as a regulation of trade and the latter alone objectionable. This distinction, Hutchinson pointed out, was fallacious when, as in the case of the American Act of 1764, the external taxes were admittedly for revenue and not primarily for the regulation of trade. "How," in this case, said he, "are the Privileges of the People less affected than by an internal tax? Is it any difference to me whether I pay three pounds ten shillings for a Pipe of wine to an officer of Impost [customs] or whether I pay the same Sum by an excise of ninepence per Gallon to an excise Officer?" And he made the same point in pointing out to Ebenezer Silliman of Connecticut the fallacy of assuming all "duties upon trade to be imposed for the sake of regulating trade, whereas the professed design of the duties by the late act is to raise a revenue."

Hutchinson also questioned the validity of Jackson's assumption that the colonists ought willingly to accept British taxation in gratitude for British protection of the colonies at great expense in the late war. "Let me ask," wrote Hutchinson in reply to this, "whether it was from a parental Affection to the Colonists and to save them from french Vassalage that Britain was at this Expence or was it from the fear of losing that advantageous trade she had so long carried on with her Colonies?"

Hutchinson's remarks as to requiring the colonists to pay for the British troops stationed in North America are also highly interesting. "I am very sensible," he wrote, "that if in any future wars any Nation of Europe should make the colonies their object, a British Navy must protect or they will become a prey and in case of such a war I cannot doubt the Colonies would contribute as liberally to their own protection as they have done in the last. But when there is peace in Europe what occasion is there for any national expence in America. . . . New York, Pensilvania, Maryland, Virginia and the Carolinas are as able to defend their respective frontiers as the New England Colonies were to defend theirs and if they had no aid from the Crown they would do it. The Indians may harass them for a short time but as soon as the Inhabitants have learned to hunt the Indians as the New England Men did in their own territories and lay waste their Corn fields and break up their Settlements they will grow tired and sue for peace. And as the Governments who have been molested heretofore have born the charge of their own defence it seems reasonable that those Governments who are now molested should bear their Charges and no doubt they had rather do the whole of it by a tax of their own raising than pay their proportion in any other way."

The unreasonableness of taxing the colonists for the support of British regiments, unsuited for Indian warfare and unrequested and undesired by them, was pointed out by others besides Hutchinson. Jared Ingersoll wrote his English friend Thomas Whately, "You say America can and ought to Contribute to its own defence; we one and all say the same on this Side the water—we only differ about the means; we perhaps should first of all Rescind great part of the present Expence and what remains should difray by the Application of our own force and Strength." And Cortlandt Skinner of New Jersey wrote Governor Boone of South Carolina, "The protection of the colonies is made the pretence for taxing them. This is assistance indeed. Garrisons may be necessary at Quebec and Montreal, but what occasion is there for garrisons and forts hundreds of miles in the Indian country. These are so far from protecting, that they are the very cause of our Indian wars, and the monstrous expenses attending them. . . . All we want with them is their trade, which we can never enjoy with any advantage until we remove their Jealousy [suspicion]. When this is done we shall live in all the security we have heretofore enjoyed, when a few independent Companies were sufficient for the continent. And why cannot we do without so many regiments when every [European] enemy is removed at least a thousand miles from our borders?"[9]

As pointed out by Dyer in the letter quoted at the beginning of the chapter and stressed by Governor Stephen Hopkins of Rhode Island in his *The Rights of Colonies Examined* (1764), the most serious objection to the tax was the establishment of a precedent for future taxes. "Whatever burdens are laid upon the Americans," wrote Hopkins, "will be so much taken off the Britons; and the doing this, will soon be extremely popular; . . . the [British] people's private interest will be concerned, and will govern them; they will have such and only such representatives as will act agreeably to this their interests."[10]

This danger was particularly grave because of the temptation to exploit the colonists, as the people of Great Britain and Ireland long had been exploited, as a source of public revenue to be spent in excessive salaries, sinecures, and unearned pensions to members of the British ruling class.[11] With the Government finding it difficult "to find pasturage enough for the beasts that they must feed"[12] in the heavily grazed British Isles, and with India reserved as the private domain of the British East India Company, once the precedent for taxing the colonists for revenue was established, the natural place to turn for further pasturage would be the relatively uncropped British colonies in America.

The seriousness of this danger to the colonies was pointed out by a number of colonists familiar with the situation in Great Britain. Otis in his *Considerations On Behalf of the Colonists* wrote, "If places, pensions and dependencies shall be ever increased in proportion to new resources instead of carefully applying such resources to the clearing off former incumbrances, the game may be truly infinite"; and Daniel Dulany in his *Considerations on the Propriety of Imposing Taxes in the British Colonies* . . . maintained that the solution for Great Britain's financial problem lay not in taxing the colonies but in "the Reduction of exhorbitant Salaries, the Abatement of extravagant, and the Abolition of illegal Perquisites, the Extinction of useless Places, or the disbanding of undeserving or ill deserving Pensioners."[13]

Dulany's fellow Marylander, Charles Carroll of Carollton,* demanded to know "what security remains for our property" if "a set of

---

*On Carroll, consult Ronald Hoffman, *Princes of Ireland: A Carroll Saga, 1500–1782* (Chapel Hill: University of North Carolina Press, 2000); Pauline Maier, *The Old Revolutionaries: Political Lives in the Age of Samuel Adams* (New York: Alfred A. Knopf, 1980), ch. 5. [B. W. S.]

men at so great a distance, so little acquainted with our circumstances, and not immediately affected with the taxes laid upon us," were conceded the right to tax the colonies. "Men," he went on to say, "who have been so profuse and lavish of their constituents' money—will they be sparing of ours?"[14] And the Reverend Ezra Stiles, pastor of the Second Congregational Church of Newport, Rhode Island (later President of Yale), claiming for the colonists the protection of the "fundamental Principle of the British or rather English, Constitution that no Body of the King's Subjects be taxed but by their own Consent," added "Or must there be an american List of Pensioners, and we [like Ireland] be saddled with supporting Pensioners who hate and dispise us?"[15]

The colonial protests were accompanied by efforts in most of the northern colonies to curtail imports from Great Britain and the West Indies and to promote local manufacturing.* Ingersoll wrote Whately, "the more wealthy merchants in N. York and Boston have turned to our own Manufactures, urging the absolute necessity of it. They have actually Entered into Associations, have advanced monies and set number of hands to Spinning, have erected works for the Distilling of Corn Spirits [that is, whisky, to replace rum], are planning ways and means for the increase of the Stock of Sheep in this Country, and have gone so far as actually to send to Europe for Artificers in the several branches of the Woolen and Linnen manufacture." And throughout the year, the northern colonial newspapers carried accounts of concerted movements at Boston, New Haven, New York, and Elizabeth, New Jersey, to abstain from the use of imported luxury products, such as lace, ruffles, mourning clothes, and foreign liquor; to use native leather instead of imported cloth for work clothes; to establish woolen mills for the manufacture of cloth from native wool and to build up the flocks of colonial sheep.[16]

In most of the publicity regarding the disuse of imported luxuries and the encouragement of colonial manufacturing, there was no intimation of putting pressure on Parliament to repeal or modify the act of

---

*Edmund S. Morgan, "The Puritan Ethic and the American Revolution," *William and Mary Quarterly*, 3rd ser., 24 (1967): 3–43, places the boycott of British goods in a moral context. [B. W. S.]

1764; only the immediate advantage to the colonies of economizing and of developing home industries was mentioned. (The declared objects, for example, of the Society for the Promotion of Arts, Agriculture and Economy of New York City were solely "to advance husbandry, promote Manufactures, and suppress Luxury.")[17] But, in at least two instances, a boycott by the colonists to influence the action of Parliament was plainly suggested. An anonymous writer in the *Providence Gazette*, urging the increase of colonial manufacturing and reduction in the consumption of sugar and molasses, declared this "must end in a Repeal of the Tax Act," and the *Connecticut Courant*, commenting on the "disposition of many of the inhabitants of this and the neighbouring governments to cloath themselves with their own manufactures" and on "the severity of the new a____t of p_____t," added that the colonies must "unite in such measures as *will be effectual* to obtain redress."[18]

One other manifestation of colonial resentment at this time must be noted: the outbreaks at Newport, Rhode Island, and New York City against the impressment of colonial seamen for the royal navy.

Cruel at best, impressment was particularly so in the case of colonial sailors because, as Governor Trelawny of Jamaica pointed out, men on vessels from the North American colonies were generally only part-time sailors, most of whom had "small familys and propertys at home, and when they are press'd their desire is so strong to return to their families and the life they were used to" that, if not able to escape, they were likely to "die soon."[19] Even in time of war, when the British navy was defending the colonial seacoast and shipping, there was much colonial opposition to impressment not only among sailors but among the shipowners and merchants whose trade was interrupted by impressment raids on merchantmen crews. Though the violent outbreak in the great Boston impressment riot of November 1747, during King George's War, is best known, the opposition extended to other colonial ports, and broke out again in the French and Indian War.[20] Indeed, according to Franklin, writing in 1759, merchants at Boston and New York had become indifferent to whether or not naval vessels were stationed there to protect their trade from enemy raids because of "the Pressing of their men and thereby disappointing Voyages often hurting their Trade more than the Enemy hurts it."[21] Now that the vessels were stationed in colonial waters not primarily to protect the colonists but to enforce British restrictions on their trade, colonial impressment was, of course, less tolerable than ever.

The resentment was all the greater because, though the legality of impressment was firmly established in Great Britain by 1764, its legality in the mainland colonies was far from clear. In 1708, during the War of the Spanish Succession, Parliament passed an act, entitled "An Act for the encouragement of the trade to America," providing "That no mariner or other person who shall serve on board, or be retained to serve on board, any privateer, or trading ship or vessel, that shall be imployed in any part of America, nor any mariner, or other person, being on shoar in any part thereof, shall be liable to be impressed . . . by any . . . officers of or belonging to any of her Majesty's ships of war . . . unless such mariner shall have before deserted from such ship." Some of the other sections of the act were limited to "the continuance of the present war" but there was no such limitation in the section relating to impressment.[22]

The Crown's legal advisers gave opinions in 1716 and 1740 that the act as a whole expired at the end of the war; but they gave no reasons for their opinions and there is nothing in the language of the act of 1708 or the reported proceedings of Parliament supporting these opinions. Nor did an act of 1746 relating to impressment in the British West Indies repeal the Act of 1708.[23] The question of the legality of impressments in the colonies arose in the case of Michael Corbet, indicted for murder in Massachusetts for having killed an officer trying to impress him; but the indictment was dismissed without occasion to pass on whether the provision of the act of 1708 for colonial exemption from impressment was still in force in the mainland colonies,[24] and this question was apparently still undecided at the outbreak of the Revolution.

Late in the spring of 1764, Admiral Lord Colville, commander of the British fleet in North American waters, sent four small armed vessels, including the *St. John* and the *Chaleur*, to visit the principal harbors between Casco Bay in Massachusetts (now Maine) to Cape Henlopen in Delaware to raise men by enlistment, if possible, but, if not, to impress them.[25]

On arrival at Newport, Rhode Island, the *St. John* impressed a man who escaped. A party sent ashore to recapture him was attacked by a crowd who seized the officer in charge and stoned and drove away the other members of the party. Later in the day, the acting commander of the *St. John* refused to permit a provincial civil officer to board the schooner with a warrant for the arrest of two members of the crew implicated in a recent theft ashore. Whereupon, members of the Rhode Island Council instructed the gunner of the provincial fort in Newport harbor to prevent the vessel from leaving the harbor, and, when her commander set sail to join a British warship lying at the mouth of the harbor, the gunner fired several shots at the *St. John*, one of which pierced her mainsail.[26] Soon afterward (July 10, 1764) the *Chaleur* impressed a man in each of five fishing vessels in an unnamed harbor off Long Island. Though the men were released the next day on threat of death to the *Chaleur*'s master if they were held, a barge from the *Chaleur* was seized by a mob in New York City, dragged to the front of the City Hall, and burned.[27]

Thus at the very time when new issues were causing severe friction between the colonies and Great Britain, revival, under exceptionally aggravating circumstances, of the old issue of impressment to help man the royal navy contributed to the rising tide of colonial indignation against the mother country.

LEGISLATIVE PROTESTS—
MASSACHUSETTS AND
CONNECTICUT

NEWS OF THE resolutions for colonial taxation for revenue in the House of Commons reached Massachusetts early in May 1764, and at a Boston town meeting on May 15 a committee headed by Richard Dana, a Boston lawyer, and including Samuel Adams, not yet in the Legislature or much in the public eye, was chosen to draw up instructions for the town's four representatives in the Massachusetts House. These representatives were a distinguished group, consisting of Thomas Cushing, the merchant whose correspondence as to renewal of the old Sugar Act was quoted in Chapter 11, Royall Tyler, also a leading Boston merchant, and the lawyers James Otis and Oxenbridge Thacher whom we met in Chapter 4.

The committee's draft of the instructions, approved at a town meeting on May 24, after expressing concern over the proposed duties for revenue on colonial imports and exports, continued, "But what still [more] hightens our Apprehensions is that those unexpected proceedings may be preparatory to new Taxations upon us; For if our Trade may be taxed why not our Lands? Why not the produce of our Lands

and every Thing we possess or make use of? This we apprehend anni-
hilates our Charter Right to Govern and Tax ourselves—It strikes at
our British Privileges which as we have never forfeited them we hold
in common with our Fellow Subjects who are Natives of Britain. . . .
¶ We therefore earnestly recommend it to you to use your utmost endeavors, to obtain in the General Assembly all necessary Instructions
and advice to our Agent . . . to remonstrate [claim] for us all those
Rights and Privileges which Justly belong to us either by Charter or
Birth. ¶ As his Majestys other North American Colonys are embark'd
with us in this most important Bottom, we further desire you to use
your Endeavors, that their weight may be added to that of this Province; that by the united Applications of all who are Aggrieved, All
may happily obtain Redress."[1]

Boston's priority in public action in this case, as in so many others
throughout the Revolutionary period, does not warrant the conclusion
that its inhabitants were at this period more alert, freedom loving, or
contentious than those of the other colonial towns (New York, Philadelphia, and Charleston) of similar size and importance. Being nearer
to England than these other towns, Boston was likely to be the first to
receive word of new measures taken in England, and, having in common with other Massachusetts towns, a form of local government enabling any small, interested group of citizens to secure a town meeting,[2] had means at hand for prompt action by the town.

Soon after the Massachusetts Legislature convened at the end of
May, the House chose a committee headed by the Speaker, Samuel
White of Taunton, and including Otis, Thacher, and Cushing, to consider recent letters from the colony's London Agent, Jasper Mauduit,
several of which dealt with the proposed levy by Parliament of taxes
for revenue on the colonies. The House also chose a committee consisting of all four of the Boston members and Captain Edward Sheafe
of neighboring Charlestown to correspond with the assemblies of the
other British colonies on the North American continent, which, on
June 25, 1764, sent a circular letter to them urging united action.[3]

The report of the committee to consider Mauduit's letters took the
form of proposed instructions to him, condemning the high rate of
duty levied on foreign molasses by the American Act of 1764; direct-

ing him to try to secure the repeal of the act and prevent the imposi-
tion of any other taxes on the colonies; and stating that measures
would be taken to have the London Agents of other colonies cooperate with him. On the question of Parliament's right to tax the colonies,
the instructions were somewhat self-contradictory, at one point tending to deny the right of Parliament to impose any kind of taxes on the
colonies, at another suggesting the expediency of reducing the rate of
duty on foreign molasses imported into the colonies to a penny a gallon as a means of raising a revenue. The instructions were approved
by the House, which ordered them sent to Mauduit together with a
paper entitled "State [Statement] of the Rights of the Colonies" asserting that Parliament was bound by limitations imposed by Magna
Carta, the common law, "the laws of nature and of nations, the voice
of universal reason, and of God," and implying that immunity of the
colonies from taxation by Parliament was among these limitations.[4]

A few weeks later Otis published a pamphlet, *The Rights of the British
Colonies Asserted and Proved,* expanding the argument set forth in the
"State" and bristling with references to Vattel, Harrington, Rousseau,
Grotius, Puffendorf, Thucydides, Montesquieu, Coke, and Viner, besides at least eight to Locke. Otis has many striking phrases, such as
"One single act of Parliament, we find, has set people, a thinking, in
six months, more than they had done in their whole lives before";
"nothing can eradicate from their hearts their natural and almost mechanical affection to Great Britain, which they conceive under no
other sense nor call by any other name than that of *home*"; and the
right "to be free from all taxes but what he consents to in person, or
by his representative . . . is part of a British subjects birthright, and as
inherent and perpetual as the duty of allegiance." But he is diffuse and
contradictory, repeating, for example, at one point his contention in
the writs of assistance case that acts contrary to natural law are void
and will be so adjudged by the courts, yet declaring at another that
"The power of parliament is uncontroulable, but by themselves."[5]

Later in the summer, Thacher, too, published a pamphlet — *Sentiments of a British-American, occasioned by an Act to lay Certain Duties in the
British Colonies and Plantations* — asserting that the colonists, as members
of the British Empire, have "the same British rights inherent in them,

as the inhabitants of the Island itself," among which is a "right that no person shall be subject to any tax but what in person, or by his representatives, he hath a voice in laying," and that in protesting against the violation of this basic right by Parliament, the colonists were in the same position as Parliament had been in earlier times in vindicating this right "against the attempts of Kings to invade it." Thacher, however, dealt chiefly with the trade features of the American Act of 1764 — the Black Act, as John Rowe called it — criticizing its restrictions along the lines outlined in Chapter 15, with particular condemnation of the new admiralty courts at Halifax, the changes in court procedure in cases involving alleged violations of the acts of trade, the new requirement for bonds on practically all intercolonial shipments even in small, undecked boats, and the prohibition on shipments of colonial lumber directly to Ireland.[6]

Several weeks after the publication of his *Rights*, Otis and the other Boston representatives of the House asked Governor Francis Bernard to convene a special session of the Massachusetts Legislature, stating that Grenville had said an internal tax on the colonies by Parliament "might be prevented; if they would tax themselves to the same purposes" and that they "were desirous of immediately setting about such taxation themselves or at least of doing something to prevent a parliamentary tax." Bernard said he saw no way for the Massachusetts Legislature to levy a substitute tax without knowing the colony's quota, which was not yet fixed, but promised nevertheless to call a special session for October.[7]

Soon after the special session convened, the House chose a committee of eleven members, headed by Speaker White and including Otis and Thacher, which drafted an Address to the King and Parliament claiming exemption from any kind of colonial taxes for revenue levied by Parliament, including the duties imposed by the Act of 1764. These duties, the Address declared, will "deprive us of the most essential rights of Britons," for "we look upon those duties as a tax," and "have ever supposed this to be one essential right of British subjects, that they shall not be subjected to taxes which, in person or by representative, they have no voice in laying." The House approved the Address; but the provincial Council declined to concur in it, and a joint committee of twenty-one members, including Otis, Thacher, Cushing, and White of the House and Thomas Hutchinson and James Bowdoin of the Council, was chosen to prepare a revised statement.[8]

The Committee's statement, adopted by both Houses, was a Petition exclusively to the House of Commons, which contained a vigorous and able protest against the new restrictions on colonial trade and some of the new enforcement provisions of the Act of 1764 but weakened the protest concerning taxation by substituting "priviledge" for "right" of freedom from taxation by Parliament and by referring only to "internal" taxes, thus implying that "external" taxes were not objectionable in principle.[9]

In his letter to Agent Mauduit enclosing the Petition with instructions to present it to the House of Commons, the provincial Secretary said the legislature considered any taxation of the colony by Parliament a violation of the rights of the colony and had refrained from stating this in the Petition only as a matter of policy. Cushing likewise wrote Mauduit privately that he should "collect the sentiments" of the House of Representatives, not from the Petition but "from what they have heretofore sent you."[10] Yet whatever might be said collaterally for Mauduit's information, the Petition itself was the decisive official statement of the colony's position, and the implication in it that "external" taxes, even though for revenue, were not objectionable in principle, was extremely dangerous. For, once it was conceded that Parliament had the right to levy duties on the colonies for revenue as distinguished from duties for regulation of colonial trade, the way, of course, was opened for burdening the colonies with ever-increasing taxes raised by duties for revenue on colonial imports and exports.

Curiously, the person mainly responsible for weakening the Massachusetts Petition was Chief Justice Hutchinson, who, as we saw in Chapters 11 and 16, had been foremost to point out the danger of conceding a distinction between internal and external taxation. Hutchinson's leading part in securing the modifications is described by him in a letter of November 5, 1764, to Richard Jackson, stating:

"The heads of the popular party had prepared an Address to the King, Lords and Commons which was passed in the House and sent to the Council for concurrence. It was informal and incautiously expressed and therefore rejected by the Council. A conference ensued. The major part of the House were convinced and a Committee of the two Houses was appointed to consider of a more proper form. . . . Ten days were spent in this manner which I thought time not ill spent as I had the more opportunity of shewing them the imprudence of every measure which looked like opposition to the determinations of Parliament. I declined any concern in framing an address until I found them perplexed and tired and then fearing they would unite upon something worse, at the general request of the Committee, I drew a Petition to the House of Commons. . . . ¶ I had by this means an opportunity of communicating to the Committee your letter of the 16. of April which . . . greatly contributed to the unanimity which appeared in the Committee."[11]

The letter of April 16 from Jackson mentioned by Hutchinson was the one to which he had replied in the admirable statement of July 1764, quoted in Chapter 16, pointing out Jackson's error in not recognizing that import or other "external" duties levied for revenue were indistinguishable in principle from stamp duties or other "internal" taxes levied for revenue. Hutchinson justified his effort to persuade the Committee to draw a distinction which he himself considered unsound, on the ground of public policy. But there was also a private motive, presumably fear of losing his Crown office or jeopardizing his chance of advancement by the Crown, for his conduct, as appears from his statement to Jackson, "I have been thus particular in relating this proceeding lest any ill construction should be put upon my being at the head of a Committee for a thing of this nature [protesting against an act of Parliament] which will appear from the General Courts records." A similar motive probably accounts for his request to Jackson in the letter enclosing the statement of July 1764 that, if the statement was published, it be "so disguised as to . . . prevent fixing upon the author."[12]

It also is questionable if Jackson, who was one of Grenville's secretaries, was disinterested in his advice to the colonists. Writing a Massachusetts friend concerning Jackson in May 1765, William Bollan warned that "Modern ministers frequently manage public affairs by getting under their power and influence the persons to whom they are entrusted; and I am sorry to say that you have exposed yourself to the censure of your best friends by chusing the man [Jackson] to oppose the master [Grenville] who by his sole representation and management occasion'd a heavy tax to be laid on your trade last year, and another tax that is not very light to be laid upon you in this." And some months later, Ezra Stiles wrote that Jackson was reportedly "aiming at Promotion, Preferment and Figure in the Nation and in his Conduct made every Thing bow to these ultimate Views"—suspicions given color by a letter from Charles Jenkinson, senior Secretary to the Treasury, to Grenville stating that Jackson was not inclined to accept the proffered post of London Agent for Massachusetts, unless "his acceptance of it would be of service to Government."[13]

But there was no hint of this in 1764. Eliphalet Dyer wrote Jared Ingersoll from London in April 1764 that he esteemed Jackson "of more Consequence than all the other Agents for the Continent, . . . not only most knowing but heartily Engag'd for the Interest of the Colonies . . . [and] believe by his Influence the proposed Stamp duty is at present postponed," and, six months later, William Allen of Pennsylvania, recently returned from England, wrote, "No person in Brittain has, or can do more to assist the Colonys than Mr. Jackson; he already deserves a statue for his noble and disinterested regard to our rights."[14]

At its session in May–June 1764, the Connecticut Legislature, like that of Massachusetts, appointed a committee—Governor Thomas Fitch, Ebenezer Silliman, senior member of the Council, George Wyllys, Secretary of the colony, and Jared Ingersoll—"to collect and set in the most advantageous light all such arguments and objections as may justly and reasonably [be] advanced against creating and collecting a revenue in America . . . and especially against effecting the same by Stamp Duties etc." to be transmitted to the colony's London Agent, Jackson. The committee's statement, approved at the October session of the Legislature, while strongly protesting against Parliament's levying internal taxes in the colonies, conceded the right and propriety of levying external duties for revenue on the colonies. It even suggested that if Parliament considered such duties necessary at this time, duties on the importation of Negroes and on the colonial fur trade (in neither of which Connecticut participated) would be particularly suitable.[15] The committee probably was influenced in drawing this imprudent distinction by a missing letter of March 10, 1764, from Jackson, mentioned by the Connecticut Legislature,[16] which presumably expressed substantially the same views as those in his letter of April 16 to Hutchinson previously discussed.

Thus, by the end of October 1764, the legislatures of the two leading New England colonies, influenced apparently by Jackson, were on record, Massachusetts by implication, Connecticut explicitly, as accepting the principle of Parliamentary taxation of the colonies for revenue provided the taxes were in the form of external taxes—customs duties—and not in the form of stamp duties or other internal taxes.

CHAPTER 18

LEGISLATIVE PROTESTS – THE MIDDLE COLONIES

ON SEPTEMBER 11, 1764, the New York Assembly, answering Governor Cadwallader Colden's opening message, said, "We hope your Honour will join with us in an Endeavour to secure *that Great Badge of English Liberty, of being taxed only with our own Consent*, to which, we conceive, all his Majesty's Subjects at home and abroad equally intitled; and also in pointing out to the Ministry, the many Mischiefs arising from the Act, commonly called *the Sugar Act*, both to us and to Great Britain." Colden declined the invitation to participate but stated he would do nothing to prevent the Assembly's "making a Representation of the State of this Colony, which you think best." Whereupon the Assembly chose a committee to draw up a petition to the House of Commons setting forth "the many Inconveniences that must attend the infringing the Liberty we have so long enjoyed of being taxed only with our own Consent" and also those arising from the restrictions imposed by the recent American and Currency Acts of 1764.[1]

On October 4, soon after the receipt of Colden's message recommending annulment of the Kayaderosseras grant discussed later in this Chapter, the committee submitted a statement, which, though bolder than that suggested by the resolution appointing the committee,

was adopted without change by the Assembly. The latter also now appointed committees to draw statements on the same subjects to the
King and to the House of Lords.[2]

The three statements, of which the "Representation and Petition"
to the House of Commons quoted below is typical, setting forth fully,
forcefully, and without concession to supposed expediency the Assembly's claim of right not to be taxed for revenue by Parliament, are
among the great state papers of the pre-Revolutionary period.

By long-established custom, the Assembly declared, the "Rights
and Privileges" of the colonists included "an Exemption from the
Burthen" of all taxes not granted by themselves, which, even if a mere
privilege, could not, unless abused, be justly taken from the people,
and there had in fact been no abuse. But the exemption was more
than a privilege; it was "a Right . . . inseparable from the very Idea of
Property, for who can call that his own which can be taken away at the
Pleasure of another? And so evidently does this appear to be the natural Right of Mankind that even conquered tributary States, though
subject to the Payment of a fixed periodical Tribute, never were reduced to . . . yield to all the Burthens which their Conquerors might
at any future Time think fit to impose. The Tribute paid, the Debt was
discharged; and the Remainder they could call their own."

It would be dangerous enough if power to tax the colonists for revenue without their consent was lodged in a King, who "will naturally
consider his Relation to be . . . equal to all his good Subjects," but it
must be more so if lodged in the House of Commons, for "who that
considers the natural Reluctance of Mankind to Burthens and their
Inclination to cast them upon the Shoulders of others, cannot foresee
that, while the people on the one side of the Atlantic enjoy an Exemption from the Load, those on the other must submit to the most unsup-
portable Oppression and Tyranny."

Nor was it material whether such taxes took the form of internal
or of external taxation, since "all Impositions, whether they be internal Taxes, or Duties paid for what we consume, equally diminish the
Estates upon which they are charged."

These arguments must not, however, the Assembly continued, be
construed as a contention that Parliament had no legislative power

over the colonies. On the contrary, the authority of Parliament "to model the Trade of the whole Empire, so as to subserve the Interest" of Great Britain was recognized "in the most extensive and positive Terms."[3]

The Petitions to the two Houses and the King were drafted by three able lawyers of New York City, William Livingston, the great Governor of New Jersey during the Revolutionary War, William Smith, Jr., later a mild Tory and, after the war, Crown-appointed Chief Justice of Quebec, and John Morin Scott, one of the leaders of the Revolution in New York.[4] Smith drafted the statement to the House of Commons quoted above, but his views followed closely and were probably greatly influenced by the views of Livingston, who had written a friend as early as March 1764:

"I have long remarked a deep-formed and steadily-prosecuted Plan of the British Ministry either arising from their own Ignorance of his Majesty's Plantations in America and the misrepresentation of disgusted officers in the Military (often traducing the People in the Colonies to varnish over their own Misconduct) or from worse motives, to reduce us by degrees to perfect Vassalage. This Project has already been so Far carried into Execution that the Judges of our highest Courts of Judicature hold their Commissions on the unconstitutional Tenure of the King's Pleasure. . . . Add to this that the Point of a standing Army among us (a measure absolutely inconsistent with civil Liberty) is doubtless determined. And what is now on the carpet before the Parliament, is the crushing the Trade of North America in such essential Articles, as must approach very near to the reducing us to Beggary. Should they also carry another favourite Point, which is that of subjecting us to the Payment of the national Tax, we should certainly have reason to envy the superior political Happiness of the French . . . governed by a Prince who can really have no interest separate from that of his People, whereas if we are taxed by a British Parliament, the Commons of England will be eased in Proportion to the Burden they throw on us."[5]

The New York Assembly's adoption of so uncompromisingly bold a protest was probably attributable in large measure to the members' indignation over the recent message from Governor Colden, under directions from the Board of Trade, proposing the annulment of title to a great tract of former Crown land in northern New York[6] which, if adopted, would cast a cloud on the title to a large part of the privately owned land in the province.

When New York was permanently wrested from the Dutch in 1674, ungranted land in the province became Crown land, which the British Governors were long empowered, subject to the advice of the provincial Council, to grant without any limit as to acreage and at such quit rent (a perpetual rent payable to the Crown) as they "shall think fitt."[7] From 1698 to 1701 Governor Lord Bellomont was instructed to include in his grants a stipulation for an annual quit rent of two and a half shillings per hundred acres, and this instruction was revived in 1708 and thereafter continued.[8] But it was not included in the commission or instructions to Governor Lord Cornbury, a cousin of Queen Anne, who succeeded Bellomont in 1701 and held office until December 1708.[9]

The Governor and other provincial officials were entitled as perquisites of office to fees for grants of Crown land in the province proportionate to the amount of land granted. The greater the number of acres granted, the larger the fees; and the lower the quit rents, the more the acres prospective grantees presumably would request and pay fees for. It is therefore not surprising that Cornbury and other early Governors, who seem to have had little or no difficulty in getting the Council to concur, made grants of Crown lands in New York running into millions of acres at extremely low quit rents.[10]

In addition to paying fees for grants of Crown land in New York the prospective grantee was required by a New York act of 1684 to acquire Indian title to the land before the grant was made. But until this act was supplemented by regulations issued by the Governor and Council of New York in 1736 and the Crown in 1755,[11] the act gave the Indians relatively little protection, because the prospective grantee might obtain a deed from the Indians so loosely worded as to bear almost any construction as to boundaries and then secure a clearly defined Crown grant covering perhaps many times the acreage the Indians thought they were selling.

One of the largest of the earlier grants, known as the Kayaderosseras or Queensborough patent, situated in an angle between the north bank of the Mohawk river and the west bank of the Hudson, was granted by Cornbury in 1708 to thirteen grantees. By 1754, ownership of the tract was widely distributed, and by 1766 was said to include "every family of any consideration in the Province . . . as well as the principal Lawyers of the Country." The quit rent stipulated for this tract, later estimated to contain about 800,000 acres, was only four pounds New York currency a year.[12] How much in fees the grantees paid Cornbury is not known; but, under a New York act passed the following year, Cornbury's fee alone (besides fees payable to the provincial Secretary and other provincial officers) on a grant of 800,000 acres would have been about £4,000.[13] The bounds of the grant were reasonably well defined but whether they were compatible with those loosely stated in the deed conveying Indian title to the land[14] is not now determinable.

In June 1754, some Mohawk Indians, at a conference with Governor James De Lancey of New York and others in Albany, complained of the Kayaderosseras grant, which, they said, covered land that "upon enquiry among our old Men we cannot find was ever sold."[15] After his appointment in 1755 as Superintendent of the Northern Indians, William (later Sir William) Johnson wrote the Board of Trade about the Mohawks' complaints concerning the grant, and pursuant to the Board's order, De Lancey's successor, Governor Sir Charles Hardy, tried to get the Assembly to pass a bill annulling the grant, but in vain.[16] In July 1764, apparently without making any independent effort to ascertain the facts, the Board again issued instructions — to Governor Colden — to recommend passage of a bill annulling the grant, adding the threat that if the Assembly failed to act "it will be our duty to advise His Majesty to apply to Parliament."[17]

For the British Government to have Colden recommend annulment by legislative act of a land title fifty years old which, in form at least, was perfectly valid, without giving the owners their day in court, would be unjust and provoking at best, but was all the more so because both the Crown and Colden and, it was suspected, Johnson stood to profit financially by the proposed annulment.

The quit rent payable to the Crown under the existing grant was, as previously noted, only four pounds New York currency a year, whereas, by regranting the land at the current rate of two shilling sixpence sterling per hundred acres, the tract would, as Johnson pointed out to the Board, "yield a Revenue to the Crown of about £1,700 pr annum currency."[18] As to Colden, if the land was reacquired by the Crown and regranted while Colden was acting Governor, he would get £10,000 New York currency (about £5,400 sterling) in fees for himself, and his son an additional £4,000 in fees as Surveyor-General of Land in New York.[19]

Furthermore, there was reason to suspect that Johnson, too, had private reasons for seeking the annulment. A Crown grant of Johnson's, known as the Kingsborough patent, was said to overlap the Kayaderosseras grant by about 12,000 acres, and, being a later grant, would be reduced to this extent if the Kayaderosseras grant was not annulled.[20] Moreover, in 1760, the Mohawks had deeded him a huge tract of "Verry fine" land in the upper Mohawk Valley[21] for only "£480 Currency in Specie together with a handsome present." This transaction, dubious at best, was the more so because Johnson took the deed without complying with any of the Crown instructions of 1755 as to purchases of Indian land and because of his conflicting statements as to the cost and acreage of the land.[22] Was not Johnson's revival of activity to have the Kayaderosseras grant annulled part of a bargain for the Indians' grant to him?

Johnson, of course, denied that there was any ground for suspicion. He wrote Colden, "I am aware of many mean as well as false insinuations of Interested People, as if it was an Affair of mine, whereas no decision relative thereto is of the smallest consequence and importance to me"[23] and to the Board of Trade that "the affair of Kayaderosseras has drawn upon me a load of scurrility & detraction, but I comfort myself it proceeds from those who always did, and always will, traduce everry officer of the Crown that is not of their Party."[24] But his conduct belied his fine words.

It is hardly surprisingly therefore that the New York Assembly not only rejected Colden's proposal to annul the Kayaderosseras grant but was exceptionally tart in its reply. After making a thrust at Johnson and pointing out that "it is very common for the Indians to Deny the Sales of their Ancestors, as well as their own, . . . to force repeated payments for the same Lands," the Assembly declared that "an easy attention to Indian Claims of Lands long since Patented has a natural Tendency to excite new and Repeated Complaints," and that "This House Therefore upon *General principles* (for they know nothing of the peculiar state of Kayaderosseras, other than that it is a large Tract thinly Settled, because formerly much exposed to Incursions from Crown Point) conceive it extremely dangerous, at this late day, to enter into an Enquiry, in which Sufficient light probably CANNOT be obtained to direct a just and Accurate determination, and that the Precedent of Annulling the Crown Grants . . . Will render all property insecure; Give the highest disatisfaction to His Majesty's Subjects; Alarm their fears; and discourage the Settlement, Cultivation and Prosperity of the Colony."[25]

Colden attributed the Assembly's action to "the influence of several leading Men in the Assembly, who are interested in the Grants of Large Tracts of Land in this Province,"[26] and this may well have been an important factor. But members having no personal interest at stake must have recognized the injustice of annulling the Kayaderosseras grant without trial by judge or jury, and suspected that Colden and Johnson were using, if not encouraging, the Indians' complaint to feather their own nests.

Turning to Pennsylvania,* we find the action of its Assembly much less bold than New York's. Though asserting the right to freedom from taxation by Parliament, the Pennsylvania Assembly, in September, made no protest to the King or Parliament, voting merely to send a letter to Richard Jackson, its London Agent, directing him to try to prevail on Parliament not to tax the colonies and to repeal or amend the American Act of 1764 because detrimental to colonial trade. The Assembly even added a promise to send him a plan, undescribed, for raising a colonial revenue to contribute to the general defense of the colonies by a temporary act of Parliament. At its October session the

---

* The complexities of Pennsylvania politics are elucidated in William S. Hanna, *Benjamin Franklin and Pennsylvania Politics* (Stanford, Calif.: Stanford University Press, 1964); James H. Hutson, *Pennsylvania Politics, 1746–1770: The Movement for Royal Government and Its Consequences* (Princeton, N.J.: Princeton University Press, 1972); James H. Hutson, "Benjamin Franklin and Pennsylvania Politics, 1751–1755: A Reappraisal," *Pennsylvania Magazine of History and Biography,* 93 (1969): 31–71. [B. W. S.]

Assembly voted to withdraw this promise, but otherwise affirmed the earlier letter.[27]

The conduct of the Pennsylvania Assembly probably resulted largely from the long struggle between the so-called Quaker party in the Assembly, consisting of the Quaker members and a number of non-Quakers, including Franklin, who enjoyed the lucrative printing business at the Assembly's command,[28] and the Proprietaries of Pennsylvania, Thomas and Richard Penn, sons and heirs of the great William.

Under the charter granted by Charles II to Penn in 1681, his heirs had much the same authority as the Governors of the royal colonies, including the power to prevent the passage of any act by refusing assent to it personally or by the Deputy Governor to whom their power was delegated, a power which led to numerous disputes between successive Deputy Governors and the Assembly[29] (the provincial Council of Pennsylvania had no legislative power). One of the most bitter of these was in 1757 over a tax bill for £100,000 to provide funds to defend the province from the French and their Indian allies during the French and Indian War, which Governor William Denny would not assent to because the bill did not conform to his instructions from the Penns to negative any tax bill imposing a tax on the Penns' unimproved land in Pennsylvania. To meet the emergency the Assembly passed a new tax bill conforming to the instructions, but at the same time chose Franklin as a special Agent to London to try to have the instructions changed.[30]

Franklin was still in England unsuccessfully pursuing his mission[31] when, in 1759, the Assembly passed a tax bill for £100,000, similar to the rejected bill of 1757, which Denny, in spite of his instructions, assented to. Whereupon the Penns dismissed him and sought to have the act disallowed by the Privy Council in England. The Council eventually allowed the act to stand pursuant to a recommendation in August 1760, by the Council's Committee on Plantation Affairs, based on a promise by Franklin and the regular Agent for the Assembly, Robert Charles, that the Assembly would amend the act. The amendments were to exempt from tax all the Penns' unsurveyed ("waste") land; provide against assessment of the Penns' surveyed ("located") but uncultivated land at a higher rate than the lowest rate at which the surveyed land of others was assessed; and classify the Penns' town and borough lands for assessment as surveyed but uncultivated land and not as town lots. In addition, the Governor was to be given joint control with the Assembly over public expenditures.[32] The Assembly failed to carry out the promise of its Agents as to taxation, whereupon Charles resigned. But Franklin continued as Agent until late in 1762 when he returned to Pennsylvania and resumed his seat in the Assembly, apparently without making any protest against its failure to redeem his promise.[33]

In March 1764, during the great Indian uprising of 1763–1764 described in Chapters 8 and 9, the Assembly passed a bill similar to the act of 1759, which Governor John Penn, a son of Richard, refused to sign unless it was amended to accord exactly with the Franklin-Charles agreement of 1760 relating to the assessment of the Penns' surveyed, unimproved land and the classification of their town and borough land. In May the Assembly passed a new bill conforming to his demand but, at the same time, chose a committee, of which Franklin was a member, to prepare a petition to the Crown for a change from proprietary to royal government in Pennsylvania.[34] Despite a powerful speech by John Dickinson of Philadelphia pointing out the advantages enjoyed under the charter of 1681 that might be lost if the province became a royal colony, the petition was adopted by a great majority.[35]

Soon after the adoption of this petition, the Penns yielded concerning the taxation of their lands.[36] Nevertheless, the Assembly voted, nineteen to eleven, at its October session, to adhere to its decision to seek a change in the province's form of government from proprietary to royal, and chose Franklin, who had been defeated for reelection to the Assembly, to go to London again as its Agent.[37]

The seemingly irrational decision of the majority to proceed with the petition was probably owing in large measure to the hope of perpetuating Quaker control over legislation in the province. Heretofore, though by now a minority in Pennsylvania, the Quakers had been able to retain control of the Assembly because of the disproportionate representation of Chester, Philadelphia, and Bucks counties, where most of the Quakers lived. These counties (excluding the population of the city of Philadelphia, which had its own representatives apart from the county of Philadelphia) contained much less than half the population of the province in 1760 and somewhat less than half the property value. Yet they had twenty-four seats in the Assembly while all the rest of the province, comprising the city of Philadelphia and the relatively new counties of Lancaster, York, Cumberland, Berks, and Northampton, settled chiefly by Scotch-Irish Presbyterians, Germans of Lutheran and Reformed faiths, and Anglicans, had only twelve.[38] Demands for fairer representation of the newer counties were becoming so pressing[39] that if Quaker control over legislation in the province was to be perpetuated, some other means, it seemed, must be devised.

If the petition for a royal government in Pennsylvania was granted, the Crown would almost certainly adopt the usual pattern of royal government, including a Council having legislative power and appointed by the Crown, and the Quakers in England were so influential a minority group there that they might well be able to secure the appointment of a Council composed of a majority favorable to the Quakers of Pennsylvania. Thus the Quaker party in Pennsylvania might retain ultimate control over provincial legislation through the Crown-appointed Council. This object, though of course not openly declared, is disclosed in a number of surviving letters of 1764–1765, including an assurance by Franklin from London that English Quakers would "give their whole force and weight" to the petition for a change of government and thus prevent "their friends in Pennsylvania falling totally under the domination of Presbyterians."[40]

The determination of the Pennsylvania Assembly to petition for a change in the form of provincial government had a very material bearing on its approach to the threatened taxation of the colonies by Parliament. Since this was a favorite measure of the Grenville Ministry and since the Ministry's support of the Assembly's petition would be essential to its success, the Assembly was naturally hesitant to risk offending the Ministry by taking a strong stand against colonial taxation.

New Jersey was the third of the middle colonies to protest against colonial taxation by Parliament. In August 1764, Robert Ogden, Speaker of the New Jersey House, sent a copy of the Massachusetts circular letter of the preceding June to Cortlandt Skinner, Attorney-General of the colony and member of the House, with a letter saying,

"The affair is Serious and Greatly Concerns all the Colonies to unite and Exert themselves to the utmost to Keep off the Threatening blow of Imposing Taxes, Duties etc so Distructive to the Libertys the Colonies hitherto enjoyed. . . . If you think it of Importance Beg you would Loose no Time in Consulting Mr. Nevill and Mr. Johnston on the Subject and write to his Excellency [Governor William Franklin] and Desire him to Give us a Meeting as Early in September as Possible."[41]

So far as is known, no meeting of the New Jersey legislature was called at this time. But a protest, dated September 10, was sent to the colony's London Agent, Joseph Sherwood, by Charles Reade and Samuel Smith, members of the provincial Council, and Jacob Spicer, a member of the House, signing themselves "Committee of Correspondents for West-Jersey," stating, "If anything comes on the Stage next Session of Parliament either for repealing the Duties laid on the Trade of the Northern Colonies and prohibiting a paper currency at last Session, or for adding any thing new by way of Tax on this Colony, the Committee of Correspondents direct that you will humbly and Dutifully Set forth, in the name and on Behalf of this Colony that we look upon all Taxes laid upon us without our Consent as a fundamental infringement of the Rights and Privileges Secured to us as English Subjects; and by charter. And that our paper Currency . . . being prohibited from . . . being Legal tender . . . we esteem a very great provincial hardship. . . . The more active and Expensive part of the Opposition we expect will lie upon the other Colonies who are abundantly more Concerned in Trade, yet it is necessary so far to cooperate with them as to Show the Colonies are unanimously of One Mind."[42]

CHAPTER 19

LEGISLATIVE PROTESTS —
THE CAROLINAS, VIRGINIA, AND
RHODE ISLAND

IN AUGUST 1764, the South Carolina House, first of the southern assemblies to take action concerning the American Act of 1764 and the
proposed stamp tax, ordered its Committee of Correspondence to instruct Charles Garth, London Agent for the colony, "to oppose the
passing of the Bill for Laying a Stamp Duty or any other Tax, on this
Colony, and to give him such other Directions for the Benefit of the
Inhabitants thereof, as they Judge necessary and expedient."[1]

Pursuant to this order, the Committee, a distinguished group including Rawlins Lowndes, Speaker of the House, Thomas Bee, Christopher Gadsden, Thomas Lynch, Isaac Mazyck, Charles Pinckney,
and John Rutledge, wrote Garth, "We have particularly in charge
from the House to direct you to make all opposition you possibly can,
in conjunction with the agent of the other colonies, in the laying a
stamp duty, or any other tax by act of Parliament on the colonies," as
inconsistent with "that inherent right of every British subject, not to
be taxed but by his own consent or that of his representative."[2]

Furthermore, said the Committee, there were other serious grievances, including the recent refusal by the Board of Trade to support a
petition from South Carolina for an act of Parliament permitting it to
import salt directly from Europe, and passage of the Currency Act of
1764, which latter would result, the Committee declared, in reducing
the colony's total outstanding currency to only £15,000 for conduct-
ing the colony's business, which in exports alone was over £250,000
sterling a year.[3]

Soon after the Legislature of Virginia met in October, John Robinson, Speaker of the House of Burgesses, submitted a copy of the
Massachusetts circular letter of June 1764, reporting the action taken
by the Massachusetts Assembly concerning British taxation of the colonies and inviting other colonies to follow suit. The House directed
the colony's Committee of Correspondence to send a favorable reply
to the Massachusetts letter and chose a strong committee, headed by
Peyton Randolph, with Richard Henry Lee, Landon Carter, George
Wythe, Edmund Pendleton, Benjamin Harrison, Archibald Cary, John
Fleming, and Richard Bland, to draft addresses to the King and to
each House of Parliament asserting the colony's rights.[4]

Randolph, now in his middle forties, was easily one of the most distinguished and influential men in Virginia. Elder son of Sir John Randolph, former Speaker of the Virginia House, and Susanna Beverley
Randolph, he had studied at William and Mary College and the Middle Temple, London, where he was called to the bar in 1744. Returning to Virginia he took up the practice of law, served for many years
in the House as member for William and Mary College or the town of
Williamsburg, and was now and had been for many years King's Attorney for Virginia. Like most of the political leaders in Virginia, he
had important family connections. Peter Randolph, prominent member of the Virginia Council, and Richard Bland were among his first
cousins, and his wife was a sister of his fellow committee member,
Benjamin Harrison.[5] (Two others destined to be even more famous
and influential, young Thomas Jefferson and John Marshall, were first
cousins once removed of Randolph.)

The Virginia protests, consisting of an Address to the King, a Memorial to the House of Lords, and a Remonstrance to the House of

Commons, although claiming freedom from taxation by Parliament as a right, not a mere privilege, were weaker than those of the New York House in not clearly indicating that this claim of right referred to taxes for revenue of all kinds and not to internal taxes only.[6] Nevertheless, they were of signal importance not only because of Virginia's leading position among the colonies but because they were adopted by the Crown-appointed provincial Council as well as by the lower House and touched on two important points not previously brought out in the protests of other colonial legislatures.

The first was that the essentials of "British Liberty" included freedom from taxation except by a body of persons who "sustain a Proportion of the Burthen laid on them," thus anticipating and meeting the British argument, mentioned in Chapter 13, that the colonists, like residents of Manchester or other English towns or boroughs having no representatives in Parliament, were, nevertheless, "virtually" represented by the members as a whole.[7] The Virginia protests pointed out that there was a vital distinction in the two cases, in so far as taxation was concerned, because, since taxes levied by Parliament on English residents were levied on the nation as a whole, any taxes burdening Manchester or other unrepresented English boroughs or towns would likewise burden constituencies represented in Parliament, whereas taxes levied by Parliament on the colonies, far from adding to the tax burden of the constituencies having members in Parliament, would lighten the burden by shifting part of it to colonial taxpayers.

The other was the rejection, not explicitly but by clear implication, of representation of the colonies in Parliament as a practicable and acceptable solution of the taxation issue.[8] Exclusive home rule in the matter of taxation was, the Virginia protests indicated, alone acceptable.

The protests were ordered sent to Edward Montague, London Agent for the House, with instructions to present them to the King and the respective Houses of Parliament, and the committee of correspondence wrote Montague that if the House of Commons declined to receive the Remonstrance addressed to it (a standing rule in the Commons prohibited acceptance of petitions against money bills) he was to publish it, or at least have its substance made public, so there would be no question in Great Britain as to Virginia's stand.[9]

At its October 1764 session the North Carolina House, drawing no distinction between internal and external taxes, expressed its concern to Governor Arthur Dobbs at having "our Commerce Circumscribed . . . and Burthened with new Taxes and Impositions laid on us without our Privity and Consent, and against what we esteem our Inherent right and Exclusive privilege of Imposing our own Taxes."[10] But apparently the House sent no directions to its London Agent to protest against the American Act of 1764 or the proposed stamp tax.

So far as is known, none of the other colonial Legislatures took action[11] except Rhode Island's, which, after long delay, strongly protested against the new restrictions on colonial trade but dealt rather gingerly with the question of British taxation of the colonies.

In July 1764, the Rhode Island Legislature chose a committee composed of Governor Stephen Hopkins, Daniel Jenckes, an outstanding member of the Providence delegation in the House, and Nicholas Brown, not in the Legislature but a leading merchant of Providence, "to confer and consult with any committee or committees that are, or shall be, appointed by any of the British colonies upon the continent of North America, and to agree with them upon such measures . . . as shall appear to them necessary and proper, to procure a repeal of the act . . . passed at the last session of Parliament, for levying several duties in the colonies . . . ; also to prevent the levying a stamp duty."[12]

Hopkins, perhaps best known to Americans today as one of the Signers of the Declaration of Independence, unlike most of the leading men in New England at this time, was not a college graduate and had had little formal schooling. Born in 1707, he lived in the rural town of Scituate about ten miles west of Providence, working as a farmer and surveyor until 1742 when he moved to Providence and opened a store. Active in politics, he served in the legislature both before and after moving to Providence, was one of the Rhode Island delegates to the Albany Congress of 1754, and was elected Governor a year later. His popularity is evident, since, despite strong opposition, he was annually reelected in all but four years from 1756 to 1767. In 1762 he was one of the founders of the *Providence Gazette* (a rival of the more conservative *Newport Mercury*), which carried various items attributed to him, including an "Essay on the Trade of the Northern Colonies" in the

January 14 and 21, 1764, issues, urging united action of the northern colonies to secure relief from the Sugar Act of 1733.[13]

For reasons unknown, Hopkins's committee took no action (perhaps it was waiting to learn what other colonial legislatures would do) until reappointed at the September session with instructions "to write to the neighboring governments, and remonstrate to the Parliament etc." Pursuant to this instruction the committee sent a circular letter to other colonial governments in North America stating it had been directed "to correspond, confer, and consult, with any committee or committees that are or shall be appointed by any of the British colonies on the continent, and, in concert with them, to prepare and form such representations . . . as may be most likely to be effectual to remove or alleviate the burdens which the colonists at present labor under, and to prevent new ones being added," and asking "to be informed whether your colony hath taken these matters under consideration; and if it hath, what methods have been thought of, as most conducive to bring them to a happy issue."[14]

Though sent too late to be of any immediate effect, this letter is important for its suggestion of a conference to secure united colonial action, which British colonial officials or former officials had repeatedly warned would be a grave threat to the continued dependence of the colonies on Great Britain.[15]

At its October session the Rhode Island Legislature took further action, this time choosing a large committee consisting of the members of the original committee and several others to prepare an Address to the King for a redress of grievances, which was adopted by the legislature at its November session with directions that it be sent to the colony's London Agent, Joseph Sherwood, for presentation to the King.[16] The Legislature also voted that a statement submitted by Governor Hopkins be completed by him, reviewed by the committee, and, if approved, sent to Sherwood to be circulated in England as he thought best. This statement has not been found; but it probably was a draft of the important pamphlet, *The Rights of Colonies Examined,* soon afterward published at Providence, copies of which were sent to Sherwood.[17]

The Address and the pamphlet both contain a strong protest against the restrictions on trade in the Act of 1764 and its provisions for the enforcement of these restrictions in the colonial admiralty courts, thereby depriving defendants of the right to trial by jury. But in dealing with taxation of the colonies by Parliament, the protest refers only to "stamp duties and other internal taxes,"[18] thus implying, as had the recent Massachusetts protest, that "external" taxes, that is, import and export duties, even if for revenue, were not in principle objectionable.

CHAPTER 20

THE PROTESTS FAIL:
THE STAMP ACT IS PASSED

IN AUGUST 1764, Lord Halifax, as Secretary of State for the Southern Department, sent a circular letter to the colonial Governors referring to the recent resolution of Parliament concerning a colonial stamp tax and directing them to send him without delay a list of "all instruments made use of in public transactions, law proceedings, Grants, conveyances, securities of Land or money within your Government" to assist Parliament in case it "should think proper to pursue the intention of the aforesaid resolution."[1] Some of the Governors promptly replied.[2] Whereupon, with the assistance of several collaborators, Thomas Whately, joint Secretary to the Treasury, prepared a detailed plan for the proposed tax, following with some modifications the general lines of the British stamp duties. This was approved at a meeting of the Treasury Board on December 17, 1764.[3]

At the time this fateful decision to proceed with the stamp tax was made, Grenville probably had not yet received word of most of the colonial legislative protests against the proposed tax. But English newspapers had carried numerous reports indicating widespread colonial opposition, and at least two of the legislative protests—those of the Massachusetts Assembly in June 1764 and of the New York Assembly in October discussed in Chapters 17 and 18—had been pre-sented to the King.[4] Yet Grenville apparently made no effort to ascertain from the colonial agents, merchants trading to the colonies, or anyone else if the opposition in the colonies must be taken seriously. Though full of protestations of kindly feelings toward the colonists, his attitude seems to have been, if they balked at the tax so much the worse for them; say what they would, he would ask Parliament to cram the tax down their throats without further ado.

This attitude was reflected in the hearing granted by Grenville to the colonial agents pursuant to his promise in May 1764 mentioned in Chapter 12, which took place on February 2, 1765, four days before the details of the proposed colonial stamp tax were laid before the House of Commons.*

"The Agents of the Colonies," wrote Jared Ingersoll, co-Agent for Connecticut, to Thomas Fitch, Governor of the colony, "have had several Meetings at one of which they were pleased to desire Mr. Franklin & myself as having lately Come from America & knowing more Intimately the Sentiments of the people, to wait on Mr. Grenville, together with Mr. Jackson & Mr. Garth who being Agents are also Members of Parliament, to remonstrate against the Stamp Bill, & to propose in Case any Tax must be laid upon America, that the several Colonies might be permitted to lay the Tax themselves. This we did Saturday before last.

"Mr. Grenville gave us a full hearing—told us he took no pleasure in giving the Americans so much uneasiness as he found he did—that it was the Duty of his Office to manage the revenue—that he really was made to believe that considering the whole of the Circumstances of the Mother Country & the Colonies, the later could and ought to pay something, & that he knew of no better way than that now pursuing to lay such Tax, but that if we could tell of a better he would adopt it. We then urged the Method first mentioned as being a Method the people had been used to—that it would at least seem to

---

*For Grenville's dealings with the agents, see Edmund S. Morgan and Helen M. Morgan, *The Stamp Act Crisis: Prologue to Revolution* (Chapel Hill: University of North Carolina Press, 1995), 60–68; Thomas, *British Politics and the Stamp Act Crisis*, 75–77; Bullion, *A Great and Necessary Measure*, 125–32, 144–53. [B. W. S.]

be their own Act & prevent that uneasiness & Jealousy which otherwise we found would take place—that they could raise the Money best by their own Officers &c &c. . . .

"Mr. Grenville asked us if we could agree upon the several proportions Each Colony should raise. We told him no. He said he did not think any body here was furnished with Materials for that purpose; not only so but there would be no Certainty that every Colony would raise the Sum enjoined & to be obliged . . . to compel some one or two provinces to do their Duty & that perhaps for one year only, would be very inconvenient. . . .

"Upon the whole he said he had pledged his Word for Offering the Stamp Bill to the house, that the house would hear all our Objections & would do as they thought best; . . . that their Ears will always be open to any remonstrances from the Americans with respect to this bill both before it takes Effect & after, if it shall take Effect, which shall be exprest in a becoming manner, that is, as becomes Subjects of the same common Prince."[5]

Grenville's statement that he "did not think any body here was furnished with Materials" from which to estimate what would be a fair apportionment of tax among the colonies, was disingenuous. He knew as well as anyone that the files of the Board of Trade in London contained the only central pool of information concerning the colonies from which a fair apportionment might be drawn, and he, not the Agents, had full access to these files.

The proposed tax, when presented in Grenville's budget message of February 6, was attacked by a number of speakers, including Jackson, Garth, Isaac Barré, and two members with large West Indian interests, William Beckford and Rose Fuller. Beckford alone denied that Parliament had any authority to levy taxes on the colonies; the others conceded the right, but maintained it should not be exercised "untill or unless the Americans are allowed to send Members to Parliament."[6] Barré's speech, according to Ingersoll, was particularly impressive.

"Mr. Barre," he wrote, "having been some time in America as an Officer in the Army, & having while there . . . contracted many Friendships with American Gentlemen, & I believe Entertained much more favourable Opinions of them than some of his profession have done, Delivered a very handsome & moving Speech upon the bill. . . .

"After him Mr Charles Townsend [Townshend] spoke in favour of the Bill—took Notice of several things Mr Barre had said, and concluded with the following or like Words:—And now will these Americans, Children planted by our Care, nourished up by our Indulgence untill they are grown to a Degree of Strength & Opulence, and protected by our Arms, will they grudge to contribute their mite to releive us from the heavy weight of that burden which we lie under? When he had done, Mr Barre rose and . . . took up the beforementioned Concluding words of Mr. Townsend, and in a most spirited & I thought an almost inimitable manner, said—

" 'They planted by your Care? No! your Oppressions planted em in America. They fled from your Tyranny to a then uncultivated and unhospitable Country—where they exposed themselves to almost all the hardships to which human Nature is liable. . . .

" 'They nourished up by *your* indulgence? they grew by your neglect of Em:—as soon as you began to care about Em, that Care was Exercised in sending persons to rule over Em, in one Department and another . . . whose behaviour on many Occasions has caused the Blood of those Sons of Liberty to recoil within them. . . .

" 'They protected by *your* Arms? they have nobly taken up Arms in your defence, have Exerted a Valour amidst their constant & Laborious industry for the defence of a Country, whose frontier, while drench'd in blood, its interior Parts have yielded all its little Savings to your Emolument. And beleive me, remember I this Day told you so, that same Spirit of freedom which actuated that people at first, will accompany them still. . . . I claim to know more of America than most of you, having seen and been conversant in that Country. The People I beleive are as truly Loyal as any Subjects the King has, but a people Jealous of their Lyberties and who will vindicate them, if ever they should be violated—but the Subject is too delicate & I will say no more.'

"These sentiments were thrown out so intirely without premeditation, so forceably and so firmly, and the breaking off so beautifully abrupt, that the whole house sat awhile as Amazed, intently Looking and without answering a Word."[7]

Barré's eloquence may have held the House spellbound, as Ingersoll believed, but it failed to win extensive support; when the House divided, the vote was five to one (245 to 49) in favor of proceeding with the proposed tax, whereupon a bill was introduced on February 13 for a colonial stamp tax "towards further defraying the Expences of defending, protecting and securing" the colonies.[8]

On the second reading of the bill (February 15), Fuller offered a petition against it on behalf of merchants in London trading to America, to whom the colonists were said to owe about four million pounds; but, upon citation of a precedent barring the consideration by the House of petitions against revenue bills, Fuller withdrew the protest. No member of the House was willing even to try to introduce the petition of the New York Assembly, discussed in Chapter 18, because it was considered so "inflammatory"; but Sir William Meredith presented a petition drawn by Edward Montagu, Agent for Virginia, along the lines of the protests sent him by the Virginia Legislature.[9] He was warmly supported by Henry Seymour Conway, who, like Beckford in the earlier debate, denied the right of Parliament to tax the colonies, urging "with Great Vehemence the many Hardships and what he was Pleased to Call Absurdities that would follow from the contrary Doctrine and practice"; but after a "pretty warm debate," in which Charles Yorke denied that the colonial charters limited the right of Parliament to tax the colonies, the petition was rejected by "a great Majority."[10]

No list of those voting in the minority in this or the previous division on the proposed stamp tax has been found; but, according to Ingersoll, the opposition was confined to "the Gentlemen Interested in the West Indies . . . a few Members . . . Particularly connected with some of the colonies & a few of the heads of the minority who are sure to athwart & oppose the Ministry in Every Measure of what Nature or kind so-ever."[11] As brought out in Chapter 1, Pitt was opposed to Parliament's taxing the colonies; but, ill with the gout, he was not present, and, even if he had been, probably could have made little headway against a tax supported by the Ministry and attractive financially to members and their constituents.

The extreme importance of the stamp tax as a precedent was recognized by the Ministry no less than by the colonists. On February 9, 1765, Whately declared, "The great Measure of the Sessions is the American Stamp Act; I give it the appelation of *a great measure* on account of the important point it establishes, the Right of Parliament to lay an internal Tax upon the Colonies," and a few days later Edward Sedgwick, Under Secretary of State, wrote, "What you have heard of the Refractoriness of the Colonies is very true. There are several Resolutions of American Assemblies in which they almost deny or strongly remonstrate against the Right of Parliament to tax them, which are directed by Order in Council to be laid before Parliament. But first it is thought proper to establish the Right by a new execution of it, and in the strongest instance, an internal Tax, that of the Stamp Duty."[12]

After the debate on February 15, the stamp tax bill met no further opposition, and, with a few amendments, to which the Ministry seems to have offered no objections, passed the House of Commons on February 27 and the Lords on March 8.[13]

The act, effective November 1, 1765, levied stamp duties on a wide range of colonial legal and commercial documents, including pleadings and judgments in civil cases in all courts of law, probate of wills, licenses to practice law, liquor licenses, deeds, leases, mortgages, insurance policies, bonds, ship charters and various other contracts, bills of lading, customs clearances, pamphlets, almanacs, newspapers and newspaper advertisements, playing cards, and dice.[14] Some of the rates were extremely high, especially the tax of two shillings sterling per advertisement on newspaper advertisements, equal in many cases to a tax of over 200 per cent ad valorem,[15] in addition to a tax of a halfpenny sterling per copy on the newspaper itself. Furthermore, the act apparently contemplated that the only documentary stamps to be supplied were on embossed paper furnished by the British Board of Stamp Commissioners,[16] thus giving this Board and its colonial distributors a virtual monopoly of the sale of much of the paper used in the colonies.

Documents requiring stamps if not stamped were inadmissible as evidence in any court. Furthermore, heavy penalties recoverable in the colonial admiralty courts without trial by jury were imposed on public officials for recording such documents and on lawyers for proceeding in any suit without them, and on persons selling unstamped newspapers, almanacs, or pamphlets.[17]

Because of the King's illness, the act did not become law until March 22, when his assent was given by commission.[18] Many writers have said the King was insane at this time, in which case Bancroft's statement that he must be exonerated from any immediate responsibility for enactment of the stamp tax would be unimpeachable.[19] But the contemporary evidence indicates that the King was mentally competent and, had he wished, could have exerted his powerful influence against the introduction and passage of the act.[20]*

*On the illness of George III, see John Brooke, *George III* (New York: McGraw-Hill, 1972) 209–10, 318–43; Ida Macalpine and Richard Hunter, *George III and the Mad-Business* (New York: Pantheon Books, 1969). [B. W. S.]

COLONIAL NULLIFICATION OF
THE STAMP ACT

On May 30, 1765, the Virginia House of Burgesses, fired by the or-
atory of Patrick Henry, responded to the Stamp Act by passing five
resolutions declaring, among other things, that the King's subjects in
Virginia were "entitled to all the Liberties, Privileges and Immunities"
enjoyed by his subjects in Great Britain; that these privileges included
the "inestimable Right of being governed by such Laws respecting
their Internal Policy and Taxation as are derived from their own Consent, with the approbation of their Sovereign, or his Substitute . . ."
and that "every Attempt to vest such Power in any Person or Persons
whatsoever other than the General Assembly [of Virginia] Aforesaid
has a manifest Tendency to destroy British as well as American Freedom."[1] The next day the last of these resolutions was rescinded and
two even more fiery ones — that the people of Virginia were not bound
by any law imposing taxes other than those imposed by their own Legislature and that anyone who maintained otherwise should be deemed
an enemy to the colony — which a group of "young, hot and giddy"
members of the House had prepared, were withheld.[2]

The Massachusetts Assembly acted next. On June 8, it directed its Speaker to write those in the other mainland colonies that the Assembly had appointed a committee to meet at New York in October with delegates from other colonial Assemblies "to consider of a general and united, dutiful and humble representation of their condition to his Majesty and the Parliament, to implore relief."[3] Responding to this message, delegates from Connecticut, Rhode Island, New York, New Jersey, Delaware, Pennsylvania, Maryland, and South Carolina, chosen in various ways, met with those from Massachusetts in New York from October 7 to 25.[4]*

This Congress, presided over by Timothy Ruggles of Massachusetts, was important in bringing together leading men from all sections of North America, and for its adoption of petitions to the King and both Houses of Parliament for repeal of the Stamp Act, in which the members discarded the illogical and risky distinction between internal and external taxes for revenue previously sanctioned by some of the colonial Legislatures and also went on record that colonial representation in Parliament was impractical.[5] But since Parliament would presumably not meet until after November first, the petitions, even if eventually given favorable consideration, would foreseeably not be effective to prevent the Stamp Act from operating for a time. The same was true of a project begun late in October by merchants of New York, Philadelphia, and Boston to put pressure on British merchants and manufacturers to secure repeal of the act by agreeing not to import any but a few specifically exempted articles from Great Britain until it was repealed.[6] But a general movement launched in August to compel the Stamp Distributors, one of whom was appointed for nearly every colony, to resign,[7] thus leaving no one in authority in the colonies to sell and distribute the stamped paper, effectively prevented execution of the act in any of the thirteen colonies except Georgia.

The opening move was against Andrew Oliver of Boston, Chief Justice Hutchinson's brother-in-law and Secretary of the colony, who was appointed Distributor for Massachusetts. In the early morning of August 14, an effigy of Oliver was hung, by persons unknown, in the

*C. A. Weslager, *The Stamp Act Congress* (Newark: University of Delaware Press, 1976). [B. W. S.]

center of Boston, accompanied by a boot (a familiar English pun on Lord Bute) with the Devil peeping out of it. In the afternoon a mob carried Oliver's effigy to a building reportedly to be used for his stamp office, tore it down, and proceeded to his home, where the effigy was beheaded and the windows of the house were stoned. Then, having burned what was left of the effigy in a bonfire on a nearby hill, the mob returned to Oliver's home, broke in the doors, uttering threats to kill him, and, when he could not be found, smashed his furniture to bits. Urged by friends to resign, Oliver publicly promised the next day to give up his commission if the report of his appointment proved to be true.[8]*

The attack on Oliver (encouraged by the Virginia resolves quoted above, including those withheld, which were published in newspapers throughout the colonies as having actually been passed)[9] was apparently led by Ebenezer Mackintosh, a shoemaker, in collaboration with a group calling themselves the Loyall Nine. This was probably composed, with perhaps one exception, of the nine Boston "Sons of Liberty" listed by John Adams in January 1766 as "John Avery distiller or merchant of a liberal education, John Smith the brazier, Thomas Crafts the painter, [Benjamin] Edes the printer, Stephen Cleverly the brazier, [Thomas] Chase the distiller, Joseph Field master of a vessel, Henry Bass, George Trott jeweller."[10] Samuel and John Adams were in touch with this group some months later, but no evidence has been found of either of the Adamses having been involved in the attack on Oliver in August 1765.[11]

The next move was against Augustus Johnston of Newport, reported Distributor for Rhode Island. On the morning of August 27, a mob erected a gallows near the Newport town hall, where they hung

*On the crowd in the coming of the Revolution, see Morgan and Morgan, *The Stamp Act Crisis*, chs. 8 and 9; Gordon Wood, "A Note on Mob in the American Revolution," *William and Mary Quarterly*, 3rd ser., 23 (1966): 635–42; Jesse Lemisch, "Jack Tar in the Streets: Merchant Seamen and the Politics of Revolutionary America," *William and Mary Quarterly*, 3rd ser., 25 (1968): 371–407; Dirk Hoerder, *Crowd Action in Revolutionary Massachusetts, 1765–1780* (New York: Academic Press, 1977); Peter Shaw, *American Patriots and the Rituals of Revolution* (Cambridge, Mass.: Harvard University Press, 1981); Pauline Maier, *From Resistance to Revolution: Colonial Radicals and the Development of American Opposition to Britain, 1765–1766* (New York: Alfred A. Knopf, 1972); James H. Hutson, "An Investigation of the Inarticulate: Philadelphia's White Oaks," *William and Mary Quarterly*, 28 (1971): 3–25. [B. W. S.]

effigies of Johnston and two other local men, Martin Howard and Dr. Thomas Moffatt, alleged to have written in favor of the Stamp Act, with the copy of a song beginning

"He who for a Post or Base sordid Pelf
His Country betrays, Makes a Rope for himself.
Of this an Example before you we Bring
In these Infamous Rogues, Who in Effigy Swing."

The effigies were left hanging until evening when they were burned.

The following night a mob again assembled, broke the windows and furniture in the houses of both Howard and Moffatt, and surrounded but did not injure the home of Johnston. Fleeing for refuge to a British warship in Newport harbor, Johnston returned the next day and, following Oliver's example, publicly promised to resign his commission if the report of his appointment was verified.[12]

Shortly afterward, James McEvers of New York City, Distributor for New York, "frightened by Threats of the like Treatment that Mr. Oliver . . . had met with" sent his resignation to Governor Colden, and for some weeks it appeared that New York would be spared mob violence. But on hearing that a merchant vessel with packages of stamped paper was about due, Colden, who was determined that stamped paper should be available for sale in New York by November first, arranged for the commander of a British warship at New York to escort the vessel on its arrival to within gunshot of Fort George and unload the paper there.[13]

On the night (October 26) the stamps were landed, the following warning was pasted on the door of every public office and on street corners in New York,

"Pro Patria

The first Man that either distributes or makes use of Stampt Paper let him take Care of his House, Person & Effects.

Vox Populi
We Dare"

And the evening before the Stamp Act was to take effect, a crowd marched through the streets of New York shouting "Liberty!" breaking street lamps and windows, and threatening to bury alive Major Thomas James, commanding the troops at the Fort, reported to have bragged that his men "would cram down the Stamp Act" upon the people of New York. The following evening a mob of about two thousand, consisting largely of former privateersmen and soldiers, led by boys carrying torches and effigies of Colden and the Devil, marched to within a few feet of the gate of Fort George, broke open Colden's coach house and seized his coach, seated the effigies in the coach, paraded them around the town, and, after hanging them on a gibbet in sight of the Fort, burned them together with the coach and three other vehicles hauled out of the coach house. The mob also broke into James's home and drank his wine, smashed his furniture, and stole his books and silverware. But apparently not daring to attack the Fort, the mob dissolved around four in the morning without getting the stamps.[14]

Four days later, after armed men had thronged into the city from near and far, placards were posted throughout the city announcing an attack on the Fort that night if the stamped paper was not handed over before then. Whereupon, under pressure from frightened local bigwigs and with the acquiescence of General Gage, Colden delivered the stamped paper to the Mayor and Corporation of New York City under an agreement that the Corporation would be responsible for its safekeeping.[15]

Though the object of the mobs at Boston, Newport, and New York to compel the Distributors to resign was probably in general approved, their unruliness in carrying out their object, and particularly the gratuitous mob vandalism, such as wrecking Hutchinson's Boston home on August 26,[16] impaired colonial solidarity by disgusting and frightening many of the colonists, particularly among the well-to-do in the northern colonies. Fearful of domestic social upheaval ("levelling"), they were henceforth anxious to avoid any measures that might involve this risk.[17]

In September, the Distributors for New Jersey, New Hampshire, and Connecticut resigned; the first two, William Coxe and George Meserve, without much ado, the third, Jared Ingersoll, only after various threats were pointed up by the reception accorded him on his way from New Haven to Hartford on September 19. He was, he wrote, met by "about Five Hundred Men, all on Horseback" carrying "pretty long and large new-made white Staves." Riding two abreast and led by three trumpeters and two officers dressed in red, the whole line of horsemen, on reaching Ingersoll, wheeled and escorted him to Wethersfield, where, taken into an inn and told to resign immediately or suffer the consequences, he resigned.[18]

John Hughes of Philadelphia, Distributor for Pennsylvania and Delaware, supported by the Quaker party in Pennsylvania, held out until October 5, when the stamps for the colonies in which he was to act reached Philadelphia. Summoned by the beat of muffled drums and the tolling of church bells throughout the city, a great crowd collected at the State House and deputed seven of its number to request Hughes's resignation. Warned by friends that "the mob intended to proceed to the last extremities," Hughes told the deputies he was disposed to comply, and, two days later, signed a paper promising not to exercise his office so long as the Stamp Act was not executed in the neighboring colonies.[19]

First of the Distributors in the southern colonies to yield was Caleb Lloyd of South Carolina, who, on learning of the uproar in Charleston over the Stamp Act prior to his arrival from England on October 26, promptly resigned his commission. A few weeks later William Houston, Distributor for North Carolina, resigned.[20] The Distributor for Virginia, Colonel George Mercer, member of an influential Virginia family and an outstanding officer in the Virginia forces during the French and Indian War, who likewise was in England at the time of his appointment, did not reach Virginia until October 30. His reception and ensuing resignation were described in a letter of November 3 from Governor Francis Fauquier to the Board of Trade.

"We were some time," wrote Fauquier, "in almost daily expectations of the arrival of Colonel Mercer with the Stamps for the use of this Colony, and rumours were industriously thrown out that at the time of the General Court parties would come down from most parts of the country to seize on and destroy all Stamped Papers. At those Courts persons engaged in business of any kind constantly attend as well as those who have suits depending before the Court; it being the time when all accompts of transactions of moment are settled, payments made and bills of exchange on Great Britain are drawn; so that there is always a vast concourse of people then in town. . . .

"Very unluckily, Colonel Mercer arrived at the time this town was the fullest of Strangers. On Wednesday the 30th October he came up to town. I then thought proper to go to the Coffee house (where I occasionally sometimes go) which is situated in that part of the town which is call'd the Exchange, tho' an open street, where all money business is transacted. . . . The mercantile people were all assembled as usual. The first word I heard was 'One and all' upon which, as at a word agreed on before between themselves, they all quitted the place to find Colonel Mercer at his father's lodgings where it was known he was. This concourse of people I should call a mob, did I not know that it was chiefly if not altogether composed of gentlemen of property in the Colony, some of them at the head of their respective Counties, and the merchants of the country whether English, Scotch or Virginian, for few absented themselves. They met Colonel Mercer on the way, just at the Capitol: there they stop'd and demanded of him an answer whether he would resign or act in this office as Distributor of the Stamps. He said it was an affair of great moment to him, he must consult his friends, and promised to give them an answer at 10 o'clock on Friday morning at that place. This did not satisfy them, and they followed him to the Coffee house, in the porch of which I had seated myself with many of the Council and the Speaker. . . . After much entreaty of some of his friends, Mr Mercer was, against his own inclination, prevailed upon to promise them an answer at the Capitol the next evening at five."

At the appointed time, Mercer, probably on the advice of his father and brother, "who were both frightened out of their senses for him," appeared at the capitol and read a paper stating "I will not, directly or indirectly, by myself or deputies, proceed in the execution of the act until I receive further orders from England, and not then without the assent of the General Assembly of this colony." Whereupon, he was "borne out of the Capitol gate, amidst the acclamations of all present" and feasted by a number of gentlemen at a nearby inn, with drums, French horns and bells playing and "the whole town . . . illuminated."[21]

The last to resign was Zachariah Hood of Maryland, who fled from Annapolis late in August when an effigy of him was carted through the town, whipped, pilloried, hanged, and burned and a house recently rented by him, reportedly as a storehouse for stamped paper, was pulled down. Turning up in New York City and driven away from the inn where he was staying, he found temporary refuge in nearby Fort George. But on retiring after a time to Flushing, Long Island, he was visited on November 28 by a crowd of three hundred men from New York City carrying banners inscribed "Liberty, Property and no Stamps" and frightened into resigning.[22]

George Angus, Distributor for Georgia, on his tardy arrival early in January 1766, sold some stamped paper; but soon left for parts unknown, and, hearing that a crowd of at least six hundred men was advancing on Savannah to seize the remaining stock of stamped paper, Governor James Wright of Georgia had the paper sent aboard a British sloop of war, thus putting a stop to further sale.[23]

In the other mainland colonies, the act was executed, though not without complaints,[24] and the same seems to have been true of most of the island colonies. The stamped paper was seized and burned in the tiny islands of St. Kitts (St. Christopher) and Nevis,[25] but was apparently used in Bermuda, Antigua, and Grenada[26] and certainly was in the two most important island colonies, Jamaica and Barbados.[27]

Henry Laurens of Charleston, one of the outstanding patriot leaders during the American Revolution, wrote a Philadelphia merchant shortly before the resignation of Distributor Lloyd, "a suspension of it [the Stamp Act] while it is in force would prove our ruin and destruction, and I am sure that if a stamp officer were so timid as to resign and a Governor so complisant as not to appoint another in his stead — we should in one fortnight, if nothing else would do, go down on our knees and pray him to give life to that law. What, else, would become of our estates, particularly ours who depend upon commerce?" A few days before the act was due to take effect, David Colden in New York was so sure it would "be quietly submitted to . . . in a few months" that he wrote the Commissioners of Stamps in London begging to be appointed McEvers' successor as Distributor for New York. And on November 2, Ingersoll wrote, "Some think the distresses which the want of the Stampt papers will Occasion will put the people upon moving the Assembly to desire me to introduce and distribute them. Should this be the Case I should not Scruple to Officiate, notwithstanding my forced resignation."[28] But these forecasts proved to be erroneous.

On November first, their regular publication date, the *New-London Gazette* of New London, Connecticut, the *Connecticut Gazette* of New Haven, and the *New-Hampshire Gazette* of Portsmouth appeared on unstamped paper, despite the heavy penalties in the Stamp Act. The *New-Hampshire Gazette* omitted the name of the publisher; but the other two appeared without even this much difference. Most of the Northern papers followed suit, some, like the *Boston Gazette* of November 4, without change, others with alterations of one kind or another.[29] All of the Southern papers suspended publication for part of the time the Stamp Act was in effect; but at least two of them resumed publication regularly before the Act was repealed.

Merchants and shipowners had anticipated the act by accelerating shipments or obtaining clearance papers dated before November first. But, after a time, cargoes accumulated and pressure on the customs officers to give clearances on unstamped paper began to build up, and, luckily for the colonists, the Stamp Commissioners had failed to send to Virginia a stock of stamped paper needed for customs clearance. On the strength of this, the Surveyor-General of Customs having control over Virginia (Peter Randolph, a cousin of Peyton Randolph, later Speaker of the Virginia House of Burgesses) authorized the Collector of Customs at Norfolk to give clearances on unstamped paper, which he did. After this opening wedge, merchants and shipowners of other colonial ports, pointing out that stamped paper was unavailable there too, put pressure on the local customs officials to grant similar clearances, and in time succeeded in obtaining these. With the sanction of Charles Stewart, Surveyor-General of the customs district which included Philadelphia and New York, the Collector at Philadelphia began to issue clearances on unstamped paper on December 2, and the Collector at New York City then or shortly afterward did the same.[30]

A surviving copy of the approved forms discloses that the procedure was for the captain of the vessel to enter at the foot of his manifest the statement, "And I, in Behalf, and at the Risque of the Owners of the said [name of ship] and Cargoe, desire a Clearance on the usual Papers as no Stampt Papers are issued in this Province" and for the Collector and Comptroller of Customs to state, "These are to certifie that Application being made to this Office to Clear out Vessells, and no Stampt Papers being distributed in this Province, We are therefore *obliged* to Grant the Clearances and Cocquets on un-stampt Papers as formerly."[31]

John Temple, Surveyor-General for the Northern District, includ-ing New England and Nova Scotia, more cautious than Stewart, de-clined to commit himself, and the customs officers at Boston held off from granting clearances until December 17, when, following Oliver's flat refusal to resume his office and furnish them with stamped paper, they too gave way. The customs officers at Newport and at New Lon-don, chief port of Connecticut, had yielded before those at Boston, and soon clearances were granted throughout New England.[32]

As to the ordinary citizen, whether farmer or city man, he was probably not too much discommoded by the lack of stamped paper. A letter from the president or principal of the college or academy stat-ing that a youth had been graduated would serve, at least temporarily, in lieu of a diploma; marriage by license was more expeditious, but marriage by banns, for which no stamped paper was required, was valid and cheaper. And wills, as pointed out by Edmund Pendleton, one of the leading lawyers of Virginia, could be legally proved, though recording would have to be deferred until the courts were will-ing or compelled to act without regard to the Stamp Act.[33] As to users of cards and dice, they had had ample opportunity before November first to lay in a supply.

The closing of the courts for lack of stamped paper was, of course, an inconvenience to some, particularly to creditors trying to collect overdue debts, but this was far from an unmitigated hardship. Henry Laurens wrote disgustedly of the desire of colonial debtors to "obtain a Credit during their own pleasure by the distruction of the Stamp'd Papers." And a letter of William Samuel Johnson of Connecticut in December 1765 stating that "Our being so excessively in debt to the Neighbouring Governments seems to be a Reason peculiar to us why we sho'd be less hasty than others in opening the Courts of Law" bears out Laurens's view. Washington doubtless had the same point in mind in writing a British correspondent that if the Stamp Act put a stop to judicial proceedings in Virginia, "I fancy the Merchants of G. Britain trading to the Colonies will not be among the last to wish for a Repeal of it."[34] But, though they were under no such pressure to act without stamps as were the customs officials, many of the colonial courts were proceeding without stamped paper by March 1766,[35] and probably others held off only because of reports from England that the Stamp Act was about to be repealed.

These reports proved to be well founded. The Stamp Act was repealed on March 18, 1766. Thus, though the Act and the colonial measures to annul it had excited fears and animosities on both sides of the water which were never wholly dispelled, the most important cause and the threat of immediate colonial rebellion were removed.[36]

NOTES

Introduction

1 Charles Andrews's statement, *A.H.R.* XXXI (1926) 219–32 at 231.

2 Independence not desired, Pownall *Administration of the Colonies* 28; Rev. Jonathan Mayhew to Thomas Hollis Aug. 19, 1765, Knollenberg "Hollis and Mayhew" 175–76.

3 Aspiration in colonies for independence, Benson *Kalm's Travels* I 139–40; John Adams to Nathan Webb Oct. 12, 1755, Adams *Works* I 23.

4 Charles Carroll of Carrollton wrote his father Charles Carroll, Sr., Nov. 12, 1763, that he would not marry an English girl who insisted on their living in England because "I can not sacrifice the future aggrandisement of our family to a woman; America is a growing country; in time it will and must be independent," *Md. Hist. Mag.* XII (1917) 21.

5 British fear of colonial desire for independence, Dummer *A Defence of the New England Charters* (London 1721) 60–61; George Clarke to N.Y. Legislature April 15, 1741 *N.Y. Legis. Council Journal* 1 768; Duke of Bedford to Duke of Newcastle March 24, 1746 Wood *Shirley* 318. I have not found Newcastle's reply.

6 *Contest in America* (attributed to Dr. John Mitchell) xxi–xxii; Col. James Murray to Gen. Jeffery Amherst, Nov. 1759, Burt *Quebec* 17; Bedford to Newcastle May 9, 1761, Pease *Anglo-French* 295. I have not found Amherst's or Newcastle's reply.

7 *Remarks* (London, 1760) 50–51. As to William Burke's authorship, Wecter *Burke* 19–22, and William Franklin to Galloway June 16, 1760, Knollenberg "Three Letters" 23–24. The Canada-Guadeloupe controversy is discussed in Grant "Canada versus Guadeloupe" 735–43.

8 The paragraph as to the British West Indies is based chiefly on Pitman *West Indies* 38–60, 113–18, 164–68, 185–86, 338–54; Saxby *The British Customs* (1757) 168–69; Gipson *Brit. Empire* II 297–98; Harper "Effect" 12; *Journal B. of T.* for 1749–1753, 267–68, and Sheffield *Observations* (1783) 65.

9 The appropriations toward support of the civil administration of Nova Scotia for 1764 and 1765 were £5,703 and £4,911 respectively, *Journals H. of C.* XXIX 877 and XXX 290.

Chapter 1

Part 1

1 The relations of the King, Newcastle, Pitt, and Lady Yarmouth with one another and with the Prince of Wales and Bute, at the opening of our period, are strik-

ingly illustrated in the correspondence from July 20 to Aug. 7, 1759, concerning the Prince's desire for army service, Sedgwick *Bute* 25–28; Namier *Eng.* 115–17; *Pitt* I 169–70 [letter of July 26, 1759, misdated July 15, 1756]; and Add. Mss. 32893:172–73, 202–3, and 318–19.

2 Newcastle wrote Pitt April 2, 1754, of Lord Hardwicke as one "with whom I do everything, and without whom I do nothing," *Pitt* I 99. For evidence of this: correspondence of Newcastle and Hardwicke, July 5, 1750, Sept. 4, 5, 1755, June 1, Oct. 23, 1757, Jan. 4, 1758, *Hardwicke* II 94, 237–49, 397, III 191, 41.

3 Favorable estimate of Newcastle, Pease *Anglo-French*, xxiii. Lodge *Chesterfield and Newcastle*, xxii comments on Newcastle's "extensive and accurate insight into the affairs of Europe" and Owen *Pelham* 128 on his "cogent and consistently-held principles, and his ample fund of common sense." But see Namier *Eng.* 76–91 for a highly unfavorable characterization.

4 Newcastle to Henry Pelham June 9, 1750, urging vigorous British defense of colonies in North America, Coxe *Pelham* II 345, and, in similar vein, to Horatio Walpole and Lord Albemarle June 29 and Sept. 5, 1754, Pease *Anglo-French* 48–49, 51. As to retaining Canada, Newcastle to Hardwicke Nov. 29, 1762, *Hardwicke* III 437.

5 Newcastle opposes alteration in colonial policy, Newcastle's memorandum of Aug. 10, 1761, Namier *Eng.* 336; opposes coercion of colonies or giving Governor of Canada power to govern without elected Assembly, Newcastle's notes of Aug. 11, 1763, Add. Mss. 32950:65–80 at 71 and Newcastle to Devonshire, Aug. 16, Add. Mss. 32950:81–83; opposes coercion of colonies, Newcastle to Lord Rockingham Sept. 12, 1768, Brooke *Chatham Administration* 373–74.

6 The importance to Great Britain of preserving its trade with the colonies was similarly stressed by Newcastle in a letter to Lord Rockingham of Jan. 13, 1766, urging repeal of the British act of 1765 levying a stamp tax on the colonies, Add. Mss. 32973:25.

7 Tory support of Pitt, Richard Rigby to the Duke of Bedford Jan. 20, 1756, *Bedford* II 223; Hardwicke to Newcastle Dec. 6 and 12, 1756, *Hardwicke* II 377–79; Lord Barrington to Andrew Mitchell Dec. 28, 1756, Namier *Eng.* 221; Newcastle to Hardwicke March 15, 1760, Namier *Structure* I 8. As to William Beckford's support, Hardwicke to Newcastle Oct. 17, 1761. As to number of Tories in House of Commons, Namier *Eng.* 487–90.

8 The Cabinet (inner Cabinet), Cabinet Council, and Privy Council are discussed in the Appendix to Chapter I of Knollenberg *Origin* (1960 ed.).

9 Jared Ingersoll to William S. Johnson as to Pitt, Dec. 22, 1759, Beardsley *W. S. Johnson* 21–22. As to Ingersoll's acquaintance with Pitt, *same* 16.

10 Pitt's procolonial views, Newcastle to Hardwicke Oct. 2, 1754, Rosebery *Chatham* 350–51 and April 17, 1761, *Hardwicke* III 315–16; Hardwicke to Newcastle April 2, 1762, Pease *Anglo-French* 412; Newcastle's notes Aug. 11, 1763, Add. Mss. 32950:71; Charles Townshend to Newcastle March 23, 1764, Add. Mss. 32957:239; George Onslow to Newcastle March 19, 1765, Winstanley *Government* 218–19n; John Calcraft to Lord Shelburne April 15, *Shelburne* I 323–24; Morgan *Stamp Act* 273–75.

11 Stalemate in Germany but British successes elsewhere in 1759, Gipson *Brit. Empire* VII 346–56, 361–64, 410–25, VIII 12–23, 32–39.

12 Unanimity in Parliament, Walpole to Sir Horace Mann Nov. 16, 1759, Toynbee *Walpole* IV 320. (Unless otherwise noted, "Walpole" refers to Horace Walpole, the famous letter writer, son of the former Prime Minister, Sir Robert.) To the same effect, Barrington to Mitchell Jan. 14, 1760, 2 *Ellis* IV 416; *Parl. Hist.* XV 965.

13 British successes in 1760, Gipson *Brit. Empire* VII 462–66, VIII 164–65. The Articles of Capitulation of Montreal, Sept. 8, 1760, are in S. & D. *Doc.* I 25–36.

14 Chesterfield to his son Philip Stanhope May 18, 1758, as to Newcastle and Pitt, *Chesterfield* IV 290–91. As to friction between Newcastle and Pitt, Torrens *Hist. of Cabinets* II 489–563 *passim*; *Hardwicke* III 54–112, 233–53 *passim*; Sherrard *Chatham* 297–367 *passim* and other biographies of Pitt, later Lord Chatham.

15 As to the Old Pretender, Mann to Walpole Nov. 8, 1760, *D.N.B.* X 640; as to Prince Charles, Hans Stanley to Pitt June 9, 1761, stating "The Pretender's eldest son is drunk as soon as he rises, and is almost senselessly so at night, when his servants carry him to bed." Thackeray *Pitt* I 522, and Charles Carroll, Jr., to Charles Carroll, Sr., Oct. 3, 1763, *Md. Hist. Mag.* XI (1916) 348.

16 Government $3\frac{1}{2}$% of 1758, which dropped from $88\frac{1}{8}$ on Oct. 24, 1760, to $85\frac{1}{4}$ bid, $85\frac{1}{2}$ asked on Oct. 25, were $87\frac{1}{4}$ on Oct. 27, and back to $88\frac{1}{8}$ on Nov. 1, Monthly Summary of each day's market, *Gentleman's Magazine* for Oct. and Nov. 1760, XXX 492, 544.

17 Favorable impression made by George III, Barrington to Mitchell Jan. 5, 1761, 2 *Ellis* IV 430; Edmund Hooper to James Harris Nov. 8, 1760, *Malmesbury* I 82; Walpole to Mann Nov. 1, 1760, Toynbee *Walpole* IV 449. Namier "George III" 610–21 has an excellent characterization of the King.

18 George III's winning thoughtfulness, Walpole to Mann Nov. 1 and to George Montagu Nov. 4, 1760, Toynbee *Walpole* IV 449, 453.

19 The current Parliament would expire, if not sooner dissolved, six months after the death of George II, 6 Anne ch. 7 sec. 4 (1707). But even if the King had lived, the current Parliament, having opened May 31, 1754, would have expired on May 30 or 31, 1761, under the Septennial Act of 1716, 1 Geo. I, session 2, ch. 38.

20 Bute's appointment to Privy Council and as Groom of the Stole, *Gentleman's Mag.* for Oct. and Nov. 1760, XXX 488, 542. Groom of the Stole was one of the four great offices of the King's household, along with Lord Chamberlain, Lord Steward, and Master of the Horse, Beatson *Pol. Index* I 284–301.

21 Prince George's correspondence evincing his love for and trust in Bute, *Bute* 2–48.

22 Prince George to Bute May 4, 1760, *same* 44–46. An omitted passage as to Pitt's ingratitude to Bute indicates that Pitt is "the blackest of hearts" referred to by the Prince. After fawning on Bute (letters of June 1755 to Sept. 1758, Sedgwick "Letters from Pitt to Bute" 108–62), Pitt had become somewhat aloof, and recently had repulsed an effort of Bute to reestablish closer relations, Namier *Eng.* 117–23.

23 The *Considerations* (London, 1760), summarized in the November 1760 issue of *Gentleman's Mag.* XXX 495–500, is attributed to Israel Mauduit, *D.N.B.* under

"Mauduit, Israel" and H. & L. *Dict.* I 417. Walpole to Mann Dec. 5, 1760, as to influence of the pamphlet Toynbee *Walpole* V 7, 7n. Rigby wrote Bedford, Dec. 22, 1760, that its arguments, repeated in the House of Commons, had not been answered and were unanswerable, *Bedford* II 426.

24 Subsidy to Prussia continued, proceedings in the House of Commons Dec. 22 and 23, 1760, *Journals H. of C.* XXVIII 1006–7, with Rigby to Bedford, Dec. 22, 1760, *Bedford* II 426 (Prussia misprinted "Russia").

25 George III to Bute Jan. 20 to June 27, 1761, concerning his search for a suitable Queen, *Bute* 51–56. The King chose Princess Charlotte, daughter of the Duke of Mecklenburg-Strelitz, deceased, whom he married Sept. 8, 1761. For a charming notice of her, Walpole to Henry Seymour Conway Sept. 9, 1761, Toynbee *Walpole* V 103–4.

26 Newcastle's preparations for election of new House of Commons, Namier *Eng.* 153, 157–59, 166–67, 172, 197–200. Bute told Newcastle, who had begun to prepare for the election a month before the death of George II, *same* 130–34, that George III intended to give Newcastle "the choice of the new Parliament," and this promise was kept, Newcastle to Joseph Yorke Oct. 31, 1760, and to John Page Feb. 7, 1761, *same* 144, 175–76.

27 Most of the constituencies had two representatives; some had one and the combined boroughs of Weymouth and Melcombe Regis and the City of London four each. Namier *Structure* (1957) 62.

28 Few contests and most members reelected, Namier *Structure* I 196 slightly modified by Namier *Eng.* 200. In many other constituencies, threatened contests were dropped before the poll was taken, Namier *Structure* I 196–97. Of the sixteen Scotch peers representing the Scottish peerage in the House of Lords, six, including Bute, were new, *Parl. Hist.* XV 322, 1100.

29 As to Newcastle's approval of Bute's appointment without consulting Pitt, Namier *Eng.* 185–90. Basil Williams (Williams *Pitt* II 72) and others have denounced this as "treachery" to Pitt. But since Pitt, without consulting Newcastle, had approved appointing five Tories to the royal household, Newcastle to Joseph Yorke and to Hardwicke, Dec. 5 and 7, 1760, Namier *Eng.* 153–54, the charge seems farfetched.

30 Bute's theatrical letter to George III May 24, 1761, accepting office of Secretary of State, *same* 190–93. Bute replaced Lord Holderness, who was appeased with a promise of future appointment to the rich sinecure of Wardenship of the Cinque Ports and, while waiting for this, a pension of £4,000 a year, *Bute* 52n.

31 Changes in Ministry, *Gentleman's Mag.* XXXI (March 1761) 141. As to Pitt's enlarged power, Order in Council May 15, 1761, *Acts P.C.* IV 157 with Basye *Board of Trade* 107–9.

32 Peace negotiations March 26 to Sept. 25, 1761, Rashed *Peace* 70–75, 79–100; Pease *Anglo-French* 290–397; Thackeray *Pitt* I 539–79, II 507–26, *Hardwicke* III 315–28; Add. Mss. 32924:311–22; 32925:335; 32926:187–93, 249, 269–70; 32927:69–70.

33 As to the importance of the Newfoundland fishery and Pitt's determination to exclude France, Innis *Cod Fisheries passim;* Lounsbury *Brit. Fishery at Newfoundland, passim,* Hotblack "Peace" 265–66; Newcastle to Hardwicke April 17 and Aug. 9,

1761, *Hardwicke* III 316 and Add. Mss. 32926:324, the latter stating "The Point of the Fisheries is, and has been almost the Sole Obstacle to our Peace."

34 The French-Spanish treaty of military alliance of Aug. 15, 1761, provided that France would support Spain in its pending claims against Great Britain and would not make peace except in concert with Spain, while Spain agreed to declare war on Great Britain by May 1, 1762, if peace had not been made by then, Blart *Rapports de la France et de l'Espagne* 214–17.

35 Dissension in Cabinet, Hardwicke's correspondence April 18 to Aug. 15, 1761, *Hardwicke* III 318–21; Newcastle's June 28 to Aug. 9, Add. Mss. 32924:311–16, 314–15; 32926:269–70, 324–27; Bedford's July 9 to Sept. 13 *Bedford* III 22–46; Namier *Eng.* 339–42. Evidence of French-Spanish alliance, *Pitt* II 139–44. Pitt outvoted, notes of Cabinet meetings Sept. 18 to Oct. 2, Hunt "Pitt's Retirement" 121–32; *Hardwicke* III 275–76.

36 Correspondence of Bute and Pitt as to Pitt's pension and peerage for his wife, Oct. 6 to 8, 1761, *Pitt* II 146–51.

37 Hardwicke to Charles Yorke predicting that Pitt would temporarily be quiet, Oct. 17, 1761, *Hardwicke* III 331. Pitt in fact gave the Ministry little opposition at the next session. As to the popular reaction against Pitt and his subsequent return to popular favor, Williams *Pitt* II 118–21.

38 Cabinet changes, Beatson *Pol. Index* I 255, 277. As to Grenville's leadership of House of Commons, Barrington to Mitchell Oct. 9, 1761, 2 *Ellis* IV 444; Hardwicke to Charles Yorke Oct. 10, *Hardwicke* III 330. As to the family and political relations of Grenville with Pitt and Temple, Wiggin *Grenvilles, passim.*

39 Lord Egremont's efforts for peace, *Parl. Hist.* XV 1152–69. French-Spanish Treaty of Aug. 15, 1761, Blart *Rapports de la France et de l'Espagne* 214–17. England declared war on Spain Jan. 4, 1762, *Gentleman's Mag.* XXXII (Jan. 1762) 42.

40 Cabinet agreement as to Havana, Newcastle to Hardwicke Jan. 10, 1762, Add. Mss. 32933:179–82 (partly in *Rockingham* I 86–87 and Namier *Eng.* 360). Prince George to Bute [Aug. 5, 1759] condemning his grandfather's partiality to Hanover and George III to Bute [Jan. 6 and April, 1762] expressing his desire for withdrawal from the German war, *Bute* 28, 79, 92–93.

41 Division in the Cabinet as to withdrawal from the German war, Henry Fox to Lord Shelburne Jan. 8, 1762, *Shelburne* I 127; Newcastle to Hardwicke Jan. 10, 16, and April 10, 1762, Namier *Eng.* 360, 362 and *Rockingham* I 105–8; Bedford's resolution for withdrawal opposed by Bute Feb. 5, *Parl. Hist.* XV 1217–19; Hardwicke to Newcastle April 14 as to Bute's indecision, *Hardwicke* III 348.

42 Newcastle outvoted in Cabinet under particularly bitter circumstances, Newcastle to Hardwicke April 30, 1762, *same* 352 and Namier *Eng.* 368; Newcastle to Joseph Yorke May 14, Riker *Fox* II 371–77 with addition in *Hardwicke* III 355–58; Bute to Bedford May 1, *Bedford* III 76–77; George III to Bute [May 7] *Bute* 101.

43 King sustains majority of Cabinet and Newcastle resigns, Newcastle to Hardwicke and to Devonshire May 3, 7, 1762, *Hardwicke* III 353, Namier *Eng.* 371–73; George III to Bute [May 3, 7] *Bute* 96–97, 101. Newcastle apparently hoped to be asked to reconsider, but was not, Newcastle to various correspondents May 14 to

17, Namier *Eng.* 375–76. He gave up his office May 26, Newcastle to Marquis of Rockingham May 27 Add. Mss. 32939:37.

44 The troops, led by Gen. Lord Granby, numbering nominally about 23,000 men exclusive of artillery, were retained in Germany and saw hard fighting before the summer was over, Manners *Granby* 241–60, Schaefer *Geschichte* II Part II 537–79. The vote of £1,000,000 sufficed to maintain the troops, Bute to Bedford Oct. 30, 1762, *Bedford* III 142; George III to Bute [about Oct. 30] *Bute* 153.

45 Grenville's supposed wish for headship of Treasury, Newcastle to Hardwicke April 10, 1762, *Rockingham* I 107; George III to Bute [May 6, 1762] *Bute* 100. The King had long desired and now insists on Bute's having the post, *same* 19–20, 21, 45, 93, 109.

46 Lord Anson's death and Cabinet changes, *London Chronicle* June 1, 8, 22, 1762.

Part 2

1 British successes in the war, *Annual Register* for 1762, 23–32; Gipson *Brit. Empire* VIII 193–96, 261–73; Corbett *England* II 246–81.

2 Peace negotiations in 1762 and secret commitments of Bute and Egremont, Pease *Anglo-French* cxxvi–clxvii, 425, 456, 554; Pease "Mississippi Boundary" 278–86; Rashed *Peace* 118–86. France was eager for peace because of the recent accession to the Russian throne of a pro-Prussian emperor, Paul III, *same* 135–37.

3 Promise to cede western Louisiana, Louis XV of France to Charles III of Spain Oct. 9, 1762, Aiton "Diplomacy of the Louisiana Cession" 717. The cession was made Nov. 3, *same* 718. (Spain took over the lower part of the ceded territory temporarily in Feb. 1766, and permanently in 1769, Lyon *La.* 44–45, 52, and the upper in 1770, *Gage* I 266.)

4 Grenville's disagreement with Bute, Rigby to Bedford Sept. 29 and 30, 1762, *Bedford* III 128–33; Newcastle to Hardwicke Oct. 3 *Hardwicke* III 418; Duc de Nivernois to Comte de Choiseul Oct. 9 *Bute* 142.

5 Changes in Cabinet, Fox's memorandum of Oct. 8, 1762, *Shelburne* I 154–55 with Ilchester *Fox* II 193; George III to Bute [Oct. 8 and 11] *Bute* 144–45. Grenville's Narrative of Events Oct. 9 to 11, 1762, *Grenville* I 451–52, 482–85; Fox and Bute to Bedford Oct. 13 and 14, 1762, *Bedford* III 134–36.

6 Differing opinions as to Fox's adding strength to the Ministry, Hardwicke to Newcastle Oct. 23, 1762; Newcastle to Charles Yorke Oct. 25, *Hardwicke* III 424, 426.

7 Newcastle to the Duke of Devonshire quoting Townshend as to the peace, Nov. 20, 1762, Ilchester *Fox* II 209; Hardwicke to Newcastle Nov. 27, *Hardwicke* III 436.

8 Terms of preliminary treaty of peace signed at Fontainebleau Nov. 3, 1762, *Parl. Hist.* XV 1241–51.

9 Newcastle's discontent in retirement and Pitt's refusal to unite with him, Namier *Eng.* 380–401, 417–52; Newcastle's notes as to conversations of Thomas Nuthall Nov. 5, 1762, and Thomas Walpole Nov. 13 with Pitt, *Hardwicke* III 430–31.

10 Pitt's speech of Dec. 9, 1762, printed in Almon *Pitt* I 347–67, discussed in James Hayes to Richard Neville Dec. 10, *Bedford* III 168; Barrington to Mitchell Dec. 13

2 *Ellis* IV 456; and several other published letters. As to vote in House of Commons Dec. 9, 1762, *Journals H. of C.* XXIX 394; as to proceedings in House of Lords, Burke to O'Hara Dec. 12, 1762, Hoffman *Burke* 302–3; Rigby to Bedford Dec. 13 *Bedford* III 170; *Parl. Hist.* XV 1251–58.

11 Tories' desertion of Pitt foretold and confirmed by vote on treaty, Hardwicke to Newcastle Nov. 27, 1762, *Hardwicke* III 436; Rigby to Bedford Nov. 26, 1762, *Bedford* III 162; analysis of the vote in House of Commons Dec. 1, 1762, Namier *Eng.* 457.

12 Vote in House of Commons Dec. 1, 1762, on motion for postponement of debate on the treaty, *Journals H. of C.* XXIX 387; Shelburne and Fox urge Bute to dismiss opposition members of Parliament from office, Shelburne to Bute Dec. 1762, *Shelburne* I 182; Fox to Bute Dec. 10, 1762, Ilchester *Fox* II 215–16. Fox from the beginning favored widespread dismissals, *same* 214–15, Namier *Eng.* 470, but Bute was more "temperate" *Bute* 175.

13 The King urges Bute to dismiss members of opposition from office, George III to Bute [Dec. 11, 1762] *same* 174. As to members dismissed, including Dukes of Newcastle and Grafton and Lord Rockingham from their county Lord-Lieutenancies, Namier *Eng.* 472–74, *Rockingham* I 155–56, *Hardwicke* III 448.

14 Treaty of Paris Feb. 10, 1763, *Annual Register* for 1762, 233–47, following further negotiations discussed in Rashed *Peace* 192–200 and Sutherland "India" 179–90. Plans for peacetime army, George III to Bute [Sept. 1762, Jan. and Feb. 1763] *Bute* 135, 185, 188; Newcastle's memorandum Feb. 19, 1763, Add. Mss. 32947:46–47; Rigby to Bedford Feb. 23 *Bedford* III 209. Reduction in King's plan to satisfy Tories, Bute to Sir John Phillips Feb. 23, 1763, Add. Mss. 36797:34.

15 Reduced plan approved, George III to Bute [Feb. 24, 1763] *Bute* 191; Sir Roger Newdigate's diary Feb. 24 Namier *Personalities* 72. The reduced plan adopted, *Journals H. of C.* XXIX 503–6. As to the number of troops before and after the war respectively, see Chapter 6.

16 Newcastle's opposition to the army increase but decision to remain silent, Newcastle to Devonshire Dec. 23, 1762, Alvord *Mississippi Valley* I 130n; Newcastle to Hardwicke March 3, 1763, Add. Mss. 32947:163.

17 As to Pitt's approval of the plan, "wishing it had been still more numerous" and the opposition's silence, Rigby to Bedford March 10, 1763, *Bedford* III 218. Apparently only one member—William Beckford—spoke against the proposed increase, James West's notes March 22 Add. Mss. 32947:265–66.

18 Increase approved March 4, 1763, by the House sitting in Committee of the Whole; motion to recommit rejected March 7, *Journals H. of C.* XXIX 527–28, 530, and embodied in annual Mutiny Bill, 3 Geo. III ch. 7 (1763). As to rapid progress of the bill, assented to by the King March 24, *Journals H. of C.* XXIX 530, 545, 564, 600, 607.

19 Report of proposed tax, Rigby to Bedford Feb. 23, 1763, *Bedford* III 210; Newcastle notes of Feb. 19, Alvord *Mississippi Valley* I 130n (date supplied from Add. Mss. 32947:46); Cecilius Calvert to Gov. Horatio Sharpe of Md. March 1 *Md. Arch.* XXXI 531; *London Chronicle* March 8. As to Welbore Ellis's mention of the proposed tax, Jasper Mauduit, London Agent for Mass., to Mass. Council March 12, 1763, Bancroft Papers, Col. Doc. Jan. 1761–Dec. 1764.

20 George III to Bute [about the middle of March 1763] condemning Charles Town-shend's premature colonial tax proposal, *Bute* 201. As to Townshend's proposal, Mauduit to Mass. Assembly March 23, 1763, Bancroft Papers "Maryland" 284. Townshend, Secretary at War from March 1761 to Dec. 1762, had just succeeded Lord Sandys as President of the Board of Trade, *London Chronicle* March 3, 1763.

21 Sharpe to Calvert June 4, 1763, as to supposed commercial concessions to colonies to offset tax, *Md. Arch.* XIV 92–93.

22 Pitt joins forces with Newcastle group, Hardwicke to Lord Royston March 8, 1763, and Newcastle to Hardwicke March 12 and 29, *Hardwicke* III 456; *London Chronicle* March 19. Opposition motion as to cider tax bill defeated March 21, 198 to 115, *Journals H. of C.* XXIX 600.

23 Bute's illness, Bute to Dr. John Campbell Jan. 30, 1763, and to Baron Mure April 9 *Bute* lxii and *Caldwell* Part II vol. I 176. The hounding of Bute by John Wilkes and other political opponents, discussed later in this chapter, was apparently encouraged by Frederick the Great of Prussia, Dorn "Frederick the Great" 557–58. Bute attacked by rowdies, Rigby to Bedford Nov. 26, 1762, *Bedford* III 159–60; Walpole to Mann Nov. 30 Toynbee *Walpole* V 278.

24 "In my opinion the Angel Gabriel could not at present govern this country, but by means too long practic'd and such as my soul abhors," Bute to Campbell Jan. 30, 1762, *Bute* lxii. Bute also complained of lack of proper support in the Cabinet, Bute to Gen. George Townshend April 8, 1763, Winstanley *Government* 151n (name of addressee supplied from Add. Mss. 36797:42).

25 King's pleading with Bute not to resign, George III to Bute Nov. 1762, *Bute* 166–67; Bute to Fox March 2, 1763, Ilchester *Letters to Fox* II 225 as to his resolution to resign. King's consent to resignation, George III to Bute [about April 4 and on April 7] *Bute* 209–10, 212.

26 George III to Bute [early March 1763] expressing his distaste for Bute's proposal of Fox as his successor, *same* 197–99. Namier *Structure* I 226–28 suggests that perhaps Fox's methods did not differ substantially from those customary at this period, but he certainly was exceptionally brazen, e.g., Fox to Peter Collinson Jan. 25, 1755, and to Horace Walpole Nov. 21, 1762, Ilchester *Fox* I 245 and Walpole *Memoirs of George the Third* I 213–14.

27 George III to Bute [about March 14, 1763] reluctantly agreeing to Fox's succeeding Bute, *Bute* 200; John Calcraft to Shelburne concerning Fox's decision not to accept, March 15, 1763, *Shelburne* I 194. Fox soon afterward changed his mind, Calcraft to Shelburne March 22, *same* 217, but nothing came of this. On April 17 Fox was created an English peer, Baron Holland, which, of course, eliminated him as Leader of the House of Commons.

28 Proposed Cabinet changes, George III to Bute [March 24, 1763] *Bute* 205; Bute to Grenville and Grenville to Bute March 25, as to Shelburne's youth, etc., *Grenville* II 32–33. (Shelburne was only twenty-five.) As to the new Cabinet, *Gentleman's Mag.* XXXIII (April 1763) 202. As to Grenville's becoming Leader of House of Commons, Grenville diary Nov. 10 and 12, 1763, *Grenville* II 221, 222.

29 Grenville's disappointment with Pitt, Grenville's narrative April 12, 1762, *Grenville* I 438–39; his industry and ability, e.g., Pitt to Hardwicke April 6, 1754, *Pitt* I 106;

Walpole to Lord Hertford Feb. 15, 1764, Toynbee *Walpole* VI 5; his prolixity, Hardwicke to Newcastle Oct. 17, 1761, *Hardwicke* III 333; George III to Bute [April 28, 1762] *Bute* 231; his rise through Bute, Bute to Grenville Feb. 11, 1761, and Charles Jenkinson to Grenville March 26 *Grenville* I 359, 361.

30 For the history of *The North Briton* and its contributors, including the poets Charles Churchill and Robert Lloyd, Nobbe *The North Briton, passim.*

31 *North Briton's* exploitation of English anti-Scotism, examples: Nos. 2, 3, 4, 6, 7, 13, 34 *North Briton* I 10–35, 45–48, 54–62, 113–23, II 111–13. As to Fox's explanation of English anti-Scotism, Henry Fox's memoir written June 17, 1762, Ilchester *Lennox* 60, 68.

32 Evidence of widespread anti-Scotism in England, William Tod to William Smellie Nov. 29, 1759, Clive and Bailyn "England's Cultural Provinces" 212; James Boswell's diary entry Dec. 8, 1762, Pottle *Boswell's London Journal* 71; Hardwicke to Charles Yorke Oct. 10, 1761, Harris *Hardwicke* III 259; Newcastle to Hardwicke Aug. 11, 1762, *Hardwicke* III 406–7; Devonshire to Fox Oct. 14, 1762, Ilchester *Fox* II 203; popular prints, 1761 to 1770, Stephens *Prints* (Satires) IV 10–352 *passim.* Johnson's and Shelburne's remarks, Johnson to Boswell Feb. 7, 1775, Hill *Boswell's Johnson* II 296–97; Shelburne's autobiography *Shelburne* I 87–89.

33 *North Briton's* playing up rumor as to Bute's supposed liaison with the Princess Augusta, No. 5, July 3, 1762, *North Briton* I 37–44. As to prevalence of this rumor (which I have not found evidence to support) Stephens *Prints* (Satires) IV 31–316, particularly 58–65.

34 Insult to the King, *North Briton* II 228–41 at 231, 237, 240.

35 This paragraph as to the proceedings against Wilkes is based on Almon *Wilkes* I 97–98n, 105–6n, III 201–8; Nobbe *The North Briton* 214–19; Howell *State Trials* XIX 1155–57; *London Chronicle* May 3, 1763.

36 Wilkes's successful application for writ of habeas corpus, May 3, 1763, Howell *State Trials* XIX 982–90. Privilege from arrest, which held during the session and for forty days before and after, usually continued for the entire term of Parliament (normally about seven years) because Parliament was rarely prorogued for more than eighty days at a time, Blackstone *Commentaries* I 165.

37 Verdict in favor of Dryden Leach's workmen, July 6, 1763, *London Chronicle* July 7; Wilkes to Temple July 7 and 9, *Grenville* II 70–75; Thomas Nuthall to Pitt July 7, *Pitt* II 230–35; Thomas Birch to Lord Royston July 9 and Hardwicke to Newcastle July 9 and 14, *Hardwicke* III 509–11. Wilkes's boasts, Wilkes to Temple July 7 and 9, *Grenville* II 70, 73–74, 75.

38 Approaches to Pitt and Hardwicke, Newcastle to Hardwicke June 20, 1763, Hardwicke to Royston Aug. 5 and Newcastle to Hardwicke Aug. 28, *Hardwicke* III 509, 512, 523; various correspondents Aug. 8 to 16, *Shelburne* I 283–88; Calcraft to Temple Aug. 10, *Grenville* II 90–91; Rigby to Bedford Aug. 15, *Bedford* III 236–37; King's talks with Pitt Aug. 27 and 29, Hardwicke to Royston, Sept. 4, *Hardwicke* III 526–27. Conflicting reports concerning Temple to head the Treasury, compare *same* with Gilbert Elliot to Sir Gilbert Elliot Aug. 30, *Elliot* 377.

39 This paragraph as to Pitt's proscriptions and Bedford's reactions is based on letters of various writers, Sept. 5 to 28, 1763, *Bedford* III 238–51 and Newcastle's mem-

orandum of Sept. 28 "Substance of Conversation . . . with Mr. Pitt yesterday,"
Add. Mss. 32951:192–205 at 193–94, 198–99. As to the King's encouragement of
Bedford's peace terms, George III to Bedford Oct. 26, 1762, *Bedford* III 140.

40 Shelburne's resignation and reason for this, Newcastle's notes Sept. 28, 1763,
Add. Mss. 32951:192–204 at 201. Changes in Ministry, *Gentleman's Mag.* XXXIII
(Sept. 1763) 465–66. Halifax's switch from the Northern to the Southern
Department had been made by Sept. 19, 1763, S. & D. *Doc.* I 153.

41 Colonial suspicion of Halifax, Benjamin Franklin to Isaac Norris March 19,
1759, Mason "Franklin and Galloway" 246 (Franklin's charge that Halifax favored a military government for Nova Scotia was apparently unjustified, Gipson
Brit. Empire IX 129–33); William Franklin to Joseph Galloway June 16, 1760,
Knollenberg "Three Letters" 24; Joseph Trumbull to Jonathan Trumbull Dec.
10, 1763, Stuart *Trumbull* 83n; Richard Jackson to Benjamin Franklin Dec. 27,
1763, *Jackson* 121–22.

42 Halifax's favoring colonial taxation, Newcastle's "Hints from Lord Halifax . . ."
Oct. 21, 1755, Add. Mss. 32996:265; colonial bishops, Thomas Secker, Archbishop of Canterbury, to Rev. Samuel Johnson Sept. 28, 1763, *N.Y. Col. Doc.* VII
566; Bernard's plan (in Bernard *Select Letters* 65–85) with Lord Barrington to Bernard Oct. 3, 1764, *Barrington-Bernard Corresp.* 81; stopping trade with French West
Indies, Halifax to B. of T. Dec. 14, 1763, C.O. 323:17: R.22:64; Crown payment
of colonial officials, Grenville Diary Jan. 6, 1764, *Grenville* II 481.

43 The collected edition of numbers 1 to 45 of *The North Briton* (2 vols., London,
1763) was published Aug. 2, 1763, Howell *State Trials* XIX 1384. The vilification
of Egremont is in No. 46 of *The North Briton* published Nov. 12 reprinted in *London
Chronicle* Nov. 15. Wilkes resented Egremont's having assumed "a supercilious, in-
solent air" during Wilkes's examination following his arrest, Wilkes to Grafton
Dec. 12, 1767, Almon *Wilkes* III 202.

44 Proceedings in House of Commons concerning Wilkes and *The North Briton* No.
45, Nov. 15, 1763, *Parl. Hist.* XV 1356–60; Walpole to Hertford and to Mann Nov.
17 Toynbee *Walpole* V 384–87, 392–93. The vote was on a motion to strike out the
words "excite them to traitorous insurrections against his Majesty's government."

45 *An Essay on Woman, and other pieces* . . . London, privately printed by J. C. Hotten,
1871. The full title page, omitting a phallic drawing, is in Bleackley *Wilkes* 116–17.
As to the probable composition of the *Essay* by Wilkes and his and Pitt's dissolute friend Thomas Potter, same 23–24, 36–37, 437–44, and Watson "Wilkes"
121–23, 143–45. As to Fanny Murray, who had become the wife of the well-
known actor, David Ross, Bleackley *Ladies* 3–49, 297–99.

46 The footnote to line 91 of the *Essay*, beginning "Hope humbly, then, clean girls;
nor vainly soar," attributed to Warburton, is as foul a passage as I have ever read.
The blasphemy is in the notes to verses 8 and 42 of the *Essay*.

47 Complaint and resolution in House of Lords as to breach of privilege Nov. 15,
1763, and resolution for prosecution Nov. 17. *Parl. Hist.* XV 1346–51; Walpole to
Hertford and to Mann Nov. 17 Toynbee *Walpole* V 387–88, 394–95; Bishop Warburton and William Strahan to Ralph Allen Nov. 17 and 21, Kilvert *Warburton*
227–30, and Peach *Allen* 191–93.

48 Edward Gibbon's journal Sept. 23, 1762, as to Wilkes, Low *Gibbon's Journal* 145.

49 Motion in House of Commons Nov. 24, 1763, as to privilege, *Parl. Hist.* XV 1362.

50 Pitt's speech Nov. 24, 1763, in favor of privilege, *same* 1363–64, Walpole to Hertford, Nov. 25 Toynbee *Walpole* V 399; Charles Yorke's great speech against privilege, Grenville to the King, Newcastle to Charles Yorke, both on Nov. 25, *George III* I 62–63, *Hardwicke* III 557 and Warburton to Allen Nov. 26 Kilvert *Warburton* 232; resolution against privilege adopted by House of Commons Nov. 24 and by House of Lords Nov. 29, *Parl. Hist.* XV 1362, 1365–71.

51 Joint resolution to burn No. 45 of *The North Briton*, Dec. 1, 1763, *same* 1378–79; riot at burning of No. 45 on Dec. 3 *London Chronicle* Dec. 6. For additional details, Lord Bath to Mrs. Elizabeth Montagu Dec. 5, Blunt *Mrs. Montagu* I 80; Walpole to Hertford Dec. 9 Toynbee *Walpole* V 407–8.

52 Wilkes's triumph in *Wilkes v. Wood, Annual Register* for 1763, 145. (*London Chronicle* Dec. 8, 1763, as to nine other suits by Wilkes pending. In one of these, against Halifax, he got a verdict in 1769 for £4,000, Nobbe *North Briton* 264.) As to Wilkes's duel with Samuel Martin, whom he had defamed (*North Briton* II 174–75), Bleackley *Wilkes* 135–37; Wilkes acclaimed, *London Chronicle* Dec. 8, 1763. For additional details, Walpole to Hertford Dec. 9 Toynbee *Walpole* V 409.

53 Wilkes's expulsion from House of Commons Jan. 19, 1764, and House of Lords' order for his arrest Jan. 24, *Parl. Hist.* XV 1352, 1388–93; found guilty of criminal libel Feb. 21, 1764, Bleackley *Wilkes* 150–51, Nobbe *North Briton* 256–57; arrival in France, Wilkes to Cotes Dec. 25, 1763, Almon *Wilkes* II 33–34; declared an outlaw Nov. 1, 1764, Nobbe *North Briton* 257 with Bleackley *Wilkes* 159–60; years abroad (1764–1768) and brief, furtive trips to England, *same* 160–85.

54 Motion as to general warrants, Feb. 14, 1764, *Parl. Hist.* XV 1399; preliminary and final debates on the motion, Walpole to Hertford Feb. 15 and 19 Toynbee *Walpole* VI 6 and 10–11. In similar vein Charles Carroll, Jr., wrote Charles Carroll, Sr., Feb. 27, that on this occasion "the house ressembled more a hospital than a Senate," *Md. Hist. Mag.* XII (1917) 37.

55 Report of Sir Fletcher Norton's and Charles Yorke's speeches, Walpole to Hertford Feb. 19, 1764, Toynbee *Walpole* VI 9; George Onslow to Newcastle Feb. 17, 1764, *Hardwicke* III 564. "Joy" to Newcastle in particular because of his love for Yorke's father, Hardwicke, who was desperately ill and died two weeks later. To same effect as to Yorke's speech, James West to Newcastle Feb. 17 *same* 563.

56 Walpole to Hertford Feb. 19, 1764, as to Pitt and other speakers, Toynbee *Walpole* VI 9–10. Other accounts are in Grenville to George III, Feb. 18, including a reference to Pitt's having been very "faint and languid," *Grenville* II 266–67; Strahan to Allen Feb. 20 Peach *Allen* 201–2; *Parl. Hist.* XV 1400–1418. As to method of "dividing" the House of Commons, Comyns *Digest* IV (1766) 309.

57 Sir Lewis Namier's statement as to vote of Scotch members, Namier *Structure* I 186–87. My estimate of the number of members from Scotch constituencies voting for and against Norton's motion is based on Namier's formula in *same* 186.

58 The sources for the statements in this paragraph and the first sentence of the next are given in the notes to Chapter 12.

59 Policy of opposition to avoid issues on which they would disagree, Newcastle to Yorke and to Charles Townshend Feb. 24 and 25, 1764. Add. Mss. 32956:83, 103.

As to Pitt's opposition to colonial taxation, Townshend to Newcastle "Friday noon" [March 23, 1764] Add. Mss. 32957:239. As to Townshend's proposals for colonial taxation, Townshend to Newcastle Sept. 13, 1754, Gipson *Brit. Empire* V 164; Mauduit to Mass. Council March 23, 1763, Bancroft Papers, "Maryland"; George III to Bute [about the middle of March 1763] *Bute* 201–2.

60 Newcastle to Pitt Oct. 19, 1764, enclosing copies of two letters concerning the proposed deal as to cider tax and Pitt's reply, *Pitt* II 293–98. Pitt had previously complained of the Opposition's failure to defend him from attack by Grenville in a speech on the budget (presumably of March 9, 1764), Newcastle to John White June 19 Add. Mss. 32960:17–19.

61 As to Townshend's and Yorke's defection, various writers, Oct. 15 to Nov. 27, 1764, *Grenville* II 448–71 and 523–31. Sandwich to Bedford Nov. 22, *Bedford* III 272; Lord Lyttelton to William Lyttelton Jan. 1, 1765, *Lyttelton* II 663. Newcastle to Rockingham and to an unidentified correspondent, Nov. 14 and 25, 1764, as to his and Cumberland's policy, Sutherland "Burke" 56, 53n. Devonshire died in Oct. 1764.

62 Motion as to general warrants defeated Jan. 29, 1765, *Journals H. of C.* XXX 70. There was no division on the final motion to condemn general warrants, but the relative strength of the two parties had just been shown on an amendment supported by the Government, which was adopted by a majority of 224 to 185, *same*.

63 The Stamp Act, 5 Geo. III ch. 12 (1765), received the royal assent March 22, 1765. Details of its passage are in Chapter 20.

64 Details concerning King's dismissal of Grenville Ministry Winstanley *Government* 214–39. See also Clark "Grenville" 383–97.

Chapter 2

1 Whites: N.H. 50,000; Mass. (including Maine) 235,000; R.I. 35,000; Conn. 140,000; N.Y. 85,000; N.J. 80,000; Pa. 180,000; Del. 25,000; Md. 115,000; Va. 200,000; N.C. 70,000; S.C. 35,000; Ga. 6,000. Negroes: N.H. 500; Mass. (including Maine) 5,000; R.I. 4,500; Conn. 4,500; N.Y. 13,500; N.J. 1,500; Pa. 10,000; Del. 4,000; Md. 50,000; Va. 140,000; N.C. 30,000; S.C. 70,000; Ga. 3,500; estimates for 1760 in Greene and Harrington *Am. Population* 15–181 *passim*.

2 West Indies 42,000 white, 290,000 Negro; Bermuda and Bahamas 6,500 white, 3,000 Negro; Nova Scotia, 8,000 white; my estimates as to the West Indies based on data in Pitman *West Indies* 373–83, as to Bermuda and the Bahamas in Gipson *Brit. Empire* II 275, 283, as to Nova Scotia in Brebner *The Neutral Yankees* 52–64.

3 Trans-Appalachian settlers driven out, James "Frontier" 55–71.

4 My estimates as to population of England and Ireland are based on Griffith *Population Problems* 6, 45 and as to Scotland on McCulloch *Statistical Account* I 428 with Macdonald *Scotland's Population* 5.

5 Volumes 2 and 3 of Gipson *Brit. Empire* give an excellent, detailed survey of the several British colonies around 1760. Newfoundland had not yet become an organized colony, Kerr "Newfoundland" 65–68.

6 Commission of Royal Governor, Labaree *Royal Government* 8–11, 30–31, 51–52, 87, 95; Pownall *Administration* 54–55.

7 Requirement in the Governors' commissions as to colonial laws conforming to British law, e.g., Commission of Gov. Benning Wentworth of N.H. June 14, 1741, *N.H. Laws* II 600–608 at 603. Conformity was also required by act of Parliament, 7 & 8 William III ch. 22, sec. 9 (1696).

8 Review of colonial acts by the King in Council, i.e., by the Privy Council, *N.H. Laws* II 603; Russell *Review* 54–58, 222–24; Labaree *Royal Government* 223–24; B. of T. to House of Lords, Jan. 23, 1734, *Talcott* 448. Details as to number, percentage, and kinds of acts disallowed are in Russell *Review* and Dorland *Royal Disallowance in Massachusetts passim;* and Smith *Appeals* 532–33, 592–97.

9 Colonial acts took effect when signed by governor, Labaree *Instructions* I 144; B. of T. to King Feb. 12, 1756, *Acts P.C.* IV 251–52. The Governor's Commission provided that upon signifying notice of disallowance to the Governor, the act shall "thenceforth" cease, *N.H. Laws* II 603.

10 Disallowance of act not ordinarily retroactive, Atty. Gen. Sir Dudley Ryder and Sol. Gen. William Murray to B. of T. July 20, 1753, Chalmers *Opinions* 292; B. of T. to King Feb. 12, 1756, *Acts P.C.* IV 251–52. Disallowance was occasionally expressly given retroactive effect when based on conflict of the colonial act with English law, Smith *Appeals* 532–36; Order in Council Aug. 31, 1699, *Calendar State Pap.* for 1699, 418–19.

11 Mass. Charter of Oct. 7, 1691, and Pa. Charter of March 4, 1682, reserving power of disallowance, Thorpe *Charters* III 1883, V 3039.

12 Opinions of Attorney-General or Solicitor-General in 1703, Labaree *Royal Government* 193 and Mitchell *Pa. Statutes* II 447–48; in 1732, Perry *Mass.* 286; in 1757, Chalmers *Opinions* 459–60, as to finality of King's approval of colonial acts. The Governor's Commission reserved to the King authority to disallow only those acts "not before confirmed by Us," *N.H. Laws* II 603.

13 As to appeals from colonial courts to the Privy Council, Smith *Appeals* 69–88, 140–45, 149, 160–63, largely superseding earlier books and articles on the same subject. The records of the Privy Council from 1745 to 1766 show that the recommendations of the Committee for Hearing Appeals were invariably adopted by the Privy Council, *Acts P.C.* IV 3–771. Hence the Committee was really the final court of colonial appeals.

14 The commission of May 15, 1696, establishing the Board of Trade is in *N.Y. Col. Doc.* IV 145–48. Records of its meetings from 1754 to 1763 are in *B. of T. Journal* for 1754–1758 and 1759–1763. Its active members are listed in *Beatson* II 373 and its ex officio members in Phillips *Early English Colonies* 119–27. As to the importance of its Secretary and legal adviser, Clarke "Board of Trade" 23 and Basye *Board of Trade* 14–15, 35–36.

15 Of the 282 members of the Board of Trade from January 1758, to Halifax's resignation in March, 1761, he attended 274, *same* 223–24. As to his dominating influence there, *same* 36 and Franklin to Isaac Norris March 19, 1759, Mason "Franklin" 246.

16 Bishop of London consulted by the Board of Trade, e.g., resolutions of the Board May 23, 1759, and May 25, 1761, *Journal B. of T.* 1759–1763, 39, 228; and Dickerson *Colonial Government* 123–27.

17 Royal Governors were instructed to recognize the Bishop's jurisdiction, Labaree *Instructions* II 489–90. But the extent of this jurisdiction was hazy. Edmund Gib-

son, Bishop of London (1720–1748) had a commission from the King, April 29, 1728, loosely defining his jurisdiction in the colonies, *N.Y. Col. Doc.* V 849–54; but his successor, Thomas Sherlock (1748–1761) had none. He considered Gibson's commission too confined, and did not have or wish to have a similar one, Sherlock to B. of T. Feb. 19, 1759, *N.C. Col. Rec.* VI 13.

18   As to the Secretary of State for the Southern Department and colonial affairs, Labaree *Royal Government* 44–50; Andrews *Colonial Period* IV 308–14; Thomson *Secretaries of State passim;* Kimball *Pitt* I and II *passim;* Egremont and Halifax correspondence (1761–1764) C.O. 5:211–16. The division of responsibility between the Board and the Secretary of State was defined in an Order in Council of March 11, 1752, and a letter of March 30, Basye *Board of Trade* 71–73.

19   As to the Privy Council Committee on Plantation Affairs occasionally not following Board of Trade's recommendation, *Acts P.C.* IV 372–74, 440–41. My statement that the Privy Council invariably adopted the Committee's recommendation is based on analysis of the published proceedings of the Committee and Council from March 7, 1745, to July 30, 1766, *same* 3–771.

20   Of many useful books and articles on the work of colonial Agents in London I found particularly helpful Penson *Agent of West Indies;* Freiberg "Bollan"; Wolff *Pa. Col. Agency;* Lonn *Agents of Southern Colonies;* Namier "Garth"; and Appleton "Partridge" and "Agents of New Eng." As to their keeping in close touch with the Board of Trade, Va. Comm. of Corresp. to Agent Edward Montague Dec. 12, 1759, *Va. Mag.* X (1903) 343.

21   As to Lord Granville's land holdings in North Carolina, Raper *N.C.* 110–12; Coulter *Granville District passim;* Bond *Quit Rents* 76–82, 298–302, 310–12. Granville's interest was in the right to quit rents on land granted and in the land itself not yet granted.

22   The paragraph as to the Privy Council Committee is based chiefly on inspection of the minutes of the Committee from 1759 to 1763, P.C. 2:106–10. For the Cholmondeleys, neither of whom is in *D.N.B.,* *Burke's Peerage* (80th ed.) 502 and Andrews *Guide to P.R.O.* II 146. The members of the Privy Council on Oct. 25, 1760, with a few later additions, are listed in *Acts P.C.* V 725–27.

23   Description of royal instructions Labaree *Royal Government* 14–15, 95–97, 420–28; Smith *Appeals* 215–16. The instructions of July 21, 1741, to Gov. Benning Wentworth of N.H. comprised 86 general and 23 trade instructions, *N.H. Laws* II 608–51.

24   Proposal to suspend effectiveness of colonial acts until approved by the King, House of Lords resolution of April 5, 1734, Stock *Proceedings* IV 237; Francis Wilks, London Agent for Conn., to Gov. Joseph Talcott of Conn. July 25, 1735, *Talcott* I 318. Colonial opposition, Wolff *Pa. Col. Agency* 55–57.

25   Proposals in House of Commons in 1744 for nullification of all colonial acts not conforming to royal instructions, Labaree *Royal Government* 33–34, 439–40; Smith *Appeals* 599–602; Wolff *Pa. Col. Agency* 129–31; in 1749, *same* 131–34, Stock *Proceedings* V 313–21, 360–67.

26   Suspending clause instruction as to acts of repeal and amendment, Labaree *Instructions* I 128. The instruction, though mentioning only "repeal," was construed to include amending acts, minutes of the Privy Council June 30, 1748, and May 31, 1750, *Acts P.C.* IV 50, 94–96, 133.

27 Action of royal Governor not void even though deviating from his Instructions, Orders in Council June 28, 1749, Nov. 30, 1749, Oct. 31, 1751, *same* 88–89, 94–96, 133, Smith *Appeals* 605–7. An opinion to the contrary by Atty. Gen. Sir Robert Raymond to B. of T. Sept. 16, 1723, Chalmers *Opinions* 270, was apparently overlooked or disregarded.

28 Board of Trade's circular letter of June 3, 1752, as to deviation from instructions, *N.Y. Col. Doc.* VI 760–61. The Board may not have intended to sanction deviation from peremptory instructions, Labaree *Instructions* I 143, 214–16, 239–40, 250–51, 258, but the instructions for a suspending clause in acts of repeal or amendment was not a peremptory one.

29 Change in rule as to suspending clause in acts amending acts approved by the Privy Council, Virginia petition April 15, 1752, Hening *Va.* V 435–36; action on Va. acts by Privy Council Committee and the Council March 1 and 7, 1753, *Acts P.C.* IV 173–75; additional instruction to Gov. Francis Fauquier of Va. May 10, 1753, C.O. 5:200: 851–52.

30 As to suspending clause and Jamaica, Gov. Charles Knowles of Jamaica to B. of T. June 27, 1753, Inst. of Jamaica, "Misc. MSS"; protest of Jamaica Assembly Oct. 29, 1753, and B. of T. to Knowles Oct. 15, 1754, approving Knowles's action, Labaree *Royal Government* 258–59 and 259n. Further details are in Herbert "Const. Issues in Jamaica" 36–260.

31 New rule as to suspending clause instruction not enforced during the war with France in America. For example, ch. 17 sec. 2 of laws of May 1755 session and ch. 5 of laws of Oct. 1755 session of the Virginia Legislature, Hening *Va.* VI 502, 568–69, amending ch. 34 of laws of the Oct. 1748 session, *same* 88, were not condemned by the Board of Trade although they contained no suspending clause.

32 Franklin to Isaac Norris concerning talk with Granville, March 19, 1759, Yale Library, M.F. Coll., published partly in Mason "Franklin" 247–49. I have not found the minutes mentioned in the letter.

33 Committee report Feb. 19, 1755, advising acquiescence in action of N.Y. Assembly *Acts P.C.* IV 327. The Board of Trade's proposed letter to Gov. Sir Charles Hardy of N.Y., dated Feb. 4, is in *N.Y. Col. Doc.* VII 32–33, and the instruction to Hardy (1755), which the N.Y. Assembly refused to accede to, in Labaree *Instructions* I 193–94. B. of T. to Gov. Thomas Pownall of Mass. Nov. 23, 1758, advising acquiescence in action of Mass. Assembly, *Mass. Acts* IV 95–96.

Chapter 3

1 Christopher Hardwicke, Bullskin Plantation, to Washington, July 11, 1758, and various writers to Washington, Aug. 14 to Sept. 7, concerning the great drought, Hamilton *Washington* II 353–54, III 30, 43, 56, 59, 68, 78, 87; William Allason to [David Allason] Oct. 5 "Allason Letters" 122. To same effect, letters of Francis Jerdone May 8 to Sept. 15, Jerdone Letter Book.

2 Tobacco or tobacco notes treated as currency in Virginia: in private dealings, Freeman *Washington* I 83, 114, II 3; Gov. William Gooch of Va. To B. of T. Feb. 7, 1731, Middleton *Tobacco Coast* 386; in public affairs Hening *Va.* III 244, IV 279,

V 38–50, VI 549. The system of issuing tobacco notes for deposits of tobacco in public warehouses, Middleton *Tobacco Coast* 121–25; Flippin *Fin. Adm. of Va.* 52.

3 Ch. 4 of Oct. 1748 session gave the established clergy a base salary of 16,000 lbs. of tobacco with incidentals equivalent to 1,280 lbs. and a glebe (parsonage with adjacent farmland) Hening *Va.* VI 88–89. Fees for marriages, funeral sermons, etc., were an additional source of income, Rev. William Dawson to Bishop of London July 15, 1751, Perry *Va.* 379.

4 Tobacco shortage raises price to 4.5 pence per pound, Virginia currency, Francis Jerdone, Louisa County, Va., to Messrs. Alexander Speirs and Hugh Brown of Glasgow, Scotland, Sept. 15, 1758, Jerdone Letter Book.

5 Rev. William Dawson and Clergy of Va. to Bishop of London July 15, 1751, and Nov. 29, 1755, valuing their annual salary of 16,000 lbs of tobacco at about £80 sterling, Perry *Va.* 379, 437, or about 1.5 pence per lb. Va. currency. This is likewise the average price of tobacco reflected in a lease of Mount Vernon in 1754, Freeman *Washington* II 3; in several Va. statutes from 1748 to 1756 Hening *Va.* V 491, VI 372, VII 47–48; and as found by Price in "Glasgow in Tobacco Trade" 189.

6 The Va. Twopenny Act of 1758, ch. 6 of Sept. 1758 session, Hening *Va.* VII 240–41, was "passed" (assented to) by the Governor in Oct. 1758, *Acts P.C.* IV 421. As to the purpose of the act, Jerdone to Speirs and Brown, Oct. 29, 1758, Jerdone Letter Book 1756–1763, William and Mary Coll. Lib.; Va. Comm. of Corresp. to Agent Edward Montague Dec. 12, 1759, *Va. Mag.* (1903) X 349; Gov. Francis Fauquier to B. of T. Jan. 5, 1759 C.O. 5:1329:229.

7 Fauquier to B. of T. Jan. 5, 1759, explaining his reasons for signing the act, C.O. 5:1329:231. The similar earlier act referred to by him was ch. 5 of Oct. 1755 session, Hening *Va.* VI 568–69.

8 Fauquier to B. of T. July 14, 1759, as to clergy alone protesting, C.O. 5:1329:336. Many of the clergy did not join in the protest, Rev. William Robinson to an unidentified English bishop, Nov. 20, 1760, Perry *Va.* 466; Landon Carter, *A Letter to the B_____ of L_____* (1760) 56. As to John Camm, Fauquier to "The Reverend Doctor [Samuel] Nicholls" July 29, 1761, Perry *Va.* 471; also Goodwin *Col. Church in Va.* 258, *D.A.B.* and Swem *Va. Hist. Index* I 296.

9 Camm's protest on behalf of Va. clergy, B. of T. minutes May 23, 1759, *Journal B. of T.* 1759–1763, 38–39; Camm's Memorial to the King and Representation to B. of T., both undated, C.O. 5:1329:265, 271–73, the latter published as Appendix III to Bland *The Colonel Dismounted* (1764). Smith *Appeals* 607–26 has a detailed discussion of the proceedings.

10 Of many books touching on the rise of the dissenters, chiefly Presbyterian and Baptist, in Virginia from 1740 to 1765, I found Sweet *Religion in Col. Am.* 294–303 and Gewehr *Great Awakening in Va.* particularly valuable.

11 Bishop of London's denunciation of the Twopenny Act, June 14, 1759, Perry *Va.* 461–63. The alleged unfairness of the similar act of 1755 was complained of in a letter of Camm and seven other clergymen to the Bishop of London Nov. 29, 1755, and by nine more of the Virginia clergy in a letter of Feb. 25, 1756, *same* 434–40 and 440–46.

12 The exception of certain contracts for tobacco, sec. 3 of the Twopenny Act, Hening *Va.* VII 241. Acts giving vestries patronage, Act I of March 1643 session, reenacted by Act IV of March 1662 session, *same* I 241–42, II 46; ch. 34, sec. 7 of Oct. 1748 session *same* VI 90, discussed in Va. Comm. of Corresp. to Montague, Dec. 12, 1759, *Va. Mag.* X (1903) 349.

13 Recommendation that Twopenny Act be disallowed and instruction issued, B. of T. minutes June 27, 1759, *Journal B. of T.* 1759–1763, 46, with Board's report to the King July 4, 1759 (misprinted 1757) Perry *Va.* 458–60. The Board refused Camm's request for a recommendation that the act be declared void from its inception, Smith *Appeals* 611–12.

14 Committee report on Twopenny Act Aug. 3, 1759, *Acts P.C.* IV 420–21, with James Abercromby, London Agent for the Va. Council, to John Blair, President of Va. Council, Aug. 3, 1759, Smith *Appeals* 614. As to the merchants' petition against Va. acts allegedly favoring Va. debtors to the detriment of British creditors, Beer *Brit. Col. Policy* 181–82; B. of T. minutes July 25, 1759, *Journal B. of T.* 1759–1763, 53–54.

15 Members of committee present, committee minutes, Aug. 4, 1759, P.C. 2:107:84. Halifax attended none of the other seventeen meetings of the committee in 1759; Hardwicke, one; and Secker two, P.C. 2:106:332–490 and P.C. 2:107:11–220.

16 Privy Council's orders on review of Twopenny Act, Privy Council minutes, Aug. 10 and 29, 1759, *Acts P.C.* IV 420–21. The peremptory instruction of Sept. 21, 1759, issued pursuant to the Privy Council's order of Aug. 29, is in Labaree *Instructions* I 130–31. Peremptory instructions previously issued, (*same* 143, 214–16, 239–40, 258) were of narrower scope than the suspending clause instruction now made peremptory.

17 My statement as to the nonattendance of Pitt and Newcastle is based on inspection of the records of the committee from 1759 through 1761, P.C. 2:106–10. The surmise as to what Pitt and Newcastle would probably have done is based on their attitude toward the colonies outlined and documented in Chapter 1.

18 Petition to King for modification of suspending clause order, Oct. 20, 1760, C.O. 5:1330:105. The Board of Trade recommended to the Privy Council Committee that the petition be not granted, May 20, 1761, C.O. 5:1368:179–85, and there is no record of further action. The date and method of delivering the Privy Council's order is stated in Fauquier to B. of T. June 30, 1760, *Va. Journals* 1758–1761, 285.

19 Copy of Bishop of London's derogatory letter obtained and published, Bland *Letter to the Clergy* (1760) 3. As to membership of Richard Bland and Landon Carter in the Church of England, Bland to Thomas Adams Aug. 1, 1771, *Va. Mag.* (1899) VI 132; Rev. William Kay to Bishop of London June 14, 1752, Perry *Va.* 389.

20 Bland, *D.A.B.*, Rossiter *Seed Time of the Republic* 247–80 and Rossiter "Richard Bland" 33–79. The description of his looks is quoted from Roger Atkinson to Samuel Pleasants Oct. 1, 1774, *Va. Mag.* (1908) XV 356. (An able essay by Bland on the pistole fee controversy, "A Modest and True State of the Case," was published in 1891 in Ford *A Fragment on the Pistole Fee.*)

21 For details as to Carter, Morton *Robert Carter passim;* Morton "Robert Wormely Carter" 345–65; Swem *Va. His. Index* I 325; Glenn *Some Colonial Mansions* I

253–60; Greene "Carter" 66–69. Carter's writings on the pistole fee controversy were *A Letter from a Gentleman in Virginia* (London, 1754) and a letter in the *Maryland Gazette* on Oct. 24, 1754. The characterization of him is in Rev. William Kay to Bishop of London June 14, 1752, Perry *Va.* 389.

22 Bland's remarks on the royal prerogative, Bland *A Letter to the Clergy* (1760) 18.

23 Argument that Twopenny Act was void because against Instructions, "The Appellant's Case," undated, in *Camm* v. *Hansford and Moss* Hardwicke Pap. Add. Mss. 36220:201–23 at 220–22.

24 Rev. Alexander White's case, Rev. William Robinson to Bishop of London, undated but before April 1763, Perry *Va.* 479–82. Rev. Thomas Warrington's case, *Warrington* v. *Jeggitts*, decided March 2, 1763, 1 *W. & M. Q.* XX (1912) 172–73; Robinson to the Bishop of London Aug. 17, 1764, Aug. 12, 1765, Perry *Va.* 496–97, 513.

25 Rev. James Maury's case, Maury to Camm, Dec. 12, 1763, *Va. Journals* 1761–1765, li. As to the loss of the records in this case, Hon. Leon Bazile, Judge of the Fifteenth Judicial Circuit of Virginia, including Hanover County, to me Oct. 19, 1946.

26 Value of tobacco payable to Maury, *Va. Journals* 1761–1765, lii. The salary for 1758 was payable by statute before the end of May; ch. 51 sec. 33 of Oct. 1748 session Hening *Va.* VI 172.

27 Patrick Henry's early success as lawyer, Meade *Henry* 81–113; Eaton "Mirror" 524–25, 531–32.

28 Hanover County was the center of the "New Lights" or "New-Side" (evangelistic) wing of the Presbyterian church, Brydon *Va. Mother Church* II 168–69. The act of 1748 providing for assessment, collection, and payment of the salaries of the established clergy made no exception in favor of Presbyterian or other Dissenters, ch. 35 of Oct. 1748 session Hening *Va.* VI 88.

29 Henry's argument and jury's verdict in Maury case, Maury to Camm Dec. 12, 1763, *Va. Journals* 1761–1765, li–liii, Meade *Henry* 125–37. As to Maury's lawyer, Peter Lyons, later judge of the Virginia Supreme Court of Appeals, Mays "Peter Lyons" *Va. Bar Assoc. Proc.* for 1926, 418–26.

30 As to the decision in the Camm case by the highest court of Virginia in April 1764, five to four against Camm, two judges not participating, and the dismissal of Camm's appeal to the Privy Council Dec. 3, 1766, Smith *Appeals* 618–19, 621–24.

31 Pamphlet war between Camm and Carter, Camm *A Single and Distinct View*, Annapolis, Md., 1763; Carter *The Rector Detected*, Williamsburg, 1764; Camm *A Review of the Rector Detected*, Williamsburg, 1764. Dates of publication and attribution, Smith "Parson's Cause" 294n, 296, 299.

32 Bland's reply to Camm and remarks on constitutional questions, Bland *The Colonel Dismounted*, Williamsburg, 1764. Date of publication and attribution, Smith "Parson's Cause" 300. Part of the pamphlet, including the passage quoted, is reprinted in 1 *W. & M. Q.* XIX (1912) 31–41 at 38.

Chapter 4

1 William Bollan to Speaker of the Mass. House, May 8, 1761, concerning Board of Trade's objection to a temporary (five years) Mass. Act, Ch. 26 Laws of

1759–1760 *Mass. Acts* IV 291–98, chiefly because of its lack of a suspending clause, *Mauduit* 15–19.

2 Mass. Charter of Oct. 7, 1791, *Mass. Acts* I 1–20.

3 King's lack of authority to revoke or modify colonial charters, Atty. Gen. Sir Edward Northey to B. of T. July 22, 1714, Chalmers *Opinions* 338–40; Atty. Gen. Philip Yorke and Sol. Gen. Charles Talbot to B. of T. Aug. 11, 1731, 2 *Maine* XI 127; opinion (date not given) of Yorke and Talbot concerning a petition of Aug. 30, 1731, from R.I., *R.I. Col. Rec.* IV 461.

4 English vested interest in charter rights, Thomas Penn to John Penn Aug. 17, 1734, Wolff *Pa. Agency* 56.

5 Mass. House to Bollan Nov. 1761, and instructions of joint legislative committee of Thomas Hutchinson and James Bowdoin from the Council and Thomas Cushing, John Phillips, and Royall Tyler from the House to Jasper Mauduit June 15, 1762, to protest against proposed enforcement of suspending clause instruction, *Mauduit* 16n, 39, 39n, 40, 41, 53.

6 Joint legislative committee's instructions to Mauduit, quoting Locke *Treatises* Book 2, par. 22. Locke's words were slightly changed by the committee.

7 Petition for renewal of writs of assistance issued from 1756 to 1760, Gray "Notes" 402–6, 412–14. These were about to expire pursuant to 1 Anne 1st session ch. 8 sec. 5 (1702). The illicit, so-called Flag of Truce and "Monte Cristi" trade is discussed in Beer *Brit. Col. Policy* 86–131; Gipson *Coming of Revolution* 28–34; Pares *War and Trade* 446–67.

8 This paragraph concerning general writs of assistance is based on Gray "Notes" 398–400, 404–5, 412–13, 418–21, 475. See also Gipson "Aspects" 20–30, and Frese "Otis" 496–508.

9 Argument by Jeremy Gridley, *same* 476. The acts relied on by Gridley were a Mass. act, ch. 3 sec. 1, Laws of 1699–1700, *Mass. Acts* I, 370–71, and two British acts, 13 & 14 Charles II ch. 11 sec. 5 (1662) and 7 & 8 William III ch. 22 sec. 6 (1696), the latter of which extended the earlier act to the colonies.

10 Oxenbridge Thacher's argument, Gray "Notes" 469–71; William De Grey's opinion Oct. 17, 1766, to Commissioners of Customs, Wolkins "Malcolm" 64, 72–73.

11 Descriptions of James Otis, *Boston Evening Post* May 2, 1763; Rev. Jonathan Mayhew to Thomas Hollis March 19, 1761, Knollenberg "Hollis and Mayhew" 120; Gov. Francis Bernard to Richard Jackson Feb. 1, 1763, Bernard Papers II 255. John Adams's diary entries of April 8, 1759, Feb. 5, 1763, and Dec. 23, 1765, describing Otis, say he was "sometimes in despondency, sometimes in a rage," Adams *Works* II 67, 143, 163. See also Brennan "Otis" 691–725.

12 Otis's argument, Gray "Notes" 471–76. In his argument Otis cited 8 [Coke's] *Reports* 118 [a], *Dr. Bonham's Case* (1610), in which Chief Justice Coke stated that "when an act of parliament is against common right and reason . . . the common law will controul it and adjudge such act to be void."

13 Hutchinson wrote for information on March 5, 1761, to Bollan in England who replied June 13 that general writs were issued there, *Mass. Hist. Soc. Proc.* vol. 59, 420. The Mass. Court's judgment was given Nov. 18; the court gave counsel a

chance to reargue before granting judgment, but apparently no new arguments were adduced, Quincy *Reports* 51–57. Writs issued in Mass. in Dec. 1761 and Jan. 1762, *same* 418–26.

14 Mass. bill in Feb. 1762 to overcome the Court's decision rejected by the governor, Gray "Notes" 495–500. I have found no evidence that the renewed writs were used in Massachusetts before 1766 (Wolkins "Malcolm" 11, 26–29) and they were apparently not applied for in other colonies except New Hampshire until after passage of 7 Geo. III ch. 46 sec. 10 (1767), explicitly providing for general writs of assistance in the colonies, Gray "Notes" 500, Dickerson "Writs" 48–75, Hickman "Writs" 96–104.

15 Adams's divergent accounts of Otis's argument, Adams's contemporary abstract, Gray "Notes" 469–77, probably the one mentioned in Adams's diary March 21, 1761, Adams *Works* II 124–25, compared with his account in 1817 *same* X 247–48. For other noncontemporary accounts by Adams and others, *same* II 523–25, X 183, 233, 276, 342–43; Gray "Notes" 479–82; Joseph Hawley's Commonplace Book N.Y. Pub. Lib. Hawley Papers II. As to Hawley, Brown *Hawley passim.*

16 Disallowance of S.C. act of 1759, Board's minutes May 29, 1761, *Journal B. of T.* 1759–1763, 200–201; Committee on Plantation Affairs recommendation June 18; Privy Council order June 25, *Acts P.C.* IV 487–89. Gov. Thomas Boone's Proclamation of Dec. 26, is in C.O. 5:479:258. As to the arrival of Boone, who had been Governor of N.J., and the details concerning the S.C. House, Smith *S.C.* 108, 338–39. As to Boone, Namier "Garth" 462–70.

17 Boone's message March 19, 1762, and the House's reply March 23 C.O. 5:480:41, 44, 48. Further details, Greene "Gadsden" 471–86.

18 Christopher Gadsden's election and Boone's highly provocative action, *Full State* (1763) 6–8, 17–18. Sec. 2 of the Election Act of Sept. 19, 1721, Cooper *S.C. Statutes* III 135–40, was ambiguous as to whether the specified special oath was required of the churchwardens as well as of persons specially chosen to act if churchwardens were lacking.

19 Quarrel between Boone and the newly elected House, *Full State* 1, 9, 11, 15–27, 51, 60–63, supplemented by the South-Carolina *Gazette* and Supplement of Dec. 11 and Dec. 18, 1762. As to the reelection of nearly all the old members, including Gadsden, Smith *S.C.* 342. As to the colonial assemblies' successful claim to privileges similar to those of the House of Commons, Clarke *Parl. Privilege*, particularly 132–72, 235–61. The House resolution (Dec. 16, 1762) quoted is in *Full State* 25.

20 As to the continued feuding between Boone and the House, Smith *S.C.* 345–47 and Greene "Gadsden" 484–87. As to grant of leave of absence to Boone, minutes of the Board of Trade March 9, 1763, *Journal B. of T.* for 1759–1763, 342. In July 1764, he was censured by the Board for his unsuitable "passion and resentment" (Namier "Garth" 469) but was apparently continued in the governorship for over a year longer, Andrews "Commissions" 436.

21 The appropriate bill passed by the House Aug. 16, 1764, was rejected by the Council Aug. 22, S.C. House Journal XXXVI 236, 244, in S.C. Archives Columbia,

S.C. Reintroduced soon afterward, it was accepted by the Council, with a mild protest, Oct. 3, 1764, *same* XXXVI 266 and S.C. Council Journal XXX 75.

22 Old instruction as to judicial commissions, Labaree *Instructions* I, 367, 369. N.J. good behavior commissions dating back to 1739, 1. *N.J. Col. Doc.* IX 209, Kemmerer *N.J.* 267, 269, 360; N.Y. dating back to 1744, O'Callaghan *N.Y. Commissions* 26, with Gov. Cadwallader Colden of N.Y. to B. of T. Aug. 12, 1761, *Colden* 1876, 105. The English act was 12 & 13 William III ch. 2 sec. 3 (1701).

23 Colden to Pitt Aug. 11, 1761, as to nonpermanent judicial salaries in N.Y., *Colden* 1876, 105; Kemmerer *N.J.* 269 indicating same in N.J.

24 Instruction for "at pleasure" commissions only, Labaree *Instructions* I 367, issued to the governors of N.Y. and N.J. in 1755 and 1758 respectively. (This instruction was not issued to Governors of Mass., presumably in deference to the provision in the Mass. charter giving jurisdiction over courts to the people of the colony, *Mass. Acts* I 14–15.)

25 Jamaica provided in 1728 for a permanent revenue sufficient to cover the ordinary expenses of the colony's government, Labaree *Royal Government* 282; provision for permanent salaries for judges in Pa. was included in the act for permanent tenure, Act of Sept. 29, 1759, *Pa. Statutes* V 462–65. The Jamaica act providing for good behavior tenure was disallowed Feb. 28, 1754, *Acts P.C.* IV 215, 217, the Pa. act, Nov. 23, 1761, *same* 441 with *Pa. Council* VIII 558.

26 Colden to Pitt and to B. of T. Aug. 11 and 12, 1761, *Colden* 1876, 104, 105–6 as to Judge David Jones's commission. It was issued Nov. 21, 1758, O'Callaghan *N.Y. Commissions* 51. Colden to Lord Halifax Aug. 7, 1760, as to tenure of judge to fill De Lancey's place, *Colden* 1876, 10. The English act requiring new commissions was 1 Anne 1st session ch. 8 sec. 2 (1702).

27 Colden's suggestion to B. of T. Aug. 11, 1761, as to judicial tenure, *Colden* 1876, 106; B. of T. report Nov. 11 in effect rejecting Colden's suggestion *Acts P.C.* IV 498–500. As to Colden, who was seventy-two when called upon to act as Governor, Keys *Colden;* Hindle *Pursuit of Science* 39–49.

28 The Privy Council's order as to judicial commissions was adopted Nov. 23, 1761, *Acts P.C.* IV 494–95, and the circular instruction Dec. 12, 1761, Labaree *Instructions* I 367–68. Two days later a N.C. act of 1760 providing for good behavior tenure of the associate judges of the N.C. Supreme Court (*N.C. Col. Rec.* IV 900–901, 986–87) was disallowed by the Privy Council, *Acts P.C.* IV 502 with N.C. *Col. Rec.* IV 986–87.

29 Benjamin Prat to Colden Oct. 3, 1761, concerning the King's mandamus for his commission, *Colden* 1922, 81. Prat's commission was issued Nov. 11, O'Callaghan *N.Y. Commissions* 58, and a salary of £500 a year was allowed him by the Crown, Colden to William Samuel Johnson April 2, 1771, *Colden* 1877, 321.

30 John Adams's diary Aug. 19, 1760, concerning Prat, Adams *Works* II 97. For additional data as to Prat's character, ability, and career, Washburn *Sketches* 224–25; *Mass. Hist. Soc. Proc.* 1864–1865, 35–36; *N.Y. Col. Doc.* VII 502n, 506. Prat to B. of T. May 27, 1762, as to salary, *same* 501.

31 N.Y. bills as to judicial tenure, Colden to B. of T. June 2 and Sept. 25, 1761, *Colden* 1876, 88–89, 119; N.Y. act as to judicial salaries, Dec. 31, *N.Y. Col. Laws* IV 550–51.

32 Prat's appeal to Speaker William Nicoil as to judicial salaries and the latter's reply March 15 and 16, 1762, *Colden* 1876, 174–75. As to Nicoll (1702–1768), who was Speaker from 1759 to 1768, Thompson *Long Island* 301.

33 Colden to Gov. Robert Monckton March 30, 1762, as to judges' acceptance of commissions, *Colden* 1876, 183; act of Dec. 11, voting judges' salaries unconditionally *N.Y. Col. Laws* IV 626–27; N.Y. House's Petition to the King for good behavior commissions Dec. 11, *N.Y. Assembly* II 718–19.

34 No revision of the instruction forbidding royal Governors to grant good behavior tenure, Labaree *Instructions* I 367.

35 Gov. Josiah Hardy of N.J. to B. of T. Jan. 20, 1762, as to having granted good behavior commissions; B. of T. to the king March 27 recommending Hardy's dismissal; Lord Egremont to Hardy Sept. 11 telling him he was dismissed, 1 *N.J. Col. Doc.* IX 346–47; 361–62; 374–75. As to Hardy, elder brother of Admiral Sir Charles Hardy, former Governor of N.Y., *same* 316–17n; Kemmerer *N.J.* 266, 272.

36 Charles Yorke's opinion as to invalidity of good behavior commissions, Jan. 18, 1763, 1. *N.J. Col. Doc.* IX 351, 380–81.

Chapter 5

1 Quincy *Harvard* I 353–76; Foote *King's Chapel* I 50–467 *passim;* Perry *Mass.* 84–330 *passim* as to friction between Congregationalists and Anglicans in Boston. The Anglicans' complaints, Reed *Church and State in Mass.* 163–87. The acts complained of were ch. 26 and ch. 46 secs. 8–11 of Laws of 1692–1693, supplemented or revised by ch. 8 of Laws of 1695–1696, ch. 17 of Laws of 1715–1716 and ch. 1 of Laws of 1718–1719, *Mass. Acts* I 62–63, 102–3, 216–17, II 26–27, 99.

2 Rev. Benjamin Coleman to White Kennet, Dean of Peterborough, Nov. 1712, Mayhew *Observations* 59–62 and ministers of Hampshire Co., Mass., to Bishop of London, Sept. 10 and 13, 1734, Perry *Mass.* 300, 302–3 as to Congregationalist complaints against the Society. For details of the Society, Introduction to Pascoe *Digest* and the Society's charter of 1701 in Batchelder *Eastern Diocese* I 106–14. Its mission churches in 1758–1759 are listed in Ellis *Sermon Preached Before the Society* (1759) 45–50.

3 For the intention to proselyte: Caleb Heathcote to Sec. of the Society Nov. 9, 1705, Fox *Heathcote* 246–47; Rev. Timothy Cutler to Dr. Zachary Gray July 2, 1735, Perry *Mass.* 674; Vestry of Trinity Church, Boston to John Thomlinson Oct. 26, 1739, Foote *King's Chapel* I 491.

4 Acts giving Anglicans right to share, temporary act of 1735, ch. 15 Laws of 1735–1736, made permanent by ch. 8 Laws of 1742–1743 *Mass. Acts* II 782–83, III 25. The Society's new mission church established in a settled community was at Hopkinton in 1748, Batchelder *Eastern Diocese* II 26–27. Another mission church, established in 1756, was on the Maine frontier, *Coll. of Prot. Episc. Hist. Soc.* II 77–80.

5 Friendly overtures by Congregationalists to Anglican churches in 1745 and 1753, *New Eng. Hist. & Gen. Reg.* LVIII (1904) 67–69; Foote *King's Chapel* II 112–15. Exhortations to common effort of British colonial Protestants against Catholic France,

Newcombe "S.P.G. Missionaries" 356; Rev. Henry Caner to Thomas Secker, Dec. 23, 1762, Perry *Mass.* 485; Ebenezer Pemberton of Boston *A Sermon* . . . (1757) 25–26; Baldwin *New Eng. Clergy* 86–88.

6   Franklin's letter of May 9, 1759, *London Chronicle* May 12, 1759, published (misdated) in Smyth *Franklin* V 207, and letters July 20, 1760, to Aug. 2, 1761, to Sec. of the Society from missionaries at Salem, Marblehead, Scituate, and Braintree, Mass., concerning friendly relations between Anglicans and Congregationalists, Perry *Mass.* 456–57, 465–66.

7   Rev. Charles Brockwell to Bishop of London, May 3, 1753, Foote *King's Chapel* II 114, as to "sin" of accepting Congregationalist invitation and Rev. Thomas B. Chandler to the Sec. of the Society April 6, 1761, deploring "moderation" of Anglicans toward non-Anglicans, Clark *St. John's* 83–84. Chandler, Yale, 1745, is in *D.A.B.* The key to the jibe at "leathern mitten" ordination will be found in Rev. Joseph Webb to Rev. Cotton Mather Oct. 2, 1722, Hawks and Perry *Conn.* I 63–64.

8   Walpole to Horatio Mann April 2, 1750, as to Secker, Toynbee *Walpole* II 437; Secker's *Sermon* (1741) decrying colonial depravity, reprinted in Klingberg *Anglican Humanitarianism* 213–33 at 216.

9   Caner to Secker April 7, 1759, suggesting Anglican mission church at Cambridge, Mass. Perry *Mass.* 452. Crudely speaking, Socinians, like later Unitarians, professed Christianity but did not accept the divinity of Christ, while Deists, as distinguished from atheists, professed belief in a God though they did not necessarily profess Christianity. As to Caner, Yale 1724, Dexter *Yale Biographies* 1701–1745, 296–99.

10   Tolerance of Anglicans at Harvard: Quincy *Harvard* I 373, 571; Gov. William Shirley to Sec. of the Society July 8, 1743, Perry *Mass.* 372; Shipton *Harvard Graduates* IV to VIII Indexes under "Church of England." Nontolerance of Dissenters at the English universities: Gibson *Thirty-Nine Articles* I 64–66. Ecclesiastical tests for students at Oxford and Cambridge were retained until the middle of the nineteenth century.

11   Rev. Samuel Johnson to Secker April 15, 1759, seconding Caner's suggestion for Cambridge mission, *N.Y. Col. Doc.* VII 374–75.

12   Secker to Caner and to Johnson July 19, 1759, reporting decision to establish the suggested mission church, Perry *Mass.* 453 and *N.Y. Col. Doc.* VII 394.

13   Rev. East Apthorp to Sec. of the Society Aug. 30, 1760, and Sept. 29, 1762, reporting progress on and opening of the new church, Perry *Mass.* 457, 473. The history of this church is outlined in Batchelder *Eastern Diocese* II 36–63; a sketch of Apthorp's life is in Sprague *Annals* V 174–78.

14   Act of Feb. 11, 1762 (signed March 6, 1762), ch. 32 Laws of 1761–1762 *Mass. Acts* IV 520–23 incorporating the Society for promoting Christian Knowledge among the Indians of North America. The list of incorporators is at 521.

15   Caner to Secker Aug. 9 and Dec. 1762, charging, without evidence, that the Preamble to the charter of the new Society was misleading, Perry *Mass.* 472. The Preamble stated, "The signal success with which it has pleased Almighty God to crown his majesty's arms, calls upon us to express our grateful acknowledge-

ments to the Author of it, and to demonstrate our gratitude by endeavouring to spread the knowledge of his religion . . . among the Indians of America," *Mass. Acts* IV 520.

16 Secker to Caner Oct. 6, 1762, as to proposed procedure to secure disallowance of Mass. missions act, Perry *Mass.* 474–75.

17 Rev. William Smith to Secker Nov. 22, 1762, which enclosed memorandum attacking the Mass. act chartering the new missionary society, *same* 477–81. B. of T. to King March 18, 1763, recommending disallowance of the Mass. act and order of disallowance May 20, *Acts P.C.* IV 559–60. Jasper Mauduit to James Bowdoin April 7, 1763, reporting Secker's activities, *Bowdoin-Temple Papers* 14. Bowdoin was President of the new society, *Boston Gazette* Feb. 14, 1763.

18 Concern over Mauduit's report, Rev. Charles Chauncy and Rev. Andrew Eliot to Mauduit May 4 and June 1, 1763, *Mauduit* 116–20. As to Eliot, Harvard 1737, Shipton *Harvard Graduates* X 128–61; Rev. Jonathan Mayhew to Hollis April 27, 1763, Knollenberg "Hollis and Mayhew" 107–8. As to the composition, work, and influence of the Dissenting Deputies, Manning *Dissenting Deputies passim.*

19 Caner to Secker Jan. 7, 1763, describing various recent signs of bitterness among Mass. Congregationalists, Perry *Mass.* 489–90; Caner wrote Secker June 8, 1763, that Mayhew was the supposed writer of the letter to the newspaper attacking the Society, *same* 497. The letter is referred to at 23 of Apthorp's *Considerations* (Boston 1763) defending the Society.

20 Mayhew *Observations on the Charter and Conduct of the Society* (Boston, 1763) replying to Apthorp. As to Mayhew, Harvard 1744, *D.A.B.*, Bradford *Mayhew* and Akers "Mayhew." Quotation from Apthorp to Sec. of Society June 25, 1763, Perry *Mass.* 500.

21 "A Form of Prayer with Fasting, to be used yearly upon the Thirtieth Day of January, being the Day of the Martyrdom of the Blessed King Charles the First" *Book of Common Prayer* division 31. Mayhew's denunciation, *A Discourse Concerning Unlimited Submission . . . With some Reflections on the Resistance made to King Charles I . . . In which the Mysterious Doctrine of that Prince's Saintship and Martyrdom is Unriddled* (Boston, 1750).

22 Mayhew's reply to Apthorp, Mayhew *Observations* 81, 90–94. The Calvinistic Articles to which Anglican clergymen had to subscribe were in the concluding (34th) division of the *Book of Common Prayer.* Mayhew had just spoken strongly against the Calvinist doctrine of predestination in sermons "On the Nature, Extent and Perfection of the Divine Goodness" delivered Dec. 9, 1762, *Two Sermons* (Boston, 1763) 34–40.

23 Mayhew's attack on the Society and on the project for colonial bishops, Mayhew *Observations* 16–23, 29–58, 108–25, 155–56.

24 Secker to Horatio Walpole Jan. 9, 1751, in favor of colonial bishops, Porteus *Secker* VI 491–509. Proposal in Bishop Sherlock's "Some Considerations" submitted to the King in Council April 11, 1750, *Acts P.C.* IV 100, published in *N.Y. Col. Doc.* VII 360–69. As to previous efforts for colonial bishops, Cross *Anglican Episcopate* 88–112; Osgood *Am. Colonies in 18th Cent.* II 45–58, III 89–93; Hawkins *Historical Notices* 375–85; Pennington *Talbot* 52–65.

25 Successful opposition of Newcastle, Archbishop Thomas Herring, Lord Hardwicke, and Horatio Walpole, Carpenter *Sherlock* 197–219; Cross *Anglican Episcopate* 324–32. Defoe *Tour* I 63 refers to the "great many meeting houses of Dissenters" at Norwich in 1724, and diary entries of 1768 and 1772 in Neville *Diary* 53, 175 mention two important dissenting churches there.

26 Horatio Walpole to Bishop Sherlock May 29, 1750, opposing movement for colonial bishops, Cross *Anglican Episcopate* 324–30. As to the jurisdiction of ecclesiastical courts in England, Maitland *Const. Hist.* 523–26; Burn *Ecclesiastical Law* (1763) *passim.* 29 Charles II ch. 9 (1676) deprived the ecclesiastical courts of authority to sentence heretics to be burned, but in other respects confirmed the wide jurisdiction of these courts.

27 Josiah Willard to Gov. Spencer Phips Dec. 12, 1750, Foote *King's Chapel* II 251. The earlier letter referred to by Willard is missing. It probably was connected with the opposition to an Anglican bishopric in the colonies voiced by the Mass. House in June 1750, *Mass. Journals* 1750–1751, 24, 32, 35.

28 The statement as to income of Anglican bishops and archbishops is in *Geo. III* I 33–43 with Namier *Additions* 14–17. As to the meager income of many of the lower Anglican clergy, Lecky *England* I 82–83. Richard Watson, Bishop of Llandaff, wrote that "6,000 of the clergy, the greater part of the whole number, had at middle rate one with another not £50 a year." *Letter to Archbishop Cornwallis* (1783) reprinted in *The Pamphleteer* VIII 574–94 at 586.

29 In his "Some Considerations," *N.Y. Col. Doc.* VII 368–69, Sherlock suggested support for colonial bishops "by annexing some preferments abroad to these Bishopricks and by giving the Bp a capacity of receiving Benefactions" but did not indicate what "preferments" he had in mind.

30 Tolerance of bishops after the American Revolution, Manross *Hist. Am. Episc. Church* 193–96; Loveland *Critical Years passim.* Various suggestions for visiting bishops, Johnson to Bishop of London, to Secker and to unnamed correspondent Sept. 25, 1751, Oct. 30, 1752, and July 13, 1753, Schneider *Johnson* I 151, 163, III 253; Rev. Hugh Neil to Sec. of the Society Oct. 18, 1764, Perry *Pa.* 366. As to the forty-three Anglican bishops in England, Ireland, and the Isle of Man, Beatson *Index* I 111–83, II 127–86.

31 Anglican clergy of N.Y. and N.J. to Secker June 22, 1758 (misdated 1768), Jones *St. Peter's* 71–72. (The correct date is from the Lambeth Mss. L. of C. transcripts.) The Archbishop of Canterbury, now ex officio president of the Society, had previously invariably been elected president, Pascoe *Digest* iv.

32 Secker to Johnson Sept. 27, 1758, Nov. 4, 1760, encouraging hope for colonial bishops but saying project must not be pushed "openly," *N.Y. Col. Doc.* VII 348, 449.

33 Secker to Johnson as to progress of their scheme for colonial bishops, March 30, 1763, and May 22, 1764, *same* 518 and Beardsley *Johnson* 281–83. Rev. Samuel Chandler D.D. was a leading Dissenting minister. The prospective "Popish" bishop, Oliver Briand, did not come until June 1766 (*Quebec Gazette* July 3, 1766), having been consecrated in France the preceding March, Gosselin *L'Eglise du Canada* 155–56.

34 Mayhew in Boston to Hollis April 6, 1762, and Rev. Richard Peters in Philadelphia to Secker Oct. 17, 1763, as to alarm among colonial non-Anglicans over rumor concerning proposed colonial bishops, Knollenberg "Hollis and Mayhew" 128–29 and Perry *Pa.* 394.

35 Mayhew's attack on plan for colonial bishops, Mayhew *Observations* 155–56.

36 Attacks on Mayhew, Browne *Remarks By a Son of the Church* (1763) 24 attributed to Rev. Arthur Browne, Perry *Mass.* 689; undated, anonymous broadside as to Mayhew's "foul Mouth," Collection of Revolutionary Broadsides, Mass. Hist. Soc. See also Foote *King's Chapel* II 266n. Caner's attack was in Caner *Candid Examination of Dr. Mayhew's Observations* (1763) to which Mayhew replied in *Defence of the Observations* (1763).

37 Hollis to Mayhew April 22 and Oct. 10, 1764, attributing to Secker the *Answer to Dr. Mayhew's Observations* Knollenberg "Hollis and Mayhew" 148, 157; Apthorp's reply, Apthorp *Review of Dr. Mayhew's Remarks* (1765), and Mayhew's decision to let the controversy drop, Mayhew to Hollis Sept. 26, 1765, Knollenberg "Hollis and Mayhew" 178. As to Thomas Hollis, *same* 102–9, Robbins "Hollis" 406–53, *D.N.B.* and Blackburne *Hollis passim.*

38 Influence of Mayhew's pamphlet, Harrison Gray to Mauduit May 3, 1763, *Mauduit* 103; Rev. Solomon Palmer to Sec. of the Society May 5, 1763, Hawks and Perry *Conn.* II 62; Secker to Rev. Jacob Duché Sept. 16, 1763, Perry *Pa.* 390.

39 Ill-feeling against Mayhew and Harvard College for unorthodoxy, Mayhew to his father, Experience Mayhew, Oct. 1747, Mayhew Pap.; Rev. Timothy Cutler to Secker Aug. 28, 1754, *N.Y. Col. Doc.* VI 907; Apthorp to Sec. of the Society June 25, 1763, Perry *Mass.* 500; Lefavour "Proposed College" 66, 72–73. As to earlier closing of ranks by Mass. Congregationalists, Edmund Randolph to Bishop of London, May 29, 1682, Hutchinson *Collection* 532.

40 Mayhew estimated 50 Congregationalists to 1 of all other denominations in Massachusetts, while Rev. Ezra Stiles, also a Congregational minister, estimated 440,000 Congregationalists to 12,600 Anglicans throughout New England, Mayhew to Mauduit, April 26, 1762, *Mauduit* 37; Stiles *Discourse* (1760) 112–13. Caner questioned Stiles's figures but gave no counterestimate, Caner to Secker Aug. 16, 1763, Perry *Mass.* 504.

Chapter 6

1 As to conquest of Canada furnishing security to British colonies, Pitt to Gen. Jeffery Amherst Dec. 29, 1758, Kimball *Pitt* I 433; Franklin to John Hughes Jan. 7, 1760, Smyth *Franklin* IV 8; King's speech March 19, 1761, *Annual Register* for 1761, 245–46; *A Letter Addressed to Two Great Men* (1760) 31; *Reflections on Domestic Policy* (1763) 30, 68–72; *Comparative Importance of our Acquisitions* (1762) 23–24; *St. James Chronicle* (London) Nov. 18, 1762; *Annual Register* for 1762, 59–60; *Boston Post-Boy* Feb. 28, 1763.

2 British prewar infantry in North America, army estimates for 1754, Nov. 21, 1753, *Journals H. of C.* XXVI 849–50. Regiments are listed as "in the Plantations" without distinction between North America and the West Indies, but the particular location is given in Millan *Army List* for each year. The rangers were in the estimates for Nova Scotia, Jan. 25, 1764, *Journals H. of C.* XXVI 921. As to the regiment from Ireland, the 47th (Colonel Lascelles's), *Northcliffe* 6, 76.

3 Artillery and engineers, Pargellis *Military Affairs* 47 and Pargellis *Loudoun* 318–20. One of the artillery companies had 107 men, Stock *Proceedings* V 584, and I assume the other was similar in size. Apparently no British cavalry was stationed in the colonies.

4 British postwar infantry forces in North America, army estimates for 1763, Feb. 25, 1763, *Journals H. of C.* XXIX 506, with Secretary at War Welbore Ellis to Amherst May 10, 1763, naming the regiments to be stationed in North America and the West Indies respectively, W.O. 34:72:387–89. Temporary retention of the 55th, *Gage* II 210, 217, 270. The artillery, Gen. Lord Ligonier, Master-General of the Ordnance, to Amherst March 10, 1763, Amherst Papers Can. Arch. 116.

5 No provision for any independent companies or rangers was made in the estimates either for Nova Scotia or for the army in 1763, *Journals H. of C.* XXIX 468 (Nova Scotia), 506 (army). Goreham's and Hopkins's corps of rangers were ordered disbanded, Ellis to Amherst May 18, 1763, Add. Mss. 21634:260.

6 British army estimates outside North America for 1763, Feb. 25, 1763, *Journals H. of C.* XXIX 503, 506 with Ellis to Amherst W.O. 34:72:387–89 stating which regiments for the colonies were to be stationed in the West Indies.

7 As to the missing letters of Lord Bute to George III, Romney Sedgwick in his Introduction, *Bute*, vii.

8 George Beer's explanation of the British army increase, Beer *Brit. Col. Policy* 261–62.

9 Army increase decided upon before Pontiac's Rebellion was foreseen, Grant "Pontiac's Rebellion" 75–83. Supporting evidence is given in Chapter 8 below.

10 Discontinuance of rangers, army estimates for 1763 *Journals H. of C.* XXIX 506 and note 5 above. As to dismissal of the Georgia mounted rangers, Lord Barrington, Sec. at War, to Gage Dec. 13, 1766, Gage Mss. Clements Lib.; Gage to Barrington Feb. 2 and May 27, 1767, *Gage* II 409, I 140.

11 Richard Jackson on inability of regular British troops to protect colonial frontiers, *An Historical Review of the Constitution and Government of Pennsylvania* (London, 1759) reprinted in Sparks *Franklin* III 105–577 at 569–71. As to Jackson's authorship and Franklin's assistance, *Jackson* 7–8.

12 Franklin's and Sir William Johnson's comments similar to Jackson's, Franklin *Interest of Great Britain* in Smyth *Franklin* IV 41–44; Johnson to B. of T. Aug. 20, 1762, *Johnson* III 868. The *Interest*, published in London April 1760, was widely republished, Ford *Franklin Bibliography* 117–19, and reviewed, Crane *Franklin's Letters to Press* 17.

13 The shift in regiments can be followed in the annual Millan *Army List* and various lists in Gage Papers and W.O., including a published one for Feb. 22, 1767, *New Regime* 512. As to the assignment of the 14th (Keppel's) regiment to North America, Henry Seymour Conway to Gage May 20, 1766, *Gage* II 38.

14 Amherst's correspondence with Lord Egremont and successive Secretaries at War in 1762–1763 is in C.O. 5:214 and W.O. 3:4:71. Egremont to Amherst Nov.

27, 1762, C.O. 5:214 Part 2:302–3 touched on the question of troops needed in North America after the war but so vaguely that Amherst in his reply, Jan. 27, 1763, did not even refer to the point, C.O. 5:63:1–3. Egremont wrote Amherst Aug. 13, 1763, of the King's "uninterrupted Satisfaction" with his "whole conduct," *Gage* II 207.

15 Colonial suspicion that the purpose of enlarging the British forces in America was to coerce the colonies, Eliphalet Dyer to Jared Ingersoll April 14, 1764, "Ingersoll Letters" 290–91; Dickinson *Late Regulations* in Ford *Dickinson* I 243. To similar effect, Johnson to B. of T. May 24, 1765, reporting what others said, *N.Y. Col. Doc.* VII 713–14, and Mayhew *Snare Broken* (Boston, 1766) in *Patriot Preachers* 25.

16 Gov. William Shirley of Mass. to Sir Thomas Robinson Aug. 15, 1755, as to large British force in America to keep the colonists under control, C.O. 5:46 Part 1:139–53, partly quoted in Bancroft *History* IV 214–15.

17 Suggestions in 1759–1761 as to keeping British troops in America to keep the colonists "in proper subjection," Robert R. Livingston, Jr., to Robert R. Livingston, Sr., March 16, 1760, Livingston Papers N.Y. Pub. Lib.; [Anonymous] *Reasons for Keeping Guadaloupe at a Peace preferable to Canada* (London, 1761) 6–7. (The modern spelling "Guadeloupe" had not yet been adopted.)

18 Capt. Walter Rutherfurd to Gilbert Elliot Dec. 14, 1759, Namier *Eng.* 326. As to Rutherfurd, *same* 325 and Rutherfurd *Family Records* 85–124. Elliot and his relations with Bute, *Elliot passim;* sketch of Elliot in *D.N.B.;* Namier *Eng.* 117–23; Bute to George Grenville March 25, 1763, *Grenville* II 32.

19 Egremont's letter of May 5, 1763, to the B. of T. asking for advice, S. & D. *Doc.* I 127–30, is discussed in Chapter 7.

20 The Canadians in general seemed contented with British rule, Colonels Thomas Gage, Ralph Burton, and James Murray, military Governors of Canada, to Amherst March 20, April (no date), and June 6, 1762 (S. & D. *Doc.* I 95, 87, 79–80), enclosed in Amherst to Egremont May 12, June 15, and July 20, 1762, C.O. 5:62:19, 169, 335.

21 Undated paper as to British troops to "awe" the colonists under pretense of "keeping of the Indians in subjection and making of roads," Shelburne Papers 85:26–34 at 31, discussed in Humphreys "Shelburne" 247–48. The passage quoted is in an unidentified hand.

22 Plan for increased British forces to assist the Indians in keeping back the colonists and to "exact a due obedience" from them, Shelburne Papers 67:107–8, quoted in Humphreys "Shelburne" 247–48. Similarly, "Mr. Pownall's Sketch," discussed in Chapter 7, suggested that the Indians' "dominion . . . be protected for them by forts and military establishments in proper places," *same* 260.

23 Suspicion that the increase in the army was designed to increase the King's influence in Parliament, Newcastle to Lord Hardwicke March 3, 1763, Add. Mss. 32947:163; *Serious Considerations* (London, 1763) 15–16, attributed to the Rev. John Butler, later Bishop of Oxford; Burke *Speeches* 26.

24 Eighty-five seats in the House of Commons in 1761 were held by service members, Namier *Eng.* 254–55, and many in the House of Lords, *Court Kalendar* for 1764, 162–65. Furthermore, nonservice members having sons, brothers, or close

friends in service were, of course, subject to Crown influence because of what the King might do for or against them.

25 Salaries and subsistence money of colonels ranged from £766 a year in the infantry regiments to £1,314 in the Horse Guards, *same* 169. Perquisites, including profit from clothing the regiment (*Gage* II 214n), made the actual income much higher, Walpole to Horace Mann Sept. 13, 1759, Toynbee *Walpole* IV 300, Thomas Whately to Grenville June 13, 1766, *Grenville* III 247–48 and Memorandum of George Clinton, Gov. of N.Y., 1743 *N.Y. Col. Doc.* VI 246–47 as to income from regiments and independent companies.

26 Colonels absent from Minorca, Corbett *England* I 103; from America, list of absent officers in return of the "Corps of His Majesty's Forces in North America," March 24, 1764, W.O. 17:1490. (Henry Bouquet, in active command in Pennsylvania in 1763–1764, was only a brevet colonel at that time.)

27 George III's readiness to use his control of army for political ends, George III to Bute [early Nov. 1762 and April 10, 1763] *Bute* 155, 213 and to Grenville [Nov. 25, 1763] *Grenville* II 166.

28 Traditional British prejudice against a large standing army, Lecky *History* I 550–59; Turberville *House of Lords* 243; Omond *Parliament and the Army* 35, 41–43; Williams *Whig Supremacy* 203–4, 210–11; Clode *Military Forces* I 87, 262, 271–72; Walpole to Mann April 29, 1742, Lewis *Walpole* XVII 410; *Seasonable Observations* (1750) 3–9, 54–62 especially among the Tories, *same, passim*.

29 Prejudice against large standing army still strong, *Letter Addressed to Two Great Men* (1760) 48; *Letter to Charles Townshend* (1763) 21–22; Quincy *Observations* (1774) 52–56. The annual so-called Mutiny Act providing for the pay, conduct, and discipline of the army, the quartering of troops, etc., was still invariably limited to a period not extending beyond the next session of Parliament.

30 As to the highly successful British operations in the West Indies during the recent war, Gipson *Brit. Empire* VIII 83–105, 186–96, 260–68; Pares *War and Trade in West Indies passim;* Smelser *Campaign passim;* Kimball *Pitt* II 346–84; Corbett *England* II 143–281. The value of British North America as a base for future operations against the French and Spanish West Indies was pointed out in the *London Chronicle* of Dec. 9, 1762.

31 Troops in North America to enforce the acts of trade and revenue, Lord Halifax to Amherst Oct. 11, 1763, *Gage* II 3. As to other proposed uses for the troops, unsigned "Plan" among papers sent to B. of T. by Egremont May 5, 1763 (*Journal B. of T. 1759–1763*, 363), published in *Critical Period* 5–11. The editors of *Critical Period* attributed the plan to Amherst (5n); but this is erroneous, Grant "Pontiac's Rebellion" 83–87.

32 As brought out in Chapter 1, the decision to tax the colonies had apparently been reached by the middle of Feb. 1763, Richard Rigby to the Duke of Bedford Feb. 23, 1763, *Bedford* III 210, but the Cabinet minutes from Dec. 1762 through Feb. 1763, P.R.O. 30:47:21, contain no reference to the matter, and hence furnish no clue to responsibility for the decision.

33 Early suggestions for colonial taxation by Parliament, Col. Robert Quary and Gov. Robert Hunter of N.Y., 1703, 1710 *N.Y. Col. Doc.* IV 1052–53, V 180; Caleb

Heathcote, Surveyor-Gen. of Customs N.Y., 1716, Fox *Heathcote,* 181; Archibald Cummings, Surveyor of Customs Boston, 1716, 1724, 1726, Pitman *West Indies* 207, 214; Col. David Dunbar 1730, 2 *Maine Hist. Soc. Coll.* XI 50–51; Sir William Keith 1726, 1728, 1739, 1742, Preston "Keith" 168–82, *N.C. Col. Rec.* II 635.

34 Later suggestions for colonial taxation, Gov. William Shirley of Mass., 1749, 1755, 1756, *Shirley* I 479, *N.Y. Col. Doc.* VI 958, Beer *Brit. Col. Policy* 48–49; Gov. George Clinton of N.Y., 1750, *N.Y. Col. Doc.* VI 554, 557; Chief Justice Robert Hunter Morris of N.J., 1752, Kemmerer *N.J.* 2; Gov. Horatio Sharpe of Md. 1754, 1757, *Sharpe* I 99, II 100; II 85–86; II 105; Gov. Robert Dinwiddie of Va. June 1754 to Feb. 1756, *Dinwiddie* I 204–493 *passim* and II 16, 17, 340–44.

35 British officers in America propose colonial taxation, Gen. Edward Braddock to Sir Thomas Robinson April 19, 1755, 1 *W. & M. Q.* XVIII (1910) 9; Gage to Lord Albemarle Jan. 22, 1756, *Keppel* I 442; Gen. Lord Loudoun to Duke of Cumberland Nov. 23, 1756, and to Pitt April 25, 1757, Pargellis *Loudoun* 186 and Kimball *Pitt* I 44. I have not found Cumberland's reply to Loudoun; in Pitt's reply, July 18, 1757, the suggestion was ignored, C.O. 5:212: Part 1:73–74.

36 B. of T.'s plan for a colonial revenue, B. of T. to Robinson April 30, 1754, Add. Mss. 33029:109; Cabinet meeting June 13 Add. Mss. 32995:266–70; Robinson to B. of T. June 14, B. of T. to Robinson with enclosures Aug. 9, *N.Y. Col. Doc.* VI 844, 902.

37 Charles Townshend and William Murray to Newcastle Sept. 13, 1754, and Oct. 6 favoring immediate taxation of colonies by Parliament, Gipson *Brit. Empire* V 164; Osgood *Eighteenth Century* IV 327 (date supplied from Add. Mss. 32737:45); Newcastle's statement of "Hints from Lord Halifax" for colonial taxation, Oct. 31, 1755, Add. Mss. 32996:265. Halifax suggested a stamp tax on the colonies as the "most eligible."

38 As to McCulloh, Bond *Quit Rents* in Index under "McCulloh, Henry"; High "McCulloh" 24–38; *Jenkinson* 228–31; *Grenville* II 374n, Cannon "McCulloh" 71–73, and sources cited in the next note.

39 McCulloh's proposal to Bute for colonial taxation, "Miscellaneous Representations . . . submitted to the Earl of Bute . . . Turnham Green, 1761," Item 407 Sotheby's Catalogue of sale on Feb. 17, 1905, of "Manuscripts, The Property of a *Nobleman,*" published in Shaw *Miscellaneous Representations.* McCulloh made similar suggestions to other Ministers, Sellers "McCulloh" 548–51, and helped prepare the colonial stamp tax bill, Ritcheson "Stamp Act" 549–52.

Chapter 7

1 Population of Canada, Amherst to Pitt Oct. 4, 1760, Kimball *Pitt* II 339; B. of T. to Committee for Plantation Affairs Sept. 2, 1765, S. & D. *Doc.* I 237; of La., 4,100 whites in 1746, Caldwell *French in Miss. Valley* 35 and apparently little later increase, Gipson *Brit. Empire* IV 118–22; of Fla., Siebert "Pensacola" 54 and "East Florida" 145–50; of Indians, Sir William Johnson's estimate of Northern Indians Nov. 18, 1763, with Johnson to Gov. William Tryon of N.Y. Oct. 22, 1773, *N.Y. Col. Doc.* VII 582–84, VIII 458–59; John Stuart's estimate of Southern Indians, Alden *Stuart* 7n.

2 *A Sermon Preached Before His Excellency Thomas Pownall* (Boston, 1759) 46. Many other published Thanksgiving Sermons on this occasion are listed in Love *Fast and Thanksgiving Days* 536–38.

3 Lord Egremont to B. of T. May 5, 1763, asking advice concerning Great Britain's new possessions, S. & D. *Doc.* I 127–31 with *B. of T. Journal* 1759–1763, 362–63, and B. of T.'s reply to Egremont June 8, 1763, S. & D. *Doc.* I 131–47 at 139–41, 145. The Board's report was accompanied by a map showing the boundary between the proposed new colonies and the Indian reservation, a copy of which is in the Map Division, Can. Archives.

4 Board of Trade reply to Lord Egremont June 8, 1763, and Egremont's reply to Board July 14, *same* 139–40, 147–50. Two material changes in the Board's plan were proposed by Egremont: that the Indian territory be included in the government of Canada and that the Commander-in-Chief correspond on Indian affairs with the Sec. of State rather than with the Board.

5 B. of T. to Egremont Aug. 5, 1763, concerning settlement of new possessions and proposing royal proclamation to quiet the Indians, *same* 150–53. The Board questioned Egremont's proposal to place the Indian territory under the government of Canada, and suggested that the Commander-in-Chief in North America be commissioned Governor of the territory.

6 Lord Halifax to B. of T. Sept. 19, 1763, on various points *same* 153–55. I have found no evidence explaining the change in name from Quebec to Canada. Col. James Grant's undated statement concerning the Fla. boundary is in Mayo *St. Mary's River* 18–22. The Board approved Grant's suggestion, B. of T. to Halifax Sept. 28, 1763, *same* 23.

7 B. of T. to Halifax Oct. 4, 1763, enclosing draft of proposed royal proclamation S. & D. *Doc.* I 156–57.

8 Royal Proclamation of Oct. 7, 1763, *same* 163–68. It had been formally approved by the Privy Council Oct. 5, *same* 157–59. The Proclamation dealt with other matters besides the new colonies and the reservation for the Indians, including grants of Crown land and purchases of Indian title in the colonies, the Indian trade, and seizure of fugitives from justice in the Indian reservation.

9 An Order in Council of May 9, 1764, extended West Florida northward to a line running from the junction of the Yazoo river with the Mississippi (about 32° 30′) due east to the Apalachicola river, *Acts P.C.* IV 668, and the Commission issued to Gov. Montagu Wilmot of Nova Scotia Nov. 21, 1763, included in this colony roughly all of present New Brunswick as well as all of present Nova Scotia, S. & D. *Doc.* I 162.

10 Territory reserved in the Proclamation for the Indians, *same* 166–67. Tracts of ungranted Indian land east of the Alleghenies remained in all the colonies south of Md. and in several of the northern colonies, and the Proclamation covered these tracts as well as the land west of the Alleghenies.

11 Carter "Commander in Chief" 182–85, Alden *Stuart* 139–52. Administration of the old French settlements in the Indian territory presented interesting problems, Carter "Commander in Chief" 182–89; Carter *Illinois Country passim;* Gage to inhabitants of the Illinois Country Dec. 30, 1764, *Critical Period* 395–96. 5 George

III ch. 33 sec. 25 (1765) provided that any person charged with crime within the territory should be dealt with initially by the Commander-in-Chief.

12 B. of T. to Shelburne Dec. 23, 1767, *N.Y. Col. Doc.* VII 1004 and Farrand "Indian Boundary" 782–91 at 785 erroneously imply that protection and pacifying the Indians was the sole object in excluding white settlers from the region west of the Alleghenies. Alvord "Genesis of the Proclamation" 21 also tends to give this implication.

13 B. of T. to Committee for Plantation Affairs April 15, 1772, as to reasons for excluding white settlers, Sparks *Franklin* IV 305–6. (Hillsborough, who was president of the Board when the Proclamation was drafted in final form, was now again president.) To same effect, B. of T. to the King March 7, 1768, *N.Y. Col. Doc.* VIII 27–28.

14 B. of T. to Egremont June 8, 1763, as to reasons for excluding white settlers, S. & D. *Doc.* I 141.

15 Capt. Walter Rutherfurd to Gilbert Elliot Dec. 14, 1759, Namier *Eng.* 326. To same effect, *London Chronicle* June 8, 1758. Franklin, in his *Interest of Great Britain* (London, 1760) rebutted the argument that colonists settled west of the Appalachians would be "useless" to Great Britain, maintaining, among other points, that the high cost of carriage would not prevent their buying British manufactures, Smyth *Franklin* IV 57.

16 Unsigned, undated document as to closing the west to white settlement, enclosed in Egremont to B. of T. May 5, 1763, Crane "Hints" 370–73 at 371.

17 Unsigned, undated document of similar import, endorsed "Mr. Pownall's Sketch," Humphreys "Shelburne" 258–64 at 259. "Mr. Pownall" presumably was John Pownall, Secretary to the Board of Trade.

18 Undated draft of letter by Maurice Morgann as to proper role for colonists, Shelburne Papers 85:26–34 at 29, handwriting identified in Humphrey "Shelburne" 247–48.

19 Later colonial discontent over exclusion of white settlers is touched on in Carter "Commander in Chief" 194–95 and is treated at length in another volume (1766–1775) which I plan to publish.

Chapter 8

1 Sir Jeffery Amherst to Lord Egremont June 27, 1763, reporting Indian outbreak, C.O. 5:63:130–31.

2 Causes of Pontiac's Rebellion, Peckham *Pontiac* 74, 92–106, 112–16, 120, 174–75, 187–88. Johnson's "Review" Sept. 22, 1767, *N.Y. Col. Doc.* VII 951, 958–62 and Parkman *Pontiac* I 173–80 are also useful. Peckham brings out that prophecies by the so-called Delaware Prophet of Indian extermination by the whites if the Indians failed to strike were an important factor in causing the uprising.

3 Crown instructions in 1755 and 1756 as to grants of Crown land in New York and Virginia, Labaree *Instructions* II 467–69. B. of T. to Gov. Francis Fauquier of Va. June 13, 1760, forbidding grants in the Ohio Valley, Alden *Stuart* 265. An instruction, December 1761, to Governors of most of the royal colonies in North

America laid further restrictions on grants of Crown land in America, Labaree *Instructions* II 476–78.

4   Deed of Release to Indians by Thomas and Richard Penn Oct. 23, 1758, *Johnson* X 43–48, given pursuant to a promise by the Penns as Proprietaries of Pennsylvania to Lord Halifax, President of B. & T., referred to in Proprietaries to Gov. William Denny of Pa. Feb. 12, 1757, *same* II 684.

5   Assurances given Indians by Sir William Johnson and George Croghan, minutes of Canajoharie conference April 17, 1759, *N.Y. Col. Doc.* VII 388; minutes of Fort Pitt conference July 9, 1759, *Pa. Col. Rec.* VIII 389. These assurances confirmed a similar one made on behalf of Gen. John Forbes at an Indian conference in Philadelphia Feb. 9, 1759, *same* 268.

6   Amherst's permit April 10, 1761, for settlement at Niagara C.O. 5:61: Part I 285; Amherst to Johnson May 7 concerning the permit, *Johnson* III 387. The names of those included in the permit and the fact that a settlement at Niagara was promptly begun appear in Capt. Walter Rutherfurd to Amherst April 28, 1761, C.O. 5:61: Part I 289.

7   Protest of twenty-seven Albany merchants to the B. of T. against Amherst's Niagara permit, Jan. 28, 1762, *N.Y. Col. Doc.* VII 488; Order in Council June 19 to Amherst to disperse the Niagara settlement *Acts P.C.* IV 543–44; Amherst to Commanding Officer at Fort Niagara Oct. 17, 1762, revoking the permit C.O. 5:1070:395–96.

8   Indians' fear aroused by Amherst's Niagara settlement, minutes of Detroit Indian conference, Capt. Donald Campbell, commanding at Detroit, July 3, 1761, *Johnson* III 451; entry July 25 in "Croghan's Journal" 410.

9   Johnson to Amherst July 29, 1761, and Amherst's reply Aug. 9 concerning Indian complaints as to the Niagara settlement *Johnson* X 321–22, III 514. The speech mentioned by Johnson was delivered by Gen. Robert Monckton on Aug. 12, 1760, at an Indian conference at Easton, Pa., *Pa. Archives* III 745–46.

10 Amherst to Maj. Henry Gladwin June 22, 1761, stating he had ordered Monckton to build a fort at Sandusky, *Johnson* X 295. As to reestablishing Presque Isle and other former French forts in present western Pennsylvania, Bouquet to Monckton Dec. 20, 1760, *Aspinwall* I 386.

11 Indians' fears aroused by rebuilding of forts, July 7, 1761, "Kenny's Journal" 12; minutes of Easton conference Aug. 8, *Pa. Council* VIII 642; Johnson to B. of T. Aug. 20, 1762, to Amherst June 6, 1763, to Gov. Cadwallader Colden July 13, 1763; *Johnson* III 866, *N.Y. Col. Doc.* VII 523, *Johnson* IV 170; Gladwin to Amherst April 20, 1763, *same* 95.

12 Johnson to Amherst July 29, Amherst to Johnson Aug. 9, 1761, *Johnson* X 322, III 516. Though much "fretted" by the neighboring Indians, the officer in charge completed the blockhouse before the end of Nov., Lieut. Elias Meyer to Col. Henry Bouquet Nov. 29, 1761, *Bouquet* Ser. 21647, 214 with entry Feb. 3, 1762, "Kenny's Journal" 39.

13 Amherst to Johnson Aug. 11, 1761, as to Col. James Grant's punishment of the Cherokees *Johnson* III 517. Grant's journal of his campaign, June 7–July 9, 1761, is in *Fla. Hist. Quarterly* XII (1953) 25–36. As to the Cherokee uprising of 1760–

1761, Alden *Stuart* 101–32; Gipson *Brit. Empire* IX 67–87; Hamer "Fort Loudoun" 442–58; Wallace *Laurens* 100; Gov. William Henry Lyttelton and Gov. William Bull of S.C. to Amherst Feb. 2 and Oct. 19 and Nov. 18, 1760 C.O. 5:57 and 60.

14 As to the custom of both British and French to make the Indians gifts, Jacobs *Indian Gifts, passim* and entries of June 1759 to May 1760 in "Croghan's Journal" 316–70. In 1759 alone, Amherst gave Johnson about £9,000 sterling out of army funds, largely for Indian presents, *Johnson* III 182, 185, the nature of which appear in *same* II 898–900. Fort de Chartres was not transferred to the British until 1765, Capt. Thomas Sterling to Gen. Thomas Gage Oct. 18, 1765, *New Regime 1765–7* 107–8.

15 Indians to be punished for ill behavior, not bribed to be good, Amherst to Johnson Feb. 22, 1761, *Johnson* III 345. Johnson subject to orders of the Commander-in-Chief, Johnson's commission, dated Feb. 17, 1756, reissued March 11, 1761, *same* II 434, *N.Y. Col. Doc.* VII 459.

16 Johnson to Amherst June 21, 1761, warning of Indian unrest *Johnson* X 291; Amherst to Johnson June 24, Aug. 9 and 18, 1761, *same* III 421, 514, 520, replying to Johnson's letters of June 21, July 29 and 24, *same* X 291 and 320–23, III 513. As to relative experience, Johnson had lived in the Mohawk country for over twenty years while Amherst, who had been in America less than three years, had had little contact with the Indians.

17 As to importance of British gifts of ammunition and Indians' dire need, Johnson to Amherst March 21, June 7, June 12, 1761, *same* X 246, 279, 286–87; complaint of Huron Indian chief at Detroit Conference Sept. 10, 1761, *same* III 486; entry of May 21, 1762, in "Kenny's Journal" 156–57. Amherst also seems to have issued a temporary order forbidding even the sale of powder to the Indians, Johnson to Amherst July 7 and 29, 1761, *Johnson* X 312, 321; entry July 25, 1761, "Croghan's Journal" 410.

18 Amherst's policy of keeping Indians short of ammunition and the grave danger of this policy, Amherst to Bouquet May 2, 1762, *Bouquet* Ser. 21634, 88; Capt. Donald Campbell to Bouquet Oct. 12, 1761, July 3, 1762, *same* Ser. 21647, 161–62, Ser. 21648 Part II 1; Bouquet to Campbell May 25, 1762, *same* Ser. 21653, 136. Campbell was among the first victims of the Indian uprising in 1763, Peckham *Pontiac* 139–40, 195.

19 Johnson to Amherst June 12, 1761, warning him of the danger of his policy of keeping the Indians short of ammunition; Amherst to Johnson June 24, providing for gift of ammunition in a particular case; and Johnson to Amherst July 24 urging the necessity of a general change in policy on this point, *Johnson* X 286–87, III 421, and III 513.

20 Entries Oct. 1761–April 1762, concerning gifts of ammunition to Indian raiding parties, "Croghan's Journal" 416–37. As to encouraging these raiding parties, Johnson-Amherst correspondence April–Sept. 1762, *Johnson* III 725, 743, 877, X 451, and Croghan to Johnson Oct. 8, 1762, *same* X 548–49.

21 Amherst to Johnson Aug. 9, 1761, insisting that the surest way to avert Indian rebellion was to keep them short of powder, *same* III 515. Amherst may have discounted Johnson's advice because he reasoned that it was to the Indian Agents' "interest to treat the Indians as of more Consequence than they really are." Amherst to Bouquet June 7, 1762, *Bouquet* Ser. 21634, 90. Croghan was notoriously unscrupulous, Wainwright *Croghan, passim,* and there was considerable distrust of Johnson's integrity, as brought out in Chapter 18.

22 Gen. John Forbes to Amherst Feb. 7, 1759, questioning his attitude concerning the Indians, *Forbes* 289–90.

23 Croghan to Johnson Sept. 28, 1763, accusing Amherst of indifference to distress of frontier settlers, *Johnson* X 827. The meaning of "B____t of p____e" stumps me.

24 Reports of widespread Indian discontent, Thomas Hutchins' report April 4–Sept. 24, 1762, *Johnson* X 521–29; Croghan to Bouquet Dec. 10, 1762, Jan. 8, 1763, *same* 597, *Bouquet* Ser. 21649 Part I 6; Amherst's knowledge of such reports, Johnson to Amherst Nov. 12, 1762, March 18, 1763, *Johnson* X 568, 624, and Amherst to Johnson Jan. 10, 1763, *same* 607.

25 Amherst's dismissal of the reports as "meer Bugbears," Amherst to Johnson April 3, 1763, *same* 648. In the same vein, Amherst to Johnson Oct. 31, 1762, Jan. 31, 1763, *Johnson* III 920, X 614 and to Maj. John Wilkins as late as May 29, 1763, W.O. 34:23:120.

26 As to Indians' reaction to news of French cessions, Capt. Simeon Ecuyer to Col. William Amherst (Sir Jeffery's younger brother) March 11, 1763, *Bouquet* Ser. 21649 Part I 69; Croghan to Gen. Amherst April 30, Volwiler *Croghan* 162. To same effect, Croghan to Johnson and Bouquet March 12 and 19, 1763, *Johnson* IV 62, and *Bouquet* Ser. 21649 Part I 80; and entry of March 26, 1763, "Kenny's Journal" 192.

27 Amherst to Croghan May 10, 1763, three days after the uprising (of course not yet known to Amherst) had begun, Volwiler *Croghan* 162.

28 Attack on Detroit, Gladwin to Amherst May 14, 1763, Parkman Papers, Mass. Hist. Soc. Lieut. James McDonald wrote Croghan July 12, 1763, that the attacking Indians were Ottawas, Wyandots (Hurons), Chippewas (Ojibways), and Potawatomies, *Johnson* X 736–41; other attacks, minutes of Court of Enquiry, Detroit July 6, 1763, *same* X 730–31; entries of June 16 and 29, 1763, *Amherst Journal* 306–7, 315.

29 Whites killed near Fort Pitt, Ecuyer to Bouquet May 29, 1763, *Bouquet* Ser. 21649 Part I 114–15; entries May 27–June 26, 1763, "Trent's Journal" 393–402; attack on Fort Ligonier, Lieut. Archibald Blane to Bouquet, June 4, 1763, *Bouquet* Ser. 21649 Part I 131.

30 Attack on Fort Le Boeuf, Ensign (Second Lieut.) George Price to Bouquet June 26, 1763, *same* Part I 172–73 with Johnson to Amherst July 11, 1763, *N.Y. Col. Doc.* VII 532; on Fort Pitt, Ecuyer to Bouquet June 26, 1763, *Bouquet* Ser. 21649 Part I 175–76; on Presque Isle, minutes of Court of Enquiry, Detroit July 10, 1763, *Johnson* X 734–35.

31 Amherst widely held liable for the outbreak, Thomas Penn to Gov. James Hamilton of Pa. Dec. 9, 1763, Boyd *Susquehanna Co. Papers* II 284; Robert Stewart to Washington Jan. 14, 1764, Hamilton *Washington* III 265; *Pennsylvania Journal* April 19, 1764; *Newport Mercury* Dec. 31, 1764.

32 William Livingston to Eleazar Wheelock, head of More's Charity School for Indians (forerunner of Dartmouth College), March 22, 1764, attributing Indian outbreak to Amherst's blunders, Wheelock Papers Dartmouth College Lib. See also Johnson to Gov. Colden, Dec. 24, 1763, *Johnson* IV 276 and Halifax to Gage Jan. 14, 1764, *Gage* II 10, probably referring to, though not naming, Amherst.

Chapter 9

1 I have seen no references to Indian ravages in N.J. and only one to ravages in N.Y., Gov. Cadwallader Colden of N.Y. to Gen. Sir Jeffery Amherst Nov. 3, 1763, *Colden* 1876, 251. Loyalty of the Six Nations, Sir William Johnson to B. of T. Nov. 13, *N.Y. Col. Doc.* VII 576. Frontier service of N.Y. and N.J. militia, various papers from July to Nov. of Colden and of Gov. William Franklin of N.J. *Colden* 1876, 217, 221–24, 248–54, 1 *N.J. Col. Doc.* XXIV 276.

2 Indian raids, *Pa. Journal* July 21, 1763; *Pa. Gazette* July 21, 28, Aug. 4; *Md. Gazette* July 7, 14, 21, Aug. 4, 11, Parkman *Pontiac* II 57, 85, Dorr *Hist. Account* 141. As to Va. militia and Pa. recruits for frontier defense, Gov. Francis Fauquier of Va. to the Legislature Jan. 12, 1764, *Va. Journals* 1761–1765, 203–4; Pa. Assembly minutes July 5 to Oct. 18, 1763, 8 *Pa. Archives* VI 5426, 5429, 5430, 5438–39, 5478.

3 Renewal of Indian raids, *Pa. Journal* Sept. 15, Oct. 13, 27, Nov. 10, 17, 1763; *Md. Gazette* Sept. 1, 15, Oct. 20, Nov. 10. The most destructive (in Oct. 1763) was on a settlement of Conn. people, intruders on Indian land at Wyoming on the Susquehanna, described in Wallace *Teedyuscung* 264 and Boyd *Susquehanna Co. Papers* II 277–82.

4 Heavy loss of life, Col. Henry Bouquet to Gov. James Hamilton of Pa. Sept. 12, 1763, *Rep. on Can. Archives* 1889, Part II, 239; George Croghan to B. of T. June 8, 1764, *Critical Period* 1763–1765, 256. Such reports of deaths and captures as I have found, add up to much less than Croghan's figure; but many of the losses may, of course, have been unrecorded or the records of them escaped my search.

5 Importance of punishing rebel Indians as deterrent, Amherst to Lord Egremont Aug. 13, 1763, C.O. 5:63:399. To same effect, Amherst to Johnson and to Colden Aug. 20, Oct. 30 *Johnson* IV 193, *N.Y. Assembly* II 721; B. Franklin to Richard Jackson, June 27, Sept. 22 *Jackson* 107, 110; Johnson to Amherst Aug. 20, *N.Y. Col. Doc.* VII 541; W. Franklin to B. of T. Dec. 5, 1 *N.J. Col. Doc.* IX 398–99; Colden to Lord Halifax and to Johnson Dec. 8 and 19, *Colden* 1876, 261, 267.

6 Amherst's supreme confidence, Amherst to Bouquet June 6, 1763, *Bouquet* Ser. 21634, 182–83; Amherst to Egremont July 23 C.O. 5:63:297 and to Johnson, Aug. 20, 27, Sept. 9, 30 *Johnson* IV 193, *N.Y. Col. Doc.* VII 545, 547, *Johnson* X 857.

7 Number of British defenders at Detroit and Fort Pitt, Lieut. James McDonald at Detroit to Croghan July 12 *same* 739; Capt. Simeon Ecuyer at Fort Pitt to Bouquet June 26 *Bouquet* Ser. 21649 Part I 175–76.

8 Amherst's orders to Maj. John Wilkins and to Bouquet June 10 and 12, 1763, W.O. 34:23:121 and Bouquet Ser. 21634, 186.

9 Amherst to Egremont July 23, 1763, C.O. 5:63:303 and to Johnson Aug. 14, concerning Capt. James Dalyell's mission, *Johnson* IV 186; Maj. Henry Gladwin to

Amherst Aug. 8, as to arrival of Dalyell's detachment at Detroit, Amherst Papers W.O. 34:49:455; McDonald to Croghan July 12 as to arrival of previous reinforcements, *Johnson* X 744.

10 Amherst's orders to Capt.-Lieut. Valentine Gardner Aug. 10, 1763, Amherst Papers, Clements Library. Knollenberg "Amherst and Germ Warfare" *Miss. Vall. Hist. Rev.* XLI 489–94, with correction in 762–63, deals with the attempt to kill off hostile Indians by spreading smallpox among them in 1763.

11 As to Dalyell's defeat and Amherst's ensuing orders to Wilkins, Gladwin to Amherst Aug. 8, 1763, Amherst Papers W.O. 34:49:455; Maj. Alexander Duncan to Johnson Sept. 8, *Johnson* IV 200 and X 762–66; Amherst to Wilkins Sept. 3 ordering him forward, W.O. 34:23:135.

12 The Niagara "Carrying-Place" disaster, entry of Sept. 30, 1763, *Amherst Journal* 322 with Amherst to Egremont Oct. 13, C.O. 5:63:726; Capt. George Etherington and Duncan to Johnson Sept. 17 and Oct. 1 and Johnson to Amherst Oct. 6, Johnson X 817, 863, 867; Maj. Thomas Moncrieffe to Amherst Sept. 26, 1763, W.O. 34:95:160–68.

13 Wreck delays Wilkins's departure, Moncrieffe to Johnson Oct. 4, Johnson IV 212–13, entry of Nov. 7, 1763, *Amherst Journal* 326. The details of the accident are in the diary entry Aug. 28, 1763 (the day the vessel was wrecked) of Lieut. John Montresor, Webster "Montresor" 14.

14 Return of Wilkins's detachment to Niagara, Gen. Thomas Gage to Lord Halifax Dec. 23, 1763, *Gage* I 5. I have found nothing in the Amherst or Gage papers attributing the failure to quell the Indian rebellion to the heavy losses of experienced British troops from North America in the Havana campaign of 1762, but this may have been an important contributing factor.

15 Gladwin's statement on Oct. 12 to Indians besieging Detroit, Gladwin to Amherst Nov. 1, 1763, *Mich. Pioneer Coll.* XXVII 675–76.

16 Neyon de Villiers to Indians Sept. 27, 1763, urging them to make peace with the British *same* 653–54; Pontiac to Gladwin Oct. 30, 1763, proposing peace, *Bouquet* Ser. 21649 Part II 117–18; Gladwin to Pontiac (undated) indicating all would be well, *same* 118–19.

17 Bouquet to Gladwin Aug. 28, 1763, as to his expedition to Fort Pitt, Ad. Mss. 21649:313; Amherst to Bouquet Aug. 31, 1763, as to his poor opinion of colonial scouts, *Bouquet* Ser. 21634, 255. In similar vein Gen. Wolfe wrote Lord George Sackville, Aug. 7, 1758, "The Americans are in general the dirtiest most contemptible cowardly dogs that you can conceive . . . rather an encumbrance than any real strength to an army," Willson *Wolfe* 392.

18 Bouquet to Amherst July 26, 1763, as to hiring colonial woodsmen *Bouquet* Ser. 21634, 223. Other British officers besides Bouquet, who had served on the frontier, recognized the value of colonial troops in Indian warfare, e.g., Col. James Grant, *Fla. Hist. Quart.* XII 24, and Gage *Mich. Pioneer Coll.* XIX 243–44, *Rep. on Can. Archives* 1889 A 8, 61.

19 Battle of Bushy Run, Bouquet to Amherst Aug. 5 and 6, 1763, Parkman *Pontiac* II 338–41 and to Gladwin Aug. 28, Add. Mss. 21649:313. The distance stated is from a Table of Distances from Philadelphia to Fort Pitt in *Bouquet's Expedition*

148, the losses from "Return of Killed and Wounded" *Pa. Frontier Forts* II 533–34. The Indians' loss was thought to be "60 killed or mortally wounded," entry Aug. 25, 1763, *Amherst Journal* 318.

20 Bouquet to Amherst Aug. 11, 1763, reporting his arrival at Fort Pitt the day before, *Bouquet* Ser. 21634, 243.

21 Amherst to Bouquet July 2, 7, 16, 1763, as to proceeding to Presque Isle, Bouquet to Amherst Aug. 26 and 27 reporting his inability to advance beyond Fort Pitt, Amherst to Bouquet Sept. 18 expressing hope that Bouquet would at least punish the hostile Indians in the neighborhood of Fort Pitt, and Bouquet's reply of Oct. 24 that even this was impracticable, *same* 206–88 *passim*.

22 Indian Congress at Augusta Nov. 1763, Alden *Stuart* 181–85. Apparently neither Johnson nor Amherst proposed a similar Congress of the Northern Indians, perhaps because of the heavy expense of such Congresses coupled with the consideration that a Congress of the Northern Indians had been held (at Detroit) as recently as September 1761.

23 The terrible punishment of the Cherokees in 1761 was described in Chapter 8. The location of the Cherokee and Creek settlements is shown in the map of the Southern Indian country in the pocket at end of Alden *Stuart*.

24 Amherst to Gage Oct. 11, 1763, telling of his plan to go to England on leave of absence, W.O. 34:7:178. Amherst's decision to leave at this critical juncture was justified by the mental breakdown of his wife, owing, he believed, to "the dread of my being in this country and my long [five years] absence from home," Amherst to John Calcraft April 26, 1763, W.O. 34:99:203. As to Lady Amherst's illness, Long *Amherst* 188–89.

25 Amherst's parting injunction to Gage Nov. 17, 1763, to crush the Indian rebellion and punish those implicated in it, *Gage* II 211–12.

26 Amherst's call for provincial troops, Amherst to Colden Oct. 30, 1763, *N.Y. Assembly* II 721 and Gage to Halifax Dec. 9 summarizing orders as to provincial troops given by Amherst, *Gage* I 3. Gage requested troops from the New England colonies, too, but only Connecticut voted any, Gage to Halifax Dec. 9, 1763, to May 12, 1764, *same* 3–27 *passim*.

27 William Smith, Jr., to unidentified correspondent Nov. 22, 1763, deriding Amherst, Parkman *Pontiac* II 104n.

28 Gage to Gladwin Dec. 22, 1763, authorizing peace with Indians subject to final settlement with Johnson, Gage Papers. No punishment was exacted when this final settlement took place in 1766, Johnson's minutes of Indian conference at Detroit July 1766, *N.Y. Col. Doc.* VII 854–67.

29 Col. John Bradstreet's expedition, Gage to Halifax May 12, 1764, *Gage* I 28; undated statement and entries Aug. 9 and 12, 1764, in journal of Montresor, Bradstreet's chief engineer, *Montresor* 275, 279, 280. An undated copy of Gage's instructions to Bradstreet is in Gage Papers.

30 Treaty of Aug. 12, 1764, *Johnson* XI 328–33, ratified at Presque Isle, present Erie, Pa., Aug. 15, *Montresor* 281. As to the Indians' overture, Montresor's journal Aug. 12, *same* 280; as to location of L'Ance aux Feuilles, *Johnson* XI 329n. Bradstreet wrote Gage Aug. 14 enclosing a copy of the treaty, Hough *Siege* 281.

31 Ratification by Bradstreet of Gladwin's truce with Ottawas and other Indians, minutes of Indian conference at Detroit Sept. 7–10, 1764, *Johnson* X 349–51, IV 526–33, enclosed in Bradstreet to Gage Sept. 12, "Bradstreet Manuscripts" 126. As to failure of Delawares and Shawnees to appear at Sandusky and Bradstreet's message to them, Montresor's journal Sept. 9, 18, 25 *Montresor* 290, 294, 298–99.

32 Gage to Bradstreet Sept. 2, 1764, denouncing his treaty with the Indians, Gage Papers, partly in Parkman *Pontiac* II 178n, 179n. As to recent massacres referred to by Gage, John Penn of Pa. to Johnson, June 9 *Johnson* XI 224; the particularly gruesome murder of a schoolmaster and nine pupils in Pennsylvania on July 22 described in Parkman *Pontiac* II 90 and the *London Chronicle* of Sept. 20; and Bouquet to Gage Aug. 27 *Mich. Pioneer Coll.* XIX 271.

33 Bouquet to Gage (not, as printed, to Amherst) denouncing Bradstreet's peace treaty Aug. 27, 1764, *same.*

34 Gov. Horatio Sharpe of Md. to Cecilius Calvert Sept. 18, 1764, as to indignation over Bradstreet's treaty, *Sharpe* III 178. To similar effect: Hugh Wallace, New York City, to Johnson Oct. 29 *Johnson* IV 575; Lieut. Col. John Reid to Bouquet, Sept. 3, *Bouquet* Ser. 21650 Part II 117–18. Gage's faulty instructions to Bradstreet were apparently not made public.

35 Bradstreet's and Six Nations' conduct, Montresor's Journal Sept. 26 to Oct. 18, 1764, *Montresor* 300–311.

36 Bouquet's force, Return of Effectives Nov. 5, 1764, *Bouquet* Ser. 21651, 34. As to provision for provincial troops, Pa. act of May 30, 1764, *Pa. Statutes* VI 344–45; Bouquet to Gov. John Penn, Aug. 10 and 22, *Pa. Arch.* IV 198–99.

37 Bouquet's plan of operations, Bouquet to Gage May 2, 1764, Gage Papers, published in part in *Montresor* 526–27, approved in Gage to Bouquet May 14, *same* 527. An injunction that the Indians must "deliver the Promoters of the War into your Hands, to be put to Death" was added in Gage to Bouquet Aug. 27, Add. Mss. 21638:371 (Bouquet Papers).

38 "An Onondaga and an Oneida Indian" to Bouquet Oct. 2, 1764, begging him to defer action, *Pa. Council* IX 209–10.

39 Bouquet to Gage Oct. 2, 1764, reporting his message to Delawares and Shawnees, Bouquet Papers, Can. Arch., with Bouquet's journal for Oct. 3, *Pa. Council* IX 211–13; Gage's order to disregard Bradstreet's treaty is in Gage to Bouquet Sept. 2, 1764, *Mich. Pioneer Coll.* XIX 272.

40 Bouquet's march and his conditional promise of lenity, Alexander McKee, Indian Agent, to Johnson Oct. 21, 1764, and minutes of Bouquet's Indian conferences and related matters Oct. 17 and 20, *Johnson* XI 386, 438–46. A map of Bouquet's march from Fort Pitt by way of Tuscarawas to the mouth of the Tuscarawas river is in *Bouquet's Expedition* facing p. 1.

41 Delivery of captives and Bouquet's further negotiations, minutes of Indian conferences and related matters Oct. 22–Nov. 14, 1764, *Johnson* XI 447–67 and Bouquet to Johnson Nov. 15, *same* IV 585–86. As to Gage giving Bouquet carte blanche, Gage to Bouquet Oct. 21 and Bouquet's reply Nov. 5, *Mich. Pioneer Coll.* XIX 278–80.

42 McKee wrote Johnson Nov. 17, 1764, that the army would return to Fort Pitt "tomorrow," *Johnson* XI 475; as to its arrival at Fort Pitt on Nov. 28, Bouquet to Johnson Nov. 30, *same* IV 606.

43 Shawnee hostages decamp, Bouquet to Johnson Dec. 3, 1764, *same* 608. Final terms of peace, minutes of Johnson's Indian conferences April to July, 1765, *N.Y. Col. Doc.* VII 718–41, 750–55. No restitution whatever was exacted for losses of frontier settlers, even those whose homes were on land which had unquestionably been previously ceded by the Indians and was open to white settlement. A list of the captives delivered by the Shawnees May 10, 1765, is in Ewing "Indian Captives" 197–202.

44 Resolution of Va. House of Burgesses thanking Bouquet Dec. 11, 1764, *Va. Journals* for 1761–1765, 289–90; Samuel Wharton of Pa. to Franklin Dec. 19 *Critical Period* 376; Address of thanks to Bouquet of Pa. Assembly Jan. 15, 1765, 8 *Pa. Arch.* VII 5704–5.

Chapter 10

1 Early recognition in England of value of colonial white pine for naval masts, Albion *Forests and Sea Power* 211–35 *passim;* Pepys's diary Dec. 3, 1666, Braybrooke *Pepys* 449. For other early references, Mayo "The King's Woods" 50; Beer *Origins* 381–82.

2 Reservation of white pines for the Crown, Mass. charter of Oct. 7, 1691, *Mass. Acts* I 20. N.H. had no charter, but it early (1708) passed an act forbidding the felling of any white pine not "the perticuler property of any private person" if 24 inches or more in diameter a foot from the ground and "fitt to make Masts for her Majesties [Queen Anne's] Royal Navy," *N.H. Laws* II 82.

3 9 Anne ch. 17 secs. 1 and 2 (1711); 8 Geo. 1 ch. 12 secs. 5 and 6 (1722); 2 Geo. II ch. 35 secs. 1 and 2 (1729). The unrepealed section of the act of 1711 merely forbade anyone but the Surveyor-General or his deputies to mark trees with the broad arrow, symbol of Crown ownership.

4 The Surveyors' source of authority, e.g., Commission of Surveyor-General John Bridger Dec. 24, 1705, signed by Lord Godolphin, Lord High Treasurer, *N.H. Papers* III 334–35. The practice of corresponding with the B. of T. will appear in subsequent footnotes.

5 Colonial admiralty courts given jurisdiction over offenses under the White Pine Acts, 8 Geo. I ch. 12 sec. 5 (1722). The colonial admiralty courts are discussed in the Appendix to Chapter 14.

6 Description of clashes between the Surveyors and loggers in Mass. and N.H., Lord *Indust. Esp.* 91–99, 109–23; Albion *Forests and Sea Power* 262–63; Palfrey *New Eng.* IV 399–401; 2 *Maine* IX, X, XI *passim.*

7 Chief Justice Thomas Hutchinson in his *History of Massachusetts-Bay* II 191 (1767) estimated that a white pine tree suitable for a naval mast was worth twenty times its value for lumber. I have found no other estimate but have no reason to doubt this one, if limited, as Hutchinson probably intended, to trees near navigable water.

8 Recommendation for reasonable limitation, Gov. Joseph Dudley to B. of T., July 23, 1702, *Calendar State Pap.* for 1702, 482–83; Gov. William Burnet to B. of T., June 25, 1723, enclosing undated paper by Cadwallader Colden, *N.Y. Col. Doc.* V 685, 688–89. Limitation in instructions to Governors of Nova Scotia, N.H., and N.Y., Labaree *Instructions* II 599, 549, 598, but not in White Pine Acts, 8 Geo. I ch. 12 sec. 5 (1722), 2 Geo. II ch. 35 sec. 1 (1729).

9 Surveyor David Dunbar's proclamation Dec. 2, 1729, C.O. 5:871:28 with Dunbar to Alured Popple, Secretary to B. of T., Dec. 10, 2 *Maine* X 455. B. of T. to Dunbar May 7, 1730, requiring revocation of the proclamation C.O. 5:916:382–83; Dunbar's revocation Aug. 22, 1730, *Boston Gazette* Aug. 31 and Dunbar to Popple Aug. 19, concerning this, 2 *Maine* XI 29–30. As to Dunbar, Index under "Dunbar, David" *Cal. State Papers* for 1728–1729 and Stock *Proceedings* IV 66.

10 Surveyor John Wentworth to Secretary of State Oct. 12, 1778, as to unreasonable features of the White Pine Acts, C.O. 5:175:81–96 at 81–82. Wentworth recommended (fol. 89) a bonus for preserving, as well as a penalty for felling white pines fit for naval masts.

11 Former Governor Thomas Pownall and Hutchinson point out unreasonableness of the White Pine Acts, Pownall *Administration* 196; Hutchinson *Hist. of Mass.* II 191. Similarly, Gov. Colden of N.Y. to B. of T. Feb. 28, 1761, *Colden* 1876, 65.

12 Bridger's proclamation Feb. 7, 1709, ruling that lands held in common by town proprietors were not "the property of any private person," and statement of Elisha Cooke to the Mass. Legislature read July 1, 1718, protesting against this ruling 2 *Maine* IX 271–72, 412.

13 Misunderstanding as to the nature of ownership of town lands held in common, Pownall *Administration* (1764) 126. The issue as to trees on town lands held in common became of diminishing importance as the land was from time to time divided among the town proprietors.

14 Surveyors' interpretation of "logs" to include lumber, Dunbar to unidentified deputy Nov. 25, 1730, ordering him to seize white pine logs "and boards," *N.H. Papers* XVIII 37–38; Surveyor Benning Wentworth's commission to deputy Jan. 17, 1753, authorizing seizure of white pine logs "or other timber," *Wolcott* 232; Wentworth to B. of T. Oct. 21, 1754, complaining of the Admiralty Court's refusal to sustain his seizures of lumber as "logs," C.O. 5:926:220.

15 Exeter riot, depositions of April 24, 1734, Gov. Jonathan Belcher's proclamation May 6 and minutes of N.H. Assembly Oct. 19, *N.H. Papers* XVIII 52–54, 55–56, IV 678; minutes of N.H. Council April 26, 2 *Hist. Mag.* IV (1868) 190–91.

16 The grant to Sir Ferdinando Gorges was made by Charles I, April 3, 1639, and confirmed by Charles II, March 12, 1664, Thorpe *Charters* III 1625–1640, 1641–1644. As to the boundaries of the grant, Palfrey *New Eng.* I 524–25. As to the deed from Ferdinando Gorges (Sir Ferdinando's grandson) to John Usher March 13, and from Usher to the Governor and Company of Mass. March 15, 1678, 2 *Maine* VII (1901) 343–50, 351–56.

17 Richness of Gorges grant in mast trees and people's idolization of the Mass. Charter, Bridger to B. of T. July 14, 1718, *same* IX 419.

18 Mass. Charter of 1691, *Mass. Acts* I 1–20, quotations at 8, 20.

19 Richard West's opinion Nov. 12, 1718, conceding the validity of the grant to Gorges, a private person, but holding nevertheless, on grounds irrelevant to the point at issue, that trees in the Gorges grant were reserved to the Crown, Chalmers *Opinions* 134.

20 As to the Surveyors' position, Dr. Elisha Cooke's complaint to the Mass. Assembly July 1, 1718, concerning Bridger's instructions as to woods in Berwick, a town in the Gorges tract, and Bridger to B. of T. July 14, 1718, 2 *Maine* IX 407, 418; Jeremiah Dunbar [misprinted Dummer] to Surveyor David Dunbar March 26, 1729, *same* X 432.

21 As to Cooke, Shipton *Harvard Graduates* IV 349–56. Shipton says (p. 351) that Cooke and his associates offered land for sale "with the understanding that they would fix the local courts against convicting poachers on the King's woods"; but he cites no evidence for this charge and I have seen none. As to Cooke's holdings, Bridger to B. of T. April 8, 1720, 2 *Maine* X 135.

22 Statement of Mass. joint legislative committee condemning Bridger for invading rights of inhabitants, Dec. 4, 1718, *Mass. Journals* II 109; also proceedings of the Mass. Assembly Feb. 14 to July 1, 1718, *same* I 272, II 47, 108. As to Cooke's continuing opposition, Dunbar to Alured Popple, Sec. to the B. of T., Dec. 10, 1729, and May 25, 1730, 2 *Maine* X 454, XI 26.

23 The facts of the Frost case are in John Frost's petition to the Governor and Legislature of Mass. Dec. 17, 1735, Adm. 1:3817 and papers on appeal to the Privy Council in *Frost v. Leighton* April 2, 1736, *Acts P.C.* III 462–66.

24 Frost's suit was based on a Mass. Act of June 27, 1726, sec. 1 entitling the owner to damages of one pound for every tree under a foot in diameter and two pounds plus treble the value of the tree for every tree over a foot in diameter, *Mass. Acts* II 383–84. William Leighton's defense is in papers on appeal April 2, 1736, *Acts P.C.* III 464–65.

25 Appeal to and decision by the Privy Council in England, Smith *Appeals* 329–30 with *Acts P.C.* III 466. As to failure of Mass. court to enforce Privy Council's order, Davis "Frost v. Leighton" 233–40. The Court's failure to act was blamed on Gov. Belcher and contributed to his replacement as royal Governor of Mass. and N.H. by William Shirley, Ford "Shirley" 352–56.

26 Privy Council's third order, Smith *Appeals* 332; Frost's repayment to Leighton, Shirley to Duke of Newcastle and to others Nov. 14, 1743, Wood *Shirley* 151–52, Smith *Appeals* 332. Shirley as Leighton's counsel, Shirley to Admiralty Board May 6, 1739, Adm. 1:3817.

27 I have found no evidence of proceedings by Frost to obtain a new trial. As to prospective costs probably deterring Frost, though the Mass. Legislature in 1735 had the colony's London Agent pay thirty guineas toward Frost's costs, Shirley to Admiralty Board May 6, 1739, Adm. 1:3817 with *Mass. Journals* XIII 170, 194, in 1737 the Legislature denied Frost aid, *same* XIV 143, 248.

28 Benning Wentworth's commission as Surveyor, dated Dec. 12, 1743, is in *N.H. Papers* VI 914–15. My supposition as to Wentworth's laxity is based on the dearth of evidence of opposition to the acts from 1743 to 1763 and on the report of an unidentified writer, sent by the B. of T. to the Admiralty Board Jan.

30, 1747, Adm. 106:2183:18, and a complaint of Deputy Surveyor Daniel Blake considered by the B. of T. Oct. 25, 1759, C.O. 5:323:102 with *Journal B. of T.* 1759–1763, 28.

29 No reservation of any trees to the Crown in Conn. charter of April 23, 1662, Thorpe *Charters* I 536. Wentworth's commission and instructions to Blake Jan. 17 and June 26, 1753, improperly construing the White Pine Acts, *Wolcott* 232–33, 310–11. (Wentworth had earlier appointed William Prout deputy for Connecticut, Wentworth to Gov. Jonathan Law of Conn. May 30, 1747, *Law* III 41–42; but I have found no evidence of Prout having acted.)

30 Wolcott to Wentworth Feb. 5, 1753, pointing out invalidity of Wentworth's construction and Wentworth's reply June 25 *Wolcott* 235, 309. Wentworth possibly thought that a long-expired act of Parliament of 1705, 3 & 4 Anne ch. 10 sec. 6 (extended to 1725 by 12 Anne ch. 9) for the preservation of colonial pitch pine, which referred to trees on land "not being within any fence or actual inclosure," was still in force.

31 Wentworth to Wolcott June 25, 1753, and May 15, 1754, concerning assault on Blake and threatened prosecution, *Wolcott* 310, Fitch I 1–2. In 1759 Blake sought compensation for his sufferings in Connecticut, *Journal B. of T.* for 1759–1763, 28, but apparently in vain. In 1763 he was again active, Blake's "An Account of all White Pine Logs seized" Nov. 10, 1763, Ingersoll Papers.

32 Wentworth to B. of T. Jan. 15, 1758, concerning his recent seizure of logs, C.O. 5:927.

33 Notices of seizures and suits for forfeiture of logs in the admiralty court in Mass., *Boston Post-Boy* June 13 and 20, July 11 and 25, Aug. 1 and 8, Sept. 19 and 26, and Dec. 12, 1763. The records of this Court for 1745 to 1765 are meager; those surviving for other years, listed and briefly described in Noble "Notes on Mass. Admiralty" 99–100, generally throw little light on the evidence on which the court acted.

34 Blake to Jared Ingersoll Nov. 7 and Nov. 10, 1763, concerning seizures of logs in Conn., Ingersoll Papers. As to Ingersoll's recent masting operations, Gipson *Ingersoll* 96, 99–102; "Ingersoll Letters" 255–64.

35 Statements concerning Benning Wentworth's laxity are cited in footnote 28 above. His being under fire in 1765 appears from John Wentworth to Lord Rockingham March 10, 1765, defending his uncle Benning's record as Surveyor, *N.H. Papers* XVIII 566.

36 As to the Wentworth family's masting interests and probable antagonism to Ingersoll as a competitor, Gipson Ingersoll 93–94, 102–6; *N.H. Papers* XVIII 179, 182.

37 Proclamation of Gov. Francis Bernard of Mass. to assist Surveyors July 9, 1763, *Mass. Gazette* July 14; report of refusal of magistrates to do so, Eleazer Burt and Elijah Lyman to Bernard April 24, 1764, Judd Papers V 131, Forbes Library, Northampton, Mass., partly published in Holland *Western Mass.* I 182–83.

38 Samuel Willis and Matthew Talcott to Ingersoll April 9, 1764, as to inhabitants' hostility to them, "Ingersoll Letters" 266–67. Before the new White Pine Acts enforcement campaign was launched, they had written (July 12, 1762) that "most of

the People seem willing to affoord us what assistance they can with good will," Ingersoll Papers.

Chapter 11

1 Background and primary purpose of the Sugar Act, 6 Geo. II ch. 13 (1733), Stock *Proceedings* IV 87, 93–144, 153, 156–70, 176–95, 206–12; Thomas Hutchinson to Richard Jackson Aug. 3, 1763, *Mauduit* 130n; Southwick "Molasses Act" 391–404; Pitman *West Indies* 248–70; Andrews "Anglo-French Rivalry" 766–73; Wolff *Pa.* 42–52. The rates were 6d. a gallon on molasses, 9d. a gallon on rum, and 5sh. per 112 lbs. on sugar, raw or refined.

2 Boston letter to Agent Jasper Mauduit Nov. 28, 1764, stating that molasses "generally" sold for sixpence a gallon at the foreign islands, *Mauduit* 175. At this price the duty was 100 per cent. Earlier, the price of foreign molasses had been even lower, Pitman *West Indies* 204, 309. The earliest extension of the Sugar Act was 11 Geo. II ch. 18 (1738), the latest, prior to 1764, 1 Geo. III ch. 9 (1761).

3 Indulgence to Spanish vessels at Jamaica, Pitman *West Indies* 147n, 152, 153n, 195; Nettels *Money Supply* 27–28; Pares *War and Trade* 116–17, Beer *Old Colonial System* I 362–64, Armytage *Free Port System* 22–24, 31n. Slaves were held to be a "commodity" within the meaning of the act of 1660, Chalmers *Opinions* 562–63. Jamaica, long a Spanish colony, was not ceded to England until 1670.

4 Indulgence of direct imports of wine and fresh fruit, Thomas Wharton of Pa. Feb. 28, 1759, to Gerard G. Beekman Bezanson *Prices* 245; Gov. Francis Bernard of Mass. 1763–1764 to various persons *Select Letters* 2, 4, Quincy *Reports* 423n; "Essay" *Providence Gazette* Jan. 14, 1764; Gov. Francis Fauquier of Va. to Lord Halifax Nov. 20, 1764, Beer *British Col. Policy* 237; Sampson Toovey Salem, Mass., Sept. 27, 1764, in *Boston Gazette* June 12, 1769.

5 Indulgence as to foreign colonial molasses, Jamaica Legislature to the King, Nov. 21, 1749, Pitman *West Indies* 404; Bernard to various correspondents 1763–1764, *Select Letters* 3, 5, Quincy *Reports* 423–24n, *Boston Evening Post* Nov. 30, 1764, Bernard Pap. III.

6 Andrews *Col. Period* IV 243 and Andrews "Col. Adm. Courts" 53 speak of the "grim determination" of British customs officers in Mass. after 1740 to enforce the Sugar Act. But the effort was apparently shortlived; no suit under the Sugar Act from Dec. 1744 to May 1760 is entered in the records of Northern Admiralty District 1740–1774, 14–121 *passim*. For further details, Gipson "Aspects" 12–15.

7 Rate of molasses duty paid at Boston, James Otis *A Vindication of the British Colonies* (1765) 145–46; at N.Y., testimony in 1766 of "Mr. [William] Kelly," Dickerson *Navigation Acts* 98. To similar effect, Gov. William Franklin of N.J. to B. of T. Feb. 8, 1764, 1 *N.J. Col. Doc.* IX 403–4. But see Jared Ingersoll to Thomas Whately July 6 "Ingersoll Letters" 296–97, repeated in Thomas Whately *Regulations* (1765) 79, indicating that the rate commonly paid was nearly 1½d a gallon.

8 Rate of molasses duty paid at Salem, Mass., Timothy Orme to Capt. George Dodge July 18, 1758, Orme Papers, Essex Institute. The full rate was being enforced a year later, Orme to Dodge April 30, 1759, Orme Papers, Essex Institute.

At Charleston, S.C., no duty whatever was collected if the foreign molasses, sugar, or rum was reshipped, Gov. James Glen of S.C. to B. of T. March 1753, Labaree *Instructions* II 900.

9 Small amount of molasses duty reported prior to 1760, Pitman *West Indies* 275. Bernard wrote Richard Jackson Nov. 30, 1764, that the Collector of Customs at Salem had paid to the Treasury £2,000 in duties which, "according to the practice of other officers," he might have pocketed for himself, Bernard Pap. III.

10 The statements in this paragraph concerning the value of the foreign molasses trade in the colonial economy are based on evidence discussed later in this chapter; on Gov. Stephen Hopkins of R.I. to Pitt Dec. 20, 1760, Kimball *Pitt* II 377 and on Ingersoll to Whately July 6, 1764, "Ingersoll Letters" 297. As to British restrictions on importation into Great Britain of many colonial products, Beer *Comm. Policy* 74.

11 Foreign molasses trade chiefly with French West Indies, Pitman *West Indies* 193–309, 401–30, *passim;* Andrews "Anglo-French Rivalry" 764–71; Pares *Yankees and Creoles, passim.* Protecting market for French brandy, Declaration du Roy Jan. 24, 1713, Wroth and Annan *French Acts* 43 with Memorial to B. of T. Oct. 18, 1750, Pitman *West Indies* 415; Postlethwayt *Britain's Interest* (1757) I 491. Cheapness of foreign molasses, Pitman *West Indies* 201, 213; Kistler "Allen" 54–55; and note 2 above.

12 Threat to foreign molasses trade, 12 Charles II ch. 18 sec. 1 (1660) forbidding foreign vessels to enter British colonial ports coupled with Ordonnance du Roy June 10, 1670, Reglement du Roy Aug. 20, 1698, and Lettres Patentes du Roy en Forme d'Edit Oct. 1727, forbidding foreign vessels to enter French colonial ports, Ford "French Edicts" 256, 262, 278 listing printed copies in the Arch. Nationales.

13 French Minister of Marine to Governor of Guadeloupe July 23, 1726, authorizing importation of certain items in foreign vessels, Satineau *Guadeloupe* 49.

14 Authorization widened, Mémoire du Roy pour servir d'instruction générale aux Gouverneurs et Intendants de ses Colonies April 18, 1763, Arch. Nationales, Colonies A-8:46. As to regulations issued pursuant to this authorization, order of Governor and Intendant of Guadeloupe Aug. 18, 1763, copy in C.O. 323:17:R30:95–97; Pitman *West Indies* 332.

15 Relatively little foreign sugar imported, *Boston Evening-Post* Nov. 21, 1763; Rhode Island Remonstrance Jan. 1764, *R.I. Col. Rec.* VI 383; Boston letter to Mauduit Nov. 28, 1764, *Mauduit* 173–74. Relatively little foreign rum made, Pitman *West Indies* 208n; Harper "Mercantilism" 11n; speech in Parliament of John (later Sir John) Barnard Feb. 23, 1732, Stock *Proceedings* IV 140.

16 Molasses trade with Dutch colonies in America, entries under Surinam and St. Eustatius in Indexes to Hedges *The Browns* and Pitman *West Indies;* Serionne *Commerce de la Hollande* (1768) I 262–64; Fermin *Description de Surinam* (1769) I 105–6; Colden's report in Gov. Burnet of N.Y. to B. of T. June 25, 1723, *N.Y. Col. Doc.* V. 686.

17 Trade with Danish colonies, Pitman *West Indies* Index under "St. Thomas" and "Santa Cruz." As to sugar production in Brazil, *same* 156, 309–10; speeches in House of Commons Feb. 21, 1733, Stock *Proceedings* IV 179–83. Trade with Brazil could legally be carried on only from Portugal, Christelow "Great Britain and

the Trades from Cadiz and Lisbon" 4–7. Nicholas Brown & Co. to Esek Hopkins Dec. 30, 1764, as to opening direct trade between R.I. and Brazil, Hedges *The Browns* 76.

18 Early sugar production in Santo Domingo, Wright "Commencement of Cane Sugar Industry in America," 755–80. As to no sugar exports from Cuba prior to 1746, Hussey *Caracas Company* 211. Foreign trade with the Spanish colonies, unless by special dispensation, was illegal, Haring *Trade between Spain and the Indies, passim;* Christelow "Great Britain and the Trades from Cadiz and Lisbon" 2–4. Wartime trade with Monte Cristi, Beer *Brit. Col. Policy* 96–103.

19 Smuggling of European and East Indian products frowned upon by British colonial "fair traders," Henry Lloyd to Aaron Lopez April 3, 1756, *R.I. Commerce* I 66; *Boston Evening-Post* Dec. 6, 1756; Thomas Cushing to Jasper Mauduit Nov. 11, 1763, *Mauduit* 136–37; John Watts to Robert Monckton Dec. 29, 1763, *Watts* 212; statement of N.Y. merchants in 1764, *N.Y. Assembly* II 741–44n.

20 British colonial imports of foreign colonial molasses averaged 3,208,000 gallons a year in 1768–1770, Harper "Mercantilism" 11, and 4,013,246 gallons were imported in 1771, Channing *History* III 109.

21 British West Indian efforts to have foreign molasses trade stopped, including suggested peacetime use of British navy for this purpose, Pitman *West Indies* 283, 298–300; Stock *Proceedings* IV 801, 804, V 460–86; Richard Partridge to Gov. John Wanton of R.I. Aug. 10, 1739, Kimball *R.I.* I 116. As to rigorous enforcement of the Sugar Act during the Seven Years' War as means of breaking up trade with the enemy, Beer *Brit. Col. Policy* 105–8, 114–16.

22 Mauduit wrote the Massachusetts Council March 23, 1763, "Some days ago the first Lord of Trade [Charles Townshend] proposed lowering the duties on foreign molasses to 2d. pr. gallon, in order more effectually to secure the payment" Bancroft Papers "Maryland," N.Y.P.L. As to postwar renewal of the indulged foreign molasses trade, Thomas Hutchinson to Jackson Sept. 17, 1763, Quincy *Reports* 430.

23 New enforcement act, 3 Geo. III ch. 22 (1763). The act also facilitated condemnation of small vessels hovering off the colonies. List of vessels sent to the colonies, *Providence Gazette,* Sept. 24, 1763, in aid of the customs service, William Wood, Sec. to Customs Board to Philip Stephens, Sec. to the Admiralty June 20 with instructions Adm. 1:3866, Lord Egremont to colonial governors July 9, *Fitch* II 248.

24 Treasury to Customs Board July 22, 1763, directing that customs officers be sent to their posts, T. 29:35; George Grenville to Horace Walpole Sept. 8 saying order for this had been given, *Grenville* II 114. Egremont to colonial Governors July 9 ordering them to assist customs officers, *Fitch* II 247–49, and Halifax to Amherst Oct. 11, ordering that the army do the same, *Gage* II 3.

25 *Providence Gazette* Jan. 21, 1764, as to John Temple's reported earlier assurance of granting the usual indulgence in his district with respect to the Sugar Act, and Tench Francis to Nicholas Brown & Co. Nov. 15, 1763, concerning similar assurance at Philadelphia, Wiener "R.I. Merchants" 471.

26 English Customs Commissioners' circular letter Nov. 3, 1763, threatening dismissal of customs officers for neglect of duty, T. 1:426:459. Notice Dec. 26 in

Pennsylvania Gazette Dec. 29, 1763, and *Boston Gazette* Jan. 2, 1764, warning of proposed enforcement of Sugar Act. Bernard to Jackson Jan. 7, 1764, as to alarm over this, Bernard *Select Letters* 9 (Jackson's name supplied from Bernard Papers III 120–23).

27 Political influence and activity in Great Britain of British West India sugar interests, Penson "West India Interest" 373–92; Namier *Eng.* 271–79; Penson *Agents of West Indies, passim;* Pitman *West Indies, passim; New-York Mercury* Jan. 2, 1764; Israel Mauduit to unidentified correspondent March 3, 1764, *Mauduit* 149n; *Gentleman's Magazine* of May 1766 (XXXVI 229), stating there were over forty members of Parliament having West Indian backgrounds or "concerns."

28 Charles Jenkinson to Grenville April 20, 1764 (misprinted 1763), *Grenville* II 47–48, Grenville's reply April 29 *Jenkinson* 291; and B. of T. to Gov. William Henry Lyttleton of Jamaica May 12 as to continued indulgence to Jamaica contraband trade with Spanish colonies, Christelow "Contraband Trade" 323. William Allen to Rev. Jonathan Mayhew Oct. 15 as to Grenville's wooing of West Indians in Parliament, Mayhew Papers.

29 Thomas Cushing to Jasper Mauduit Oct. 28, Nov. 11, 1763, as to merchants' willingness to pay a light molasses duty, *Mauduit* 130–35, 139. To same effect, Ingersoll to Whately July 6, 1764, "Ingersoll Letters" 297.

30 Hutchinson to Jackson Aug. 3, 1763, as to merchants' willingness to pay light duty on molasses but danger in this, Quincy *Reports* 435.

31 Petitions of Mass. "merchants and traders" to the Mass. Legislature Dec. 27, 1762, against renewal of the Sugar Act, *Mass. Journals* 1763–1764, 132. In colonial parlance, "merchant" seems to have meant a dealer who was exclusively or partly a wholesaler, while "trader" meant one who was exclusively a retailer; but the differentiation is not clear.

32 Andrews "State of Trade" 382–90 concerning importance of foreign molasses trade to Mass. was similar to an anonymous letter in the *Boston Evening-Post* Nov. 21 and 28, 1763. It was later published with slight revisions as *Reasons Against the Renewal of the Sugar Act* (Boston, 1764). I assume that "hogshead" as used in the "State" was 100 gallons as fixed by act of Parliament for the British customs, 22 Geo. II ch. 22 (1749).

33 Instructions to Mauduit to protest against proposed colonial taxation, minutes of Mass. House Dec. 27, 1763, Jan. 26, 1764, *Mass. Journals* 1763–1764, 132, 231; minutes of Mass. Council Dec. 27, 1763, Mass. Arch., Court Records XXV 100; Cushing to Mauduit Jan. 1764, *Mauduit* 145–46 with Mauduit to Andrew Oliver, Secretary of Mass., March 21, 1764, Mass. Arch. XX 360.

34 Thomas Gray, Joshua Winslow, Joseph Green, Edward Payne, and others to Simon Pease and Godfrey Malbone of Newport, R.I., and to Gurdon Saltonstall and Nathaniel Shaw of New London, Conn., Jan. 4 and 9, 1764, for united action to counteract influence of the West Indians and prevent renewal of the Sugar Act, Wiener "R.I. Merchants" 476–77, Andrews "State of Trade" 380–81.

35 Elisha Brown of R.I. to Nicholas Brown & Co. Oct. 28, 1763, proposing a meeting for united action against enforcement of the Sugar Act, Wiener "R.I. Merchants" 471; summons by Gov. Stephen Hopkins of R.I. to Sheriff of Newport

County Jan. 13, 1764, for special session of R.I. Legislature on request of merchants and traders, Kimball *R.I.* II 357–58; remonstrance of Jan. 1764 by R.I. Legislature *R.I. Col. Rec.* VI 378.

36 Remonstrance of R.I. Legislature Jan. 27, 1764, bringing out the great importance of its foreign molasses trade to the colony, *R.I. Col. Rec.* VI 378–83 with Wiener "R.I. Merchants" 493. "Elephants' teeth" are ivory; "camwood" is a wood yielding a red dye.

37 Nicholas Brown to David Van Horne Jan. 24, 1764, encouraging N.Y. action similar to R.I.'s, Wiener "R.I. Merchants" 491–92; N.Y. merchants committee chosen Jan. 27, *New-York Mercury* Jan. 30; action by N.Y. Council March 8, *N.Y. Council Cal.* 464 with John Watts to Gov. Robert Monckton March 11, *Watts* 234–35; N.Y. merchants' statement approved by the N.Y. House April 20, *N.Y. Assembly* II 740–44.

38 Petition by Ingersoll on behalf of Gurdon Saltonstall and others Jan. 20, 1764, for opposition by Conn. Legislature to renewal of the Sugar Act *Fitch* II 275–76; appointment by Conn. Legislature of a committee, in March, *Conn. Records* XII 240n. The importance to Connecticut of the foreign molasses trade was brought out in an unsigned statement dated "New London January 1764," *Fitch* II 277–79.

39 Appointment of committee in Philadelphia to oppose renewal of the Sugar Act, "Letter from a Gentleman in Philadelphia . . . dated February 22, 1764" *Boston Post-Boy* March 26.

40 Mauduit to Oliver March 21, 1764, reporting the arrival of the Mass. petition against renewal of the Sugar Act, Mass. Arch. XXII 360. The bill for a duty of 3d. a gallon on foreign molasses had been introduced March 4, *Journals H. of C.* XXIX 933.

41 Mauduit to Timothy Ruggles, Speaker of Mass. House Dec. 30, 1763, and Feb. 11, 1764, as to probable duties on foreign molasses, 1 *Mass. Hist. Soc. Coll.* VI 193–95. Mauduit's statement endorsed "9th Feb. 1764" acquiescing in rate of 2d. per gallon on foreign molasses, J. C. Brown Lib. As to similar action by Jackson and John Huske, Jackson to Franklin Nov. 12, 1763, *Jackson* 113; Huske, M.P. for Malden, to Boston merchants Aug. 14, 1764, *Providence Gazette* Nov. 3.

42 The French proclamation referred to by Huske was Mémoire du Roi April 18, 1763, effective Jan. 1, 1764, Arch. Nationales, Colonies, A-8:46 (partly quoted without citation of source in Sée "French Commerce" 735) permitting foreign vessels to import a wide range of specified products into French colonial ports and to export molasses and rum received in exchange for these products.

43 4 Geo. III ch. 15 levying new perpetual rates of colonial duty on foreign colonial molasses and refined sugar and forbidding British colonial imports of foreign colonial rum, was assented to April 5, 1764, *Journals H. of L.* XXX 551–52.

Chapter 12

1 Lord Egremont to B. of T. May 5, 1763, asking for proposal as to best method of having colonies contribute to imperial expense and Board's reply June 8 that it would collect information and report S. & D. *Doc.* I 128, 147. No record of the promised report has been found.

2 Treasury Board to Commissioners of Stamp Duties Sept. 22, 1763, ordering preparation of bill for colonial stamp tax T:29:35. The background of the proposed tax is discussed in Chapter 6. Proceedings House of Commons March 9 and 10, 1764, as to colonial taxation *Journals H. of C.* XXIX 933–35. (The minutes for March 9 are unenlightening because the House was sitting as a Committee of the Whole, and its proceedings when so sitting were not recorded.)

3 George Grenville's comments on colonial taxation in his budget speech are reported in Israel Mauduit to unidentified, March 10, 1764, Mass. Arch. XXII 357–58; Jasper Mauduit to Speaker of Mass. House March 13 Morgan *Stamp Act* 55; Cecilius Calvert to Gov. Horatio Sharpe of Md. March 30 *Sharpe* III 144; Edward Montague to Va. Comm. of Corresp. April 11 *Va. Mag.* X (1903) 3–4.

4 Duties imposed by American Act of 1764, *Journals H. of C.* XXIX 934–35 and 4 Geo. III ch. 15 secs. 1–14 (1764). The duties payable in Great Britain were imposed by repealing as to the colonies, though not as to foreign nations, the refund of British import duties previously allowed on certain goods imported into Great Britain and reexported.

5 Revenue from colonial duties to be applied to defending the colonies, 14th resolution March 10, 1764, *Journals H. of C.* XXIX 934–35, embodied in 4 Geo. III ch. 15 secs. 1, 11 (1764).

6 Grenville's views as to object and amount of taxes on the colonists, Israel Mauduit to unnamed Mass. correspondent March 10, 1764, Mass. Arch. XXII 357–58; Montague to Va. Comm. of Corresp. April 11, 1764, *Va. Mag.* X (1903) 3–4; Charles Garth to S.C. Comm. of Corresp. June 5 Namier "Garth" 647. Mauduit, Montague, and Garth indicated respectively that £225,000, £350,000, and £400,000 a year were to be raised.

7 The concept of the relationship between restrictions on colonial trade and taxation of the colonies by Parliament was well stated in Franklin to Gov. William Shirley of Mass. Dec. 4, 1754, *Shirley* II 106 and Dickinson *Regulations* (1765) 237–39. Burke's quoted statement on this point was in his famous Speech on American Taxation April 19, 1774, Burke *Speeches* 25–26.

8 Proceedings on the tax bill, March 14 to April 4, 1764, *Journals H. of C.* XXIX 949, 978, 983, 987, 1015 and *Journals H. of L.* XXX 550. The King's assent April 5, *same* 551–52. Failure of the colonial agents' appointed interview with Grenville, John Thomlinson, Jr., M.P. for Steyning and London Agent for N.H., to John Thomlinson, Sr., March 26, Howard *Long Family* I 226. As to the Thomlinsons, Namier *Eng.* 273, 283n, 285–92.

9 Charles Townshend wrote Newcastle on "Friday" [March 23, 1764] that "in civility to Sir W. Baker" he had "divided" the day before "upon the Molasses duty," Add. Mss. 32957:239, presumably on a motion to reduce the duty from 3 to 2d. per gallon, referred to in a London letter March 24, 1764, in the *Newport Mercury* of June 11, of which there is no official record because the House was sitting in Committee of the Whole on March 22, *Journals H. of C.* XXIX 978.

10 Speakers in favor of motion to reduce proposed rate of molasses duty, John Huske to Comm. of Boston Merchants Aug. 14, 1764, in *Boston Gazette* Oct. 29. Col. Isaac Barré, M.P. for Chipping Wycombe, likewise at some point opposed "the oppressive Views of Parliament," John Watts to Barré May 24, *Watts* 258.

11 Calvert to Sharpe March 30, 1764, *Sharpe* III 144 (Huske misprinted "Hurst"); Huske to Committee Aug. 14 in *Boston Gazette* Oct. 29. Joseph Reed wrote Charles Pettit June 11 that Huske, a recent recruit to the colonial cause, had earlier proposed raising £500,000 a year from the colonies, Reed *Reed* I 33, perhaps in his speech "upon American Busyness" referred to in Grenville to George III Nov. 16, 1763, *George III* I 58.

12 Details concerning Jackson, *Jackson* 1–30. As to his family being of the same "persuasion" as Jasper Mauduit and Dennys De Berdt, who were Dissenters, Jackson to Thomas Hutchinson Jan. 9, 1767, Mass. Arch. XXV 145. His secretaryship to Grenville, Thomas Penn to Gov. James Hamilton of Pa. June 18, 1763, Boyd *Susquehanna Co. Papers* II 257.

13 Jackson's relations with Jared Eliot and other Conn. residents, Jackson to Eliot Sept. 17, 1753, Feb. 10, 1755, June 12, 1760, Eliot Papers, Yale Lib.; Rev. William Johnson and Jared Ingersoll to W. S. Johnson May 5, 1756, Dec. 22, 1759, Beardsley *Johnson* 219, Beardsley *W. S. Johnson* 20. Jackson's appointment as Conn. Agent March 1760, *Conn. Col. Rec.* XI 357–58; his long acquaintance with Franklin, Peter Collinson to Franklin Sept. 27, 1752, *Jackson* 5.

14 Ellis Huske, *Col. Soc. Public.* IX 465–68. As to John Huske, Huske to Committee of Boston Merchants Aug. 14, 1764, *Boston Gazette* Oct. 29; John Hancock to Thomas Hancock Jan. 14, 1761, *M.H.S. Proc.* vol. 43 (1910) 197. A very popular pamphlet denouncing French encroachments in America, *The Present State of North America* (London, 1755), was probably by Huske, Wroth *An American Bookshelf* 134–37.

15 John Huske and the Maldon election, Bamber Gascoyne and William Hunter to Charles Jenkinson April 21 and 26, 1763, *Jenkinson* 147, 149–50; *London Chronicle* July 19; Namier *Structure* I 137–39.

16 Richard Partridge, Appleton "Partridge" 293–309, Wolff *Pa.* 87–196 *passim*, and Indexes under "Partridge, Richard" in *Belcher Papers* I, II; *Fitch* I, II; *Wolcott*; Kimball *R.I.*; Burns *Col. Agents*, Bollan's dismissal; *Mauduit* 26n.

17 Warnings to colonists of proposed colonial taxation by Parliament, Calvert to Sharpe March 1, 1763, *Md. Arch.* XXXI 531; Mauduit to Andrew Oliver March 12 Bancroft Papers, "Col. Doc. 1761–4"; Joseph Sherwood, Agent for R.I. and N.J., to correspondents in R.I. and N.J. Aug. 4 and 12, *R.I. Col. Rec.* VI 368; *N.J. Hist. Soc. Proc.* V 141.

18 Franklin chosen member of Pa. comm. of corresp. and notification to Jackson of this, Pa. Assembly resolution April 2, 1763, 8 *Pa. Arch.* VI 5425 and Franklin to Jackson April 11, *Jackson* 100–101.

19 Franklin's statement to Gov. William Shirley Dec. 4, 1754, as to colonial opposition to taxation by Parliament, *Shirley* II 103 and (misdated Dec. 18) Smyth *Franklin* III 232, contrasted with his letters to Jackson in 1763–1764. (After further study of Franklin, I think I erred in crediting him with striking consistency in political thought and action, as I did by implication in *Meet Dr. Franklin* 127–33.)

20 Jackson to Franklin as to British Ministry's tax plans and Franklin's seemingly unconcerned replies, March 10, 1763, to Jan. 16, 1764, *Jackson* 105, 113–14, 136. In writing Jackson Feb. 11, 1764, Franklin even went so far as to suggest tea and other named items as additional objects of taxation if Parliament was deter-

mined to raise a colonial revenue, *same* 140, but this was probably too late to have influenced Jackson's action.

21 Franklin's salary from the Crown, Butler *Franklin Postmaster Gen.* 42, 69–70. Franklin's commission as Postmaster has not been found but it was evidently held "at pleasure," since he referred to himself November 1764 as a person "who holds a profitable Office under the Crown" and "can expect to hold it no longer than he behaves with . . . Fidelity and Duty," Franklin *Remarks* in Smyth *Franklin* IV 275.

22 Probable influence of William Franklin's governorship on his father's conduct, Penn to Hamilton Feb. 11, 1763, Sparks *Franklin* VII 242–43; Joseph Chew to Ingersoll June 8, 1763, "Ingersoll Letters" 281. Similarly, Calvert to Sharpe March 1, 1763, *Md. Arch.* XXXI 531. The appointment was probably procured through Dr. John Pringle, Lord Bute's physician, unpublished passage in Penn's letter of Feb. 11 Sparks Mss. #19, Harv. Coll. Lib.

23 Garth to S.C. Comm. of Corresp. June 5, 1764, reporting colonial agents' conference of May 17 with Grenville, Namier "Garth" 647–48. For further light on this conference, Mauduit to Andrew Oliver May 26, *Mauduit* 147n and Morgan *Stamp Act* 58–60.

Chapter 13

1 Claims of James I and Charles I to exclusive jurisdiction over the colonies, Beer *Origins* 301–2; Keith *Const. Hist.* 3–6; McIlwain *Am. Rev.* 18–44 criticized in Edward S. Corwin's review in *A.H.R.* XXIX 775–78 and in Schuyler *Parliament* 1–71. The statements quoted in the text are in *same* 22–23.

2 Two acts of Parliament passed after the colonies were founded, I Charles I ch. 1 sec. 1 (1625) and 16 Charles I ch. 8 sec. 1 (1640), the latter levying import and export duties, included the "Dominions" as well as the realm of England, but no evidence has been found of their publication or enforcement in the colonies. The same is true of acts referred to in Schuyler *Parliament* 13, 19–22, passed before the colonies were founded.

3 Maryland charter of June 20, 1632, granting exemption from taxation, Thorpe *Charters* III 1685.

4 Acts of 1649, 1650, 1651 Firth and Rait *Acts and Ordinances* II 122, 427, 559–60. Navigation Act of 1660 12 Charles II ch. 18 (1660). List of British acts of trade applying to the colonies, trade instructions of 1761 to Gov. Benning Wentworth of N.H., *N.H. Laws* III 281–88, republished with unimportant differences in Labaree *Instructions* II 752–60.

5 Initial colonial opposition to Parliament's restrictions on colonial trade, Harper *Navigation Laws* 246n; Andrews *Col. Period* IV 134–42. Earlier suggestions for colonial taxation, Chapter 6.

6 British Declaratory Act recognizing difference in principle between duties for revenue and duties for regulation of trade, 18 Geo. III ch. 12 (1778).

7 Statement as to commercial purpose of the Act of 1673 (25 Charles II ch. 7) levying duties on certain intercolonial exports, resolution for the bill Stock *Proceedings* I 398; statements in sec. 2 of the act itself and of Auditor-General of the King's

Revenues arising in America (1692) and Customs Board (1692) *Calendar Treas. Books* IX Part IV 1504, IX Part V 1965.

8 Post Office Act, 9 Anne ch. 10 (1711) amended by 6 Geo. I ch. 21 sec. 51, 4 Geo. II ch. 33 and later acts; Greenwich Hospital Acts, 7 & 8 William III ch. 21 (1696), 8 & 9 William III ch. 23 (1697), 10 Anne ch. 17 (1711), 2 Geo. II ch. 7 (1729); Prize Goods Act, 6 Anne ch. 37 sec. 2 (1708).

9 George Grenville to Horace Walpole Sept. 8, 1763, as to cost of collection far exceeding revenue from colonial duties, *Grenville* II 114. To same effect, B. of T. to Governor and Company of Conn. Oct. 11 *Fitch* II 255.

10 Colonial protests against Parliament's levying colonial duties even though for services or regulation of trade, Smith "Col. Post-Office" 268–69; Forbes "Greenwich Hosp. Money" 523–24; Richard Partridge to Gov. William Wanton of R.I. Feb. 28, 1733, and to Newcastle March 28 as to Sugar Act, *Kumball* R.I. I 34, Beer *Brit. Col. Policy* 41.

11 Declaratory Act concerning Ireland 6 Geo. I ch. 5 sec. 1 (1719), repealed by the Renunciation Act of 1783, 23 Geo. III ch. 28 (1783). Examples of British regulation of Irish trade, 9 Anne ch. 12 sec. 27 (1710), 19 Geo. II ch. 12 secs. 19, 21 (1746).

12 My statement as to no British taxation of Ireland until after granting of representation by the Act of Union, 40 Geo. III ch. 67 Article 4 (1800), is based on inspection of the statutes of Ireland from 1660 to 1800.

13 Bill of Rights, 1 William and Mary second sess. ch. 2 secs. 1 and 11 (1689). As to Magna Carta and its influence, Adams and Stephens *Documents* 42–52; Radin "Magna Carta" 1060–91; Mott *Due Process* 32–36, 52–53, 61–63, 117–19; Corwin "Higher Law" 175–79, 374n, and 377–78; Corwin *Liberty* 23–57 *passim;* Malden *Magna Carta Commemoration Essays* 78–226; Care *English Liberties* 5–32; Otis *Rights* (1764) 31, 35, 44, 60.

14 Act of Union with Scotland, 5 Anne ch. 8 articles 6, 7, 25 (March 6, 1706/7).

15 Locke on natural law, *Two Treatises* (1690) Part 2 par. 135. Locke's influence in England, Stephen *Eng. Lit.* 46–47, and Bourne *Locke, passim.* Locke's influence in colonial New England, Baldwin *New Eng. Clergy* 24–96; Otis *Vindication* (1762) 19–20; Mass. Legislature (1762) *Mauduit* 40; Williams *Election Sermon* (1762) 23; John Adams (in 1760 and 1774–1775) *Works* I 53, IV 82–83; Samuel Adams (from 1768 to 1772) Cushing *S. Adams* I 251, II 210–452 *passim.*

16 *Cato's Letters,* appearing originally from 1720 to 1723 as a series of articles in *The London Journal* and *The British Journal,* were published in a collected edition in 1724 and often later republished, *D.N.B.* under John Trenchard, Rossiter *Seed Time* 141–45 has a good discussion of the character and of the influence in the colonies of *Cato's Letters.*

17 Lords Bolingbroke and Chesterfield on the English constitution, Bolingbroke *Parties* (1735) 91; *Chesterfield* II 28–29.

18 Recognition by English judges and law commentators as to limitations on the legislative authority of Parliament, Plucknett "Bonham's Case" 30–49; McGovney "British Origin" 7; repeated statements in *Coke's Institutes* cited in Corwin "Higher Law" 372n.

19 Statement in Blackstone *Analysis* (Oxford, 1756) 2 as to unlimited legislative power of Parliament qualified in Blackstone *Commentaries* (Oxford, 1765) Introduction 41, which, however, at I 162 repeats the doctrine of the *Analysis*.

20 Furneaux *Letters* 82–83n as to limitations on Parliament. Furneaux, who was the pastor of the independent (Dissenting) congregation at Clapham, a suburb of London, wrote chiefly to refute Blackstone's statements concerning the legal status of Dissenters in England.

21 Limitations on Parliament, *Magna Charta* 9, Bill of Rights, 1 William and Mary second sess. ch. 2 sec. 1 (1689); Locke *Two Treatises* (1690) Part 2 par. 142. See also McIlwain *High Court* 42–108.

22 English colonists have same constitutional rights as Englishmen in England, Va. charter 1606; Mass. charter 1629; Conn. charter 1662; Ga. charter 1732, Thorpe *Charters* VII 3788, III 1856–1857, I 533, II 773; Colonial Naturalization Act of 1740, 13 Geo. II ch. 7 sec. 1.

23 Lord Camden's denunciation of the bill for the Declaratory Act, 6 Geo. III ch. 12 (1766), asserting Parliament's authority to legislate for the colonies "in all cases whatsoever" March 1766, *Parl. Hist.* XVI 178. Camden's speech was probably on March 5 or 7, *Journals H. of L.* XXXI, 291 and 297 with Lord Charlemont to Henry Flood March 13, Rodd *Charlemont* 14. Pitt, too, denied Parliament's power to tax the colonies but on the curious and dubious ground that taxation was not legislation, *same* 99. As to English writers from 1765 to 1776 who agreed with Camden, Mott *Due Process* 63n.

24 British argument as to "virtual representation" in Parliament, Charles Garth to S.C. Comm. of Corresp. Feb. 8, 1765, Namier "Garth" 649; Whately *Regulations* (1765) 104–9. The colonial answer to the argument is discussed in Chapter 19.

25 Obligation of British courts to execute acts of Parliament without regard to constitutionality, now undisputed, Maitland *Const. Hist.* 526–28, has been well established since the *Wensleydale Peerage* case (1856), in which Lord Brougham, in harmony with the decision in the case, declared that in Great Britain "things may be legal and yet unconstitutional," 5 *H.L.* 979. The earlier doctrine of the authority of English judges to declare acts of Parliament void had waned in England by 1764, Plucknett "Bonham's Case" 59. Even so strong a colonial sympathizer as Camden implied in 1768 that an unconstitutional act of Parliament was not void, Gray "Notes" 516–17.

26 Thomas Hutchinson to Jackson Sept. 12, 1765, and in similar vein to Thomas Pownall March 8, 1766, *same* 441, 445. For evidence of Coke's strong influence on colonial thought, Warren *Hist. of Am. Bar* 169, 171–74; Corwin "Higher Law" 394–95; Goebel "Const. Hist." 564; Dickinson *Letters of a Farmer* (1768) 330, 375, 382.

27 Otis *Rights* 41 asserting authority of judges to adjudge laws void. The term "executive" courts, I presume, was used by Otis in the sense of judicial courts engaged in executing the law, as distinguished from "general" courts, such as the "General Court" or Legislature of Massachusetts, which exercised a variety of functions, legislative, advisory, judicial, and administrative.

28 R.I. decision March 1762, denying petitions for naturalization of Aaron Lopez and Isaac Elizer under Colonial Naturalization Act of 1740, 13 Geo. II ch. 7,

Stiles *Itineraries* 52; Goodman *Am. Overture* 52–58; McKinley *Suffrage* 451–52. As to Chief Justice Samuel Ward, Knollenberg *Samuel Ward* 3–35.

29 Gov. Horatio Sharpe of Md. to Cecilius Calvert Aug. 22, 1764, *Sharpe* III 175 as to people's view that the courts would hold void an act of Parliament in conflict with the Md. charter. Franklin later queried if it was not a breach of faith for the King to assent to an act of Parliament infringing a royal charter, Franklin's observations on Tucker *A Letter* (1766), Sparks *Franklin* IV 218.

30 Justice Littleton Eyre, Feb. 1766, and Edmund Pendleton to Col. James Madison Feb. 15, as to invalidity of the Stamp Act because unconstitutional, *Va. Mag.* XXXIV (1927) 366, *W. & M. Q.* XIX (1911) 224, Mays *Pendleton* I 170.

31 Examples of declarations in Governors' commissions and colonial charters as to invalidity of colonial acts, Commission of Gov. Francis Bernard of N.J., 1758, Greene *Provincial Governor* 228–29; Charter of Conn., 1662, Thorpe *Charters* I 533. Similarly, 7 & 8 William III ch. 22 sec. 9 (1696) declared that any colonial statute repugnant to any English act relating to the colonies was "illegal, null and void."

32 Colonial acts held void, McGovney "Brit. Origin" 10–20, 27–28, 48–49; Smith *Appeals* 531–51.

33 Colonial danger from unequal Parliamentary legislation because of abandonment of royal veto power, William Livingston to Eleazar Wheelock, March 22, 1764, Wheelock Papers, Dartmouth Coll. Lib.; Jefferson *Summary View* (1774) 14. As to last exercise (in 1708) of Crown's power to disallow acts of Parliament, Everett "Last Royal Veto" 156–63.

34 British protection of colonies as compensation for British restrictions on colonial trade, Jackson to Franklin Dec. 27, 1763, *Jackson* 123–24; Hutchinson to Jackson Aug. 1764, Morgan "Hutchinson" 483; *Late Occurrences in North America* (London, 1766) 29. Passages in Charles Carroll, Jr., of Carrollton to Edmund Jennings May 29, 1766, *Carroll Letters* 116, lead me to think that Jennings probably wrote the *Late Occurrences*.

35 Further statements along same line as preceding note, B. of T. to Gov. William Shirley April 13, 1756, *Mass. Acts* III 743–44, justifying disallowance of ch. 8 of Mass. Laws of 1753–54, levying a tax for funds to encourage the manufacture of linen in Mass., *same* 680–82; Kennedy *Essay* (1752) 3, quoting Montesquieu *The Spirit of Laws* (1750), II 61; Gov. Arthur Dobbs of N.C. to Lord Halifax Jan. 14, 1764, *N.C. Col. Rec.* VI 1021. As to Montesquieu's influence in the colonies, Spurlin *Montesquieu* 48–72, 99–122.

36 Comparatively light debt and taxes of some of the colonies compared with Great Britain's, Gipson *Coming of Revolution* 121–53 *passim;* Gipson *Ingersoll* 162, 244–49.

37 Negotiations with the Scotch for union with England and advantages offered the Scotch, Johnston "Union with Scotland 1707" 466–72.

Chapter 14

1 Requirements as to ownership and crew of vessels in colonial trade under Navigation Act of 1660, 12 Charles II ch. 18, and other acts discussed in the appendix

to this chapter. This Act contained an exception (sec. 15) permitting the importation of bullion (silver and gold) in foreign vessels; but the Act of 1696, 7 & 8 William III ch. 22 sec. 1, reenacted the prohibition without the exception. Restriction on exports of colonial enumerated products 12 Charles II ch. 18 sec. 18 (1660). Touching at an English port did not suffice in the case of colonial enumerated products consigned to a foreign country; they must be put ashore in England and reloaded, Beer *Old Col. System* I 77–78n.

2   Act of Union of England (including Wales) and Scotland putting Scotland on same footing as England, 5 Anne ch. 8 (1707).

3   15 Charles II ch. 7 secs. 5, 6, 7 (1663) requiring shipment of most European and Irish products to colonies only by way of England, modified by 3 & 4 Anne ch. 8 (1704), and 3 Geo I ch. 21 sec. 1 (1716) as to Irish linen and by 13 Geo. I ch. 5 (1727), 3 Geo. II ch. 12 (1730), 2 Geo. III ch. 24 (1762), 4 Geo. III ch. 19 (1764) as to salt.

4   Further restrictions on colonial exports, 22 & 23 Charles II ch. 26 secs. 11 and 12 (1671). As to the construction of sec. 12 of this act, opinion of Attorney-General and Solicitor-General Aug. 21, 1699, Chalmers *Opinions* 563–64.

5   25 Charles II ch. 7 sec. 2 (1673) levying duties as regulation of trade on intercolonial shipments of enumerated products. The act also levied a duty on intercolonial shipments of cocoa beans ("cocoa-nuts"), which were not classified as an enumerated commodity until 1764, 4 Geo. III ch. 15 sec. 27.

6   7 & 8 William III ch. 22 (1696), for better enforcement of acts restricting colonial trade and (sec. 14) banning colonial exports direct to Ireland, the latter modified by 4 Geo. II ch. 15 (1731) to permit export of nonenumerated products to Ireland.

7   7 & 8 William III ch. 20 secs. 8, 9 (1696) banning export of knitting frames to the colonies. As to the industrial importance of these frames, Felkin *Hist. of Machine Wrought Hosiery* 49.

8   East India Company Act of 9 & 10 William III ch. 44 secs. 61, 81 (1698), with extensions of the act listed in Pickering *Statutes* X 194, excluding colonists from trading to the East Indies. A similar monopoly granted by royal charter to Hudson's Bay Company was confirmed by 6 Anne ch. 37 sec. 23 (1707) and a trade monopoly covering the west coasts of North and South America and part of the east coast of South America (conflicting in part with the East India Company monopoly) was granted to the South Sea Company by 9 Anne ch. 21 sec. 46 (1710).

9   Complaint to House of Commons in 1698 as to Irish competition with English woolen goods and Board of Trade's recommendation in 1699 for restricting exports of both Irish and colonial woolens, Stock *Proceedings* II 212, 265–67.

10 10 & 11 William III ch. 10 secs. 1, 2, 3, 19, 20 (1699) restricting exports of Irish woolen goods and the trade in colonial wool and wool products. As to colonial woolen manufacture, largely household, Beer *Comm. Policy* 77–81; Clark *Manufactures* index under "Woolen Manufactures" and "Worsteds"; Cole *Wool* I 5–53, II 277–80; Dickerson *Col. Govt.* 302–4; Lord *Indust. Exp.* 129–33, 136; Nettels *Money Supply* 136–37, 149–51; Weeden *Econ. Hist.* index under "Sheep" and "Wool."

11 Addition of rice and other colonial products to list of enumerated products, 3 & 4 Anne ch. 5 sec. 12 and ch. 10 sec. 8 (1704). Exclusion of colonial vessels from

permitted rice trade with southern Europe 3 Geo. II ch. 28 (1730) with 8 Geo. II ch. 19 (1735) extended by later acts. A similar restriction as to export of colonial sugar was made by 12 Geo. II ch. 30 sec. 2 (1739), amended by 15 Geo. II ch. 33 sec. 5 (1742) and extended by later acts.

12 Colonies forbidden to import East Indian products except from Great Britain, 7 Geo. I first sess. ch. 21 sec. 9 (1721). Though forbidden to trade with the East Indies, the colonists had previously been able legally to import directly from Holland or elsewhere tea, spices, etc., brought from the East Indies by the Dutch East India Company or other foreign competitors of the English East India Company.

13 Fur and copper added to list of enumerated commodities, 8 Geo. I ch. 15 sec. 24 and ch. 18 sec. 22 (1722).

14 Hat and Felt Act of 1732, 5 Geo. II ch. 22. The act also forbade employment as a hat or felt maker of any Negro, slave or free, sec. 8. Martin Bladen's proposal for retrial in England of offenses against the Act, April 13, 1732, Stock *Proceedings* IV 168. As to the colonial hat industry, Beer *Comm. Policy* 81–83.

15 Hops Act of 1732, 5 Geo. II ch. 9, following complaint in the House of Commons March 10, 1732, as to competition of colonial hops Stock *Proceedings* IV 150–51.

16 Sailcloth Act of 1736, 9 Geo. II ch. 37 sec. 4, supplemented by 19 Geo. II ch. 27 secs. 7–13 (1746) and extended by later acts.

17 Iron and Steel Act of 1750, 23 Geo. II ch. 29 secs. 9, 10. Parliament had previously (1710) sought to discourage the manufacture of hardware in the colonies by abolishing the drawback of British import duty on foreign iron and steel reexported to the colonies, Bining *Col. Iron Indust.* 35. The drawback, allowed by 12 Charles II ch. 4 (1660), was repealed by 9 Anne ch. 6 sec. 55 (1710).

18 Circular letter May 5, 1732, to Governors of six colonies, later extended to others, instructing them not to sign any act levying import duties on British manufactures, Labaree *Instructions* I 146–47.

19 Examples of provisions as to penalties, 12 Charles II ch. 18 sec. 1 (1660) ; 15 Charles II ch. 7 sec. 6 (1663); 9 & 10 William III ch. 44 sec. 81 (1698); 13 & 14 Charles II ch. 11 sec. 6 (1662) extended to colonies by 7 & 8 William III ch. 22 sec. 6 (1696).

20 Early methods of enforcing restrictions on colonial trade, Andrews *Col. Period* IV 148, 179–81.

21 Beginning in 1673, 25 Charles II ch. 7 sec. 3, charged the English Customs Board with enforcing the tax on intercolonial exports of enumerated commodities, and in 1696, 7 & 8 William III ch. 22 sec. 6 gave customs officers in the colonies the same broad powers of search as those in England. As to the development of the customs service in the colonies, Andrews *Col. Period* IV 120–21, 160–77, 195–221; Hoon *Eng. Cust. System, passim.*

22 As to the Customs Districts, Customs Board to Treasury Oct. 16, 1764, and Treasury warrant Nov. 7, T:11:28:151–53. Some of the colonies were redistricted in 1764, with an Eastern Middle District and a Western Middle District added. Bermuda was part of the Northern Customs District, Temple to Colden Dec. 12,

1763, *Colden* 1922, 261; Temple's notice to Collectors of the Northern District *Boston Gazette* Feb. 6, 1764. Delaware was presumably included in the Southern District as an appendage of Pennsylvania.

23 "A List of the Commissioners and Officers of His Majestys Customs in England and the Plantations with their respective Salaries," 132 folios, undated but 1765 or 1766, Yale Lib.

24 The requirements for bonds, etc., and details of the colonial admiralty courts and the extent of their jurisdiction relative to the acts of trade and customs are discussed in the Appendix to Chapter XIV of Knollenberg *Origin* (1960 ed.).

25 Colonial smuggling and nonenforcement of the British restrictions on colonial manufacturing are discussed in the appendix to this chapter.

26 British tariff preferences to certain colonial products, Saxby *The British Customs* (1757) 82, 173, 178–79, 200–201, 209, 216, 223, 241, 250, 254–61. As to the volume of British imports, Harper "Effect" Tables II and III, 14–16.

27 British bounties: naval stores, 2 Geo. II ch. 35 sec. 3 (1729); indigo, 21 Geo. II ch. 30 sec. 1 (1749) — both later extended. Amounts paid, Channing *History* 35n; Albion *Forests and Sea Power* 418. (British bounties on certain British exports, Dickerson *Navigation Acts* 71–73, were not confined to exports to the colonies and therefore cannot count as special benefits to the colonies offsetting British restrictions on colonial trade.)

28 Access of colonial-built vessels to the British as well as colonial carrying trade, Harper *Navigation Laws* 338–90. A third of British merchant marine tonnage in 1775 was colonial-built, Albion *Forests and Sea Power* 246. As to the important colonial shipbuilding industry, Hutchins *Am. Maritime Industries* 144–57.

29 Importance of the northern fisheries to colonial New England, particularly Mass., which then included most of the present state of Maine, Harper *Navigation Laws* 260, 334, and sources there cited. As to Mediterranean passes, Beer *Brit. Col. Policy* 7–8n.

30 Estimated value of exports of mainland colonies to British West Indies, Bell "West India Trade" 273–74. For other details as to economic importance to the mainland colonies of their trade with the British West Indies, Pitman *West Indies* App. III, IV, IX; Huntley "Va." 301–6; Sellers *Charleston* 157; Channing *History* II 526; Harper "Mercantilism" 11; Harrington *N.Y. Merchant* 356–68; Carman *Am. Husbandry*, Index under "West Indies"; Nettels *Money Supply* 80–87.

31 British tariff preference in favor of colonial tobacco: Schedule of Rates Inward 12 Charles II ch. 4 (1660) rated foreign tobacco at 10 sh. per pound, English colonial at 1 sh. 8 pence. See also Saxby *The British Customs* 244 (London, 1757). Planting of tobacco in England or Ireland, except in small plots for medicinal use, was forbidden, 12 Charles II ch. 34 (1660), but this restriction was probably of little commercial importance.

32 In 1773, 96,734,000 out of 100,482,000 pounds or 96 per cent of the British colonial tobacco imported was reexported, Harper "Effect" 14 (Table 2) with 5n. In 1762 and 1763 the proportions were 94 per cent and 88 per cent, Gray *Hist. of Agriculture* I 214.

33 As to the price in a so-called protected market being determined by the price in the world market, Faulkner *Am. Economic Hist.* 628–29, Wallace *Farmers and the Ex-*

port Market 2–5, Knollenberg "Our Solemn Farce: Re-enter the Tariff" 688–89. That the price of colonial tobacco was no exception to the general rule is confirmed by the studies of Dr. Jacob Price, whose "Glasgow in Tobacco Trade" is a pioneer study in this field, Dr. Price to me May 18, 1957.

34   Cost to Virginia and Maryland tobacco planters of British restrictions on colonial exports of tobacco, Dulany *Considerations* (1765) 75–76; Harper "Effect" 34–35, 37. N.C., later a leading source of tobacco for export, had not yet become a great tobacco exporting region, Chittenden *N.C. Commerce* 74, 161. Cost to British colonies of other British restrictions on colonial trade, Harper "Effect" 35–37.

35   Dickerson's view of the restrictions being of no disadvantage to colonial tobacco growers, Dickerson *Navigation Acts* 38–39. Average colonial tobacco exports, 86,237,963 pounds for 1767–1775; 99,665,656 for 1790–1794; 70,625,518 for 1795–1799; 85,925,914 for 1800–1804; 54,525,206 for 1805–1809, *same* 38. Dickerson does not give the prices of tobacco at these several periods, which would be a pertinent point.

Chapter 15

1   Additional restrictions on colonial trade, sections 27, 28, and 30, of 4 Geo. III ch. 15 (1764).

2   Madeira, Azores, and Canary wine taxed £7 a tun in the colonies if imported directly, 10 sh. if by way of Great Britain, 4 Geo. III ch. 15, sec. 1 (1764). Adding the net duty payable in Great Britain (Saxby *The British Customs* 267–75) still left a heavy balance against direct import. As to consumption of Madeira wine in, and importance of the Madeira trade to the colonies, Wallace *Laurens* 30; Huntley "Va." 304–5, Whately *Regulations* 74; "Madeira" and "Wine" in indexes to Barker *Md.*, Baxter, *Hancock*, Fitzpatrick *Washington* II, Harrington *N.Y. Merchants, Watts.*

3   Cockets and bonds required for intercolonial shipments, sections 23 and 29 of 4 Geo. III ch. 15 (1764). The quotations are taken from an original copy of the Act.

4   Complaints as to interference with intercolonial trade, William Allen to David Barclay & Sons Nov. 20, 1764, Walker *Burd Papers* 65; protests in *Massachusetts Gazette* May 17, 1764, and *Newport Mercury* June 25; Franklin to Richard Jackson June 1, *Jackson* 160; Benjamin Marshall to James Brooks June 23, Marshall Letter-Book, 207, Hist. Soc. of Pa.; Mass. Assembly to Jackson Nov. 7, 1765, Wells *Adams* I 81.

5   Customs clearance of small vessels in colonial coastwise trade not previously required, Gov. Jonathan Belcher of Mass. to Sir Robert Walpole Nov. 3, 1733, *Belcher* I 400; Gov. James Glen of S.C. to B. of T. March 1753, Labaree *Instructions* II 887; Allen to William Nelson Dec. 3, 1761, Walker *Burd Papers* 48.

6   Exemption of certain colonial coastwise traffic, 30 Geo. II ch. 9 sec. 6 (1757). Somewhat similarly, 7 & 8 William III, requiring registration of vessels engaged in colonial trade, exempted open boats and vessels engaged exclusively in intracolonial trade, and 2 Geo. II ch. 7 sec. 1 (1729), requiring withholding part of the wages of seamen in the colonies toward maintaining Greenwich Hospital, exempted open boats and vessels that "trade only from place to place within any river."

7 William Gregory's diary, Oct. 6, 1765, 1 *W. & M. Q.* XIII (1905) 221, 227, speaks of the "Thousands of vessels going up and Down the Deleware." As to the swarm of little boats on the Hudson and in New York harbor, Benson *Kalm's Travels* I 326; De Voe *Market Book* 310; Pownall *Topographical Description* 42.

8 As to the burdensomeness and complexity of the custom regulations now extended to intercolonial coastwise trade, Martin "King's Customs" 202.

9 Earlier provisions for distribution of the proceeds of forfeitures (for example, 12 Charles II ch. 18, secs. 1, 18, 19) were consolidated and supplemented by sec. 42 of the American Act of 1764 (4 Geo. III ch. 15) and an Order in Council of Oct. 12, 1764, *London Chronicle* Oct. 16, 1764.

10 Secs. 43, 46 of 4 Geo. III ch. 15 encouraging reckless seizures and suits for alleged violations of acts of trade and customs. The Customs Board referred to in the act had nine members, Beatson *Index* I 454.

11 Sec. 41 of 4 Geo. III ch. 15 providing for new colonial admiralty court having general colonial jurisdiction.

12 The commission of the judge, Dr. William Spry, for the new admiralty court at Halifax was issued June 15, 1764, and the court was opened Oct. 9, 1 *Mass. Hist. Soc. Proc.* XVII (1879–1880) 292–93. Halifax had a population of less than 1,500 in 1764, Brebner *New Eng. Outpost* 171n. For an example of the colonial reaction to the establishment of this court, John Watts of N.Y. to Moses Franks, Dec. 22, 1765, *Watts* 407. As to colonial alarm proving to be unfounded, Ubbelohde *Vice-Admiralty Courts* 82, 94n.

13 Adm. Lord Colville to Philip Stephens Oct. 25, 1763, recommending Halifax as place for new admiralty court, Adm. I:482:615.

14 Sec. 45 of 4 Geo. III ch. 15 laying burden of proof on the defendant. (Earlier acts, for example 7 & 8 William III ch. 22 sec. 7, had laid the burden of proof on the defendant as to particular facts but not in all respects.)

15 Sec. 41 of 4 Geo. III ch. 15 clearly giving colonial admiralty courts jurisdiction in all cases under acts of trade and customs. Previous confusion concerning their jurisdiction is discussed in the Appendix to Chapter XIV of Knollenberg *Origin* (1960 ed.).

16 Genesis of 4 Geo. III ch. 15, minutes of Treasury Board July 29, 1763, T:29:35; Commissioners of Customs to Treasury Board Sept. 16 T:1:426:295; minutes of Treasury Board Sept. 21 T:29:35, present George Grenville, Lord North, and Thomas Orby Hunter. The bill, drawn by John Tyton, solicitor to the Customs Commissioners, and Robert Yeates, a chief clerk in the Treasury, was apparently designed to plug every possible loophole without regard to the effect on colonial prosperity or opinion. As to the draftsmen, *Jenkinson* 245.

17 William Wood to Commissioners of Customs Jan. 10, 1764, *Jenkinson* 254. Wood (1679–1765), author of the well-known *A Survey of Trade* (1718) and Secretary to the Commissioners of Customs, had held this office for over twenty years, Hoon *Eng. Cust. System* 68–69.

18 The merchants' complaints against currency inflation and the recommendations of the Board of Trade and Privy Council, Feb. 10 and March 9, 1763, are in *Acts P.C.* IV 623–31, 641–46. As to the complaints concerning Va., Edward

Montague, London Agent for the Va. House, to unnamed addressee Feb. 5, 1763, Carter (Landon) Papers. Tables showing inflation in the currency of Va., Pa., and N.Y. at this period are in Brock "Col. Currency." The act restricting issues of currency in New England was 24 Geo. II ch. 53 (1751).

19 Currency Act of 1764, 4 Geo. III ch. 34. Currency not having the quality of legal tender could still be issued. As to revision of the bill so as not to cut short the life of outstanding legal tender currency, Namier "Garth" 640. An act of 6 Anne ch. 30 (1708) relating to coin in the colonies had failed to prevent inflation.

20 The depression in the colonies may well have been incident to the general business depression in western Europe which followed the close of the Seven Years' War in 1763, rather than to the recent British restrictions on colonial trade to which the colonists, perhaps mistakenly but quite naturally, attributed their troubles.

21 Extreme business depression in R.I. and N.Y., Nicholas Brown & Co. to David Van Horne May 14, 1764, and Van Horne to Brown Aug. 4 Hedges *The Browns* 164, 348. Jonathan Trumbull, Jr., to Joseph Trumbull June 8, postscript to letter on May 27, Trumbull (Joseph) Corresp. Box 295. To same effect, John Van Cortlandt to Abraham Maer March 19 Harrington *N.Y. Merchant* 318; John Watts to William Brymer May 15 and to George and John Riddell Sept. 18 *Watts* 254, 286.

22 As to widespread economic distress in Conn., Jared Ingersoll to Thomas Whately July 6, 1764, "Ingersoll Letters" 297; John Ledyard to Jonathan Trumbull, Sr., Nov. 6, 1764, Zeichner *Conn.* 47; Joseph Trumbull at Norwich, Conn., to Thomas Collinson Jan. 20, 1765, *same*. The farm products mentioned by Ingersoll as a drug on the market were "horses, cattle, sheep, hogs, poultry, wheat, oats, Indian corn and lumber of all sorts."

23 Business depression in Boston, Thomas & John Hancock to Barnard & Harrison June 23 and July, 1764, Baxter *Hancock* 232, Brown *Hancock* 44; James Otis to Francis Pybot Dec. 24, and to George Johnston and others Jan. 25, 1765, *Mass. Hist. Soc. Proc.* vol. 43, 202–5; John Rowe's diary Jan. 19 Rowe 74; and in N.H., *New Hampshire Gazette* Dec. 7, 1764.

24 Trade very dull in Philadelphia, too, Samuel Rhoads, Jr., to Neate, Pigou, and Booth May 4 and Oct. 20, 1764, "Rhoads" 422–23; Benjamin Marshall to Dr. James Tapscott June 22, Oct. 22 and to James Brooks July 28, "Marshall" 206–8; Roberdeau to Meyler & Hall of Jamaica July 6, Bezanson *Prices* 280; William Allen to David Barclay & Sons of London Dec. 19, Walker *Burd Papers* 66, "The Farmer" (unidentified) in the *Pennsylvania Journal* Aug. 23.

25 William Allason to Alex. Walker June 24, 1764, as to financial distress in Va., "Allason Letters" 133–34. Va.'s financial woes at this time were presumably caused chiefly by the sharp drop in the price of tobacco from an average of around 20 sh. sterling per hundred pounds in 1756 to 1759 to around 10 sh. sterling in 1763–1765, data in 1 *W. & M. Q.* XVI 127, 130, Jerdone Letter Book, William and Mary Coll. Lib. and Mays *Pendleton* I 142–43 and "Allason Letters" 122, 124, 133.

26 Further evidence of extreme distress in Va., Allason to Bogle & Scott July 29, 1764, *same* 134; John Baylor to John Norton Sept. 18, 1764, *Norton* 11–12; Lee *Vin-*

dication (1764) 20; Richard Corbin to former Gov. Robert Dinwiddie Aug. 11, 1764, Corbin Letter-Book. There is evidence of a severe business depression in Md., too, but not until 1765, Barker *Md.* 295–97, Giddens "Md." 519–21.

27 Parliament grants some colonial benefits in 1764; direct import of salt into Quebec allowed, 4 Geo. III ch. 19; direct export of rice from S.C. and Ga. to any part of America "southward of South Carolina or Georgia" allowed on payment of export duty, 4 Geo. III ch. 27.

28 Bounty on hemp and flax granted, 4 Geo. III ch. 26. The bounty proved to be relatively unimportant £5,560 total for the years 1766 to 1772, Channing *History* III 35n, and £59 for 1773–1775, Comptroller-General's Account Aug. 29, 1777, T:38:363 and 667.

29 B. of T. to the King Feb. 9, 1764, proposing bounty on colonial exports of flax to Great Britain because, "unless some Channel of beneficial exploration" of flax was opened, colonial manufacture of cordage and linen competing with British would be "greatly increased," 1 *N.J. Col. Doc.* IX 418–19. The same would apply to the bounty on hemp. For Franklin's jeer at the claim of British generosity to the colonies in granting this bounty, Sparks *Franklin* IV 225.

30 4 Geo. III ch. 29 reduced the British tariff on colonial whalebone; 4 Geo. III ch. 11 sec. 3 prolonged the admission of colonial lumber into Great Britain duty free; and 4 Geo. III ch. 22 contained favorable provisions as to colonial whale oil. British duties on colonial beaver skins were adjusted in 1764, 4 Geo. III ch. 9, but whether beneficially or not to the colonies I cannot determine. Extension and revision in 1764 of the Sugar Act of 1733 was discussed in Chapter 11.

Chapter 16

1 Eliphalet Dyer to an unidentified correspondent about March 1, 1764, voicing his suspicion concerning the army, *Connecticut Courant* Sept. 16, 1765 Date of Dyer's letter identified by reference to Grenville's budget speech of 1764 as of "about a Fortnight since." As to Dyer, *D.A.B.* and Groce "Dyer" 290–304.

2 My statements as to Arthur, Richard, Francis, and William Lee are based on sketches of them in *D.A.B.* and on lists of members of the Va. House, *Va. Journals* 1761–1765, 201–2.

3 Richard Henry Lee's protest to unidentified correspondent May 31, 1764, Ballagh *Lee* I 5–7. (Lee applied—unsuccessfully—in Nov. 1764 for the prospective office of Collector of Stamps for Virginia; his humiliating explanation of this is in *same* 16–18.)

4 John Watts to Gen. Robert Monckton May 16, 1764, concerning colonial anger, *Watts* 255. To same effect, and attributing recent British harshness to the colonies to acquisition of Canada, Dickinson *The Late Regulations* 243; Diary of a French Traveller June 6, 1765, *A.H.R.* XXVI 747.

5 Thomas Hutchinson to Richard Jackson July 23, 1764, in reply to Jackson's letter of April 16, Mass. Arch. XXVI 99–100. The description of Hutchinson is from *Boston Gazette* Jan. 31, 1763, and Jonathan Mayhew to Thomas Hollis March 19, 1761, Knollenberg "Hollis and Mayhew" 119.

6 My sketch of Hutchinson is based chiefly on Freiberg "Hutchinson" 35–55; Freiberg "Hutchinson and Mass. Politics"; and Shipton *Harvard Graduates* VI 156, VII 222, 384–91, VIII 149–217, which give many details concerning Hutchinson not in *D.A.B.* or Hosmer *Hutchinson*. As to the Otis affair, Edmund Trowbridge to William Bollan, July 15, 1762, *Mauduit* 66; statement of James Otis, Jr., in *Boston Gazette* April 4, 1763.

7 Decision against the province in *Province of Massachusetts Bay* vs. *Paxton* Feb. 1762, term Mass. Superior Court, Quincy *Reports* 548–52; Hutchinson to Bollan March 6, 1762, giving reasons for his unpopularity Mass. Arch. XXVI 8; reelection to Council in 1763–1765, Whitmore *Mass. Civil List* 61–62. As to Hutchinson's currency anti-inflationist principles, Shipton *Harvard Graduates* VIII 154, 158, 170–71 and Freiberg "Hutchinson and the Currency" *passim*.

8 Hutchinson's memorandum to Jackson of July 1764, analyzed in this and succeeding paragraphs, is in Morgan "Hutchinson" 480–92 with minor gaps filled by me in *New Eng. Q.* XXII (1949) 98. Hutchinson's remark as to the "fallacy" of lumping duties for revenue with those for the regulation of trade, Hutchinson to Ebenezer Silliman Nov. 9, 1764, Morgan *Stamp Act* 216.

9 Unreasonableness of taxing the colonists for British troops not wanted, Jared Ingersoll to Thomas Whately July 6, 1764, "Ingersoll Letters" 229; Cortlandt Skinner, Att. Gen. of N.J., to Thomas Boone Oct. 5, 1765, Whitehead *Perth Amboy* 103. As to Skinner, Kemmerer *N.J.* Index under "Skinner, Cortlandt."

10 *The Rights* reprinted in *R.I. Col. Rec.* VI 416–27, at 423. To similar effect, William Livingston of N.Y. to Eleazar Wheelock of N.H. March 22, 1764, Wheelock Papers Dartmouth Coll. Lib.

11 The Appendix to Chapter XVI of Knollenberg *Origin* (1960 ed.) this chapter describes some of the wastage of the public revenue of Great Britain, Ireland, and the British West Indies on lavish sinecures, unearned pensions, and exorbitant salaries and perquisites to members of the British ruling class.

12 Lord Chesterfield to Solomon Dayrolles Nov. 16, 1753, as to shortage of "pasturage" *Chesterfield* IV 98. In announcing to Newcastle Feb. 2, 1760, the conquest of Martinique Admiral George Rodney stressed the power this would give Newcastle "to oblige many of your friends by the posts and employments . . . which are very lucrative in this island" Namier *Eng.* 73n.

13 Colonial remarks on wastage of British revenue, Otis *Considerations* (1765) 115; Dulany *Considerations* (1765) 27.

14 Charles Carroll of Carrollton (the younger) to Henry Graves Sept. 15, 1765, on the danger of the wastage of British public revenue being extended to the colonies, *Carroll Letters* 90.

15 Ezra Stiles to John Hubbard June 12, 1764, on danger of an American list of pensioners, Knollenberg "Stiles" 151.

16 Colonial efforts to curtail colonial imports and promote colonial manufacturing, Ingersoll to Whately July 6, 1764, "Ingersoll Letters" 297–98; Schlesinger *Col. Merchants* 63–65; Morgan *Stamp Act* 32; Brown *Democracy in Mass.* 211; Hindle *Pursuit of Science 1735–1789*, 107, 109.

17 Circular letter of the Society for the Promotion of Arts, etc., Dec. 10, 1764, signed by Charles W. Apthorp, Walter Rutherford, Wm. Smith, Jr., John Morin

Scott, and James Duane, announcing its objects *N.Y. Doc. Hist.* IV 344–45. Other leading members of the Society were Benjamin Kissam, Frederick Philipse, and Philip and William Livingston, *Newport Mercury* Dec. 24, 1764.

18 Boycott of British imports with intent to secure repeal of British taxation, *Providence Gazette* Oct. 6, 1764; *Connecticut Courant* Oct. 29.

19 Gov. Edward Trelawney of Jamaica to Newcastle July 29, 1742, as to particular cruelty of impressment for the navy when applied to colonial seamen, Pares "Manning the Navy in West Indies" 45.

20 Colonial opposition to impressment Clark "Impressment in the Colonies" 198–224; Pares "Manning the Navy in West Indies" 31–60; Adams *Rev. New Eng.* 192–94; Letters from America June 1741–July 1743, enclosed in Admiralty Board to Lord Justices Sept. 26, 1743, *Law* I 112–22; Gov. William Shirley of Mass. to B. of T. Dec. 1, 1747, *Shirley* I 412–19; Mass. Legislature to Bollan Sept. 11, 1756, 1 *Mass. Hist. Soc. Coll.* VI 97–100; Gov. Cadwallader Colden of N.Y. to B. of T. Aug. 30, 1760, *Colden* 1876, 17.

21 Franklin to Joseph Galloway April 7, 1759, concerning injury of impressment to colonial trade, Mason-Franklin Coll.

22 Legality of impressment in Great Britain, Maitland *Const. Hist.* 280, 461–62; Clark "Impressment in the Colonies" 198–201; act forbidding impressment in colonies, 6 Anne ch. 37 (1708). The exemption quoted is in sec. 9.

23 Weak legal opinions upholding impressment in the colonies, Sir Edward Northey Feb. 10, 1716, and Sir Dudley Ryder and Sir John Strange July 17, 1740, Chalmers *Opinions* 232. Proceedings in House of Commons Nov. 19, 1707, to March 17, 1708, concerning the act of 6 Anne ch. 37 (1708) Stock *Proceedings* III 142–95 *passim*. Sec. 9 of the Act of 1708 was not repealed by 19 Geo. II ch. 30 (1746). The debates concerning the latter are in Stock *Proceedings* IV 235–36.

24 Trial of Michael Corbet for killing Lieut. Henry B. Panton, undated notes of John Adams, counsel for Corbet, Adams *Works* II 224–26, 526–34; testimony at the trial, *M.H.S. Proc.* vol. 44 (1911) 429–52. Corbet was acquitted on the ground of justifiable homicide, Dickerson *Boston* 110–11, Panton having acted without authority of a press warrant, Hutchinson *Hist. of Mass.* III 167n corroborated by John Adams's diary Dec. 23, 1769, Adams *Works* II 224–26.

25 Adm. Lord Colville to Philip Stephens July 26, 1764, concerning his orders as to impressment, *R.I. Col. Rec.* VI 428. Lt. Thomas Laugharne, master of the *Chaleur*, wrote Colville Aug. 11, *Acts P.C.* VI 384–85, of having given orders "to impress such men as could be reasonably spared, not exceeding one out of five exclusive of the master."

26 The *St. John* affair at Newport, R.I., July 1764, *Newport Mercury* July 16; Colville to Stephens July 26 and Aug. 24 enclosing statements of Lieut. Thomas Hill of the *St. John* and Lieut. Hugh Backie of the *Squirrel, R.I. Col. Rec.* VI 428–30; John Robinson and John Nicoll, Collector and Comptroller at R.I., to unidentified correspondent Aug. 30, 1765, digested in Privy Council minutes Nov. 5 *Acts P.C.* VI 385–86; Gov. Samuel Ward of R.I. to B. of T. Oct. 23 Ward Papers R.I. Hist. Soc.

27 The *Chaleur* affair at New York, July 10–11, 1764, *New-York Gazette* July 12 quoted in
Dawson *Sons of Liberty* 54–55; Laugharne to Colville Aug. 11 *Acts P.C.* VI 384–85.

Chapter 17

1 Instructions of committee appointed at Boston town meeting May 15, 1764 *Boston
Records* 1758–1769, 116, 121–22. The handwriting of the draft instructions in the
Boston Public Library is apparently that of Samuel Adams (Zoltán Haraszti,
Keeper of Rare Books at the Library, to me June 9, 1955). The *Boston Gazette* of
May 7 reported arrival of news of the House of Commons resolution of March
10 to tax the colonies.

2 Provisions for easy calling of town meetings in Mass., ch. 28 sec. 11 of Laws of
1692–1693 *Mass. Acts* I 68 with Gov. Shirley to B. of T. Dec. 1, 1747, *Shirley* I 418.

3 Committees chosen by Mass. House June 1 and 13, 1764, to consider letters of the
Agent and write to other colonies *Mass. Journals* for 1764–1765, 14, 77. Circular
letter of June 25, *Fitch* II 284–85.

4 Proposed instructions to London Agent, *same* 72–77 with "State of the Rights of
the Colonies" Mullett *Writings* of Otis I 94–101. The "State" was probably written by James Otis; its style and reasoning are similar to those of his *Rights*.

5 Otis *Rights* (Boston, 1764) 73–74, 78–88. The *Rights* (70–71) recommended colonial representation in Parliament and by implication suggested that, if so represented, the colonists could not rightly object to taxation by Parliament.

6 Thacher *Sentiments* (Boston, 1764) 4–13. As to Thacher, who is not in *D.A.B.*, Shipton *Harvard Graduates* X 322–28; *Mass. Hist. Soc. Proc.* XX (1882–1883) 46–56; indexes to Brennen *Mass. 1760–1780* and Adams *Works* under "Thacher, Oxenbridge." The reference by John Rowe to "The *Black Act*" is in his diary Sept. 29,
1764, *Rowe* 64.

7 Gov. Francis Bernard of Mass. to Richard Jackson Aug. 18, 1764, Morgan *Stamp
Act* 60–61. (Bernard was on familiar terms with Jackson, having employed him as
his personal lawyer in 1762, *Barrington-Bernard* Corresp. 57.)

8 Committee chosen by Mass. House and proceedings to petition the British Government for relief, Oct. 19 to 25, 1764, *Mass. Journal* 1764–1765, 97–98, 102,
111–12 with *Mass. Hist. Soc. Proc.* XX (1882–1883) 50–51.

9 Joint petition of Mass. House and Council for modification of the American Act
of 1764, Nov. 3, 1764, *Mass. Journals* 1764–1765, 135, published in *Bowdoin-Temple
Papers* 32–36. The harmful effects of the trade restrictions of the Act of 1764
were also pointed out by Bernard to Lord Halifax Nov. 10, Bernard *Select Letters*
17, and an unidentified writer to Mauduit Nov. 28 *Mauduit* 171–79.

10 Letters supplementing the Mass. Legislative petition, Andrew Oliver to Mauduit
Nov. 3, 1764, Mass. Arch. vol. 56, 427–31; Thomas Cushing to Mauduit Nov. 17
Mauduit 171. Oliver wrote that a letter from a member of Parliament (probably
Jackson's letter of April 16 mentioned in the next footnote) advising that a "de-
cent" remonstrance might procure relief, had influenced the decision not to "set
up in opposition to Parliament."

11 Thomas Hutchinson to Jackson Nov. 5, 1764, as to his strategy to secure an innocuous petition, Mass. Arch. XXVI 110–11. To same effect, Bernard to Jackson
concerning Hutchinson's strategy, Nov. 17, 1764, Bernard Papers III 262. Jackson's influential letter of April 16 to which Hutchinson referred has not been
found, but its tenor is indicated by Hutchinson's reply of July 23, discussed in
Chapter 16.

12 Hutchinson to Ebenezer Silliman of Conn. Nov. 9, 1764, justifying his recent
conduct as to Mass. petition, Morgan *Stamp Act* 216; Hutchinson to Jackson July
23 and Nov. 5, 1764, disclosing fear of injury to his reputation in Great Britain,
Mass. Arch. XXVI 99–100, 110–11.

13 Suspicion of double-dealing by Jackson, William Bollan to Edmund Trowbridge
May 2, 1765, Dana Mss. Mass. Hist. Soc.; Ezra Stiles memorandum Dec. 26
Stiles Papers. Charles Jenkinson to George Grenville April 11 concerning Jack-
son, *Jenkinson* 359.

14 Praise of Jackson's regard for and help to colonies, Eliphalet Dyer to Jared Ingersoll April 14, 1764, "Ingersoll Letters" 289; William Allen to Rev. Jonathan
Mayhew Oct. 15 Mayhew Papers.

15 Instructions to committee of Conn. Legislature in May 1764 to prepare a statement as to colonial taxation and legislative approval of the committee's statement in Oct. *Conn. Col. Rec.* XII 256, 299. The statement published under the title
Reasons Why, etc. (New Haven, 1764), is reprinted in *Conn. Col. Rec.* XII 651–71.
Copies of the statement reached Jackson, the colony's London Agent, by Dec.
14, Fitch to Jackson Dec. 7 with Jackson to Fitch Dec. 14, *Fitch* II 304, 312.

16 Missing letter of Jackson to unidentified addressee March 10, 1764, "relative to
creating a revenue in America," considered by the Conn. Legislature at its
May–June 1764 session *Conn. Col. Rec.* XII 256.

Chapter 18

1 Gov. Cadwallader Colden's Message to N.Y. Legislature, Assembly's reply, Colden's response, Assembly's appointment of a committee to draw up a petition.
Sept. 5–17, 1764, *N.Y. Assembly* II 746–54. The only member of the committee
whose name is mentioned (764), presumably its chairman, was William Bayard,
a leading merchant of New York City, later a Tory, Sabine *Loyalists* I 217–18, *Appleton's Cyclopedia* under "Bayard."

2 N.Y. Assembly's adoption of petition to House of Commons and appointment
of committees to draft representations to the King and House of Lords Oct. 4,
1764, *N.Y. Assembly* II 764. The drafts prepared by the committees were approved
by the Assembly Oct. 18, *same* 769–75.

3 N.Y. Assembly's petition ("Representation") to House of Commons Oct. 4, 1764,
reaffirmed Oct. 18 *same* 776–79, reprinted in Morgan *Declaration of 1764* 7–15.

4 The petitions to both Houses of Parliament and the King were drafted by William Livingston, William Smith, Jr., and John Morin Scott, note by Smith headed

"Autumn 1764," Sabine *William Smith* 24. As to these men, all three of whom were Yale graduates and New York lawyers, *D.A.B.* under name of each and Dillon *New York Triumvirate, passim.*

5 William Livingston to Eleazar Wheelock, later President of Dartmouth College, March 22, 1764, denouncing British encroachments on colonial liberties Wheelock Papers Dartmouth Coll. Lib.

6 Colden's message to N.Y. Assembly Oct. 2, 1764, proposing annulment of title to a large tract of former Crown land *N.Y. Assembly* II 762. The direction from the B. of T. to propose this was in B. of T. to Colden July 10, *N.Y. Col. Doc.* VII 633.

7 Early British Governors of N.Y. required to reserve in grants of Crown land only such quit rents as they "shall think fitt," e.g., instructions and Commission of Gov. Benjamin Fletcher March 17 and 18, 1692, *same* III 818–33 at 832.

8 Reservations to the Crown of annual quit rent of 2s. 6d. per 100 acres required in instruction to Gov. Lord Bellomont of N.Y. Nov. 10, 1698, *same* IV 424–25. For resumption of this instruction in 1708 and its continuation thereafter, instruction to Gov. Lord Lovelace of N.Y. July 20, 1708, *same* V 54–55 and Labaree *Instructions* II 579.

9 Gov. Lord Cornbury of N.Y. required to reserve only such quit rent as he "shall see fitt," Commission and instructions to Cornbury Nov. 26, 1701, C.O. 5:1118:426–65. Cornbury's successor, Lovelace, reached New York Dec. 18, 1708, *N.Y. Col. Doc.* V 67.

10 Some of the huge grants of Crown land at extremely low quit rents are listed in Bellomont to B. of T. May 3, 1699, *same* IV 514, others in Higgins *N.Y. Expansion* 22–27. The readiness of the Council to acquiesce in these grants perhaps was because its members were often among the participants, e.g., Rip Van Dam, one of the grantees in 1708 of the great Kayaderosseras tract.

11 Requirements in N.Y. for acquisition of Indian title to land, N.Y. act of Oct. 23, 1684, *N.Y. Col. Laws* I 149; N.Y. Council order of Dec. 2, 1736, N.Y. Council Minutes, State Archives Albany, N.Y.; Crown instruction of 1755 Labaree *Instructions* II 467–68.

12 Kayaderosseras grant Nov. 2, 1708, *Colden* 1922, 360–64; ownership of the grant widely distributed, Gov. James De Lancey of N.Y. to B. of T. July 22, 1754, and Gov. Sir Henry Moore of N.Y. to Lord Shelburne Nov. 8, 1766, *N.Y. Col Doc.* VI 851 and VII 876–77; estimated acreage of the grant and amount of quit rent reserved, Sir William Johnson to B. of T. Nov. 13, 1763, *same* VII 576. Other estimates ran from 256,000 to 900,000 acres, *same* VI 851, VII 562, 876.

13 Estimate of fees payable for the Kayaderosseras grant based on N.Y. act of May 24, 1709, *N.Y. Col. Laws* I 638–53 fixing a fee of 10 sh. per 100 acres for the Governor and smaller amounts for various other officials.

14 The Indian deed to the grantees of the Kayaderosseras tract dated Oct. 6, 1704, and the Crown grant of Nov. 2, 1708, are in *Colden* 1922, 359–60 and 360–64.

15 Indian complaints of Kayaderosseras grant, minutes of Albany meeting with Indians June 27, 1754, enclosed in De Lancey to B. of T. July 22 *N.Y. Col. Doc.* VI

851, 866. The Indians later admitted giving a deed, but said that there was no intention to convey so much; that one of the interested tribes had not concurred in the deed; and that the goods to be given in payment were burned before the Indians got them, Gov. Moore to Shelburne Nov. 8, 1766, *same* VII 876.

16 Johnson to B. of T. July 1755 to Nov. 1763 as to Indians' complaints concerning the Kayaderosseras grant, *same* VI 962, VII 8, 433, 561–62, 576–77, *Johnson* III 867. B. of T. to Gov. Sir Charles Hardy March 19, 1756, instructing him to secure legislative annulment of the Kayaderosseras grant *N.Y. Col. Doc.* VII 77–78; Hardy's messages to N.Y. Assembly in 1756 and 1757 recommending annulment and the Assembly's replies, *N.Y. Assembly* II 497, 499, 501, 503, 523, 525.

17 B. of T. to Colden July 10, 1764, giving him instructions similar to Hardy's *N.Y. Col. Doc.* VII 633.

18 Johnson to B. of T. Nov. 13, 1763, pointing out increased quit rent to Crown if Kayaderosseras grant was annulled, *same* 576. (£1.85 N.Y. currency was worth about £1 sterling in 1764, John Watts to various correspondents April to Nov. 1764, *Watts* 239, 246, 257, 267, 271, 308.)

19 The Governor's fee, at this period, was 25 shillings per hundred acres N.Y. currency (amounting to £20,000 on 800,000 acres) and was to be equally divided between Colden, the acting Governor, and Gen. Robert Monckton, the absent titular Governor, Colden to B. of T. Oct. 13, 1764, *Colden* 1876, 387. Surveyor-General Alexander Colden to Gov. Moore about April 1767, stating his rate of fees, *N.Y. Col. Doc.* VII 926.

20 Johnson's grant said to overlap the Kayaderosseras grant, Witham Marsh and John Watts to Johnson Dec. 11, 1763, March 26, 1765, *Johnson* IV 267, XI 663. The two grants were contiguous, Claude J. Southier's 1779 map of N.Y., reprinted in *N.Y. Doc. Hist.* I 775, but I have not been able to ascertain if the supposed overlap in fact existed.

21 The grant of Indian title to the upper Mohawak tract was made to Johnson in December 1760, Johnson to Alexander Colden Jan. 28, 1761, *Johnson* III 313. Johnson to Cadwallader Colden April 6, 1764, described the land as "verry fine" *same* IV 388. The statements of acreage and of purchase price are in Johnson to Goldsbrow Banyar Jan, 2, 1761, and to John Pownall April 18, 1763, *same* III 297 and IV 90.

22 As to the Crown instructions, disregarded by Johnson, Labaree *Instructions* II 467–68. As to Johnson's conflicting statements, he first (1761) described the Indian grant as a "gift," *Johnson* III 296, 313, 326, later said he had given "£480 Currency in Specie together with a handsome present" *same* IV 90. He first (1761) said the grant was of "about 40 thousand Acres," later (1764) "about 40 or 50," still later (1765) "near 80,000," and, in the end (1767), "about 130 thousand," *same* III 297, IV 89, 615, V 476.

23 Johnson to Cadwallader Colden Feb. 27, 1765, denying any selfish interest in the Kayaderosseras affair *same* IV 653. Colden had at first been cool toward Johnson's recent acquisition because of his failure to observe the Crown instructions as to acquiring Indian title, Colden to Amherst June 29, 1761, *Colden* 1876, 94–95; but after Johnson offered Colden 10,000 acres to waive his official fee for signing the grant, *Johnson* IV 388, Colden strongly supported a Crown grant to Johnson based on the Indian title questionably acquired, Colden to B. of T. June 8, 1765, *Colden* 1877, 17–18.

24 Johnson to B. of T. May 24, 1765, denying the justice of attacks on him concerning the Kayaderosseras (or, as he spelled it, "Kayader usseras") affair, *N.Y. Col. Doc.* VII 713.

25 N.Y. Assembly's reply Oct. 5, 1764, to Colden's recommendation for annulment of the Kayaderosseras grant *Colden* 1922, 356–57. As to the thrust at Johnson, Colden to Johnson Oct. 15, 1764, *same* 1876, 378. (In 1768 the Indians, on advice of counsel that "there were not sufficient grounds to proceed against the Patent with any Prospect of Success in a Court of Law," finally released their claim for 5,000 dollars, Johnson to Gen. Thomas Gage and to Lord Hillsborough Aug. 5 and 17, 1768, *Johnson* VI 308, *N.Y. Col. Doc.* VIII 94.)

26 Colden to B. of T. Nov. 6, 1764, concerning the Assembly's refusal to annul, Colden 1876, 392–98 at 392. For a detailed discussion of the interest by members of both the Assembly and Council of N.Y. in land, the title to which was disputed, Mark *Agrarian Conflicts in N.Y.*, *passim*.

27 Proceedings of Pa. Assembly Sept. 22 and Oct. 20, 1764, concerning British taxation of the colonies 8 *Pa. Arch.* VII 5643–45, 5678. The "plan" referred to by the Assembly was probably Franklin's plan for a general colonial currency including payment of interest to the British Government on the amount issued, Crane *Franklin's Letters to the Press* 25–30; Thomas Pownall and Franklin to George Grenville Feb. 12, 1765 (photostat), Mason-Franklin Coll.

28 Franklin had the Pa. Assembly's printing business, Franklin's Autobiography and Franklin to William Strahan April 29, 1749, Smyth *Franklin* I 350, II 373.

29 Power of Governors of Pa. to block legislation by refusing assent, Pa. Charter March 4, 1682, Thorpe *Charters* V 3037–39, and controversies with the Assembly arising out of this, Thayer *Pa. Politics 1740–1776* 12–65; Wolff *Pa.* 150–200; Shepherd *Pa.* 422–50.

30 Proceedings relative to Pa. tax bill, including Gov. William Denny's message and appointment of Franklin as special London Agent, Jan. 22 to Feb. 3, 1757, 8 *Pa. Arch.* VI 4495–98, 4505–6. Thomas Penn, the older and chief Proprietary, forsook Quakerism in fact by 1743 and formally in 1758, Shepherd *Pa.* 216, 216n.

31 Franklin's unsuccessful London mission, 1757–59, Mason "Franklin and Galloway" 236–60; Van Doren *Franklin* 272–300. The Penns were antagonized after Franklin's arrival in London by learning of a letter from him to Isaac Norris, Speaker of the Pa. Assembly, Jan. 14, 1758, comparing Thomas Penn to a "low jockey" and expressing "thorough contempt for him" Franklin to Galloway April 7, 1759, Mason-Franklin Coll.

32 Passage of new tax bill including the Penns' unimproved land as taxable property, April 5, 1759, assented to by Gov. Denny April 17, 8 *Pa. Arch.* VI 4972, 4985; Denny's replacement in Nov. 1759, by James Hamilton, Thayer *Pa. Politics 1740–1776* 73–74; Privy Council Committee's recommendation Aug. 28, 1760, and Privy Council's action concerning the act, Sept. 2, *Acts P.C.* IV 440–42.

33 Resignation of Robert Charles, Wolff *Pa.* 210 with Richard Jackson to Franklin April 4, 1763, *Jackson* 98. Franklin's continuance as Pa. Agent and resumption of

seat in the Assembly, Van Doren *Franklin* 287–88, 301, 313–15. I have not found any evidence of any protest by him.

34 Tax bill for raising £55,000, passed in March 1764 and rejected by Gov. John Penn, who had succeeded Hamilton on the latter's resignation in 1763; and passage in May of new bill conforming to Penn's demand 8 *Pa. Arch.* VII 5571–86, 5604–18 *passim*.

35 Petition for change in the form of government of Pa., prepared by a committee including Franklin, adopted May 25, 1764, *same* 5607–10, published in Eddy *Franklin & Hall* facing p. 11. John Dickinson's speech in opposition, *A Speech on a Petition for a Change of Government* (Philadelphia, 1764), reprinted Ford *Dickinson's Writings* 21–49. Speaker Isaac Norris, though a leader of the Quaker party, concurred with Dickinson in opposing the change, *same* 14. Norris resigned as Speaker and Franklin was elected to succeed him for the brief remainder of the session, 8 *Pa. Arch.* VII 5611.

36 Penns yield as to taxing their land, Thomas and Richard Penn to Gov. Penn June 1 and 8, 1764, Shepherd *Pa.* 471n; Dickinson's statement Oct. 26 Ford *Dickinson's Writings* 151–52.

37 Assembly's adherence to its petition for a change of government and vote to send Franklin to London, Oct. 1764, 8 *Pa. Arch.* VII 5688–90. As to Franklin's defeat for reelection to the Assembly, Charles Pettit to Joseph Reed Nov. 3, *Reed* I 36–37 with Allen *Answer* (1764) 105; Franklin to Jackson Oct. 11 *Jackson* 188; Franklin *Remarks* (1764) reprinted Smyth *Franklin* IV 276.

38 Quakers, no longer in the majority in Pa., Smith *Brief State* (1755) 4 and Tolles *Meeting House* 232, were concentrated in Chester, Philadelphia, and Bucks counties, Proud *Pa.* II 339. As to overrepresentation of these counties in the Assembly, table of representation, Lincoln *Rev. Movement in Pa.* 47 with lists of valuations and representatives in 1760 8 *Pa. Arch.* VI 5141, 5157.

39 Pressure for redistribution of seats in the Pa. Assembly, Petition of "Freemen of the County of Berks" March 29, 1763, *same* 5419–20; Remonstrance of "the Inhabitants of the Frontier Counties" Feb. 13, 1764, *Pa. Council* IX 138–42; petitions from Cumberland and other "back Counties" Feb. to Sept., 8 *Pa. Arch.* VII 5542–43, 5582–83, 5597, 5608, 5626; *Pennsylvania Journal* April 19; *The Plain Dealer*, Philadelphia, May 14; Douglass *Rebels and Democrats* 221–22.

40 Fear of Quaker party of losing control of Assembly and plan to gain control of provincial Council if royal government for Pa. secured, James Pemberton to John Fothergill March 7, 1764, to John Hunt April 11, and to Samuel Fothergill June 13 (date supplied from Pemberton Papers) Hindle "Paxton Boys" 483, Thayer "Quaker Party" 34, Sharpless *Quaker Experiment* II 67; Thomas Wharton to Franklin Dec. 4, 1764, Sparks *Franklin* VII 280–81n; Franklin to John Ross Feb. 14, 1765, Smyth *Franklin* IV 361–62. As to close connection between colonial and English Friends, Boorstin *Americans* 64–67.

41 Robert Ogden to Cortlandt Skinner Aug. 24, 1764, for united colonial action against British taxation 1 *N.J. Col. Doc.* IX 449–51. Neville and Johnston mentioned by Ogden probably were Samuel Nevill and John L. Johnston of Perth Amboy, N.J.

42 N.J. Committee for West-Jersey to Agent Joseph Sherwood Sept. 10., 1764, Woodward *Ploughs and Politics* 149–50. As to Reade, Smith, and Spicer, Kemmerer *N.J.* 360 with 1 *N.J. Col. Doc.* XXIV 625.

Chapter 19

1 Resolution of S.C. House Aug. 25, 1764, against British taxation of the colonies, S.C. House Journal 252.

2 S.C. Comm. of Corresp. to Agent Charles Garth Sept. 4, 1764, to oppose British taxation of the colonies, Gibbes *S.C. Doc. Hist.* 1764–66 1–6 at 2. (I have not found the original of this letter, the printed copy of which is defective; Gibbes's collection of documents is said to have been burned about the time of the American Civil War, Prof. Robert H. Woody of Duke University to me July 6, 1955.)

3 S.C. Comm. of Corresp. to Garth Sept. 4, 1764, protesting as to salt and as to Currency Act of 1764. In recommending no relaxation as to salt, the Board of Trade (*Journal B. of T.* 1764–1767, 9) ignored the colonial plea that English salt, whatever its price, was unsatisfactory because too mild and that only salt from the Bay of Biscay was suitable for curing meat for use in a hot climate, Gov. Arthur Dobbs of N.C. to B. of T. March 29, 1764, *N.C. Col. Rec.* VI 1030.

4 Proceedings of Va. House Nov. 1 and 14, 1764, in response to Mass. circular letter concerning British taxation of the colonies, *Va. Journals* 1761–1765, 233, 256–57.

5 As to Peyton Randolph and his family relations and influence, sketches in *D.A.B.* and Stannard "Randolph Family" and Sydnor *Gentlemen Freeholders* 97. As to Randolph and other colonial Middle Templars, Bedwell "American Middle Templars" 681–88.

6 The Va. protests against colonial taxation Dec. 18, 1764, *Va. Journals* 1761–1765, 302–4.

7 Va. Remonstrance to House of Commons as to levy of taxes only by those who share the burden, *same* 303. The "virtual" representation argument anticipated by this remonstrance was justly called by the colonists "fantastical and frivolous." Morgan *Stamp Act* 78. It was ably answered in Dulany *Considerations* (1765) 1–12 and Moore *Justice* (1765) reprinted in Boyd *Tracts* 165–74 at 167–71.

8 Va. Memorial to the House of Lords stating colonies "cannot" be represented in Parliament, *Va. Journals* 1761–1765, 303, thus in effect repudiating the plea for colonial representation in Parliament implicit in Otis *Rights* (1764) 70–71, 87. Later, in his *Considerations* (Boston, 1765), Otis stated that the proposal for colonial representation in Parliament is "generally much disliked in the colonies, and thought impracticable" Mullett *Writings of Otis* II 121.

9 Va. Comm. of Corresp. to Agent Edward Montague Dec. 20, 1764, transmitting the Va. protests *Va. Mag.* IX 354–55.

10 Address of N.C. House concerning British taxation of the colonies prepared by a committee headed by Thomas McGuire and adopted Oct. 21, 1764, *N.C. Col. Rec.* VI 1259, 1261.

11 My statement as to the other colonial legislatures not protesting is based on examination of their proceedings from May to December 1764, so far as available. Those, if any, of Delaware for 1764 are missing, Leon de Valinger, Jr., State Archivist of Delaware, to me April 7, 1953. No session of the Md. Legislature was held from Nov. 1763 to Sept. 1765, *Md. Arch.* vol. 59, xvii.

12 Proceedings of R.I. Legislature relative to British taxation July 1764 *R.I. Col. Rec.* VI 403.

13 The facts concerning Gov. Stephen Hopkins are drawn from the sketch of him in *D.A.B.* and Foster *Hopkins*. As to the attribution of the "Essay," *same* Part 2, 50 and Wiener "R.I. Merchants" 483–84.

14 Instructions of R.I. Legislature Sept. 1764 to its committee to circularize other colonies for united action, *R.I. Col. Rec.* VI 406, and the committee's circular letter of Oct. 8 to officials of other colonies, e.g., to the Speaker of the Pa. Assembly and to the Governor of Conn., Sparks *Franklin* VII 264–65, *Fitch* II 290–92. (The better known Mass. circular letter initiating the Stamp Act Congress of 1765 was not sent until June 1765, Bradford *Mass. Papers* 36.)

15 Warnings by British officials or former officials as to danger to Great Britain of a union of the colonies, Sir William Keith "Short Discourse" (1728) Hart *Am. History* II 140; statement of Comptroller Nathaniel Weare (Ware) 1 *Mass. Hist. Soc. Coll.* I 76–77; "Some Thoughts" March 10, 1763, Shelburne Papers 48:525–42; Sir Jeffery Amherst to Lord Egremont April 12, 1763, Amherst Papers Can. Arch.; Pownall *Administration* 36–37.

16 Proceedings of R.I. Legislature Oct. and Nov. 1764 as to colonial grievances, *R.I. Col. Rec.* VI 411–16.

17 *Rights of the Colonies Examined* dated "Providence in New-England, Nov. 30, 1764" reprinted *R.I. Col. Rec.* VI 416–27. Its official character appears from the inscription "Published by Authority" and the colony's payment for its printing, Alden *R.I. Imprints* 135. Attribution to Hopkins, *same* 134–35; copies sent to Agent Joseph Sherwood, Sherwood to Hopkins April 11, 1765, Kimball *R.I.* II 361–62.

18 Protests as to taxation in R.I. Address to the King and in Hopkins *The Rights* were confined to "stamp duties and other internal taxes," *R.I. Col. Rec.* VI 415, 421–25, at 422.

Chapter 20

1 Halifax to colonial Governors Aug. 11, 1764, for data as basis for colonial stamp tax *N.Y. Col. Doc.* VII 646, following reminder by Charles Jenkinson, joint Secretary to the Treasury, to George Grenville, July 2, 1764, that this information should be obtained, *Grenville* II 373.

2 Requested data sent to Halifax in Oct. 1764 by Governors Cadwallader Colden of N.Y., Horatio Sharpe of Md., Francis Bernard of Mass., Thomas Fitch of Conn., and Francis Fauquier of Va., *Colden* 1876, 405, *Sharpe* III 182, Bernard Papers III 188 Harv. Coll. Lib., *Fitch* II 296–98, (Fauquier) C.O. 5:1345:66–69.

3 Thomas Whately's plan accompanied by a table of British stamp duties, submitted to the Treasury Board Dec. 17, 1764 (Add. Mss. 35910:167–203, 310–23),

is in Hughes "Eng. Stamp Duties" 259–64. Its progress can be followed in a bill for services Sept. 1763 to July 1, 1765, probably by Thomas A. Cruwys, Solicitor to the Commissioners of Stamp Duties, who with Henry McCulloh, discussed in Chapter 6, were apparently Whately's chief collaborators, Add. Mss. 35910:137, 35911:1–37, 36226:353–55.

4   English newspaper reports of colonial opposition to proposed stamp tax, Laprade "Stamp Act" 764n; *London Chronicle* Sept. 1, 4, Oct. 2, 11, 25, 30, Nov. 29, Dec. 6, 8, 11, 1764; Mass. and N.Y. Assemblies' protests received by King, Privy Council minutes Dec. 19, *Acts P.C.* IV 692.

5   Conference of Grenville with colonial Agents as to the proposed colonial stamp tax, Jared Ingersoll to Fitch Feb. 11, 1765, *Fitch* II 317–26 at 324–25. To similar effect, Charles Garth to S.C. Comm. of Corresp. Feb. 8, Namier "Garth" 649. Thomas Pownall and Franklin wrote Grenville Feb. 12, enclosing an alternative plan to raise a colonial revenue by an act of Parliament providing for the issue of a general colonial paper currency, Franklin Mss. Yale Lib., Crane *Franklin's Letters to Press* 28–30.

6   Proceedings House of Commons Feb. 6 and 7, 1765, on proposed colonial stamp tax *Journals H. of C.* XXX 90, 97–101 with Garth to S.C. Comm. of Corresp. Feb. 8, Namier "Garth" 649–50; Richard Jackson and Ingersoll to Fitch Feb. 9 and 11, *Fitch* II 316–26; John Nelson to John Temple [between Feb. 15 and 27, 1765] *Bowdoin-Temple Papers* 46. The attack on the proposed tax was launched by a motion to adjourn the proceedings, Namier "Garth" 650.

7   Ingersoll to Fitch Feb. 11, 1765, reporting Col. Isaac Barré's speech *Fitch* II 321–23.

8   Garth to S.C. Comm. of Corresp. Feb. 8, 1765, as to vote, 245 to 49, in favor of a resolution for bill to levy a colonial stamp tax, Namier "Garth" 650; and proceedings of the House of Commons concerning the resolution and the bill Feb. 7 and 13, *Journals H. of C.* XXX 98–101, 131.

9   Proceedings House of Commons Feb. 15, 1765, *same* 147–48, with Ingersoll to Fitch March 6, 1765, *Fitch* II 332–35. On Dec. 11, 1764, the B. of T. had denounced the petitions of the Mass. and N.Y. Assemblies, discussed in Chapters 17 and 18, as showing "indecent disrespect" to Parliament and avowing "principles of a dangerous nature," *Journals B. of T.* 1764–1767, 122; also *Acts P.C.* IV 692.

10 Action on petitions submitted on second reading of stamp tax bill Feb. 15, 1765, and Gen. Henry Seymour Conway's speech denying the right of Parliament to tax the colonies, *Journals H. of C.* XXX 147–48 with Garth to S.C. Comm. of Corresp. Feb. 17, Namier "Garth" 650–51 and Ingersoll to Fitch March 6, *Fitch* II 332–35; *Boston Gazette* June 5; *Maryland Gazette* June 13; *Georgia Gazette* Aug. 1. The quotations are from *Fitch* II 334.

11 Ingersoll to Fitch March 6, 1765, describing the limited circle of members who opposed the tax bill, *Fitch* II 334.

12 Whately to Temple Feb. 9, 1765, as to importance of the proposed colonial tax as a precedent, Temple-Whately Letter Book, Stowe Coll. Huntington Lib., partly quoted in Morgan *Stamp Act* 63; Edward Sedgwick to Edward Weston Feb. 14, 1765, *Weston-Underwood* 382.

13 The stamp tax bill adopted, after some amendment, by the House of Commons Feb. 27, 1765, and the House of Lords March 8, *Journals H. of C.* XXX 192–93, 235. The amendments can be followed in the House of Commons minutes from Feb. 18 to 27, *same* 157, 160–61, 172, 192 and by comparing the resolutions adopted Feb. 6 and 7, *same* 97–101, with sections 1–11 of the act itself. I have found no evidence of any speech against the bill in the House of Lords.

14 The Stamp Act, 5 Geo. III ch. 12 (1765).

15 Heavy tax on newspaper advertisements and newspapers themselves secs. 1 and 12. As to the advertising rates of colonial newspapers, Schlesinger *Prelude* 68n. Franklin thought the new taxes would "go near to knock up" half the circulation and advertising of the colonial newspapers, Franklin to David Hall Feb. 4, 1765, Smyth *Franklin* IV 363. Another conspicuously high rate was the tax of £2 on diplomas from a college or academy. Sec. 58 provided that the duties and penalties imposed by the act should be payable in sterling money of Great Britain or its equivalent valued at 5s.6d. per ounce of silver.

16 Stamps procurable only on paper supplied by the British Government 5 Geo. III ch. 12 secs. 14 and 49. All the references I have seen concerning the arrival of stamps in the colonies refer to stamped paper, not stamps; perhaps dependable adhesives had not yet been developed.

17 5 Geo. III ch. 12 secs. 16, 21, 22, 32, and 58.

18 Stamp Act assented to March 22, 1765, by persons commissioned by the King on March 20, *Journals H. of C.* XXX 293, *Journals H. of L.* XXXI 91–93. Other acts relating to the colonies passed at this session included 5 Geo. III ch. 45, somewhat alleviating the hardships of the American Act of 1764 discussed in Chapter 15 and granting bounties on colonial lumber shipped to Great Britain, and 5 Geo. II ch. 33, containing a provision requiring the colonies to furnish supplies to British troops.

19 Historians' statement that the King was insane at this time, Lecky *History* III 96 (1888); Winstanley *Government* 219 (1910); Sedgwick *Bute* vii, lxv (1939); Namier *Personalities* 56 (1955); Bancroft *History* V 248 (1857), which states, "Be every sentiment of anger towards the King absorbed in pity. At the moment of passing the Stamp Act, George the Third was crazed."

20 The Appendix to Chapter XX of Knollenberg *Origin* (1960 ed.) gives my reasons for querying the view that George III was insane in 1765. I have found no evidence as to his attitude concerning the proposed stamp tax on the colonies.

Chapter 21

1 Va. Resolutions of May 29, 1765, denouncing the stamp tax, the first four in *Va. Journals* for 1761–1765, 360, the fifth in *same* lxvii; Meade *Henry* 171. In supporting these resolutions, Patrick Henry made his famous speech comparing George III to "a Tarquin, a Caesar, a Charles the First" and threatening him with "a Brutus or an Oliver Cromwell," *A.H.R.* XXVI 727, 745, quoting the *London Gazeteer* of Aug. 13, 1765, and the May 30 diary entry of an unidentified Frenchman.

2 The more fiery withheld resolutions are in Meade *Henry* 171 and *Va. Journals* for 1761–1765 lxvii. The reference to the "young, hot and giddy" members is in Gov. Francis Fauquier of Va. to B. of T. June 5, 1765, *same* lxviii.

3 Mass. resolutions and circular letter signed by Samuel White, Speaker, June 8, 1765, for an intercolonial congress are in Bradford *Mass. Papers* 35–36. The Mass. delegates were James Otis, Oliver Partridge, and Timothy Ruggles.

4 Members and proceedings of the Stamp Act Congress Oct. 7 to 25, 1765, Niles *Principles* 155–69; Morgan *Stamp Act* 102–15. Its members included Thomas Lynch, Christopher Gadsden, and John Rutledge of S.C., John Dickinson and John Morton of Pa., Thomas McKean and Caesar Rodney of Del., Eliphalet Dyer and William S. Johnson of Conn., Robert R. and Philip Livingston of N.Y., Edward Tilghman of Md., Metcalf Bowler of R.I., and Robert Ogden of N.J.

5 Proceedings of Stamp Act Congress Oct. 7 to 24, 1765, Niles *Principles* 155–68; Morgan *Stamp Act* 103–11. Eight colonial assemblies besides Virginia's House of Burgesses protested, Sept.–Dec. 1765, against the Stamp Act as violating colonial rights, Morgan *Prologue* 50–69. As to Timothy Ruggles, President of the Congress, Harvard, 1732, *D.A.B.* and Shipton *Harvard Graduates* IX 199–223.

6 Nonimportation movement of 1765–1766 Schlesinger *Col. Merchants* 78–82. A copy of the New York nonimportation agreement dated Oct. 31, 1765, is in Stevens *Col. Records* 313–14.

7 Gen. Thomas Gage wrote Secretary of State Henry Seymour Conway Sept. 23, 1765, "The general Scheme, concerted throughout, seems to have been first by Menace or Force to oblige the Stamp Officers to resign" *Gage* I 67. The Stamp Distributors are listed in Matthews "Book of America" 186–87.

8 Attack on Andrew Oliver of Mass. Aug. 14, 1765, Gov. Francis Bernard of Mass. to Lord Halifax Aug. 15 and 16 Bernard Papers IV 137–50; John Avery to John Collins Aug. 19 Stiles *Itineraries* 436–37. As to Oliver, Harvard, 1724, Secretary of Mass. and a member of the provincial Council, *D.A.B.* and Shipton *Harvard Graduates* VII 383–413.

9 Misrepresentations in colonial newspapers as to the Virginia resolves, *Newport Mercury* June 24, 1765; *Boston Gazette* July 1; *Maryland Gazette* July 4. As to the effect, Gage to Conway Sept. 23, 1765, stating "The Resolves of the Assembly of Virginia . . . gave the Signal for a general outcry over the Continent" *Gage* I 67. To same effect, Bernard to B. of T. Aug. 15, Bernard Papers IV 149–50; Chief Justice Thomas Hutchinson of Mass. to Thomas Pownall March 8, 1766, Quincy *Reports* 445.

10 Probable responsibility of Ebenezer Mackintosh, Boston shoemaker, and the "Loyall Nine" for the attack on Oliver, Henry Bass to Samuel Phillips Savage Dec. 19, 1765, Anderson "Mackintosh" 355–56. Though Bass's letter refers primarily to the Nine's putting renewed pressure on Oliver on Dec. 17, it speaks of their and Mackintosh's part in "the First Affair," presumably meaning the affair of Aug. 14. As to Mackintosh and the Loyal Nine, *same* 15–64, 348–61. As to the nine "Sons of Liberty," John Adams's diary Jan. 15, 1766, Adams *Works* II 178.

11 Later connection of Samuel and John Adams with the Sons of Liberty, Bass to Savage Dec. 19, 1765, Anderson "Mackintosh" 356; John Adams's diary for Dec.

19, 1765, and Jan. 15, 1766, and the Sons of Liberty and Thomas Crafts, Jr., to John Adams Feb. 5 and 15, 1766, Adams *Works* II 156, 178, 183–84, 184–85.

12 Attack on Augustus Johnson of R.I. at Newport, William Almy to Elisha Story Aug. 29, 1765, *M.H.S. Proc.* vol. 55 (1922) 235–37.

13 Resignation of James McEvers of N.Y. McEvers to Gov. Cadwallader Colden of N.Y. undated but marked "Received friday 30th of Aug [1765]" *Colden* 1923, 56–57 with Colden to Conway Sept. 23, 1765, *same* 1877, 34. Colden's determination to have stamped paper available for sale in N.Y. and storage of it in Fort George, Colden to Conway and David Colden to Comissioners of Stamps Oct. 26, 1765, *same* 47–49, 51.

14 "Vox Populi" notice Oct. 26, 1765, *N.Y. Col. Doc.* VII 770. Threat against Maj. Thomas James and riots of Oct. 31 and Nov. 1, Capt. John Montresor diary Oct. 31, 1765, *Montresor* 336–37 with Robert R. Livingston to Gen. Robert Monckton Nov. 8 *Aspinwall* II 560–67 and Colden to Conway Nov. 5, *Colden* 1877, 54–55. Colden had made himself highly unpopular by his position in the case of *Forsey v. Cunningham*, as to which see Labaree *Royal Government* 409–18; Smith *Appeals* 390–412.

15 Armed men throng to New York City, followed by taking of steps to assure nonissuance of stamped paper, Montresor diary Nov. 4 and 5, 1765, *Montresor* 338 with Colden to James Nov. 6 and to Conway Nov. 9 *Colden* 1877, 58–61, and Livingston to Monckton Nov. 8 *Aspinwall* II 563–67.

16 Attack on Hutchinson's home, Morgan *Stamp Act* 126–27; Shipton *Harvard Graduates* VII 174–76. As to probable reasons for the attack, Freiberg "Prelude" 113–20. As to similar vandalism at Newport, Morgan *Prologue* 109–13.

17 Alarm over mob violence, Gage to Conway Sept. 23, Dec. 21, 1765, *Gage* I 67–68, 78–79; Colden to Conway Sept. 23 *Colden* 1877, 36; Livingston to Monckton Nov. 8, *Aspinwall* II 566; James Otis to Henry Sherburne Nov. 26, sketch of Otis in *D.A.B.;* Samuel Gray to William S. Johnson Dec. 9 Schneider *Johnson* I 360; Ezra Stiles to Hutchinson Dec. 28, Zeichner *Conn.* 67; Roger Sherman to Matthew Griswold Jan. 11, 1766, Boardman *Sherman* 91.

18 Resignations of William Coxe of N.J. on Sept. 2, 1765, and George Meserve of N.H. on Sept. 10, Morgan *Stamp Act* 153–154; threats against Jared Ingersoll of Conn. and his resignation, Ingersoll's statement in *Connecticut Gazette* Sept. 23, and to Commissioners of Stamps Nov. 2 "Ingersoll Letters" 343–48, 354.

19 Pressure on John Hughes of Pa. and his promise not to serve, Hughes to various persons Sept. 7 to Nov. 7, 1765, *Prior Documents* 24, 45–57; Morgan *Stamp Act* 247–52.

20 Resignation of Caleb Lloyd of S.C., McCrady *South Carolina* 563–71; of William Houston of N.C., *N.C. Col. Rec.* VII 123–25, 131, 143–44, and vi–xi; Haywood "Stamp Act" 331–37; Haywood *Tryon* 32–36; Morgan *Stamp Act* 156.

21 Pressure on Col. George Mercer of Va. and his resignation, Supplement to *Virginia Gazette* (Royle) Oct. 31, 1765, and Fauquier to B. of T. Nov. 3 *Va. Journals* for 1761–1765 lxviii–lxx. As to Mercer and his distinguished family, Freeman *Washington* II and IV, Indexes under "Mercer, Col. George, James and John"; sketch of James Mercer in *D.A.B.*

22 Pressure for resignation of Zachariah Hood in Md., Smith *Carroll* 71–72; Gov. Horatio Sharpe to Cecilius Calvert Sept. 10, 1765, *Sharpe* III 222–26. Hood's flight to N.Y. and treatment there, Hood to Colden Sept. 16, Colden to Hood Sept. 16, and Colden to Conway Sept. 23 *Colden* 1923, 77–78, *same* 1877, 33 and 35–36. Hood's resignation, Montresor diary Nov. 28 *Montresor* 340 with *New York Mercury* Dec. 9.

23 George Angus's flight after selling some stamped paper in Ga., Morgan *Stamp Act* 157, 165–66. For related facts, Abbot *Ga.* 115–19; Coleman *Ga.* 21–22.

24 Execution of the Stamp Act in the other continental colonies—Nova Scotia: Kerr "Stamp Act in Nova Scotia" 552–66; Kerr "Merchants of Nova Scotia" 22–23; Brebner *The Neutral Yankees* 157–63; Barnes "Legge" 420–21. Quebec: Gov. James Murray of Quebec to Conway Feb. 14, 1766, *Can. Arch.* for 1890, Part 2, 15. East and West Fla.: Kerr "Stamp Act in the Floridas" 463–70; Mowat *East Florida* 34, 180; Howard *West Florida* 124–26. Various: Dickerson *Navigation Acts* 206.

25 Destruction of the stamped paper in St. Kitts and Nevis, *New-York Mercury* Dec. 9 and 23, 1765; *Maryland Gazette* Dec. 10, 1765, Jan. 13, 1766, April 17, 1766; Gov. George Thomas of the Leeward Islands to unnamed correspondent Dec. 21, 1765, Oliver *Antigua* I cxx; *Virginia Gazette* March 7, 1766; John Pinney to unnamed correspondent May 1766, MacInnes *Gateway of Empire* 271.

26 Stamped paper in the minor Island colonies—Bermuda; Kerr *Bermuda and the Am. Rev.* 26–27 and Wilkinson *Bermuda* 365; Bahamas: resignation of Distributor forced, *Pa. Gazette* Oct. 31, 1765, and Gov. William Shirley to Robert Treat Paine Jan. 31, 1766, saying no stamps had yet arrived, Paine Papers M.H.S.; Antigua: Harper and Hartshorne to Thomas Clifford Nov. 25, 1765, Clifford Papers, Hist. Soc. of Pa., letter from Antigua Dec. 20, *Dartmouth Papers* II 495 and *Maryland Gazette* Feb. 20, 1766; Grenada: George Champlin to Christopher Champlin Feb. 17, 1766, *R.I. Commerce* I 144.

27 Stamped paper in Jamaica and Barbados—Jamaica: Gov. William Lytellton to William Knox March 30, 1766, *H.M.C.* (Knox Papers) VI (1909) 92; Herbert "Constitutional Issues in Jamaica" (thesis) 183. Barbados: Barbados Assembly's statements Nov. 26 and Dec. 17, 1765, Whitson "West Indies" 80–81; Gov. Charles Pinfold to B. of T. Feb. 21, 1766, Pitman "Slavery" 588; Barbados Comm. of Corresp. to London Agent, undated, Ford *Dickinson's Writings* I 254. Both islands: Dickerson *Navigation Acts* 206.

28 Forecasts that difficulties from stoppage of business would induce use of stamped paper, Henry Laurens to Joseph Brown Oct. 11, 1765, Wallace *Laurens* 116–17; David Colden to Commissioners of Stamps Oct. 26 *Colden* 1877, 51; Ingersoll to Thomas Whately Nov. 2 "Ingersoll Letters" 352.

29 Newspapers published without stamps, Schlesinger *Prelude* 77–79 with Brigham *Am. Newspapers* I and II *passim*, under listings of the various colonial newspapers.

30 Customs clearances granted without stamps—Western Middle District, Randolph to Collector at Norfolk Nov. 2, 1765, *Pa. Mag. Hist.* II (1878) 298–99; Morgan *Stamp Act* 159–60; Eastern Middle District, Stewart to Commissioners of Customs, Dec. 7 *Md. Hist. Mag.* IV (1909) 135–37; Morgan *Stamp Act* 160–62, 168.

As to attitude of British naval officers in the colonies toward unstamped clearances, *same* 162, 165–66, 168; Kerr "Stamp Act in Nova Scotia" 563–64.

31 Customs forms (dated Dec. 31, 1765, in an unidentified hand) showing procedure in granting unstamped clearances, Miscellaneous Papers, Hist. Soc. of Pa.

32 Unstamped clearances in Northern District—Boston, Benjamin Hallowell, Comptroller at Boston to Charles Jenkinson Dec. 17, 1765, *Jenkinson* 402–3; New London, Conn., Duncan Stewart, Collector of Customs at New London, to John Temple Dec. 19, stating he began issuing clearances on unstamped paper December 14, *Pitkin* 276–77. Other ports and additional details as to Boston, Morgan *Stamp Act* 134–39, 151, 163–64.

33 Edmund Pendleton to James Madison Dec. 11, 1765, as to proving wills not made on stamped paper, 2 *Mass. Hist. Soc. Proc.* XIX (1905) 109.

34 Colonial debtors glad to have colonial courts shut, Henry Laurens to Joseph Brown Oct. 22, 1765, and William S. Johnson to Eliphalet Dyer Dec. 31, Morgan *Stamp Act* 169; George Washington to Francis Dandridge Sept. 20, 1765, *Washington* II 426.

35 Proceedings of various colonial courts and lawyers from Nov. 1, 1765, to March 1766, Morgan *Stamp Act* 139–43, 173, 176–77; Quincy *Reports* 198–217; *Adams* II 176–93 *passim;* Lovejoy *R.I. Politics* 118.

36 The Stamp Act was repealed on March 18, 1766, effective May 1, by the assent of George III acting by commission. *Journals H. of C.* XXX 667. The act of repeal was 6 Geo. III ch. 11. For details of the movements towards and proceedings for repeal: Morgan *Stamp Act* 263–80.

BOOKS AND OTHER PUBLICATIONS CITED

Unless otherwise stated, all publications cited are in the Yale University Library, some in photocopies only. In attributing authorship to anonymous books or pamphlets, I usually have followed attributions by others, especially Halkett and Laing (*H. & L. Dictionary of Anonymous . . . Literature*); unless otherwise stated, I have made no investigation of my own. The distinction between editor and compiler is often difficult to draw; some of those to whom I refer as "ed." (editor) would perhaps be more accurately described as compiler.

Where the title of a book or pamphlet is followed by a reference to the place and date of first publication in parentheses and also to a reprint, my citation or citations are to the reprint. Otherwise, the date given is the date of publication of the edition which I used, which in many cases was not the first edition. I usually have omitted the place of publication of items published after 1775 unless the item was published in more than one place in the same year, in which case the place of publication is given to identify the edition cited.

Giving 1775 as the closing date of a newspaper (e.g., 1731–1775) means that it was continued at least until 1775; in most cases it was continued beyond that date. Unless otherwise noted, the information as to colonial newspapers in the thirteen colonies is drawn from Brigham *History and Bibliography of American Newspapers 1690–1820*. All colonial newspapers were weeklies at the period dealt with in this book.

A.H.R. — *The American Historical Review.*

Abbot *Ga.* — William W. Abbot *The Royal Governors of Georgia 1754–1775* (1959).

Accarias De Serionne *Commerce de la Holland* — [Jacques Accarias de Serionne] *La Commerce de la Holland . . . dans les Quatres Parties du Monde . . .* (1768).

Acts PC. — William L. Grant and James Munro (eds.) *Acts of the Privy Council of England, Colonial Series* [1613–1783] 6 vols. (1908–1912).

Adams *Works* — Charles Francis Adams *The Works of John Adams* 10 vols. (1850–1856).

Adams & Stephens *Documents* — George Burton Adams and H. Morse Stephens *Select Documents of English Constitutional History* (1910).

Adams *Rev. New Eng.* — James Truslow Adams *Revolutionary New England 1691–1776* (1927).

Adams *Pol. Ideas* — Randolph G. Adams *Political Ideas of the American Revolution . . . 1765 to 1775* (1939).

Addison *Bass*—Daniel D. Addison *The Life and Times of Edward Bass* (1897).

Adolphus *History*—John Adolphus *The History of England from the Accession to the Decease of King George the Third* 7 vols. (1840–1845).

Aiton "Louisiana"—Arthur S. Aiton "The Diplomacy of the Louisiana Cession" *A.H.R.* XXXVI (1931) 701–20.

Albion *Forests and Sea Power*—Robert G. Albion *Forests and Sea Power: The Timber Problem of the Royal Navy 1652–1862* (1926).

Alden *R.I. Imprints*—John E. Alden *Rhode Island Imprints 1727–1800* (1949).

Alden *Gage*—John R. Alden *General Gage in America* . . . (1948).

Alden *Stuart*—John R. Alden *John Stuart and the Southern Colonial Frontier* . . . (1944).

Alden "Why the March"—John R. Alden "Why the March to Concord" *A.H.R.* vol. 49 (1944) 446–54.

"Allason Letters"—"The Letters of William Allason, Merchant, of Falmouth, Virginia" *Richmond Coll. Hist. Papers* II (1916–1917) 118–52.

Allen *Answer*—[William Allen] *Answer to Mr. Franklin's Remarks* (1764) in *Walker-Burd Letters* 99–131.

Almon *Pitt*—[John Almon] *Anecdotes of the Life of* . . . *William Pitt* . . . *with his Speeches in Parliament* 3 vols. (1810).

Almon *Prior Documents*—See *Prior Documents*.

Almon *Treaties*—[John Almon] *A Collection of all the Treaties* . . . *between Great-Britain and Other Powers* . . . [1688–1772] (London, 1772).

Almon *Wilkes*—[John Almon] *The Correspondence of the Late John Wilkes, with his Friends* . . . 5 vols. (1805).

Alvord "Genesis of the Proclamation"—Clarence W. Alvord "The Genesis of the Proclamation of 1763" *Mich. Pioneer Coll.* XXXVI (1908) 20–52.

Alvord *Mississippi Valley*—Clarence W. Alvord *The Mississippi Valley in British Politics* . . . 2 vols. (1917).

Am. Antiq. Soc. Proc.—*Proceedings of the American Antiquarian Society.*

American Chronicle—The *American Chronicle* New York City, March 20–July 22, 1762.

Am. Hist. Assoc. Rep.—*Annual Report of the American Historical Association.*

Amherst Journal—J. Clarence Webster *The Journal of Jeffery Amherst* . . . (1931).

Anderson "Mackintosh"—George P. Anderson "Ebenezer Mackintosh: Stamp Act Rioter and Patriot" *Col. Soc. Public.* XXVI (1927) 15–64, 348–61.

Andrews "The American Revolution"—Charles M. Andrews "The American Revolution: An Interpretation" *A.H.R.* XXXI (1926) 219–32.

Andrews "Anglo-French Rivalry"—Charles M. Andrews "Anglo-French Commercial Rivalry, 1700–1750 . . ." *A.H.R.* XX (1915) 539–56, 761–80.

Andrews "Col. Adm. Courts"—Charles M. Andrews "Vice-Admiralty Courts in the Colonies" in Towle *R.I. Admiralty* (1936) 1–79.

Andrews *Col. Period*—Charles M. Andrews *The Colonial Period* . . . 4 vols. (1934–1938).

Andrews "Commissions"—Charles M. Andrews "List of the Commissions and Instructions Issued to the Governors . . . 1609 to 1784" *Am. Hist. Assoc. Rep.* for 1911, I 393–528.

Andrews *Guide to Materials in Brit. Museum*—Charles M. Andrews and Frances G. Davenport *Guide to the Manuscript Materials for the History of the United States to 1783, in the British Museum* . . . [and certain minor English archives] (1908).

Andrews *Guide to P.R.O.*—Charles M. Andrews *Guide to the Materials . . . in the Public Record Office of Great Britain,* 2 vols. (1912–1914).

Andrews "State of Trade"—Charles M. Andrews "State of Trade," *Col. Soc. Publ.* XIX (1918) 379–90.

"Andrews Letters"—"Letters of John Andrews, Esq. of Boston 1772–1776" *Mass. Hist. Soc. Proc.* for 1864–1865, 316–412.

Andrews "The King's Pines"—Henry N. Andrews, Jr., "The King's Pines" *Historical N.H.* March 1947.

Annual Register—*The Annual Register, or a View of the History . . . of the Year* (1782 reprint).

Anson "Cabinet"—William R. Anson "The Cabinet in the Seventeenth and Eighteenth Centuries" *E.H.R.* XXIX (1914) 56–78.

Aplin *Verses*—[John Aplin] *Verses on Doctor Mayhew's Book of Observations . . . With Notes, critical and explanatory. By a Gentleman of Rhode-Island Colony.* (Providence, R.I., 1763). Attribution, Alden *R.I. Imprints* 112–13.

Appleton "Agents of New Eng."—Marguerite Appleton "The Agents of the New England Colonies in the Revolutionary Period" *New Eng. Q.* VI (1933) 371–87.

Appleton "Partridge"—Marguerite Appleton "Richard Partridge: Colonial Agent" *New Eng. Q.* V (1932) 293–309.

Appleton's Cyclopaedia—James Grant Wilson and John Fiske (eds.) *Appleton's Cyclopaedia of American Biography* (1887–1889).

Apthorp *Considerations*—East Apthorp *Considerations on the Institution and Conduct of the Society for the Propagation of the Gospel in Foreign Parts* (Boston, 1763).

Apthorp *Review of Dr. Mayhew's Remarks* (1765)—East Apthorp *A Review of Dr. Mayhew's Remarks on the Answer to his Observations . . .* (London, 1765).

Army List (Millan's)—*A List . . . of the Officers in the Several Regiments . . .* published annually by J. Millan, London.

Armytage *Free Port System*—Frances Armytage *The Free Port System in the British West Indies . . . 1766–1822* (1953).

Ashton *Economic Hist. of Eng.*—Thomas S. Ashton *An Economic History of England: The Eighteenth Century* (1955).

Aspinwall I and II—*The Aspinwall Papers* 4 *Mass. Hist. Soc. Coll.* IX and X.

Atlantic—*The Atlantic Monthly.*

B. of T. Journal—See *Journal B. of T.*

Balch *Letters*—Thomas Balch (ed.) *Letters and Papers Relating Chiefly to the Provincial History of Pennsylvania . . .* (1855). (Shippen family papers.)

Baldwin *New Eng. Clergy*—Alice M. Baldwin *The New England Clergy and the American Revolution* (1928).

Ballagh *Lee*—James C. Ballagh (ed.) *The Letters of Richard Henry Lee* 2 vols. (1911).

Ballantyne *Carteret*—Archibald Ballantyne *Lord Carteret: A Political Biography, 1690–1763* (1887).

Bancroft *History*—George Bancroft *History of the United States . . .* 10 vols. (1857–1874).

Barker *Md.*—Charles A. Barker *The Background of the Revolution in Maryland* (1940).

Barnes *English Corn Laws*—Donald G. Barnes *A History of the English Corn Laws from 1660–1846* (1930).

Barnes "Legge"—Victor F. Barnes "Francis Legge, Governor of Loyalist Nova Scotia 1773–1776" *New Eng. Q.* IV (1931) 420–47.

Barrington-Bernard Corresp.—Edward Channing and Archibald C. Coolidge (eds.) *The Barrington-Bernard Correspondence and Illustrative Matter 1760–1770* (1912).

Basye *Board of Trade*—Arthur H. Basye *The Lords Commissioners of Trade* . . . (1925).

Basye "Secretary of State"—Arthur H. Basye "The Secretary of State for the Colonies, 1768–1782" *A.H.R.* XXVIII (1923) 13–23.

Batchelder *Eastern Diocese*—Calvin R. Batchelder *A History of the Eastern Diocese* 2 vols. (1876, 1910).

Baxter *Hancock*—W. T. Baxter *The House of Hancock: Business in Boston 1724–1775* (1945).

Bean "War and the Brit. Col. Farmer"—Walton E. Bean "War and the British Colonial Farmer" *Pac. Hist. Rev.* XI (1942) 439–47.

Beardsley *Johnson*—Eben Edwards Beardsley *Life and Correspondence of Samuel Johnson, D.D. . . . First President of King's College, New York* (1874).

Beardsley *W. S. Johnson*—Eben Edwards Beardsley *Life and Times of William Samuel Johnson L.L.D. . . .* (1876).

Beatson *Naval and Military Memoirs*—Robert Beatson *Naval and Military Memoirs of Great Britain from 1727 to 1783* (1804).

Beatson *Pol. Index*—Robert Beatson *A Political Index* . . . (1788).

Beaven *Aldermen*—Alfred B. Beaven *The Aldermen of the City of London* 2 vols. (1913).

Becker *New York*—Carl L. Becker *The History of Political Parties in . . . New York, 1760–1776* (1909).

Bedford—John Russell (ed.) *Correspondence of John, Fourth Duke of Bedford* 3 vols. (1842–1846).

Bedwell "American Middle Templars"—C. E. A. Bedwell "American Middle Templars" *A.H.R.* XXV (1920) 680–89.

Beer *Brit. Col. Policy*—George Louis Beer *British Colonial Policy 1754–1765* (1907, reprinted 1933).

Beer *Comm. Policy*—George Louis Beer *The Commercial Policy of England Toward the American Colonies* (1893).

Beer *Old Colonial System*—George Louis Beer *The Old Colonial System 1660–1754* (runs only to 1688) 2 vols. (1912).

Beer *Origins*—George Louis Beer *The Origins of the British Colonial System 1578–1660* (1933).

Belcher *First Am. Civil War*—Henry Belcher *The First American Civil War* 2 vols. (1911).

Belcher Papers—Papers of Jonathan Belcher, 6 *Mass. Hist. Soc. Coll.* VI, VII.

Bell "West India Trade"—Herbert C. Bell "The West India Trade Before the American Revolution" *A.H.R.* XXII (1917) 272–87.

Benedict *American Admiralty*—Erastus C. Benedict *The American Admiralty: Its Jurisdiction and Practice* . . . (1870).

Benson *Kalm's Travels*—Adolph B. Benson (ed.) *Peter Kalm's Travels in North America: The English Version of 1770* 2 vols. (1937).

Bernard *Select Letters*—[Francis Bernard] *Select Letters on the Trade and Government of America* . . . (London, 1774).

Bezanson *Prices*—Anne Bezanson, Robert D. Gray, and Miriam Hussey *Prices in Colonial Philadelphia* (1935).

Bibl. Soc. Papers—*The Papers of the Bibliographical Society* [American].

Bibl. Soc. Transactions—*Transactions of the Bibliographical Society* [English].

Billington *Westward Expansion*—Ray A. Billington *Westward Expansion: A History of the American Frontier* (1949).

Bining *Col. Iron Indust.*—Arthur C. Bining *British Regulation of the Colonial Iron Industry* (1933).

Blackburne *Hollis*—[Francis Blackburne] *Memoirs of Thomas Hollis* . . . 2 vols. (1780).

Black's Law Dictionary—Henry C. Black *Black's Law Dictionary* (1933).

Blackstone *Analysis*—William Blackstone *An Analysis of the Laws of England* (Oxford, 1756). My references are to the 1756 edition, which (though the article on Blackstone in *D.N.B.* lists a 1754 edition) was, I think, the first.

Blackstone *Commentaries*—William Blackstone *Commentaries on the Laws of England,* first volume published in 1765. Unless otherwise noted, my citations are to Cooley's edition listed below under Cooley.

Bland *The Colonel Dismounted* (1764)—"Common Sense" [Richard Bland] *The Colonel Dismounted . . . In a Letter . . . Containing a Dissertation on the Constitution of the Colony* (Williamsburg, Va., 1764). Attribution, Earl G. Swem, sketch of Bland in *D.A.B.*

Bland *Inquiry* (1766)—Richard Bland *An Inquiry into the Rights of the British Colonies* (Williamsburg, Va., 1766).

Bland *Letter to the Clergy* (1760)—Richard Bland *A Letter to the Clergy of Virginia* (Williamsburg, Va., 1760).

Bland, Richard—See Ford *Fragment on the Pistole Fee.*

Blart *Rapports de la France et de l'Espagne*—Louis Blart *Les Rapports de la France et de l'Espagne après le pacte de famille* . . . (1915).

Bleackley *Ladies*—Horace Bleackley *Ladies Fair and Frail* . . . (1925).

Bleackley *Wilkes*—Horace Bleackley *Life of John Wilkes* (1917).

Blunt *Mrs. Montagu*—Reginald Blunt *Mrs. Montagu* . . . 2 vols. [1923].

Boardman *Sherman*—Roger S. Boardman *Roger Sherman: Signer and Statesman* (1938).

Bolingbroke *Parties*—Henry St. John, Viscount Bolingbroke *A Dissertation upon Parties* . . . Dublin (1735).

Bolton *Percy Letters*—Charles K. Bolton (ed.) *Letters of Hugh Earl Percy from Boston and New York 1774–1776* (1902).

Bond *Quit Rents*—Beverly W. Bond, Jr., *The Quit Rent System in the American Colonies* (1919).

Book of Common Prayer—*The Book of Common Prayer of the Church of England* . . . (Cambridge, England, 1761).

Boorstin *Americans*—Daniel J. Boorstin *The Americans: The Colonial Experience* (1958).

Boorstin *Blackstone's Commentaries*—Daniel J. Boorstin *The Mysterious Science of the Law: An Essay on Blackstone's Commentaries* (1941).

Boston Evening-Post—*The Boston Evening-Post* 1735–1775.

Boston Gazette—*The Boston-Gazette, and Country Journal* 1719–1775 (fervently Whig paper, after 1755 published by Benjamin Edes and John Gill).

Boston Massacre—*A Short Narrative of the Horrid Massacre in Boston* . . . (1849).

Boston Post-Boy—Green & Russell's *Boston Post-Boy & Advertiser* Jan. 1, 1759–May 23, 1763; *The Boston Post-Boy & Advertiser* May 30, 1763–1775.

Boston Records—A Report of the Record Commissioners of the City of Boston containing the Boston Town Records.

Boudin *Govt. by Judiciary*—Louis B. Boudin *Government by Judiciary* 2 vols. (1932).

Bouquet—Sylvester K. Stevens and Donald H. Kent (eds.) *The Papers of Col. Henry Bouquet* 18 vols. (1940–1943).

Bouquet Forbes—Sylvester K. Stevens *et al.* (eds.) *The Papers of Henry Bouquet* Vol. II *The Forbes Expedition* (1951).

Bouquet's Expedition—[William Smith 1727–1803] *Historical Account of Bouquet's Expedition . . . in 1764* (1868).

Bourne *Locke*—Henry R. Fox Bourne *Life of John Locke* 2 vols. (1876).

Bowdoin-Temple Papers—The Bowdoin and Temple Papers, 6 Mass. Hist. Soc. Coll. IX (1897).

Boyd *Jefferson*—Julian P. Boyd (Ed. in Chief) *The Papers of Thomas Jefferson; Volume I: 1760–1776* (1950).

Boyd *Susquehanna Co. Papers*—Julian P. Boyd (ed.) *The Susquehanna Company Papers* 4 vols. (1930–1933).

Boyd *Tracts*—William K. Boyd (ed.) *Some Eighteenth Century Tracts Concerning North Carolina* (1927).

Boyd *Union*—Julian P. Boyd *Anglo-American Union: Joseph Galloway's Plans . . . 1774–1788* (1941).

Bradford *Mayhew*—Alden Bradford *Memoir of the Life and Writings of Rev. Jonathan Mayhew, D.D.* (1838).

Bradford *Mass. Papers*—[Alden Bradford (ed.)] *Speeches of the Governors of Massachusetts . . . and Other Public Papers . . .* (1818).

"Bradstreet Manuscripts"—"A Calendar of the Manuscripts of Col. John Bradstreet . . ." *Am. Antiq. Soc. Proc.* XIX (1909) 103–81.

Braybrooke *Pepys*—Richard Neville, Lord Braybrooke (ed.) *The Diary of Samuel Pepys F.R.S. Secretary to the Admiralty . . .* (1906).

Brebner *New Eng. Outpost*—John B. Brebner *New England's Outpost: Acadia Before the Conquest of Canada* (1927).

Brebner *The Neutral Yankees*—John B. Brebner *The Neutral Yankees of Nova Scotia . . .* (1937).

Brecknock *Droit le Roy*—[Timothy Brecknock] *Droit le Roy; or, a Digest of the Rights and Prerogatives of the Imperial Crown of Great Britain* (London, 1764).

Brennan *Mass. 1760–1780*—Ellen E. Brennan *Plural Office-Holding in Massachusetts 1760–1780* (1945).

Brennan "Otis"—Ellen E. Brennan "James Otis: Recreant and Patriot" *New England Q.* XII (1939) 691–725.

Bridenbaugh *Cities*—Carl Bridenbaugh *Cities in the Wilderness* (1955).

Bridenbaugh *Cities in Revolt*—Carl Bridenbaugh *Cities in Revolt; Urban Life in America, 1743–1776* (1955) with separate pamphlet of footnotes.

Bridenbaugh *Myths and Realities*—Carl Bridenbaugh *Myths and Realities; Societies of the Colonial South* [1730–1776] (1952).

Bridenbaugh *Rebels and Gentlemen*—Carl and Jessica Bridenbaugh *Rebels and Gentlemen: Philadelphia in the Age of Franklin* (1942).

Bridgwater "Franklin"—Dorothy W. Bridgwater "Benjamin Franklin and Joshua Babcock . . ." *Yale Lib. Gazette* XXV (1951) 63–69.

Brigham *Am. Newspapers*—Clarence S. Brigham *History and Bibliography of American Newspapers 1690–1820* (1947).

Brooke *Chatham Administration*—John Brooke *The Chatham Administration 1766–1768* (1956).

Brown *Hancock*—Abram English Brown *John Hancock His Book* (1898).

Brown *Hawley*—E. [Ernest] Francis Brown *Joseph Hawley Colonial Radical* (1931).

Brown *Democracy in Mass.*—Robert E. Brown *Middle-Class Democracy and the Revolution in Massachusetts, 1691–1780* (1955).

Brown "Spanish Claims"—Vera Lee Brown "Spanish Claims to a Share in the Newfoundland Fisheries . . ." *The Canadian Historical Society Report for 1925* (1926) 64–82.

Browne *Remarks by a Son of the Church*—[Arthur Browne] *Remarks on Dr. Mayhew's Incidental Reflections . . . By a Son of the Church of England* (Portsmouth, N.H., 1763). Attribution, Perry *Mass.* 689.

Brydon *Va. Mother Church*—George Maclaren Brydon *Virginia's Mother Church . . .* 2 vols. (1947–1952).

Burke's *Peerage*—Bernard Burke and Ashworth P. Burke *A Genealogical History of the Peerage and Baronetcy* (80th ed., 1921).

Burke *Speeches*—Edmund Burke *Speeches and Letters on American Affairs* (Everyman's Library ed., 1942).

Burlamaqui *Principles of Natural Law*—Jean Jacques Burlamaqui *Principles of Natural Law . . .* (London, 1748). English translation of *Principes du droit naturel . . .* (1747).

Burn *Ecclesiastical Law*—Richard Burn *Ecclesiastical Law* 2 vols. (London, 1763).

Burnett *Letters*—Edmund C. Burnett (ed.) *Letters of Members of the Continental Congress* vol. 1 (1921).

Burns *Col. Agents*—James J. Burns *The Colonial Agents of New England* (1935).

Burns *Controversies*—John F. Burns *Controversies Between Royal Governors and Their Assemblies* (1923).

Burt *Quebec*—Alfred L. Burt *The Old Province of Quebec* (1933).

Bute—Romney Sedgwick *Letters from George III to Lord Bute 1756–1766* (1939).

Butler *Franklin, Postmaster General*—Ruth Lapham Butler *Doctor Franklin, Postmaster General (1928)*.

Caldwell—William Mure (ed.) *Selections from the Family Papers at Caldwell* 2 parts in 3 vols. (1854). *See also* Mure.

Caldwell *French in Miss. Valley*—Norman W. Caldwell *The French in the Mississippi Valley 1740–1750* (1941).

Calendar H.O. Papers—Joseph Redington and Richard A. Roberts (eds.) *Calendar of Home Office Papers . . . 1760–1775* 4 vols. (1878–1899).

Calendar State Papers—William Noel Sainsbury and others (eds.) *Calendar of State Papers, Colonial Series, America and West Indies*.

Calendar Treas. Books—*Calendar of Treasury Books*, W. A. Shaw (ed.).

Calendar Treas. Books and Pap.—*Calendar of Treasury Books and Papers,* W. A. Shaw (ed.).

Calendar Treas. Pap.—*Calendar of Treasury Papers,* Joseph Redington (ed.).

Camm *A Review of the Rector Detected* (1764)—[John Camm] *A Review of the Rector Detected; or, the Colonel Reconnoitred. Part the First* . . . (Williamsburg, Va., 1764). Attribution, Smith "Parson's Cause" 297.

Camm *A Single and Distinct View* (1763)—John Camm *A Single and Distinct View of the Act, Vulgarly Entitled the Two-Penny Act* (Annapolis, Md., 1763).

Can. Arch.—*Canadian Archives Report* (various years).

Can. H.R.—*The Canadian Historical Review.*

Canby "Gilmer"—Courtlandt Canby "The Commonplace Book of Doctor George Gilmer" *Va. Mag. Hist.* vol. 56 (1948) 379–407.

Caner *Candid Examination*—[Henry Caner] *A Candid Examination of Dr. Mayhews Observations* (Boston, 1763). Attribution, Perry *Mass.* 689, substantiated by Rev. Samuel Johnson to Archbishop Secker, Dec. 20, 1763, Beardsley *Johnson* 278.

Cannon "McCulloh"—John Cannon "Henry McCulloch and Henry McCulloh" 3 *W. & M. Q.* XV (1958) 71–73.

Cappon *Virginia Gazette Index*—Lester J. Cappon and Stella F. Duff *Virginia Gazette Index 1736–1780* (1950).

Care *English Liberties*—Henry Care and William Nelson *English Liberties or the Free-born Subjects Inheritance* (Fourth ed., London, 1719; fifth, Boston, 1721; sixth, Providence, R.I., 1774). My references are to the 1774 edition.

Carlton "New England Masts"—William R. Carlton "New England Masts and the King's Navy" *New Eng. Q.* XII (1939) 4–18.

Carman *Am. Husbandry*—Harry J. Carman (ed.) *American Husbandry* (1939).

Carpenter *Am. Pol. Thought*—William S. Carpenter *The Development of American Political Thought* (1930).

Carpenter *Sherlock*—Edward Carpenter *Thomas Sherlock, 1678–1761, Bishop of* . . . *London* (1936).

Carroll Letters—Thomas Meagher Field (ed.) *Unpublished Letters of Charles Carroll of Carrollton* . . . (1902).

Carter, Clarence E.—See *Gage.*

Carter "Commander in Chief"—Clarence E. Carter "The Office of Commander in Chief . . ." in Morris *Era* 170–213.

Carter *Illinois Country*—Clarence E. Carter *Great Britain and the Illinois Country 1763–1774* (1910).

Carter *A Letter from Virginia*—[Landon Carter] *A Letter from a Gentleman in Virginia to the Merchants of Great Britain* (London, 1754).

Carter *A Letter to the B_____ of L_____* (1760)—Landon Carter *A Letter to the . . . B_____ of L_____* . . . (1760).

Carter *The Rector Detected* (1764)—Landon Carter *The Rector Detected: Being a Just Defence of the Two-Penny Act* . . . (1764).

Carter "West Florida"—Clarence E. Carter "Some Aspects of British Administration in West Florida" *Miss. Vall. H.R.* I (1915) 364–75.

Chalmers *Opinions*—George Chalmers (ed.) *Opinions of Eminent Lawyers* . . . (1858).

Channing *History*—Edward Channing *A History of the United States* vols. 2 and 3 (1924).

Charlemont—H.M.C. *Report on the Manuscripts of Lord Charlemont* 12th Rep. (1891) App. Part 10, 276.

Chesterfield—Lord Mahon (Philip Henry Stanhope) *The Letters of Philip Dormer Stanhope, Earl of Chesterfield* . . . 5 vols. (1892).

Christelow "Contraband Trade"—Allan Christelow "Contraband Trade . . . and the Free Port Act of 1766" *Hisp. Am. Hist. Rev.* XXII (1942) 309–43.

Christelow "Economic Background of Anglo-Spanish War"—Allan Christelow "Economic Background of Anglo-Spanish War of 1762" *Journ. Mod. Hist.* XXVII (1946) 22–36.

Christelow "Great Britain and the Trades from Cadiz and Lisbon 1759–1783"—Allan Christelow "Great Britain and the Trades from Cadiz and Lisbon to Spanish America and Brazil, 1759–1783" *Hisp. Am. Hist. Rev.* XXVII (1947) 2–29.

Church History—*Church History*, a quarterly published in Chicago, Ill., by The American Society of Church History.

Churchill *Prophecy of Famine*—Charles Churchill *The Prophecy of Famine* . . . (London, 1763).

Clark "Grenville"—Dora Mae Clark "George Grenville as First Lord of the Treasury . . ." *Hunt. Lib. Q.* XIII (1950) 383–97.

Clark "Impressment"—Dora Mae Clark "The Impressment of Seamen in the American Colonies" *Essays in Colonial History*, 198–224.

Clark "Secretary to the Treasury"—Dora Mae Clark "The Office of Secretary to the Treasury in the Eighteenth Century" *A.H.R.* vol. 42 (1937) 22–45.

Clark *St. John's*—Samuel A. Clark *The History of St. John's Church, Elizabeth Town, New Jersey from the Year 1703* . . . (1857).

Clark *Manufactures*—Victor S. Clark *History of Manufactures in the United States* (1916).

Clarke "Board of Trade"—Mary Patterson Clarke "The Board of Trade at Work" *A.H.R.* XVII (1912) 17–43.

Clarke *Liturgy*—William K. Louther Clarke *Liturgy and Worship: A Companion to the Prayer Book* . . . (1932).

Clarke *Parl. Privilege*—Mary Patterson Clarke *Parliamentary Privilege in the American Colonies* (1943).

Clayton-Torrence—William Clayton-Torrence *A Trial Bibliography of Colonial Virginia, 1754–1776*, 2 vols. (1908–1910).

Clive and Bailyn "England's Cultural Provinces"—John Clive and Bernard Bailyn "England's Cultural Provinces: Scotland and America" 3 *W. & M. Q.* XI (1954) 200–213.

Clode *Military Forces*—Charles M. Clode *The Military Forces of the Crown* (1869).

Coffin *Quebec*—Victor Coffin *The Province of Quebec and the Early American Revolution* (1896).

Coke *Institutes*—Edward Coke *The First Part of the Institutes of the Laws of England; or, a Commentary upon Littleton* . . . (1628). My references are to the thirteenth (London, 1788) edition.

Coke *Reports*—Edward Coke *Reports*. Many editions from 1600–1615. My references are to the 1738 edition.

Colden—*N.Y. Hist. Soc. Coll.* for 1876, 1877, 1920, 1922, 1923, 1924.

Cole *Wool*—Arthur H. Cole *The American Wool Manufacture* 2 vols. (1926).

Cole and Postgate *Brit. People*—George D. H. Cole and Raymond Postgate *The British People 1746–1946* (1947).

Coleman *Ga.*—*The American Revolution in Georgia 1763–1789* (1958).

Coll. Prot. Episc. Hist. Soc.—*Collections of the Protestant Episcopal Historical Society.*

Collins "Committees"—Edward D. Collins "Committees of Correspondence of the American Revolution" *Am. Hist. Assoc. Rep.* for 1901 I 243–71.

Col. Soc. Publ.—*Publications of the Colonial Society of Massachusetts.*

Columbia Law Rev.—*Columbia Law Review.*

Commager *Documents*—Henry Steele Commager (ed.) *Documents of American History* (1938).

Comparative Importance of Our Acquisitions—*The Comparative Importance of Our Acquisitions from France in America* (London, 1762). Author unidentified.

Comyns *Digest*—Sir John Comyns *A Digest of the Laws of England* 5 vols. (London, 1762–1767).

Conduct—*The Detail and Conduct of the American War* (3rd ed., London, 1780). Compiler unidentified.

Conn. Col. Rec.—Charles J. Hoadly (ed.) *The Public Records of the Colony of Connecticut* vols. 11 to 14 (1880–1887).

Connecticut Courant—*The Connecticut Courant* Hartford, Conn., Oct. 29, 1764–1775.

Conn. Hist. Soc. Coll.—*Collections of the Connecticut Historical Society.*

Considerations—See Mauduit *Considerations.*

Contest in America—*The Contest in America Between Great Britain and France* (London, 1757). Attributed to John Mitchell.

Cooley's *Blackstone*—Thomas M. Cooley (ed.) William Blackstone, *Commentaries on the Laws of England* 2 vols. (1884). (Citations are to the starred numbers in the body of the text.)

Cooper, Samuel *A Sermon Preached Before His Excellency Thomas Pownall Esq. . . .* (Boston, 1759).

Cooper *S.C. Statutes*—Thomas Cooper and David J. McCord (eds.) *The Statutes at Large of South Carolina* vols. 2 to 4 (1836–1841).

Corbett *England*—Julian S. Corbett *England in the Seven Years' War . . .* 2 vols. (1918).

Corwin "Higher Law"—Edward S. Corwin "The 'Higher Law' Background of American Constitutional Law" *Harv. Law Rev.* vol. 42 (1929) 149–85, 365–409.

Corwin *Liberty*—Edward S. Corwin *Liberty Against Government . . .* (1948).

Corwin's review—Edward S. Corwin's review of McIlwain *Amer. Rev.* in *A.H.R.* XXIX (1924) 775–78.

Coulter *Granville District*—E. Merton Coulter *The Granville District* (1913).

Court Kalendar—*The Court and City Kalendar; or, Gentleman's Register . . . for 1764* (London, 1764).

Coxe *Pelham*—William Coxe *Memoirs of the Administration of the Right Honourable Henry Pelham . . .* 2 vols. (1829).

Crane "Certain Writings"—Verner W. Crane "Certain Writings of Benjamin Franklin on the British Empire and the American Colonies" *Bibl. Soc. Papers* XXVIII, Part I (1934) 1–27.

Crane *Franklin's Letters to Press*—Verner W. Crane *Benjamin Franklin's Letters to the Press 1758–1775* (1950).

Crane "Hints"—Verner W. Crane "Hints Relative to . . . America" *Miss. Vall. Hist. Rev.* VIII (1922) 367–73.

Critical Period—Clarence W. Alvord and Clarence E. Carter (eds.) *The Critical Period, 1763–1765 Ill. State Hist. Lib. Coll.* X (1915).

Crittenden *N.C. Commerce*—Charles C. Crittenden *The Commerce of North Carolina, 1763–1789* (1936).

"Croghan's Journal"—Nicholas B. Wainwright (ed.) "George Croghan's Journal 1759–1763" *Pa. Mag. Hist.* vol. 71 (1947) 305–444.

Cross *Anglican Episcopate*—Arthur L. Cross *The Anglican Episcopate and the American Colonies* (1902).

Crump *Col. Adm. Jurisdiction*—Helen J. Crump *Colonial Admiralty Jurisdiction in the Seventeenth Century* (1931).

Curti *American Thought*—Merle Curti *Growth of American Thought* (1943).

Curti "The Great Mr. Locke"—Merle Curti "The Great Mr. Locke, America's Philosopher, 1783–1861" *Huntington Lib. Bull.* No. 11 (1937) 107–51.

Cushing *S. Adams*—Harry A. Cushing (ed.) *The Writings of Samuel Adams* 4 vols. (1904–1908).

Cust *Cust Family*—Lionel Cust (ed.) *Records of the Cust Family* Ser. III (1927).

D.A.B.—*Dictionary of American Biography* 21 vols. (1943), Supplement One (1944).

D.N.B.—*Dictionary of National Biography* (English) 21 vols. (1908–1909) Supplement One (1909).

Dartmouth Papers—*The Manuscripts of the Earl of Dartmouth vol. II; H.M.C.* 14th Rep., App. Part X (1895).

Davenport *Treaties*—Frances G. Davenport and Charles O. Paullin (eds.) *European Treaties Bearing on the History of the United States . . .* (1937).

Davidson *Propaganda 1763–1783*—Philip Davidson *Propaganda and the American Revolution 1763–1783* (1941).

Davis "Frost v. Leighton"—Andrew McF. Davis "The Case of Frost vs. Leighton" *A.H.R.* II (1897) 222–40.

Dawson *Sons of Liberty*—Henry B. Dawson *The Sons of Liberty in New York* (1859).

Defoe *Tour*—Daniel Defoe *A Tour Through England and Wales* 3 vols. (London, 1724–1727). I used the 1928, 2 vols., reprint.

De Voe *Market Book*—Thomas De Voe *The Market Book . . .* (1862).

Dexter *Yale Biographies*—Franklin Bowditch Dexter *Biographical Sketches of the Graduates of Yale College* [from 1701 to 1778] 3 vols. (1885–1903). See also *Ingersoll* and *Stiles Itineraries*.

Dicey *Law of the Const.*—Albert V. Dicey *Introduction to the Study of the Law of the Constitution* (1915).

Dickerson *Boston*—Oliver M. Dickerson *Boston Under Military Rule 1768–1769 . . .* (1936).

Dickerson *Col. Govt.*—Oliver M. Dickerson *American Colonial Government . . .* (1912).

Dickerson *Navigation Acts*—Oliver M. Dickerson *The Navigation Acts and the American Revolution* (1951).

Dickerson "Writs"—Oliver M. Dickerson "Writs of Assistance . . ." Morris *Era* 40–75.

Dickins *Corresp.*—Lilian Dickins and Mary Stanton (eds.) *An Eighteenth Century Correspondence, Being the Letters . . . to Sanderson Miller . . .* (1910).

Dickinson *A Speech on a Petition* (1764)—John Dickinson *A Speech Delivered in the House of Assembly . . . On Occasion of a Petition . . . for a Change of the Government . . .* (Philadelphia, 1764) in Ford *Dickinson* I 9–49.

Dickinson *Late Regulations*—John Dickinson *The Late Regulations Respecting the British Colonies Considered* (Philadelphia, 1765), Ford *Dickinson* I 207–45.

Dickinson *Letters from a Farmer* (1768)—John Dickinson *Letters from a Farmer in Pennsylvania to the Inhabitants of the British Colonies* (Philadelphia, 1768). Ford *Dickinson* I 1277–406.

Dillon *New York Triumvirate*—Dorothy R. Dillon *The New York Triumvirate . . .* (William Livingston, John Morin Scott, and William Smith, Jr.) (1949).

Dinwiddie—Robert A. Brock (ed.) *The Official Records of Robert Dinwiddie . . . 1751–1758* 2 vols. (1883–1884).

Dobrée *Geo. III*—Bonamy Dobrée (ed.) *The Letters of King George III* (1935).

Dodington—Henry P. Wyndham (ed.) *The Diary of the Late Bubb Dodington, Baron of Melcombe Regis . . .* [1749–1761] (1785).

Dorland *Royal Disallowance in Massachusetts*—Arthur G. Dorland *The Royal Disallowance in Massachusetts* (1917).

Dorn "Frederic the Great"—Walter L. Dorn "Frederic the Great and Lord Bute" *Journ. Mod. Hist.* I (1929) 529–60.

Dorr *Hist. Account*—Benjamin Dorr *A Historical Account of Christ Church, Philadelphia . . .* (1859).

Douglass *Rebels and Democrats*—Elisha P. Douglass *Rebels and Democrats: The Struggle for Equal Political Rights and Majority Rule During the American Revolution* (1955).

Douglass *Summary*—William Douglass *A Summary Historical and Political . . . of the British Settlements in North America . . .* 2 vols. (Boston 1749–1751).

Drake *Tea Leaves*—Francis Drake *Tea Leaves; Being a Collection of Letters and Documents . . .* (1884).

Dulany *Considerations* (1765)—Daniel Dulany *Considerations on the Propriety of Imposing Taxes in the British Colonies, for the Purpose of Raising a Revenue, by Act of Parliament* (Annapolis, 1765). I have used the first London (1766) edition.

Dulles *Old China Trade*—Foster Rhea Dulles *The Old China Trade* (1930).

Dummer *Defence*—Jeremiah Dummer *A Defence of the New-England Charters* (London, 1721).

Dunbar "Royal Governors"—Louise B. Dunbar "The Royal Governors in the Middle and Southern Colonies on the Eve of the Revolution . . ." [1754–1775] Morris *Era* 214–68.

E.H.R.—*The English Historical Review*.

Eaton "Mirror"—Clement Eaton "A Mirror of the Southern Colonial Lawyer . . . Fee Books" 3 *W. & M. Q.* VIII (1951) 520–34.

Eddis *Letters*—William Eddis *Letters from America . . . 1769 to 1777 inclusive* (London, 1792).

Eddy *Franklin & Hall*—George Simpson Eddy *A Work-Book of the Printing House of Benjamin Franklin and David Hall 1759–1766* (1930).

Edwards *West Indies*—Bryan Edwards *The History Civil and Commercial of the British Colonies in the West Indies* 3 vols. (1794–1801).

Elliot—George F. S. Elliot *The Border Elliots . . .* (1897).

Ellis—Henry Ellis *Original Letters Illustrative of English History . . .* 2nd Ser. (1827).

Ellis *Sermon Preached Before the Society*—Anthony Ellis, Bishop of St. David's, *A Sermon Preached Before the Incorporated Society for the Propagation of the Gospel in Foreign Parts* (London, 1759).

Elsey "Wilkes and Palfrey"—George M. Elsey "John Wilkes and William Palfrey" *Col. Soc. Publ.* XXXIV (1943) 411–28.

Ericson *Brit. Col. System*—Frederic J. Ericson *The British Colonial System and the Question of Change of Policy . . .* (Chicago, 1943).

Ericson "Stamp Act"—Frederic J. Ericson "The Contemporary British Opposition to the Stamp Act, 1764–65" *Papers Mich. Academy* XXIX (1943) 490–504.

"Essay"—"An Essay on the Trade of the Northern Colonies" in *Providence Gazette* Jan. 14 and 21, 1764.

Essay on Woman—*An Essay on Woman and other pieces . . .* (London, 1871).

Essays in Colonial History—*Essays in Colonial History Presented to Charles McLean Andrews . . .* (1931).

Essex Gazette—*The Essex Gazette* (Salem, Mass., 1768–1775).

Everett "Last Royal Veto"—William Everett "The Last Royal Veto" 2 *Mass. Hist. Soc. Proc.* V 156–64.

Ewing "Indian Captives"—William S. Ewing "Indian Captives Released by Colonel Bouquet" *West. Pa. Hist. Mag.* XXXIX (1956) 187–203.

Farrand "The Indian Boundary Line"—Max Farrand "The Indian Boundary Line" *A.H.R.* X (1905) 782–91.

Farrand "Taxation of Tea"—Max Farrand "The Taxation of Tea, 1767–1773" *A.H.R.* III (1898) 266–69.

Faulkner *Am. Economic Hist.*—Harold U. Faulkner *American Economic History* (1943).

Felkin *Hist. of Machine-Wrought Hosiery*—William Felkin *A History of the Machine-Wrought Hosiery and Lace Manufactures* (1867).

Ferguson *Dempster*—James Ferguson (ed.) *Letters of George Dempster to Sir Adam Ferguson, 1756–1813 . . .* (1934).

Fermin *Description de Surinam*—Philippe Fermin *Description générale . . . de la Colonie de Surinam* 2 vols. (1769).

Firth and Rait *Acts and Ordinances*—Charles H. Firth and Robert S. Rait *Acts and Ordinances of the Interregnum, 1642–1660* 3 vols. (1911).

Fisher *Struggle for Independence*—Sydney G. Fisher *The Struggle for American Independence* 2 vols. (1908).

Fisher *True Hist. of Am. Rev.*—Sydney G. Fisher *The True History of the American Revolution* (1902).

Fitch—Albert C. Bates (ed.) *The Fitch Papers . . . Conn. Hist. Soc. Coll.* XVII, XVIII (1918, 1920).

Fitzpatrick *Washington*—John C. Fitzpatrick (ed.) *The Writings of George Washington* vols. 1 to 3 (1931).

Fla. Hist. Q.—*The Florida Historical Quarterly.*

Flippin *Fin. Adm. of Va.*—Percy Scott Flippin *The Financial Administration of the Colony of Virginia* (1915).

Flippin *Va.*—Percy Scott Flippin *The Royal Government in Virginia 1624–1775* (1919).

Foner *Jefferson*—Philip S. Foner (ed.) *Basic Writings of Thomas Jefferson* (1944).

Foord "Influence of the Crown"—Archibald S. Foord "The Waning of 'The Influence of the Crown' " *E.H.R.* LXII (1947) 484–507.

Foote *King's Chapel*—Henry Wilder Foote *Annals of King's Chapel* 2 vols. (1882, 1896).

Forbes—Alfred P. James (ed.) *Writings of General John Forbes* . . . (1938).

Forbes "Greenwich Hosp. Money"—Allyn B. Forbes "Greenwich Hospital Money" *New Eng. Q.* III (1930) 519–26.

Force *Am. Archives*—Peter Force (ed.) *American Archives* . . . Fourth Series 6 vols. (1837–1846).

Ford *Dickinson*—Paul Leicester Ford (ed.) *The Writings of John Dickinson* (1895).

Ford *Fragment on the Pistole Fee*—Worthington Chauncey Ford (ed.) *A Fragment on the Pistole Fee, claimed by the Governor of Virginia, 1753* (1891), being Richard Bland's A Modest and True State of the Case, written about 1753.

Ford *Franklin Bibliography*—Paul Leicester Ford *Franklin Bibliography* . . . (1889).

Ford "French Edicts"—Worthington Chauncey Ford "French Royal Edicts, etc. on America" *Mass. Hist. Soc. Proc.* vol. 60, 250–304.

Ford "Shirley"—Amelia C. Ford (ed.) "William Shirley to Samuel Waldo" *A.H.R.* XXXVI (1931) 350–60.

Ford "Wilkes and Boston"—Worthington Chauncey Ford "John Wilkes and Boston" *Mass. Hist. Soc. Proc.* vol. 47, 190–215.

Foster *Hopkins*—William Eaton Foster *Stephen Hopkins (Rhode Island Historical Tracts* No. 19, 2 parts, 1874).

Fox *Heathcote*—Dixon Ryan Fox *Caleb Heathcote* . . . *1692–1721* (1926).

Frank "Sketch of an Influence"—Jerome N. Frank "A Sketch of an Influence" [Blackstone] in Sayre *Interpretations* 189–261.

Franklin *Cool Thoughts*—Benjamin Franklin *Cool Thoughts on the Present Situation of Our Public Affairs* . . . (Philadelphia, Apr. 1764) Smyth *Franklin* IV 226–41.

Franklin *Interest of Great Britain* (1760)—Benjamin Franklin *The Interest of Great Britain Considered with Regard to her Colonies* . . . (London, 1760, reprinted Boston, Philadelphia, Dublin, 1760) Smyth *Franklin* IV 32–82.

Franklin *Remarks*—Benjamin Franklin *Remarks on a Late Protest against the Appointment of Mr. Franklin as Agent for this Province* (Philadelphia, 1764) in Smyth *Franklin* IV 273–85.

Freeman *Washington*—Douglas Southall Freeman *George Washington: A Biography* 6 vols. (1948–1954).

Freiberg "Bollan"—Malcolm Freiberg "William Bollan, Agent of Massachusetts" *More Books: The Monthly Bulletin of the Boston Public Library* XXIII (1948) 43–220 *passim.*

Freiberg "Hutchinson"—Malcolm Freiberg "Thomas Hutchinson: The First Fifty Years (1711–1761)" 3 *W. & M. Q.* XV (1958) 35–55.

Freiberg "Hutchinson and the Currency"—Malcolm Freiberg "Thomas Hutchinson and the Province Currency" *New Eng. Q.* XXX (1957) 190–208.

Freiberg "Letter"—Malcom Freiberg "Missing: One Hutchinson Autograph Letter," *Manuscripts* VIII (1956) 179–84.

French *British Fusilier*—Allen French *A British Fusilier in Revolutionary Boston . . .* (1926).

French *First Year*—Allen French *The First Year of the American Revolution* (1934).

French *Gage*—Allen French *General Gage's Informers . . .* (1932).

French *The Day*—Allen French *The Day of Concord and Lexington . . .* (1925).

Frese "Otis"—Joseph R. Frese "James Otis and Writs of Assistance" *New Eng. Q.* XXX (1957) 496–508.

Frothingham "Tea Party"—Richard Frothingham "Tea-Party Anniversary" *Mass. Hist. Soc. Proc.* for 1873–1875, 155–83.

Frothingham *Warren*—Richard Frothingham *Life and Times of Joseph Warren* (1865).

Fry *New Hampshire*—William H. Fry *New Hampshire as a Royal Province* (1908).

Full State—A *Full State [Statement] of the Dispute betwixt the Governor and the Commons House of Assembly of . . . South Carolina . . . As transmitted to their Agent in Great Britain* [London] (1763).

Furneaux *Letters to Blackstone*—Philip Furneaux *Letters to the Honourable Mr Justice Blackstone . . .* (London, 1770). My references are to the Philadelphia, 1773, edition.

Ga. Col. Rec.—Allen D. Candler (ed.) *The Colonial Records of the State of Georgia* 26 vols. (1904–1906).

Ga. Hist. Q.—*The Georgia Historical Quarterly.*

Gage—Clarence E. Carter (ed.) *The Correspondence of General Thomas Gage . . . 1763–1775* 2 vols. (1931, 1933).

Gentleman's Mag.—*The Gentleman's Magazine and Historical Chronicle* (London 1731–1775).

George III—Sir John Fortescue *The Correspondence of King George the Third . . .* 6 vols. (1927–1928). Volume I, covering the years 1760–1767, of this wretchedly edited work has been corrected in Namier *Additions,* which should be consulted constantly in using this volume.

Georgia Gazette—*The Georgia Gazette* (Savannah) 1763–1775.

Gewehr *Great Awakening in Va.*—Wesley M. Gewehr *The Great Awakening in Virginia* (1930).

Gibbes *S.C. Doc. Hist. 1764–1776*—Robert W. Gibbes *Documentary History of the American Revolution . . . in South Carolina . . . 1764–1776* (1885).

Gibson *Thirty-Nine Articles*—Edgar C. S. Gibson *The Thirty-Nine Articles . . .* 2 vols. (1896–1897).

Giddens "Md."—Paul H. Giddens "Trade and Industry in Colonial Maryland, 1753–1769" *Journ. Ec. & Bus. Hist.* IV (1932) 512–38.

Giesecke *Am. Comm. Legis. before 1789*—Albert H. Giesecke *American Commercial Legislation before 1789* (1910).

Gilboy *Wages*—Elizabeth W. Gilboy *Wages in Eighteenth Century England* (1934).

Gipson "Aspects"—Lawrence H. Gipson "Aspects of the Beginning of the American Revolution in Massachusetts Bay, 1760–1762" *Am. Antiq. Soc. Proc.* vol. 67 (1957) 11–32.

Gipson *Brit. Empire*—Lawrence H. Gipson *The British Empire Before the American Revolution* 9 vols. (1936–1956).

Gipson *Coming of Revolution*—Lawrence H. Gipson *The Coming of the Revolution, 1763–1775* (1954).

Gipson *Ingersoll*—Lawrence H. Gipson *Jared Ingersoll . . .* (1920).

Glenn *Some Colonial Mansions*—Thomas Allen Glenn *Some Colonial Mansions and Those Who Lived in Them* vol. I (1898).

Goebel "Const. Hist."—Julius Goebel, Jr. "Constitutional History and Constitutional Law" *Columbia Law Rev.* XXXVIII (1938) 555–77.

Goodman *Am. Overture*—Abram V. Goodman *American Overture: Jewish Rights in Colonial Times* (1947).

Goodwin *Col. Church in Va.*—Edward L. Goodwin *The Colonial Church in Virginia* (1927).

Gordon *History*—William Gordon *The History of the Progress and Establishment of the Independence of the United States* 3 vols. (1794).

Gosselin *L'Eglise du Canada*—Auguste Gosselin *L'Eglise du Canada après la Conquete, Première Partie 1760–1775* (1916).

Grafton—William R. Anson (ed.) *Autobiography and Political Correspondence of Augustus Henry Third Duke of Grafton* (1898).

Grant "Canada versus Guadeloupe"—William L. Grant "Canada versus Guadeloupe, An Episode of the Seven Years' War" *A.H.R.* XVII (1912) 735–43.

Grant "Pontiac's Rebellion"—Charles S. Grant "Pontiac's Rebellion and the British Troop Moves of 1763" *Miss. Vall. Hist. Rev.* vol. 40 (1954) 75–88.

Gray *Hist. of Agriculture*—Lewis C. Gray *History of Agriculture in the Southern United States to 1860* 2 vols. (1933).

Gray "Notes"—Horace Gray "Notes and Appendix" in Quincy *Reports* 395–540.

Greene "American Opinion"—Evarts B. Greene "American Opinion on the Imperial Review of Provincial Legislation, 1776–1787" *A.H.R.* XXIII (1918) 104–7.

Greene *Provincial Governor*—Evarts B. Greene *The Provincial Governor . . .* (1898).

Greene and Harrington *Am. Population*—Evarts B. Greene and Virginia D. Harrington *American Population Before the Federal Census of 1790* (1932).

Greene "Carter"—Jack P. Greene "Landon Carter and the Pistole Fee Dispute" 3 *W. & M. Q.* XIV (1957) 66–69.

Greene "Gadsden"—Jack P. Greene "The Gadsden Election Controversy . . ." *Miss. Vall. H. R.* vol. 46 (1960) 469–92.

Greene "Political Power"—Jack P. Greene "Political Power in the Virginia House of Burgesses, 1720–1776" 3 *W. & M. Q.* XVI (1959) 485–506.

Gregory "Journal"—"William Gregory's Journal" *New Eng. Mag.* for May 1895.

Greig *Hume*—John Y. T. Greig (ed.) *The Letters of David Hume* 2 vols. (1932).

Grenville—William James Smith (ed.) *The Grenville Papers . . .* 4 vols. (1852–1853).

Griffith *Population Problems*—Grover Talbot Griffith *Population Problems of the Age of Malthus* (1926).

Groce "Dyer"—George C. Groce "Eliphalet Dyer: Connecticut Revolutionist," in Morris *Era* 290–304.

Guttmacher *George III*—Manfred S. Guttmacher *America's Last King: An Interpretation of the Madness of George III* (1941).

Guttridge *Eng. Whiggism*—George H. Guttridge *English Whiggism and the American Revolution* (1942).

Guttridge *Rockingham*—George H. Guttridge *The Early Career of Lord Rockingham 1730–1765* (1952).

H.L.—*House of Lords' Cases.*

H. & L. Dict.—Samuel Halkett and John Laing *Dictionary of Anonymous and Pseudonymous English Literature* (Kennedy, Smith, and Johnson, eds.) 7 vols. (1926–1934).

H.M.C.—*Historical Manuscripts Commission.*

Haines *Am. Doctrine*—Charles G. Haines *The American Doctrine of Judicial Supremacy* (1914).

Hamer "Fort Loudoun"—Philip M. Hamer "Fort Loudoun in the Cherokee War, 1758–1761" *N.C. Hist. Rev.* II (1925) 442–58.

Hamilton *Washington*—Stanislaus M. Hamilton (ed.) *Letters to Washington and Accompanying Papers* 5 vols. (1898–1902).

Hanna *Del. District*—Mary A. Hanna *Trade of the Delaware District Before the Revolution* (1917).

Hardwicke—Philip C. Yorke *The Life and Correspondence of Philip Yorke Earl of Hardwicke . . .* 3 vols. (1913).

Haring *Trade Between Spain and the Indies*—Clarence H. Haring *Trade and Navigation Between Spain and the Indies in the Time of the Hapsburgs* (1918).

Harper "Effect"—Lawrence A. Harper "The Effect of the Navigation Acts on the Thirteen Colonies" in Morris *Era* 3–39.

Harper "Mercantilism"—Lawrence A. Harper "Mercantilism and the American Revolution" *Can. H. R.* XXIII (1942) 1–15.

Harper *Navig. Laws*—Lawrence A. Harper *The English Navigation Laws . . .* (1939).

Harrington *N.Y. Merchant*—Virginia D. Harrington *The New York Merchant on the Eve of the Revolution* (1935).

Harris *Hardwicke*—George Harris *The Life of Lord Chancellor Hardwicke . . .* 3 vols. (1847).

Hart *Am. Hist.*—Albert Bushnell Hart (ed.) *American History Told by Contemporaries,* vol. 2 [1689–1783] (1950).

Harv. Law Rev.—*Harvard Law Review.*

Harvey *Burlamaqui*—Ray F. Harvey *Jean Jacques Burlamaqui; a Liberal Tradition in American Constitutionalism* (1937).

Hawes "Letters to Col. Agent"—Lilla M. Hawes (ed.) "Letters to the Georgia Colonial Agent, July 1762 to January 1771" *Ga. Hist. Q.* XXXVI (1952) 250–86.

Hawkins *Historical Notices*—Ernest Hawkins *Historical Notices of the Missions of the Church of England in the North American Colonies* (1845).

Hawks and Perry *Conn.*—Francis L. Hawks and William S. Perry (eds.) *Documentary History of the Protestant Episcopal Church . . . Connecticut* 2 vols. (1863–1864).

Hays "The Interest"—Isaac Minis Hays "On the Authorship of . . . The Interest of Great Britain Considered . . ." *Proc. Am. Phil. Soc.* vol. 63 (1924) 1–9.

Haywood "Stamp Act"—C. Robert Haywood "The Mind of the North Carolina Opponents of the Stamp Act" *N.C. Hist. Rev.* XXIX (1952) 317–43.

Haywood *Tryon*—Marshall de L. Haywood *Governor William Tryon . . . North Carolina 1765–1771 . . .* (1903).

Hazeltine "Influence"—Harold D. Hazeltine "The Influence of Magna Carta on American Constitutional Development" in Malden *Magna Carta* 180–211.

Hedges *The Browns*—James B. Hedges *The Browns of Providence Plantations: Colonial Years* (1952).

Hening *Va.*—William W. Hening (ed.) *The Statutes at Large of Virginia* 13 vols. (1809–1823).

Hertslet *Treaties*—Lewis Hertslet (ed.) *A Complete Collection of the Treaties . . . between Great Britain and Foreign Powers . . . so far as they relate to Commerce and Navigation* (1840).

Hickman "Writs"—Emily Hickman "Colonial Writs of Assistance" *New Eng. Q.* V (1932) 83–104.

Higgins *N.Y. Expansion*—Ruth L. Higgins *Expansion in New York with Especial Reference to the Eighteenth Century* (1931).

High "McCulloh"—James High "Henry McCulloh: Progenitor of the Stamp Act" *N.C. Hist. Rev.* XXIX (1952) 24–38, with comments *same* 460–64.

Hill *Boswell's Johnson*—George Birbeck Hill (ed.) and L. F. Powell (reviser) *Boswell's Life of Johnson . . .* 6 vols. (1934–1950).

Hindle "Paxton Boys"—Brooke Hindle "The March of the Paxton Boys" 3 *W. & M. Q.* III (1946) 461–86.

Hindle *Pursuit of Science 1735–1789*—Brooke Hindle *The Pursuit of Science in Revolutionary America, 1735–1789* (1956).

Hinkhouse *Preliminaries*—Fred J. Hinkhouse *The Preliminaries of the American Revolution as Seen in the English Press 1763–1775* (1926).

Hisp. Am. Hist. Rev.—*The Hispanic American Historical Review.*

Hist. Mag.—*The Historical Magazine . . .* (U.S.)

Hist. of Late Minority—[John Almon] *The History of the Late Minority . . . during the years 1762, 1763, 1764 and 1765.*

Hist. of W. & M. College—*The History of the College of William and Mary from Its Foundation, 1660 to 1874* (1874) (author not stated).

Historical Memorial (1761)—*Historical Memorial of the Negotiations of France and England* (London, 1761).

Historical N.H.—*Historical New Hampshire* (a periodical).

History—*History: the Quarterly Journal of the Historical Association* (London).

Hist. Today—*History Today* (published monthly in London).

Hoffman *Burke*—Ross J. S. Hoffman *Edmund Burke, New York Agent with His Letters to the New York Assembly and Intimate Correspondence with Charles O'Hara, 1761–1776* (1956).

Holdsworth "Conventions"—W. S. Holdsworth "The Conventions of the Eighteenth Century Constitution" *Iowa Law Review* XVII (1932) 161–80.

Holland *Western Mass.*—John G. Holland *History of Western Massachusetts* 2 vols. (1855).

Home Office Pap.—See *Calendar H.O. Papers.*

Hoon *Eng. Cust. System*—Elizabeth E. Hoon *The Organization of the English Customs System 1696–1786* (1938).

Hopkins *Grievances*—[Stephen Hopkins] *The Grievances of the American Colonies candidly examined* (London). Though dated "1766," it was reviewed in the December 1765 issues of *The Monthly Review* and *The Gentleman's Magazine*. Except for one important omission this pamphlet is nearly identical with the next.

Hopkins *The Rights of Colonies* (1764)—[Stephen Hopkins] *The Rights of Colonies Examined* (Providence, 1764) *R.I. Col. Rec.* 416–27. For ascription and dating, Alden *R.I. Imprints* 125, 134–35.

Horn *Eng. Hist. Doc.*—D. B. Horn and Mary Ransome (eds.) *English Historical Documents 1714–1783* (1957).

Hosmer *Hutchinson*—James K. Hosmer *The Life of Thomas Hutchinson* . . . (1896).

Hotblack *Chatham*—Kate Hotblack *Chatham's Colonial Policy* (1917).

Hotblack "Peace"—Kate Hotblack "The Peace of Paris, 1763" 3 *Trans. Roy. Hist. Soc.* II (1908) 235–67.

Hough *Cases*—Charles M. Hough (ed.) *Reports of Cases in . . . Admiralty . . . New York* (1925).

Hough *Siege*—Frankin B. Hough (ed.) *Diary of the Siege of Detroit* . . . (1860).

Howard *Long Family*—Robert M. Howard *Records and Letters of the Family of the Longs* . . . 2 vols. (1925).

Howard *West Fla.*—Clinton N. Howard *The British Development of West Florida, 1763–1769* (1947).

Howell *Scotland*—James Howell *A Perfect Description of the People and Country of Scotland* (London, 1649).

Howell *State Trials*—Thomas B. Howell *A Complete Collection of State Trials* . . . 21 vols. (1816).

Hughes "Eng. Stamp Duties"—Edward Hughes "The English Stamp Duties" *E.H.R.* vol. 56 (1941) 234–64.

Hughes *North Country*—Edward Hughes *North Country Life in the 18th Century* (1952).

Hulton Letters—*Letters of a Loyalist Lady . . . Anne Hulton . . . at Boston . . . 1767–1776* (1927).

Humphreys "Shelburne"—R. A. Humphreys "Lord Shelburne and the Proclamation of 1763" *E.H.R.* vol. 49 (1934) 241–64.

Hunt. Lib. Q.—*The Huntington Library Quarterly.*

Hunt *Hist. of Eng.*—William Hunt *The History of England . . . 1760–1801* (1905).

Hunt "Pitt's Retirement"—William Hunt "Pitt's Retirement from Office, 5 Oct. 1761" *E.H.R.* XXI (1906) 119–32, with additional documents supplied by H. W. V. Temperley 327–30.

Huntley "Va."—Francis C. Huntley "The Seaborne Trade of Virginia in Mid-Eighteenth Century: Port Hampton" *Va. Mag.* vol. 59 (1951) 297–308.

Hussey *Caracas Company*—Roland D. Hussey *The Caracas Company, 1728–1784: A Study in the History of Spanish Monopolistic Trade* (1934).

Hutchins *Am. Maritime Industries*—John G. B. Hutchins *The American Maritime Industries and Public Policy 1789–1914* . . . (1941). (Though dealing chiefly with the later years indicated by the title, this work has useful information on the colonial period.)

Hutchinson *Collection*—Thomas Hutchinson *A Collection of Original Papers* . . . (Boston, 1769).

Hutchinson Diary and Letters—Peter Orlando Hutchinson *The Diary and Letters of His Excellency Thomas Hutchinson* 2 vols. (1884, 1886).

Hutchinson *Hist. of Mass.*—Lawrence S. Mayo (ed.) *The History of the Colony and Province of Massachusetts-Bay* by *Thomas Hutchinson* . . . (1936) reprint of earlier editions. (I—1764, II—1767, III—1828).

Hutchinson *Letters to Great Britain*—*Copy of Letters sent to Great-Britain by . . . Thomas Hutchinson and . . . Other Persons* . . . (Boston, 1773).

Ilchester *Fox*—Lord Ilchester *Henry Fox, First Lord Holland* . . . 2 vols. (1920).

Ilchester *Lennox*—Lady Ilchester and Lord Stavordale *The Life and Letters of Lady Susan Lennox 1745–1826 . . .* (1902).

Ilchester *Letters to Fox*—Lord Ilchester (ed.) *Letters to Henry Fox . . .* (1915).

Ill. State Hist. Lib. Coll.—*Collections of the Illinois State Historical Library.*

"Ingersoll Letters"—Franklin B. Dexter (ed.) "A Selection from the Correspondence and Miscellaneous Papers of Jared Ingersoll" *New Haven Hist. Soc. Papers* IX 201–472.

Innis *Cod Fisheries*—Harold A. Innis *The Cod Fisheries; the History of an International Economy* (1940).

Irish Statutes—*The Statutes at Large of Ireland* (Dublin, 1786).

Jackson *An Historical Review*—Richard Jackson *An Historical Review of the Constitution and Government of Pennsylvania* (London, 1759).

Jackson—Carl Van Doren (ed.) *Letters and Papers of Benjamin Franklin and Richard Jackson* (1947).

Jacobs *Indian Gifts*—Wilbur R. Jacobs *Diplomacy and Indian Gifts . . . 1748–1763* (1950).

James "Frontier"—Alfred P. James "The First English-Speaking Trans-Appalachian Frontier" *Miss. Vall. Hist. Rev.* XVII (1931) 55–71.

Jefferson *Summary View* (1774)—[Thomas Jefferson] *A Summary View of the Rights of British America* (Williamsburg, Va., 1774) in Foner *Jefferson* 2–19. (See also Boyd *Jefferson* I 121–35).

Jenkinson—Ninetta S. Jucker (ed.) *The Jenkinson Papers, 1760–1766* (1949).

Jenks "Diary" — William L. Jenks "Diary of the Seige of Detroit" *Mich. Hist. Mag.* XII (1928) 437–42.

Jensen *Eng. Hist. Doc.*—Merrill Jensen (ed.) *English Historical Documents* Volume IX *American Colonial Documents to 1776* (1955).

"Jerdone Letter Book 1750–6"—"Letter Book of Francis Jerdone" 1 *W. & M. Q.* XI (1903) 153–60, 236–42.

Johnson—*The Papers of Sir William Johnson* (various editors) 12 vols. (1921–1957).

Johnson "Absenteeism in West Fla."—Cecil Johnson "A Note on Absenteeism in British West Florida" *La. Hist. Q.* XIX (1936) 196–98.

Johnson *West Florida*—Cecil Johnson *British West Florida 1763–1783* (1943).

Johnson "Britain's Fiscal Choice"—Victor L. Johnson "Internal Financial Reform or External Taxation: Britain's Fiscal Choice, 1763" *Proc. Am. Phil. Soc.* vol. 98 (1954) 31–37.

Johnson "Sugar Act"—Allen S. Johnson "The Passage of the Sugar Act" 3 *W. & M. Q.* XVI (1959) 507–14.

Johnston "Union with Scotland, 1707"—S. H. F. Johnston "Union with Scotland, 1707" *Hist. Today* VII (1957) 466–72.

Jones *St. Peter's*—William Northey Jones *The History of St. Peter's Church in Perth Amboy, New Jersey* (1924).

Journal B. of T.—*Journal of the Commissioners for Trade and Plantations* [1704–1782] 14 vols. (1920–1938).

Journ. Ec. & Bus. Hist—*Journal of Economic and Business History.*

Journ. Mod. Hist.—*The Journal of Modern History.*

Journ. Negro Hist.—*The Journal of Negro History.*

Journ. So. Hist.—*The Journal of Southern History.*

Journals Cont. Congress—Worthington C. Ford (ed.) *Journals of the Continental Congress . . .* vols. 1 to 3 (1904–1905).

Journals H. of C.—*Journals of the House of Commons.*

Journals H. of L.—*Journals of the House of Lords.*

Judd *Members*—Gerrit P. Judd *Members of Parliament, 1734–1832* (1955).

Junius—*Junius* (London, 1772), collection of Junius's letters published by Henry Sampson Woodfall.

Justice and Necessity of Taxing—*The Justice and Necessity of Taxing the American Colonies* (London, 1766). The anonymous author has not been identified.

Kalendar—See *Court Kalendar.*

Kalm *Travels*—Adolph B. Benson *Peter Kalm's Travels in North America, The English Version of 1770* 2 vols. (1937) a translation of part of Kalm's *En Resa til Norra America* (Stockholm, 1753).

Keith *Const. Hist.*—Arthur Berriedale Keith *Constitutional History of the First British Empire* (1930).

Keith "Short Discourse"—William Keith "A Short Discourse on the Present State of the Colonies" (1728) in Hart *Am. Hist.* II 138–41.

Kemble—*The Kemble Papers* vol. I *N.Y. Hist. Soc. Coll.* for 1883.

Kemmerer *N.J.*—Donald L. Kemmerer *Path to Freedom . . . N.J. 1703–1776* (1940).

Kennedy *Essay*—[Archibald Kennedy] *An Essay on the Government of the Colonies . . .* (N.Y., 1752). As to Kennedy's probable authorship, Wroth *Am. Bookshelf 1755* 31, 125.

"Kenny's Journal"—John W. Jordan (ed.) "Journal of James Kenny, 1761–1763" *Pa. Mag. Hist.* XXXVII (1913) 1–47, 152–201.

Keppel—Thomas Keppel *The Life of Augustus Viscount Keppel* 2 vols. (1842).

Kerr *Bermuda and the Am. Revolution*—Wilfred B. Kerr *Bermuda and the American Revolution, 1760–1783* (1936).

Kerr "Merchants of Nova Scotia"—Wilfred B. Kerr "The Merchants of Nova Scotia and the American Revolution" *Can. H.R.* XIII (1932) 20–36.

Kerr "Newfoundland"—Wilfred B. Kerr "Newfoundland in the Period Before the American Revolution" *Pa. Mag. Hist.* vol. 65 (1941) 56–78.

Kerr "Stamp Act in Nova Scotia"—Wilfred B. Kerr "The Stamp Act in Nova Scotia" *New Eng. Q.* VI (1933) 552–66.

Kerr "Stamp Act in Quebec"—Wilfred B. Kerr "The Stamp Act in Quebec" *E.H.R.* vol. 47 (1932) 648–51.

Kerr "Stamp Act in the Floridas"—Wilfred B. Kerr "The Stamp Act in the Floridas" *Miss. Vall. H.R.* XXI (1935) 463–70.

Keys *Colden*—Alice M. Keys *Cadwallader Colden . . .* (1906).

Kilvert *Warburton*—Francis Kilvert *A Selection from Unpublished Papers of the Right Reverend William Warburton D.D., Late Bishop of Gloucester* (1841).

Kimball *Pitt*—Gertrude Selwyn Kimball (ed.) *Correspondence of William Pitt . . .* 2 vols. (1906).

Kimball *R.I.*—Gertrude Selwyn Kimball (ed.) *The Correspondence of the Colonial Governors of Rhode Island 1723–1775* 2 vols. (1902–1903).

Kingsford *Canada*—William Kingsford *The History of Canada . . . 1763–1775* (1892) being vol. 5 of 10 vols.

Kistler "Allen"—Ruth Moser Kistler "William Allen, Pennsylvania Loyalist, 1704–1780" in *Lehigh County Hist. Soc. Proc.* 1932, 45–102.

Klett *Pa.* — Guy S. Klett *Presbyterians in Colonial Pennsylvania* (1937).

Klingberg, *Anglican Humanitarianism*—Frank J. Klingberg *Anglican Humanitarianism in Colonial New York* (1940).

Knapp "Smollett's *Continuation*"—Lewis M. Knapp "The Publication of Smollett's *Complete History . . .* and *Continuation*" *Bibl. Soc. Transactions* New Ser. XVI (1936) 295–308.

Knollenberg "Amherst and Germ Warfare"—Bernhard Knollenberg "General Amherst and Germ Warfare" *Miss. Vall. H.R.* vol. 41 (1955) 489–94, 762–63.

Knollenberg *Franklin, Williams and Pitt*—Bernhard Knollenberg *Franklin, Jonathan Williams and William Pitt* (1949).

Knollenberg "Hollis and Mayhew"—Bernhard Knollenberg (ed.) "Thomas Hollis and Jonathan Mayhew, Their Correspondence, 1759–1766" *Mass. Hist. Soc. Proc.* vol. 69, 102–93.

Knollenberg *Origin* (1960 ed.)—Bernhard Knollenberg *Origin of the American Revolution 1759–1766* (1960).

Knollenberg "Our Solemn Farce"—Bernhard Knollenberg "Our Solemn Farce: Reënter the Tariff" *Atlantic* vol. 138 (1926) 688–94.

Knollenberg *Samuel Ward*—Bernhard Knollenberg (ed.) *Correspondence of Governor Samuel Ward, May 1775–March 1776* (1952).

Knollenberg "Stiles"—Bernhard Knollenberg "Ezra Stiles on British Taxation of the Colonies" *Yale Lib. Gazette* XXVI (1952) 149–51.

Knollenberg "Three Letters"—Bernhard Knollenberg "Three Letters of William Franklin" *Yale Lib. Gazette* XXI (1947) 18–27.

Knollenberg *Washington and the Revolution*—Bernhard Knollenberg *Washington and the Revolution: A Reappraisal . . .* (1940).

Koontz *Dinwiddie*—Louis K. Koontz *Robert Dinwiddie, His Career in America . . .* (1941).

La. Hist. Q.—*The Louisiana Historical Quarterly.*

Labaree *Instructions*—Leonard W. Labaree *Royal Instructions . . .* 2 vols. (1935).

Labaree *Royal Government*—Leonard W. Labaree *Royal Government in America* (1930).

Labaree "Royal Governors"—Leonard W. Labaree "The Early Careers of the Royal Governors" *Essays in Colonial History* 145–68.

Laing "Nova Scotia Admiralty"—Lionel H. Laing "Nova Scotia's Admiralty Court as a Problem of Colonial Administration" *Can. H.R.* XVI (1935) 151–61.

Laprade "Stamp Act"—William T. Laprade "The Stamp Act in British Politics" *A.H.R.* XXXV (1930) 735–57.

Late Occurrences in North America—[Edmund Jennings?] *The Late Occurrences in North America and the Policy of Great Britain Considered* (London, 1766).

Law—Albert C. Bates (ed.) *The Law Papers, Conn. Hist. Soc. Coll.* XI, XIII, XV (1907–1914).

Law *Burke's Speeches*—Hugh Law (ed.) *Speeches and Letters on American Affairs, Edmund Burke* (1942).

Lawson *Fur*—Murray G. Lawson *Fur: a Study in English Mercantilism 1700–1775* (1943).

Lecky *History*—William E. H. Lecky *A History of England in the Eighteenth Century* 8 vols. (1888–1890).

Lee *Vindication* (1764)—"An American" [Arthur Lee] *An Essay in Vindication of the Continental Colonies of America from a Censure of Mr. Adam Smith . . . with Some Reflections on Slavery . . .* (London, 1764).

Lefavour "Proposed College"—Henry Lefavour "The Proposed College in Hampshire County in 1762" *Mass. Hist. Soc. Proc.* vol. 66, 53–79.

Legg *Dipl. Instr.*—Leopold G. W. Legg (ed.) *British Diplomatic Instructions . . . 1689–1789, France* (1922).

Lehigh County Hist. Soc. Proc.—*Annual Proceedings of the Lehigh County [Pa.] Historical Society.*

Leslie "Gaspee Affair"—William R. Leslie "The Gaspee Affair: A Study of Its Constitutional Significance" *Miss. Vall. H.R.* XXXIX (1953) 233–56.

Letter addressed to Two Great Men—*A Letter addressed to Two Great Men* (London, 1760). Attributed to John Douglas.

Letter to a Member (1757)—*A Letter to a Member of Parliament on the Importance of the American Colonies and the Best Means of Making them most Useful to the Mother Country* (London, 1757). Author unknown.

Letter to Charles Townshend (1763)—*A Letter to the Right Honourable Ch_____s T_____nd Esq.* (London, 1763). Author unknown.

Letters to Ministry—*Letters to the Ministry from Governor Bernard . . .* (London, 1769).

Lewis *Walpole*—Wilmarth S. Lewis (Ed. in Chief) *The Yale Edition of Horace Walpole's Correspondence* (1937–).

Lilly *Col. Agents*—Edward P. Lilly *The Colonial Agents of New York and New Jersey* (1936).

Lincoln *Rev. Movement in Pa.* — Charles H. Lincoln *The Revolutionary Movement in Pennsylvania 1760–1776* (1901).

Little *State of Trade in the Northern Colonies*—[Otis Little] *The State of the Trade in the Northern Colonies Considered . . .* (London, 1748).

Locke *Two Treatises*—John Locke *Two Treatises of Government* (1690). My references are to the London, 1887, edition.

Lockmiller *Blackstone*—David A. Lockmiller *Sir William Blackstone* (1938).

Lodge *Chesterfield and Newcastle*—Richard Lodge (ed.) *Private Correspondence of Chesterfield and Newcastle, 1744–1746* (1930).

London Chronicle—*The London Chronicle; or, Universal Evening Post* (1757–1775).

London Gazette—Semiweekly official British gazette.

London Gazetteer—*London Gazetteer and New Daily Advertiser.*

London Mag.—*The London Magazine; or, Gentleman's Monthly Intelligencer* (1732–1775).

Long *Amherst*—John C. Long *Lord Jeffrey Amherst . . .* (1933).

Lonn *Agents of Southern Colonies*—Ella Lonn *The Colonial Agents of the Southern Colonies* (1945).

Lord *Indust. Exp.* — Eleanor L. Lord *Industrial Experiments in the British Colonies of North America* (1896).

Lothian—H.M.S., *Report on the Manuscripts of the Marquess of Lothian* (1905).

Lounsbury *Brit. Fishery at Newfoundland*—Ralph G. Lounsbury *The British Fishery at Newfoundland, 1634–1763* (1934).

Lounsbury "Jonathan Belcher, Jr."—Ralph G. Lounsbury "Jonathan Belcher, Junior, Chief Justice and Lieutenant Governor of Nova Scotia," *Essays in Colonial History* 169–97.

Love *Fast and Thanksgiving Days*—William DeLoss Love *The Fast and Thanksgiving Days of New England* (1895).

Lovejoy "Admiralty Jurisdiction"—David S. Lovejoy "Rights Imply Obligations: The Case Against Admiralty Jurisdiction . . ." 3 *W. & M. Q.* XVI (1959) 460–84.

Lovejoy *R.I. Politics*—David S. Lovejoy *Rhode Island Politics and the American Revolution 1760–1776* (1958).

Loveland *Critical Years*—Clara O. Loveland *The Critical Years; The Reconstitution of the Anglican Church in the United States of America, 1780–1789* (1956).

Low *Gibbon's Journal*—David M. Low (ed.) *Gibbon's Journal* (1929).

Lucas *George II*—Reginald Lucas *George II and His Ministers* (1910).

Lucas *Lord North*—Reginald Lucas *Lord North, Second Earl of Guilford, K.G., 1732–1792* (1913).

Lyon *La.*—Elijah Wilson Lyon *Louisiana in French Diplomacy 1759–1804* (1934).

Lyttelton—Robert J. Phillimore *Memoirs and Correspondence of George, Lord Lyttelton from 1734 to 1773* 2 vols. (1845).

M.H.S.—See *Mass. Hist. Soc.*

McAnear "College Founding 1745–1775"—Beverly McAnear "College Founding in the American Colonies 1745–1775" *Miss. Vall. H.R.* vol. 42 (1956) 24–44.

McAnear "Raising Funds by Colonial Colleges"—Beverly McAnear "The Raising of Funds by the Colonial Colleges" *Miss. Vall. H.R.* XXXVIII (1952) 591–612.

Macauley *Historical Essays*—Thomas Babington Macauley *Historical Essays* (1901).

McCrady *South Carolina*—Edward McCrady *The History of South Carolina Under the Royal Government, 1719–1776* (1901).

McCulloch *Statistical Account*—John R. McCulloch *A Descriptive and Statistical Account of the British Empire . . .* 2 vols. (1854).

Macdonald *Scotland's Population*—Donald F. Macdonald *Scotland's Shifting Population, 1770–1850* (1937).

McGovney "Brit. Origin"—Dudley O. McGovney "The British Origin of Judicial Review of Legislation" *U. of Pa. Law Rev.* vol. 93 (1945) 1–49.

McIlwain *Am. Rev.*—Charles H. McIlwain *The American Revolution: A Constitutional Interpretation* (1923).

McIlwain *High Court*—Charles H. McIlwain *The High Court of Parliament and Its Supremacy* (1910).

MacInnes *Gateway of Empire*—C. M. MacInnes *A Gateway of Empire* (1939).

Mackenzie's Diary—*Diary of Frederick Mackenzie . . . 1775–1781 . . .* 2 vols. (1930).

McKinley *Suffrage*—Albert E. McKinley *The Suffrage . . . in the Thirteen . . . Colonies* (1905).

McLaughlin *Foundations*—Andrew C. McLaughlin *The Foundations of American Constitutionalism* (1932).

Magna Charta—*Magna Charta . . .* 1215, Senate Document 232 of the 66th Congress, Second Session (1940).

Mahon *History*—Lord Mahon *History of England . . . 1713–1783* 7 vols. (1853–1854).

Maine—James P. Baxter (ed.) *Documentary History of the State of Maine* in *Collections of the Maine Historical Society.*

Maitland *Const. Hist.*—Frederick W. Maitland *The Constitutional History of England* (1931).

Malden *Magna Carta*—Henry E. Malden (ed.) *Magna Carta Commemoration Essays* (1917).

Malmesbury—Lord Malmesbury (ed.) *A Series of Letters of the First Earl of Malmesbury . . . 1745 to 1820* 2 vols. (1870).

Manners *Granby*—Walter Evelyn Manners *Some Account of the . . . Marquis of Granby . . .* (1899).

Manning *Dissenting Deputies*—Bernard L. Manning *The Protestant Dissenting Deputies* (1952).

Manross *Hist. Am. Episc. Church*—William W. Manross *A History of the American Episcopal Church* (1935).

Mantoux *Industrial Revolution*—Paul Mantoux *The Industrial Revolution in the Eighteenth Century . . . in England* (1931).

Mark *Agrarian Conflicts in N.Y.*—Irving Mark *Agrarian Conflicts in Colonial New York 1711–1775.*

Marsden *Reports*—Reginald G. Marsden *Reports of Cases Determined in the High Court of Admiralty . . .* (1885).

"Marshall"—Thomas Stewardson "Extracts from the Letter-Book of Benjamin Marshall, 1763–1766" *Pa. Mag. Hist.* XX (1896) 206–12.

Martin "King's Customs"—Alfred S. Martin "The King's Customs, Philadelphia, 1763–1774" 3 *W. & M. Q.* V (1948) 201–16.

Maryland Gazette—*The Maryland Gazette* (Annapolis) 1745–1775.

Mason "Franklin and Galloway"—William S. Mason "Franklin and Galloway: Some Unpublished Letters" *Am. Antiq. Soc. Proc.* New Ser. XXXIV (1925) 227–58.

Mass. Acts—*Acts and Resolves of the Province of the Massachusetts Bay* 5 vols. (1869–1886).

Mass. Civil List—William H. Whitmore (ed.) *The Massachusetts Civil List for the Colonial and Provincial Periods 1630–1774 . . .* (1870).

Mass. Congress Journals—William Lincoln (ed.) *The Journals of Each Provincial Congress of Massachusetts in 1774 and 1775 . . .* (1838).

Mass. Gazette—*The Massachusetts Gazette. And Boston News-Letter* April 7, 1763–1768. For various changes of name: Brigham *Am. Newspapers* I 328.

Mass. Hist. Soc. Coll.—*Collections of the Massachusetts Historical Society.*

Mass. Hist. Soc. Proc.—*Proceedings of the Massachusetts Historical Society.*

Mass. Journals—*Journals of the Honourable House of Representatives of His Majesty's Province of the Massachustts-Bay in New-England,* the Massachusetts Historical Society reprint for 1715 to 1756 32 vols. (1919–1958).

Mass. Papers—See Bradford *Mass. Papers.*

Matthews "Book of America"—Albert Matthews "The Book of America" *Mass. Hist. Soc. Proc.* vol. 62 (1930) 171–97.

Matthews "De Berdt"—Albert Matthews "Letters of Dennys De Berdt, 1757–1770" *Col. Soc. Public.* XIII (1912) 293–461.

Matthiessen *Awakening of Scotland*—Willam Law Matthiessen *The Awakening of Scotland: A History from 1747 to 1797* (1910).

Mauduit *Considerations*—[Israel Mauduit] *Considerations on the Present German War* (London, 1760).

Mauduit—Worthington C. Ford (ed.) *Jasper Mauduit, Agent in London . . . for Massachusetts-Bay 1762–1765, Mass. Hist. Soc. Coll.* vol. 74 (1918).

May *Const. Hist.*—Thomas Erskine May *The Constitutional History of England . . . 1760–1860* 3 vols. (1896).

Mayhew *Defence of the Observations*—Jonathan Mayhew *A Defence of the Observations on the Charter and Conduct of the Society . . .* (Boston, 1763).

Mayhew *Discourse*—Jonathan Mayhew *A Discourse Concerning Unlimited Submission . . . With some Reflections on the Resistance made to King Charles I . . .* (Boston, 1750).

Mayhew *Observations*—Jonathan Mayhew *Observations on the Charter and Conduct of the Society for the Propagation of the Gospel in Foreign Parts . . .* (Boston, 1763).

Mayhew *Remarks on an Anonymous Tract*—Jonathan Mayhew *Remarks on an Anonymous Tract, entitled An Answer to Dr. Mayhew's Observations . . .* (Boston, 1764, reprinted London, 1765).

Mayhew *Snare Broken*—Jonathan Mayhew *The Snare Broken . . .* (Boston, 1766).

Mayhew *Two Sermons*—Jonathan Mayhew *Two Sermons on the Nature, Extent and Perfection of the Divine Goodness . . .* (Boston, 1763).

Mayo *John Wentworth*—Lawrence S. Mayo *John Wentworth, Governor of New Hampshire 1767–1775* (1921).

Mayo "The King's Woods"—Lawrence S. Mayo "The King's Woods" *Mass. Hist. Soc. Proc.* vol. 54, 50–61.

Mayo *St. Mary's River*—Lawrence S. Mayo *The St. Mary's River: A Boundary* (1914).

Mays *Pendleton*—David J. Mays *Edmund Pendleton, 1721–1803: A Biography* 2 vols. (1952).

Mays "Peter Lyons"—David J. Mays "Peter Lyons 1734?–1809" *Proceedings of the Virginia State Bar Association* for 1926, 418–26.

Md. Arch. — Jacob Hall Pleasants (ed.) *Archives of Maryland.*

Md. Hist. Mag.—*Maryland Historical Magazine.*

Meade *Henry*—Robert D. Meade *Patrick Henry, Patriot in the Making* (1957).

Meet Dr. Franklin—*Meet Dr. Franklin* (Thirteen talks on Franklin) (Franklin Institute, 1943).

Memoirs Hist. Soc. of Pa.—*Memoirs of the Historical Society of Pennsylvania.*

Memorials of Oswald—*Memorials of the Public Life and Character of the Right. Hon. James Oswald, of Dunniker* (1815).

Mereness *Md.*—Newton D. Mereness *Maryland as a Proprietary Province* (1901).

Mich. Hist. Mag.—*Michigan History Magazine.*

Mich. Pioneer Coll.—*Historical Collections*—*Collections and Researches Made by the Michigan Pioneer and Historical Society.*

Middleton *Tobacco Coast*—Arthur Pierce Middleton *Tobacco Coast: A Maritime History of Chesapeake Bay in the Colonial Era* (1953).

Millan *Army List*—See *Army List.*

Miller *Origins*—John C. Miller *Origins of the American Revolution* (1943).

Miller *Sam Adams*—John C. Miller *Sam Adams Pioneer in Propaganda* (1936).

Millman *Mountain*—Thomas R. Millman *Jacob Mountain, First Lord Bishop of Quebec* (1947).

Mims *Colbert*—Stewart L. Mims *Colbert's West India Policy* (1912).

Minto *Elliot*—The Countess of Minto *Life and Letters of Sir Gilbert Elliot, First Earl of Minto* (1874).

Miss. Vall. H.R. (or *Hist. Rev.*)—*The Mississippi Valley Historical Review.*

Mitchell *Pa. Statutes*—James T. Mitchell (ed.) *The Statutes at Large of Pennsylvania* . . .

Mitchell *Contest in America*—John Mitchell *The Contest in America between America and France* (London, 1757).

Montesquieu *The Spirit of Laws*—Charles Louis de Secondat, Baron de la Brède et de Montesquieu *L'Esprit des lois* translated under the title *The Spirit of Laws* by Thomas Nugent (London, 1750).

Monthly Review—*The Monthly Review* (London) 1749–1775.

Montresor—G. D. Scull (ed.) *The Montresor Journals, N.Y. Hist. Soc. Coll.* for 1881.

Moore *Justice*—Maurice Moore *The Justice and Policy of Taxing the American Colonies, in Great-Britain, Considered* . . . (Wilmington, N.C., 1765) reprinted in Boyd *Tracts* 163–74.

Moreau *Loix des colonies françaises*—Médéric L. E. Moreau de Saint-Méry *Loix et constitutions de colonies françaises de l'Amérique Sous Le Vent* . . . 6 vols. (1784–1790).

Morgan "Col. Ideas of Parl. Power"—Edmund S. Morgan "Colonial Ideas of Parliamentary Power, 1764–1766" 3 *W. & M. Q.* V (1948) 311–41.

Morgan *Declaration of 1764*—Edmund S. Morgan (ed.) *The New York Declaration of 1764, Old South Leaflets* No. 224 (1948).

Morgan "Hutchinson"—Edmund S. Morgan "Thomas Hutchinson and the Stamp Act" *New Eng. Q.* XXI (1948) 459–92 with minor gaps filled by me in *same* XXII (1949) 98.

Morgan "Postponement of Stamp Act"—Edmund S. Morgan "The Postponement of the Stamp Act" 3 *W. & M. Q.* VII (1950) 353–92.

Morgan *Prologue*—Edmund S. Morgan (ed.) *Prologue to Revolution Sources and Documents on the Stamp Act Crisis, 1764–1766* (1959).

Morgan *Stamp Act*—Edmund S. and Helen M. Morgan *The Stamp Act Crisis: Prologue to Revolution* (1953).

Morison *Mar. Hist. of Mass.*—Samuel E. Morison *The Maritime History of Massachusetts, 1783–1860* (1921).

Morison *Sources*—Samuel E. Morison (ed.) *Sources and Documents Illustrating the American Revolution, 1764–1788, and the Formation of the Federal Constitution* (1929).

Morris *Era*—Richard B. Morris (ed.) *The Era of the American Revolution* (1939).

Morris *Govt. and Labor*—Richard B. Morris *Government and Labor in Early America* (1946).

Morris *Select Cases*—Richard B. Morris (ed.) *Select Cases of the Mayor's Court of New York City, 1764–1784* (1935).

Morton *Robert Carter*—Louis Morton *Robert Carter of Nomini Hall* . . . (1941).

Morton "Robert Wormeley Carter"—Louis Morton "Robert Wormeley Carter of Sabine Hall . . ." *Journ. So. Hist.* XII (1946) 345–65.

Mott *Due Process*—Rodney L. Mott *Due Process of Law* . . . (1926).

Mott "Newspaper Coverage"—Frank Luther Mott "The Newspaper Coverage of Lexington and Concord" *New Eng. Q.* XVII (1944) 489–505.

Mowat *East Florida*—Charles L. Mowat *East Florida as a British Province 1763–1784* (1943).

Mullett *Fund. Law*—Charles F. Mullett *Fundamental Law and the American Revolution 1760–1776* (1933).

Mullett *Writings of Otis*—Charles F. Mullett (ed.) *Some Political Writings of James Otis* 2 vols. (1929).

Murdock *British in Boston*—Harold Murdock *The British in Boston, Being the Diary of Lieutenant John Barker 1774–1776* . . . (1924).

Murdock *Late News*—Harold Murdock *Late News of the . . . Nineteenth of April* . . . (1927).

Murdock *Nineteenth of April*—Harold Murdock *The Nineteenth of April, 1775* (1923).

Mure—See *Caldwell*, which includes the correspondence of Baron Mure of Caldwell from 1733 to 1776.

Murray *Eng. and Ireland*—Alice E. Murray *History of the Commercial and Financial Relations Between England and Ireland from . . . the Restoration* (1903).

Namier *Additions*—Lewis B. (now Sir Lewis) Namier *Additions and Corrections to Sir John Fortescue's Edition of The Correspondence of King George the Third (Vol. 1)* (1937).

Namier "Brice Fisher"—Lewis B. Namier "Brice Fisher, M.P.: A Mid-Eighteenth Century Merchant and His Connexions" *E.H.R.* vol. 42 (1927) 514–32.

Namier "Cabinet Council"—Lewis B. Namier "The Cabinet Council. Unnoticed end . . ." *Manchester Guardian* June 11, 1937.

Namier *Eng.*—Lewis B. Namier *England in the Age of the American Revolution* (1930).

Namier "Garth"—Lewis B. Namier "Charles Garth and His Connexions" and "Charles Garth Agent for South Carolina" *E.H.R.* vol. 54 (1939) 443–70, 632–52.

Namier "George III"—Sir Lewis B. Namier "King George III, A Study in Personality" *Hist. Today* III (1953) 610–21.

Namier *Personalities*—Sir Lewis B. Namier *Personalities and Powers* (1955).

Namier *Structure*—Lewis B. Namier *The Structure of Politics at the Accession of George III* 2 vols. (1929). Also a second revised edition (1957).

N.C. Col. Rec.—William L. Saunders (ed.) *The Colonial Records of North Carolina* vols. 1 to 11 and 23 (1886–1904).

N.C. Hist. Rev—*The North Carolina Historical Review.*

Nettels *Money Supply*—Curtis P. Nettels *The Money Supply of the American Colonies Before 1720* (1934).

Neville *Diary*—Basil Cozens-Hardy (ed.) *The Diary of Sylas Neville 1767–1788* (1950).

Newcombe "S.P.G. Missionaries"—Alfred W. Newcombe "The Appointment and Instruction of S.P.G. Missionaries" *Church History* V (1936) 340–58.

New Eng. Hist. & Gen. Reg.—*The New-England Historical and Genealogical Register.*

New Eng. Mag.—*New England Magazine.*

New. Eng. Q.—*The New England Quarterly.*

New-Hampshire Gazette—*New-Hampshire Gazette and Historical Chronicle* of Portsmouth, N.H. (1756–1775).

New Haven Hist. Soc. Papers—*Papers of the New Haven Colony Historical Society.*

New-London Gazette—*The New-London Gazette*, New London, Conn., Nov. 18, 1763–1775.

Newport Mercury—*The Newport Mercury* (Newport, R.I., 1758–1775).

New Régime 1765–1767—Clarence W. Alvord and Clarence E. Carter (eds.) *The New Régime 1765–1767 Ill. State Hist. Lib. Coll.* XI (1916).

New-York Gazette—*The New-York Gazette, or Weekly Post-Boy* (or similar name) New York City, 1747–1773.

New-York Gazette (Weyman's)—*The New-York Gazette*, New York City, published by William Weyman 1759–1767.

New-York Mercury—*The New-York Mercury*, New York City, 1752–1768. (Continued to 1783 under the title *The New-York Gazette; and the Weekly Mercury*.)

N.H. Laws—Albert S. Batchellor and Henry H. Metcalf (eds.) *Laws of New Hampshire* vols. 1 to 3 (1904–1915).

N.H. Papers—Nathaniel Bouton and Isaac W. Hammond (eds.) *Provincial and State Papers of New Hampshire* 7 vols. (1867–1873).

Niles *Principles*—Hezekiah Niles *Republication of the Principles and Acts of the Revolution in America* (1876).

N.J. Col. Doc.—Frederick W. Ricord and William Nelson (eds.) *Documents Relating to the Colonial History of New Jersey* 10 vols. (1880–1886).

N.J. Hist. Soc. Proc.—*Proceedings of the New Jersey Historical Society.*

Nobbe *The North Briton*—George Nobbe *The North Briton A Study in Political Propaganda* (1939).

Noble "Notes on Mass. Admiralty"—John Noble "A Few Notes on Admiralty Jurisdiction in . . . Massachusetts Bay" *Col. Soc. Publ.* (1906) VIII 150–86.

North Briton—*The North Briton*, collected edition (London, 1763) of *The North Briton* published weekly by John Wilkes in 1762–1763.

Northcliffe—*The Northcliffe Collection* (1926).

Norton—Frances Norton Mason (ed.) *John Norton & Sons Merchants of London and Virginia . . . Papers . . . 1750 to 1795* (1937).

Notes and Queries—*Notes and Queries A Medium of Intercommunication for Literary Men, General Readers, etc.*

N.Y. Assembly—*Journal of the Votes and Proceedings of the General Assembly of the Colony of New-York* 3 vols. (1764, 1766, 1820).

N.Y. Civil List—Edgar A. Werner (ed.) *Civil List . . . of the Colony and State of New York* (1884).

N.Y. Col. Doc.—Edmund B. O'Callaghan (ed.) *Documents Relative to the Colonial History . . . of New-York* 15 vols. (1853–1887).

N.Y. Col. Laws—*The Colonial Laws of New-York from the Year 1664 to the Revolution* 5 vols. (1894).

N.Y. Council Cal.—*Calendar of [New York Executive] Council Minutes 1668–1783* (1902).

N.Y. Doc. Hist.—Edmund B. O'Callaghan (ed.) *The Documentary History of the State of New York*, 4 vols. (1849–1851). (My references are to the small page edition.)

N.Y. Hist. Soc. Coll.—*Collections of the New-York Historical Society.*

N.Y. Legis. Council Journal—*Journal of the Legislative Council of . . . New York* 2 vols. (1861).

O.E.D.—*The Oxford English Dictionary . . .* 13 vols. (1933).

O'Callaghan *N.Y. Commissions*—Edmund B. O'Callaghan *Calendar of New York Colonial Commissions 1680–1770* (1929).

Oliver *Antigua*—Vere Langford Oliver *The History of the Island of Antigua* . . . 3 vols. (1894–1899).

Omond *Parliament and the Army*—John Stuart Omond *Parliament and the Army, 1692–1904* (1933).

Osgood *Colonies in 18th Cent.*—Herbert L. Osgood *The American Colonies in the Eighteenth Century* 4 vols. (1924).

Otis *Considerations*—[James Otis] *Considerations on Behalf of the Colonists. In a Letter to a Noble Lord* (London, 1765). Mullett *Writings of Otis* II 109–25.

Otis *Rights (1764)*—James Otis *The Rights of the British Colonies Asserted and Proved* (Boston, 1764, and London, undated) Mullett *Writings of Otis* I 45–101.

Otis *Vindication (1762)*—James Otis *A Vindication of the Conduct of the House of Representatives* . . . (Boston, 1762), Mullett *Writings of Otis* I 13–44.

Otis *Vindication of the British Colonies (1765)*—James Otis *A Vindication of the British Colonies* (Boston 1765) Mullett *Writings of Otis* II 127–51 reprinting London 1769 edition.

Owen *Pelhams*—John B. Owen *The Rise of the Pelhams* (1957).

Pa. Arch.—*Pennsylvania Archives*, First Series (1852–1856).

Pa. Assembly—*Pennsylvania Archives*, Eighth Series, "Votes of Assembly."

Pa. Col. Records—See next entry.

Pa. Council—*Minutes of the Provincial Council of Pennsylvania* (sometimes cited as *Pa. Col. Rec.*) 10 vols. (1852).

Pa. Frontier Forts—*Report of the Commission to Locate the Site of the Frontier Forts of Pennsylvania* 2 vols. (1898).

Pa. Mag. Hist.—*The Pennsylvania Magazine of History and Biography.*

Pa. Statutes—James T. Mitchell and Henry Flanders *The Statutes at Large of Pennsylvania from 1682 to 1801* 17 vols. (1896–1915).

Pac. Hist. Rev.—*The Pacific Historical Review.*

Palfrey *New. Eng.*—John G. Palfrey *History of New England* 5 vols. (1890).

Pamphleteer—*The Pamphleteer; respectfully dedicated to Both Houses of Parliament* VIII (1816).

Papendiek—*Mrs. Charlotte L. H. Papendiek: Court and Private Life in the Time of Queen Charlotte* edited by Mrs. Vernon Delves Broughton 2 vols. (1887).

Papers Mich. Academy—*Papers of the Michigan Academy of Science Arts and Letters.*

Pares "Manning the Navy in West Indies"—Richard Pares "The Manning of the Navy in the West Indies, 1702–63" 4 *Trans. Roy. Hist. Soc.* XX (1937) 31–60.

Pares *War and Trade*—Richard Pares *War and Trade in the West Indies 1739–1763* (1936).

Pares *Yankees and Creoles, The Trade Between North America and the West Indies Before the American Revolution* (1956).

Pares and Taylor *Essays to Namier*—Richard Pares and A. J. P. Taylor (eds.) *Essays Presented to Sir Lewis Namier* (1956).

Pargellis *Loudoun*—Stanley M. Pargellis *Lord Loudoun in North America* (1933).

Pargellis *Military Affairs*—Stanley M. Pargellis *Military Affairs in North America, 1748–1765* . . . (1936).

Pargellis and Medley *Bibliography*—Stanley M. Pargellis and J. D. Medley (eds.) *Bibliography of British History, The Eighteenth Century, 1714–1789* (1951).

Parkman *Pontiac*—Francis Parkman *The Conspiracy of Pontiac* . . . 2 vols. (1879).

Parl. Hist.—William Cobbett and Thomas C. Hansard (eds.) *The Parliamentary History of England* . . . *to 1803* 36 vols. (1806–1820).

Parry "West Indies" — J. H. Parry "The Patent Offices in the British West Indies" *E.H.R.* vol. 69 (1954) 200–225.

Partridge *Dictionary of Slang* — Eric Partridge *A Dictionary of Slang* . . . (1951).

Pascoe *Digest* — Charles F. Pascoe *Classified Digest of Records of the Society for the Propagation of the Gospel in Foreign Parts 1701–1892* (1893).

Patriot Preachers — [L. A. Osborne, ed.] *The Patriot Preachers of the American Revolution . . . 1766–1783* (1860).

Peach *Allen* — Robert E. M. Peach *The Life and Times of Ralph Allen* . . . (1895).

Pease *Anglo-French* — Theodore C. Pease *Anglo-French Boundary Disputes . . . Ill. Hist. Soc. Coll.* XXVII (1936).

Pease "Mississippi Boundary" — Theodore C. Pease "The Mississippi Boundary of 1763: A Reappraisal of Responsibility" *A.H.R.* vol. 40 (1935) 278–86.

Peckham *Pontiac* — Howard H. Peckham *Pontiac and the Indian Uprising* (1947).

Pemberton *Carteret* — William B. Pemberton *Carteret, the Brilliant Failure* . . . (1936).

Pemberton *A Sermon* — Ebenezer Pemberton *A Sermon Preached . . . May 25th. 1757. Being the Anniversary for the Election of His Majesty's Council for the Province* (Boston, 1757).

Pennington *Talbot* — Edgar L. Pennington *Apostle of New Jersey, John Talbot, 1645–1727* (1938).

Penn-Logan Corresp. — Edward Armstrong (ed.) *Correspondence Between William Penn and James Logan* I, II, *Memoirs Hist. Soc. of Pa.* IX, X (1870–1872).

Pennsylvania Gazette — *The Pennsylvania Gazette*, Philadelphia, 1728–1775 (B. Franklin and David Hall publishers).

Pennsylvania Journal — *The Pennsylvania Journal and Weekly Advertiser* Philadelphia, 1742–1775 (William and Thomas Bradford publishers).

Penson, *Agents of West Indies* — Lillian M. Penson *The Colonial Agents . . . West Indies* (1924).

Penson "West India Interest" — Lillian M. Penson "The London West India Interest in the Eighteenth Century" *E.H.R.* XXXVI (1921) 373–92.

Perry *Mass.* — William S. Perry (ed.) *Historical Collections relating to the American Colonial Church* III Massachusetts (1873).

Perry *Pa.* — William S. Perry (ed.) *Historical Collections relating to . . . Church* II Pennsylvania (1871).

Perry *Va.* — William S. Perry (ed.) *Historical Collections relating to . . . Church* I Virginia (1870).

Phillips *Early English Colonies* — Sadler Phillips *The Early English Colonies* . . . (1908).

Pickering *Statutes* — Danby Pickering *The Statutes at Large* (English).

Pitkin — Albert C. Bates (ed.) *The Pitkin Papers Conn. Hist. Soc. Coll.* XIX (1921).

Pitman "Slavery" — Frank W. Pitman "Slavery on British West India Plantations in the Eighteenth Century" *Journ. Negro Hist.* XI (1926) 584–668.

Pitman *West Indies* — Frank W. Pitman *The Development of the British West Indies 1700–1763* (1917).

Pitt — William Stanhope Taylor and John H. Pringle (eds.) *Correspondence of William Pitt, Earl of Chatham* 4 vols. (1838–1840).

Plain Dealer — *The Plain Dealer; or, Remarks on Quaker Politics in Pennsylvania*, Philadelphia, No. 3, May 14, 1764.

Plucknett "Bonhams Case" — Theodore F. T. Plucknett "Bonham's Case and Judicial Review" *Harv. Law. Rev.* vol. 40 (1927) 30–70.

Pol. Science Quart.—*Political Science Quarterly.*

Pomfret "Strahan"—John E. Pomfret "Some Further Letters of William Strahan, Printer" *Pa. Mag. Hist.* vol. 60 (1936) 455–89.

Porteus *Secker*—Beilby Porteus *The Works of . . . Thomas Secker . . .* 6 vols. (1825).

Postlethwayt *Britain's Interest*—Malachy Postlethwayt *Britain's Commercial Interest Explained and Improved . . .* 2 vols. (London, 1757).

Pottle *Boswell's London Journal*—Frederick A. Pottle (ed.) *Boswell's London Journal 1762–1763* (1951).

Pownall *Administration*—Thomas Pownall *The Administration of the Colonies.* There were at least six editions from 1764 to 1778. Unless otherwise indicated my references are to the third, the London, 1766, edition.

Pownall *Topographical Description*—Lois Mulkearn (ed.) [*Thomas Pownall's*] *A Topographical Description of the Dominions of the United States of America* (1949).

Preston "Keith"—R. A. Preston "Sir William Keith's Justification of a Stamp Duty in the Colonies, 1739–42" *Can. H.R.* XXIX (1948) 168–82.

Price "Glasgow in Tobacco Trade"—Jacob M. Price "The Rise of Glasgow in the Chesapeake Tobacco Trade 1707–1775." 3 *W. & M. Q.* XI (1954) 179–99.

Prior Documents—[John Almond] *A Collection of Interesting, Authentic Papers relative to the Dispute between Great Britain and America . . . from 1764 to 1775* (London, 1777).

Proc. Am. Phil. Soc.—*Proceedings of the American Philosophical Society.*

Proceedings of the Congress (1766)—*Proceedings of the Congress at New York* (Annapolis, Md., 1766) reprinted *Md. Archives* vol. 59, 327–56.

Proud *Pa.*—Robert Proud *The History of Pennsylvania . . .* 2 vols. (1797–1798).

Providence Gazette—*The Providence Gazette; and Country Journal* Oct. 20, 1762–1775.

Quarterly Review—*The Quarterly Review* (London).

Quebec Gazette—*The Quebec Gazette* (1764–1775). For details, Tremaine *Bibliography* 629–39.

Quincy *Harvard*—Josiah Quincy (1772–1864) *The History of Harvard University* 2 vols. (1840).

Quincy *Memoir*—Josiah Quincy (1772–1864), *Memoir of the Life of Josiah Quincy, Jun., of Massachusetts: 1744–1775* (1874).

Quincy *Observations*—Josiah Quincy (1744–1775) *Observations on the Act of Parliament Commonly Called the Boston Port-Bill* (Boston, 1774).

Quincy *Reports*—Samuel M. Quincy (ed.) *Reports of Cases . . . in the Superior Court of Massachusetts Bay between 1761 and 1772 by Josiah Quincy, Junior* (1865).

Radin "Magna Carta"—Max Radin "The Myth of Magna Carta" *Harv. Law Rev.* vol. 60 (1947) 1060–91. (Showing that the Great Charter's supposed influence on English political developments is not a myth.)

Raper *N.C.*—Charles L. Raper *North Carolina A Study in English Colonial Government* (1904).

Rashed *Peace*—Zenab Esmat Rashed *The Peace of Paris 1763* (1951).

Reasons for Keeping Guadaloupe—*Reasons for Keeping Guadaloupe at a Peace, preferable to Canada, explained in Five Letters . . .* (London, 1761). Copy at Boston Athenaeum.

Reasons (1764)—[Thomas Fitch and others] *Reasons Why the British Colonies, in America, Should Not Be Charged with Internal Taxes, by Authority of Parliament . . .* (New Haven, Conn., 1764) *Conn. Col. Rec.* XII 651–71.

Reed *Church and State in Mass.* — Susan M. Reed *Church and State in Massachusetts 1691–1740* (1914).

Reed *Reed* — William B. Reed *Life and Correspondence of Joseph Reed* . . . 2 vols. (1847).

Reflections on Domestic Policy — *Reflections on the Domestic Policy, Proper to be observed* . . . (London, 1763).

Remarks — [William Burke] *Remarks on the Letter Address'd to Two Great Men*, London [1760].

Rep. on Can. Archives — *Report on Canadian Archives* (various years).

"Rhoads" — Henry D. Biddle (ed.) "Extracts from the Letter-Book of Samuel Rhoads Jr. of Philadelphia" *Pa. Mag. Hist.* XIV (1890) 421–26.

Richmond Coll. Hist. Papers — *Richmond College Historical Papers* II 118–52 (1917).

R.I. Col. Rec. — John R. Bartlett *Records of the Colony of Rhode Island* . . . 9 vols. (1856–1864).

R.I. Commerce — *Commerce of Rhode Island 1726–1774*, *Mass. Hist. Soc. Coll.* vol. 69 (1914).

Riker *Fox* — Thad W. Riker *Henry Fox, First Lord Holland*. . . 2 vols. (1911).

Ripley *Financial History of Virginia* — William Z. Ripley *The Financial History of Virginia* (1893).

Ritcheson "Stamp Act" — Charles R. Ritcheson "The Preparation of the Stamp Act" 3 *W. & M. Q.* X (1953) 543–59 with comments of Edmund S. Morgan 3 *W. & M. Q.* XI (1954) 157–60.

Ritcheson *British Politics* — Charles R. Ritcheson *British Politics and the American Revolution* (1954).

Robbins "Hollis" — Caroline Robbins "The Strenuous Whig, Thomas Hollis of Lincoln's Inn" 3 *W. & M. Q.* VII (1950) 406–53.

Robbins "Hutcheson" — Caroline Robbins " 'When It Is That Colonies May Turn Independent' . . . Francis Hutcheson" (1694–1746) 3 *W. & M. Q.* XI (1954) 214–51.

Roche *Reed* — John F. Roche *Joseph Reed: A Moderate in the American Revolution* (1957).

Rockingham — Earl of Albemarle (George Thomas Keppel) *Memoirs of the Marquis of Rockingham* . . . 2 vols. (1852).

Rodd *Charlemont* — Thomas Rodd *Original Letters Principally from Lord Charlemont* . . . (1820).

Root *Pa.* — Winfred T. Root *The Relations of Pennsylvania with the British Government, 1696–1765* (1912).

Roper *North Carolina* — Charles L. Roper *North Carolina A Study in English Colonial Government* (1904).

Rosebery *Chatham* — Lord Rosebery *Chatham: His Early Life and Connections* (1910).

Rossiter "Richard Bland" — Clinton Rossiter "Richard Bland: The Whig in America," 3 *W. & M. Q.* X (1953) 33–79.

Rossiter *Seed Time* — Clinton Rossiter *Seed Time of the Republic* (1953).

Rowe — Anne R. Cunningham (ed.) *Letters and Diary of John Rowe, Boston Merchant 1759–1762; 1764–1779* (1903).

Rowland *Carroll* — Kate M. Rowland *The Life of Charles Carroll of Carrollton* . . . 2 vols. (1898).

Rowland *Mason* — Kate M. Rowland *The Life of George Mason, 1725–1792* 2 vols. (1892).

Russell *Review*—Elmer B. Russell *The Review of American Colonial Legislation* . . . (1915).

Rutherfurd *Family Records*—Livingston Rutherfurd *Family Records and Events* . . . (1894).

Ruville *Pitt*—Albert von Ruville *William Pitt, Earl of Chatham* 3 vols. (1907).

Ryder *A True Representation*—Sidney S. Ryder (ed.) *A True Representation of the Plan Formed at Albany* . . . *R.I. Hist. Tracts* no. 9 (1880).

S & D *Doc.*—Adam Shortt and Arthur G. Doughty (eds.) *Documents Relating to the Constitutional History of Canada 1759–1791* vol. I (1918).

Sabine *Loyalists*—Lorenzo Sabine *Biographical Sketches of Loyalists of the American Revolution with an Historical Essay* 2 vols. (1864).

Sabine *William Smith*—William H. W. Sabine *Historical Memoirs from 16 March, 1763, to 9 July, 1776, of William Smith Historian of the Province of New York* . . . 2 vols. (1956, 1958).

Sachse *Col. American in Britain*—William L. Sachse *The Colonial American in Britain* (1956).

St. James Chronicle—*The St. James's Chronicle; or the British Evening Post,* London.

Satineau *Guadeloupe*—Maurice Satineau *Histoire de la Guadeloupe sous L'Ancien Régime 1635–1789* (1928).

Savelle *Canadian Boundary*—Max Savelle *The Diplomatic History of the Canadian Boundary, 1749–1763* (1940).

Saxby *The British Customs*—Henry Saxby *The British Customs containing an Historical and Practical Account of each Branch of that Revenue* . . . (London, 1757).

Sayre *Interpretations*—Paul L. Sayre (ed.) *Interpretations of Modern Legal Philosophies* . . . (1947).

Schaefer *Geschichte*—Arnold D. Schaefer *Geschichte des Siebenjährigen Kriegs* 3 vols. (1867–1874).

Schlesinger *Col. Merchants*—Arthur M. Schlesinger *The Colonial Merchants and the American Revolution 1763–1776* (1918).

Schlesinger *Prelude*—Arthur M. Schlesinger *Prelude to Independence The Newspaper War on Britain 1764–1776* (1958).

Schlesinger "Col. Newspapers and the Stamp Act"—Arthur M. Schlesinger "The Colonial Newspapers and the Stamp Act" *New Eng. Q.* VIII (1935) 63–83.

Schneider *Johnson*—Herbert and Carol Schneider *Samuel Johnson* . . . *of King's College* . . . 4 vols. (1929).

Schuyler *Parliament*—Robert Livingston Schuyler *Parliament and the British Empire* . . . (1929).

Schuyler *Tucker*—Robert Livingston Schuyler (ed.) *Josiah Tucker: A Selection from His Economic and Political Writings* . . . (1931).

Seasonable Observations—*Seasonable and Affecting Observations on the* . . . *Use and Abuse of a Standing Army* (London, 1750). Author unidentified.

Secker *Answer to Dr. Mayhew's Observations*—[Thomas Secker] *An Answer to Dr. Mayhew's Observations* . . . (London, 1764). Attribution Perry *Mass.* 690, substantiated by contemporary letters in *Mauduit* 113; Beardsley *Johnson* 281, 294; Knollenberg "Hollis and Mayhew" 148; 156.

Secker *Sermon*—Thomas Secker, Bishop of Oxford, *A Sermon Preached before the Society* . . . (1741) reprinted in Klingberg *Anglican Humanitarianism* 213–33.

Second Rep. of Dep. Keep. of Publ. Rec.—*Second Report of the Deputy Keeper of* the [British] *Public Records* (Francis Palgrave) (1841).

Sedgwick—See *Bute,* edited by Romney Sedgwick.

Sedgwick *Hervey*—Romney Sedgwick (ed.) *Some Materials towards Memoirs of the Reign of King George II by John, Lord Hervey* (1931).

Sedgwick "Inner Cabinet 1739–1741"—Romney Sedgwick "The Inner Cabinet from 1739 to 1741" *E.H.R.* XXXIV (1919) 290–302.

Sedgwick "Letters from Pitt to Bute"—Romney Sedgwick "Letters from William Pitt to Lord Bute: 1755–1758" in Pares and Taylor *Essays to Namier* 108–66.

Sedgwick *Livingston*—Theodore Sedgwick *A Memoir of the Life of William Livingston . . .* (1833).

Sée "French Commerce"—Henri Sée "Commerce between France and the United States, 1783–1784" *A.H.R.* XXXI (1926) 732–52.

Sellers *Charleston*—Leila Sellers *Charleston Business on the Eve of the American Revolution* (1934).

Sellers "McCulloh"—Charles G. Sellers, Jr., "Private Profits and British Colonial Policy: The Speculations of Henry McCulloh" 3 *W. & M. Q.* VIII (1951) 535–51.

Selwyn—John Heneage Jesse *George Selwyn and His Contemporaries . . .* 4 vols. (1843–1844).

Serionne *Commerce de la Hollande*—Jacques Accarias de Serionne *Le Commerce de la Hollande . . .* 3 vols. (1768).

Serious Considerations on the Measures of the Present Administration (1763). Attributed to John Butler.

Sharpe—William H. Browne (ed.) *Correspondence of Governor Horatio Sharpe, Archives of Maryland* 1888, 1890, 1895.

Sharpless *Quaker Experiment*—Isaac Sharpless *A Quaker Experiment in Government . . . in Pennsylvania 1682–1783* (1902).

Shaw *Miscellaneous Representations*—William A. Shaw (ed.) *Miscellaneous Representations relative to Our Concerns in America . . .* London (no date).

Sheffield *Observations*—Lord Sheffield (John Baker Holroyd) *Observations on the Commerce of the American States . . .* (Second ed., London, 1783).

Shelburne—Edmond Fitzmaurice *Life of William, Earl of Shelburne afterwards First Marquess of Lansdowne . . .* 3 vols. (1875–1876).

Shepherd *Pa.*—William R. Shepherd *History of Proprietary Government in Pennsylvania* (1896).

Sherrard *Chatham*—Owen A. Sherrard *Lord Chatham: Pitt and the Seven Years' War* (1955).

Sherrard *Chatham and America*—Owen A. Sherrard *Lord Chatham and America* (1958).

Shipton *Harvard Graduates*—Clifford K. Shipton *Sibley's Harvard Graduates Biographical Sketches of those who attended Harvard College . . .* vols. 4 to 10 (1933–1958).

Shipton "New Eng. Clergy"—Clifford K. Shipton "The New England Clergy of the 'Glacial Age' " *Col. Soc. Publ.* XXXII (1937) 24–54.

Shirley—Charles H. Lincoln (ed.) *Correspondence of William Shirley, Governor of Massachusetts . . . 1731–1760* 2 vols. (1912).

Siebert "East Florida"—Wilbur H. Siebert "The Departure of the Spaniards and Other Groups from East Florida 1763–1764" *Fla. Hist. Q.* XIX (1941) 145–54.

Siebert "Pensacola"—Wilbur H. Siebert "How the Spaniards Evacuated Pensacola in 1763" *Fla. Hist. Q* XI (1933) 48–57.

Smelser *Campaign*—Marshall Smelser *The Campaign for the Sugar Islands, 1759: A Study of Amphibious Warfare* (1955).

Smith *Appeals*—Joseph Henry Smith *Appeals to the Privy Council from the American Plantations* (1950).

Smith *Brief State*—[William Smith] *A Brief State of the Province of Pennsylvania . . .* (London, 1755).

Smith *Carroll*—Ellen Hart Smith *Charles Carroll of Carrollton* (1945).

Smith *Colonists in Bondage*—Abbot Emerson Smith *Colonists in Bondage White Servitude and Convict Labor in America 1607–1776* (1947).

Smith "Col. Post-Office"—William Smith "The Colonial Post-Office" *A.H.R.* XXI (1916) 258–75.

Smith "Parson's Cause"—Glenn C. Smith "The Parson's Cause, 1755–65" *Tyler's Quarterly* XXI (1940) 140–71, 291–306.

Smith *S.C.*—William Roy Smith *South Carolina as a Royal Province 1719–1776* (1903).

Smith *Smith*—Horace W. Smith *Life and Correspondence of the Rev. William Smith D.D.* 2 vols. (1879–1880).

Smith *Wealth of Nations*—Adam Smith *An Inquiry into the Nature and Causes of the Wealth of Nations* (1838). First published in 1776.

Smollett *Continuation*—Tobias Smollett *Continuation of the Complete History of England* (1760–1765).

Smyth *Franklin*—Albert Henry Smyth (ed.) *The Writings of Benjamin Franklin* 10 vols. (1907).

So. Car. Hist. Mag.—*The South Carolina Historical and Genealogical Magazine.*

South-Carolina Gazette—*The South-Carolina Gazette* (Charleston, 1732–1775).

Southwick "Molasses Act"—Albert B. Southwick "The Molasses Act—Source of Precedents" 3 *W. & M. Q* VIII (1951) 389–405.

Sparks *Franklin*—Jared Sparks *The Works of Benjamin Franklin . . .* 10 vols. (1840).

Spotswood—Robert A. Brock (ed.) *The Official Letters of Alexander Spotswood . . . 1710–1722* 2 vols. (1882–1885).

Sprague *Annals*—William B. Sprague *Annals of the American Pulpit. . . .* 9 vols. (1857–1869).

Spurlin *Montesquieu*—Paul M. Spurlin *Montesquieu in America 1760–1801* (1941).

Stanard "Randolph Family"—W. G. Stanard "The Randolph Family" 1 *W. & M. Q* VII (1899) 122–24.

Statutes at Large [British]. I have used the Danby Pickering edition of 1762–1775, vols. 1–31.

Stephen *Eng. Lit.*—Leslie Stephen *English Literature and Society in the Eighteenth Century* (1947).

Stephens *Prints (Satires)*—Frederic George Stephens *Catalogue of Prints and Drawings in the British Museum . . . Political and Personal Satires, 1761–1770*, IV (1883).

Stevens *Col. Records*—John A. Stevens (ed.) *Colonial Records of the New York Chamber of Commerce, 1768–1784 . . .* (1867).

Stiles *Discourse*—Ezra Stiles *A Discourse on the Christian Union . . .* (Boston, 1761).

Stiles Diary—Franklin B. Dexter (ed.) *The Literary Diary of Ezra Stiles* . . . 3 vols. (1901).

Stiles Itineraries—Franklin B. Dexter (ed.) *Extracts from the Itineraries . . . of Ezra Stiles . . . with a selection from his Correspondence* (1916).

Stillé *Dickinson*—Charles J. Stillé *The Life and Times of John Dickinson 1732–1808* (1891).

Stock *Proceedings*—Leo Francis Stock (ed.) *Proceedings and Debates of the British Parliaments respecting North America* 5 vols. (1924–1941).

Stone *Johnson*—William L. Stone *The Life and Times of Sir William Johnson* . . . 2 vols. (1865).

Stopford—*H.M.C.*—*Report on the Manuscripts of Mrs. Stopford-Sackville* I (1904).

Stuart *Trumbull*—Isaac W. Stuart *Life of Jonathan Trumbull, Sen.* (1859).

Sutherland "Burke"—Lucy Stuart Sutherland "Edmund Burke and the First Rockingham Ministry" *E.H.R.* vol. 47 (1932) 46–72.

Sutherland *East India Co.*—Lucy Stuart Sutherland *The East India Company in Eighteenth-Century Politics* (1952).

Sutherland "India"—Lucy Stuart Sutherland "The East India Company and the Peace of Paris" *E.H.R.* vol. 62 (1947) 179–90.

Sweet *Religion in Col. Am.*—William Warren Sweet *Religion in Colonial America* (1947).

Swem *Va. Hist. Index*—Earl Gregg Swem *Virginia Historical Index* 2 vols. (1934–1936).

Sydnor *Gentlemen Freeholders*—Charles S. Sydnor *Gentlemen Freeholders: Political Practices in Washington's Virginia* (1952).

Sykes "Newcastle"—Norman Sykes "The Duke of Newcastle as Ecclesiastical Minister" *E.H.R.* vol. 57 (1942) 59–84.

Talcott—Mary Kingsbury Talcott (ed.) *The Talcott Papers*—*Collections of the Connecticut Historical Society* IV and V (1892–1896).

Tatham *Tobacco*—William Tatham *Essay on the Culture and Commerce of Tobacco* (1800).

Temperley "A Note on Cabinets"—Harold W. V. Temperley "A Note on Inner and Outer Cabinets; . . . in the Eighteenth Century" *E.H.R.* XXXI (1916) 291–96.

Temperley "Inner and Outer Cabinet"—Harold W. V. Temperley "Inner and Outer Cabinet and Privy Council 1679–1783" *E.H.R.* XXVII (1912) 682–99.

Temperley and Williams "18th Century Cabinet"—Harold W. V. Temperley and Trevor Williams "The Cabinet in the Eighteenth Century" *History* New Ser. XXII (1938) 332–34.

Thacher *Sentiments*—[Oxenbridge Thacher] *The Sentiments of a British American* (Boston, 1764). Thacher acknowledged his authorship in the *Boston-Gazette* Nov. 5, 1764.

Thackeray *Pitt*—Francis Thackeray *A History of . . . William Pitt, Earl of Chatham* 2 vols. (1827).

Thayer *Pa. Politics 1740–1776*—Theodore Thayer *Pennsylvania Politics and the Growth of Democracy 1740–1776* (1953).

Thayer *Pemberton*—Theodore Thayer *Israel Pemberton: King of the Quakers* (1943).

Thayer "Quaker Party"—Theodore Thayer "The Quaker Party of Pennsylvania 1755–1765" *Pa. Mag. Hist.* vol. 71 (1947) 19–43.

The North Briton—John Wilkes's weekly journal *The North Briton* published from June 5, 1762, to April 23, 1763.

Thompson *Long Island*—Benjamin F. Thompson *History of Long Island from Its Discovery and Settlement to the Present Time* (1839).

Thomson *Const. Hist.*—Mark A. Thomson *A Constitutional History of England, 1642 to 1801* (1938).

Thomson *Secretaries of State*—Mark A. Thomson *The Secretaries of State 1681–1782* (1932).

Thornton *Pulpit of the Am. Rev.*—John Wingate Thornton *The Pulpit of the American Revolution* (1860).

Thorpe *Charters*—Francis N. Thorpe (ed.) *The Federal and State Constitutions, Colonial Charters and Other Organic Laws . . .* 7 vols. (1909).

Tolles *Meeting House*—Fredrick B. Tolles *Meeting House and Counting House: The Quaker Merchants of Colonial Philadelphia, 1682–1763* (1948).

Torrens *Hist. of Cabinets*—William M. Torrens *History of Cabinets from the Union with Scotland to the Acquisition of Canada and Bengal* 2 vols. (1894).

Towle *R.I. Admiralty*—Dorothy S. Towle (ed.) *Records of the Vice-Admiralty Court of Rhode Island 1716–1752* (1936).

Toynbee *Walpole*—Mrs. Paget Toynbee *The Letters of Horace Walpole* 16 vols. (1903–1905) with 3 supplementary vols. (1918–1925).

Toynbee and Whibley *Gray*—Paget Toynbee and Leonard Whibley *Correspondence of Thomas Gray* 3 vols. (1935).

Trans. Roy. Hist. Soc.—*Transactions of the Royal Historical Society.*

Trans. Roy. Soc. Can.—*Transactions of the Royal Society of Canada.*

Tremaine *Bibliography*—Marie Tremaine *A Bibliography of Canadian Imprints 1751–1800* (1952).

Trenchard and Gordon *Cato's Letters*—[John Trenchard and Thomas Gordon] *Cato's Letters; or Essays on Liberty, Civil and Religious, and Other Important Subjects* (London, 1724).

Trent's Journal—Albert T. Volwiler "William Trent's Journal at Fort Pitt, 1763" *Miss. Vall. Hist. Rev.* XI (1925) 390–413.

Trumbull—*The Trumbull Papers,* 5 *Mass. Hist. Soc. Coll.* IX (1885).

Tucker *A Letter*—[Josiah Tucker] *A Letter from a Merchant in London to his Nephew in America* (London, 1766) in Schuyler *Tucker* 302–29.

Tunstall *Pitt*—Brian Tunstall *William Pitt, Earl of Chatham* (1938).

Turberville *House of Lords*—Arthur S. Turberville *The House of Lords in the XVIIIth Century* (1927).

Turner *Cabinet Council*—Edward R. Turner *The Cabinet Council of England . . . 1622–1784* 2 vols. (1930–1932).

Turner "Cabinet 1688–1760"—Edward R. Turner "The Development of the Cabinet, 1688–1760" *A.H.R.* XVIII (1913) 751–68, XIX (1914) 27–43.

Turner "Materials for Study of the Cabinet"—Edward R. Turner "The Materials for the Study of the English Cabinet in the Eighteenth Century" *Am. Hist. Assoc. Rep.* for 1911 I 91–98.

Turner *Privy Council*—Edward R. Turner *The Privy Council of England . . . 1603–1784* 2 vols. (1927–1928).

Turner "The Cabinet"—Edward R. Turner "The Cabinet in the Eighteenth Century" *E.H.R.* XXXII (1917) 192–203.

Tyler *Henry*—Moses Coit Tyler *Patrick Henry* (1898).

Tyler's Quarterly — *Tyler's Quarterly Historical and Genealogical Magazine*.

Ubbelohde *Vice-Admiralty Courts* — Carl Ubbelohde *The Vice-Admiralty Courts and the American Revolution* (1960).

U. of Chicago Law Rev. — *The University of Chicago Law Review*.

U. of Pa. Law Rev. — *University of Pennsylvania Law Review*.

Va. Journals — *Journals of the House of Burgesses of Virginia* 13 vols. (1905–1915).

Va. Mag. — *The Virginia Magazine of History and Biography*.

Van Doren *Franklin* — Carl Van Doren *Benjamin Franklin* (1938).

Van Doren *Franklin's Writings* — Carl Van Doren (ed.) *Benjamin Franklin's Autobiographical Writings* (1945).

Van Tyne *Causes* — Claude H. Van Tyne *The Causes of the War of Independence* . . . (1922).

Vattel *Law of Nations* — Emeric de Vattel *The Law of Nations: or Principles of the Law of Nature* . . . (London, 1760). English translations of *Droit des gens, ou principles de la loi naturelle* . . . (1758).

Venn *Alumni Cantabrigiensis* — John and J. A. Venn (eds.) *Alumni Cantabrigiensis: A Biographical List of all known Students* . . . *at the University of Cambridge* (1922).

Virginia Gazette — *The Virginia Gazette* (Hunter, etc.) (Williamsburg) 1751–1775.

Volwiler *Croghan* — Albert T. Volwiler *George Croghan and the Westward Movement 1741–1782* (1926)

W. & M. Q. — *The William and Mary Quarterly*.

Waddington *Guerre de Sept Ans* — Richard Waddington *La Guerre de Sept Ans: Histoire diplomatique et militaire* 5 vols. (1899–1914).

Wainwright *Croghan* — Nicholas Wainwright *George Croghan Wilderness Diplomat* (1959).

Walker *Burd Papers* — Lewis Burd Walker (ed.) *The Burd Papers, Extracts from Chief Justice William Allen's Letter Book* (1897).

Wallace *Appeal to Arms* — Willard M. Wallace *Appeal to Arms, A Military History of the American Revolution* (1951).

Wallace *Const. Hist. of S.C.* — David Duncan Wallace *Constitutional History of South Carolina from 1725 to 1775* (1899).

Wallace *Farmers and the Export Market* — Henry A. Wallace *Farmers and the Export Market U.S. Agricultural Adjustment Administration* G-51, Dec. 1935.

Wallace *Laurens* — David Duncan Wallace *The Life of Henry Laurens with a Sketch of the Life of Lieutenant-Colonel John Laurens* (1915).

Wallace *Teedyuscung* — Anthony F. C. Wallace *King of the Delawares: Teedyuscung 1700–1763* (1949).

Wallace *Weiser* — Paul A. W. Wallace *Conrad Weiser 1696–1760* . . . (1945).

Walpole *Memoirs of George II* — Horace Walpole *Memoirs of the Reign of King George the Second* 3 vols. (1846).

Walpole *Memoirs of Geo. III* — Horace Walpole *Memoirs of the Reign of King George the Third* 4 vols. (1845).

Ward and Alden *War of the Revolution* — Christopher Ward with John R. Alden (ed.) *The War of the Revolution* 2 vols. (1952).

Warren *Hist. of Am. Bar* — Charles Warren *A History of the American Bar* (1911).

Washburn *Sketches*—Emory Washburn *Sketches of the Judicial History of Massachusetts from 1630 to . . . 1775* (1840).

Washington—See Fitzpatrick *Washington*.

Washington Diaries—John C. Fitzpatrick (ed.) *The Diaries of George Washington 1748–1799* 4 vols. (1925).

Waterman "Mansfield"—Julian S. Waterman "Mansfield and Blackstone's Commentaries" *U. of Chicago Law Rev.* I (1934) 549–71.

Watkins *Memoir of the Duke of York*—John Watkins *A Biographical Memoir of His Late Royal Highness Frederick, Duke of York . . .* (1827).

Watson *Letter to Archbishop Cornwallis*—Richard Watson, Bishop of Llandaff, *A Letter to Archbishop Cornwallis on the Church Revenues* (London, 1783) *Pamphleteer* VIII (1816) 574–94.

Watson "Wilkes"—Eric R. Watson "John Wilkes and 'The Essay on Woman' " 11 *Notes and Queries* IX (1914) 121–242 *passim*.

Watts—*Letter Book of John Watts . . . Coll. N.Y. Hist. Soc.* for 1928.

Weatherly—Edward H. Weatherly (ed.) *The Correspondence of John Wilkes and Charles Churchill . . .* (1954).

Webster "Montrésor"—J. Clarence Webster "Life of John Montrésor" *Trans. Roy. Soc. Can.* XXII Sec. 2 (1928) 1–31.

Wecter *Burke*—Dixon Wecter *Edmond Burke and His Kinsmen . . .* (1939).

Weeden *Econ. Hist.*—William B. Weeden *Economic and Social History of New England 1620–1789* 2 vols. (1890).

Weiss *New Eng. Col. Clergy*—Frederick Lewis Weiss *The Colonial Clergy and Colonial Churches of New England* (1936).

Wells *Adams*—William V. Wells *The Life and Public Services of Samuel Adams . . .* 3 vols. (1865).

Western Pa. Hist. Mag.—*Western Pennsylvania Historical Magazine*.

Weston-Underwood—*Weston-Underwood Manuscripts H. M. C.* 10th Rep. Part 1.

Whately *Regulations*—[Thomas Whately] *The Regulations lately made concerning the Colonies and the Taxes imposed upon them considered* (London, 1765). For ascription, *Bowdoin-Temple Papers* 77.

White *Beekman Papers*—Philip L. White (ed.) *The Beekman Mercantile Papers 1746–1799* 3 vols. (1956).

White *Beekmans of N.Y.*—Philip L. White *The Beekmans of New York . . . 1647–1877* (1956).

Whitehead *Perth Amboy*—William A. Whitehead *Contributions to the Early History of Perth Amboy . . .* (1856).

Whitmore *Civil List*—William H. Whitmore *The Massachusetts Civil List . . . 1630–1774 . . .* (1870).

Whitson "West Indies"—Agnes M. Whitson "The Outlook of the Continental American Colonies on the British West Indies" *Pol. Science Quart.* vol. 45 (1930) 56–86.

Whitworth *Ligonier*—Rex Whitworth *Field Marshall Lord Ligonier: A Story of the British Army 1702–1770* (1958).

Wiener "R.I. Adm."—Frederick B. Wiener "Notes on the Rhode Island Admiralty" *Harv. Law Rev.* vol. 46 (1933) 44–90.

Wiener "R.I. Merchants"—Frederick B. Wiener "The Rhode Island Merchants and the Sugar Act" *New Eng. Q.* III (1930) 464–500.

Wiggin *Grenvilles*—Lewis M. Wiggin *The Faction of Cousins: A Political Account of the Grenvilles, 1733–1763* (1958).

Wilkinson *Bermuda*—Henry C. Wilkinson *Bermuda in the Old Empire . . . 1684–1784* (1950).

Williams *Carteret and Newcastle*—Basil Williams *Carteret and Newcastle* (1943).

Williams "18th Century Cabinet"—Trevor Williams "The Cabinet in the Eighteenth Century" *History* New Ser. XXII (1938) 240–52.

Williams *Election Sermon*—Abraham Williams *A Sermon Preach'd at Boston before the Great and General Court or Assembly . . . 1762* (Boston, 1762).

Williams *Pitt*—Basil Williams *The Life of William Pitt, Earl of Chatham* 2 vols. (1913).

Williams *Whig Supremacy*—Basil Williams *The Whig Supremacy, 1714–1760* (1945).

Wilson *Wolfe*—Beckles Wilson *The Life and Letters of James Wolfe* (1909).

Winstanley "Cabinet"—Denys A. Winstanley "George III and his First Cabinet" *E.H.R.* XVI (1902) 678–91.

Winstanley *Cambridge*—Denys A. Winstanley *The University of Cambridge in the Eighteenth Century* (1922).

Winstanley *Chatham*—Denys A. Winstanley *Lord Chatham and the Whig Opposition* (1912).

Winstanley *Government*—Denys A. Winstanley *Personal and Party Government . . . 1760–1766* (1910).

Wolcott—Albert C. Bates (ed.) *The Wolcott Papers, Conn. Hist. Soc. Coll.* XVI (1916).

Wolff *Pa. Col. Agency*—Mabel P. Wolff *The Colonial Agency of Pennsylvania, 1712–1757* (1933).

Wolkins "Boston Customs District"—George G. Wolkins "The Boston Customs District in 1768" *Mass. Hist. Soc. Proc.* vol. 58, 418–45.

Wolkins "Hancock"—George G. Wolkins "The Seizure of John Hancock's Sloop 'Liberty'" *Mass. Hist. Soc. Proc.* vol. 55, 239–84.

Wolkins "Malcom"—George G. Wolkins "Daniel Malcom and Writs of Assistance" *Mass. Hist. Soc. Proc.* vol. 58, 5–84.

Wood *Shirley*—George A. Wood *William Shirley, Governor of Massachusetts, 1741–1756* (1920).

Woodward *Ploughs and Politicks*—Carl R. Woodward *Ploughs and Politicks. Charles Read of New Jersey . . .* (1941).

Wright *Am. Interpretations*—Benjamin F. Wright *American Interpretations of Natural Law* (1931).

Wright *Am. Negotiator*—John Wright *The American Negotiator . . .* (London, 1765).

Wright *Cavendish Debates*—John Wright (ed.) *Sir Henry Cavendish's Debates of the House of Commons . . .* (1841).

Wright "Commencement of Cane Industry in America"—Irene A. Wright "The Commencement of the Cane Sugar Industry in America 1519–1538 (1563)" *A.H.R.* XXI (1916) 755–80.

Wright *Cultural Life of the Am. Colonies*—Louis B. Wright *The Cultural Life of the American Colonies 1607–1763* (1957).

Wroth *Am. Bookshelf, 1755* — Lawrence C. Wroth *An American Bookshelf, 1755* (1934).

Wroth *Colonial Printer* — Lawrence C. Wroth *The Colonial Printer* (1938).

Wroth *Printing in Col. Md.* — Lawrence C. Wroth *A History of Printing in Colonial Maryland 1686–1776* (1932).

Wroth and Annan *French Acts* — Lawrence C. Wroth and Gertrude L. Annan (eds.) *Acts of French Royal Administration Concerning Canada, Guiana, The West Indies and Louisiana, Prior to 1791* (1930).

Wyndham *Family History* — Hugh A. Wyndham *A Family History, 1688–1837: The Wyndhams . . .* (1950).

Yale Lib. Gazette — *The Yale University Library Gazette.*

Zeichner *Conn.* — Oscar Zeichner *Connecticut's Years of Controversy.*

COLLECTIONS OF DOCUMENTS CITED

Add. Mss.—The collection of papers known as Additional Manuscripts in the British Museum, London.

Adm.—Admiralty Papers, Public Record Office, London.

Am. Antiq. Soc.—American Antiquarian Society, Worcester, Mass.

Amherst Papers—Papers of Gen. Jeffrey Amherst in various named archives.

Arch. Nationales—Archives Nationales, Paris.

B.M.—British Museum, London.

Bancroft Papers—Papers of George Bancroft, New York Public Library.

Bermuda Arch.—Archives of Bermuda, Hamilton, Bermuda.

Bernard Papers—Papers of Francis Bernard, Governor of Massachusetts, Harvard College Library.

Boston U. Lib.—Boston University Library.

Bouquet Papers—The Papers of Col. Henry Bouquet in the Canadian Archives.

C.O.—Colonial Office Papers in the Public Record Office, London. To illustrate my method of citation: C.O. 5: 1329: 226 signifies Colonial Office Papers, Class 5, volume 1329, folio or page 226.

Can. Arch.—Canadian Archives, Ottawa.

Carter (Landon) Papers—Papers of Landon Carter of Sabine Hall, Va., University of Virginia Library.

Clements Lib.—William L. Clements Library, University of Michigan, Ann Arbor, Mich.

Conn. Hist. Soc.—Connecticut Historical Society, Hartford, Conn.

Conn. State Lib.—Connecticut State Library, Hartford, Conn.

Corbin Letter Book—Letter Book of Richard Corbin 1758–1768, Va. Hist. Soc. Lib.

Dartmouth Coll. Lib.—Dartmouth College Library, Hanover, N.H.

Essex Institute—The Essex Institute, Salem, Mass.

Gage Papers—Papers of Gen. Thomas Gage, Clements Library.

Hardwicke Papers—Hardwicke Papers in the British Museum.

Harv. Coll. Lib.—Harvard College Library, Cambridge, Mass.

Hist. Soc. of Pa.—The Historical Society of Pennsylvania, Philadelphia, Pa.

Huntington Lib.—Henry E. Huntington Library and Art Gallery, San Marino, Cal.

Inst. of Jamaica—Institute of Jamaica, Kingston, Jamaica.

J. C. Brown Lib.—John Carter Brown Library, Providence, R.I.

Jerdone Account Book—The Account book of Francis Jerdone, Merchant of Louisa County Va., W. & M. Coll. Lib.

Jerdone Letter Book—Letter Book of Francis Jerdone (1756–1763) W. & M. Coll. Lib.

L.C.—Library of Congress, Washington, D.C.

M.H.S.—See Mass. Hist. Soc.

Mason-Franklin Coll.—Mason-Franklin Collection, Yale Lib.

Mass. Arch.—Massachusetts Archives, State House, Boston, Mass.

Mass. Hist. Soc.—Massachusetts Historical Society, Boston, Mass.

Mayhew Papers—The Papers of Jonathan Mayhew, Chenery Library, Boston University.

N.Y. Hist. Soc.—New-York Historical Society, New York City.

N.Y. Pub. Lib.—New York Public Library, New York City.

Newcastle Papers—Newcastle Papers in the British Museum.

New Haven Col. Hist. Soc.—New Haven Colony Historical Society, New Haven, Conn.

Nova Scotia Arch.—Public Archives of the Province of Nova Scotia, Halifax, Nova Scotia.

P.C.—Privy Council Register in the Public Record Office, London.

P.R.O.—Public Record Office, London.

R.I. Arch.—Rhode Island Archives, State House, Providence, R.I.

Rec. of No. Adm. Dist.—Records of the Court of Admiralty for the Northern District of America in the Office of Clerk of the Supreme Court of Suffolk County, Mass., Boston, Mass.

S.C. Council Journal—Journal of the Upper House (Council) of South Carolina, Office of the Historical Commission of South Carolina, Columbia, S.C.

S.C. House Journal—Journal of the Commons House of Assembly of South Carolina, Office of the Historical Commission of South Carolina, Columbia, S.C.

S.P.—State Papers, in the Public Records Office, London.

Shelburne Papers—Papers of the Earl of Shelburne (later Marquess of Lansdowne) Clements Library.

State Archives of New York, Albany, N.Y.

Stiles Pap.—Papers of Ezra Stiles, Yale Library.

T.—Treasury Papers in the Public Record Office, London.

Trumbull (Joseph) Corresp.—Joseph Trumbull Correspondence, Connecticut Historical Society.

U. of Cal. Lib.—University of California Library, Berkeley, Cal.

U. of Iowa Lib.—University of Iowa Library, Iowa City.

U. of London Lib.—University of London Library.

U. of Va. Lib.—University of Virginia Library, Charlottesville.

Va. Hist. Soc. Lib.—Virginia Historical Society Library, Richmond.

W.O.—War Office Papers in the Public Record Office, London.

Ward Papers—Papers of Samuel Ward (1725–1776) Rhode Island Historical Society, Providence.

Wentworth-Fitzwilliam Mss.—Wentworth-Fitzwilliam Manuscripts, Sheffield Central Library, Sheffield, England.

Wheelock Papers—Eleazar Wheelock Papers, Dartmouth College Library, Hanover, N.H.
W. & M. Coll. Lib.—William and Mary College Library, Williamsburg, Va.
Yale Lib.—Yale University Library, New Haven, Conn.

UNPUBLISHED DISSERTATIONS CITED

Akers "Mayhew"—Charles W. Akers "The Life of Jonathan Mayhew 1729–1766" (1952) Ph.D. thesis, Boston University Library.

Berg "Philadelphia"—Harry D. Berg. "Merchants and Mercantile Life in Colonial Philadelphia 1748–1763" (1940) Ph.D. thesis, University of Iowa Library, Iowa City, Iowa.

Bever "East India Commodities"—Virginia M. Bever "The Trade in East India Commodities to the American Colonies 1690–1775" Ph.D. thesis, University of Iowa Library.

Brock "Col. Currency"—Leslie Van Horn Brock "The Currency of the American Colonies 1700–1764" (1941) Ph.D. thesis, University of Michigan Library, Ann Arbor, Mich.

Freiberg "Hutchinson and Mass. Politics"—Malcolm Freiberg "Prelude to Purgatory: Thomas Hutchinson in Provincial Massachusetts Politics, 1760–1770" (1950) Ph.D. thesis, Brown University Library, Providence, R.I.

Herbert "Jamaica"—J. W. Herbert "Constitutional Issues in Jamaica 1748–1776" (1927) M.A. thesis, University of London Library.

Ostrander "Molasses Trade"—Gilman M. Ostrander "The Molasses Trade of the Northern Colonies" (1948) M.A. thesis, University of California Library, Berkeley, Cal.

INDEX

The typeface used for this book is Monotype Baskerville, which is based on the types of the English typefounder and printer John Baskerville (1706–75). Baskerville is the quintessential transitional face: it retains the bracketed and oblique serifs of old-style faces such as Caslon and Garamond, but in its increased lowercase height, lighter color, and enhanced contrast between thick and thin strokes, it presages modern faces.

Printed on paper that is acid free and meets the requirements of the American National Standard for Permanence of Paper for Printed Library Materials, z39.48-1992. ⊗

Book design by Mark McGarry, Texas Type and Book Works, Inc.,
Dallas, Texas
Typography by Monotype Composition Company,
Baltimore, Maryland
Printed and bound by Worzalla Publishing Company,
Stevens Point, Wisconsin